HORIZONS OF ANTHROPOLOGY
SECOND EDITION

HORIZONS OF
ANTHROPOLOGY
SECOND EDITION

edited by **Sol Tax**
and **Leslie G. Freeman**

 ALDINE PUBLISHING COMPANY, *Chicago*

Second edition first published 1977 by
Aldine Publishing Company
529 South Wabash Avenue
Chicago, Illinois 60605

ISBN 0-202-01157-7 (cloth)
      0-202-01158-5 (paper)

Library of Congress Catalog Number 76-46247

Printed in the United States of America

*Dedicated to the memory of our colleague,
Tom (Lloyd A.) Fallers, whose intellectual
and moral example—and wisdom and love—
enriched our lives*

CONTENTS

Preface   ix
Contributors   xi
1. The Anthropological Tradition   *Sol Tax*   1
2. The Transition to Humanity   *Clifford Geertz*   21
3. The Study of Evolution   *Eric R. Wolf*   33
4. The Genetic Basis of Behavior   *B. J. Williams*   46
5. The Hominization Process   *F. Clark Howell*   59
6. Man, Culture, and Biology   *Aram A. Yengoyan*   75
7. Language and Thought   *Susan M. Ervin-Tripp*   88
8. Symbols and Language   *David Premack* 101
9. Language as a Part of Culture   *Michael Silverstein* 119
10. Anthropology Without Informants   *Leslie G. Freeman* 132
11. The Archeologist as Ethnographer   *Richard A. Gould* 151
12. The Origins of Agriculture   *Robert McC. Adams* 171
13. Perspectives Gained from Fieldwork   *Laura Nader* 187
14. Anthropology's Urban Progress   *Richard G. Fox* 199
15. Culture and Environment   *Marshall D. Sahlins* 215
16. The Organization of Economic Life   *Manning Nash* 232
17. Social Organization   *James L. Gibbs, Jr.* 245
18. Equality and Inequality in Human
      Societies   *Lloyd A. Fallers* 257
19. The Study of Politics in Anthropology   *Morton H. Fried* 269
20. Anthropology and the Law   *Paul J. Bohannan* 290
21. The Anthropology of Law and Order *Klaus-Friedrich Koch* 300
22. The Study of Religion   *Edward Norbeck* 319
23. Anthropology and the Arts   *Alan P. Merriam* 332
24. The Psychological Approach in
      Anthropology   *Edward B. Bruner* 344
25. Population and Environment   *Steven Polgar* 355
26. Anthropology and the Body Politic   *Cyril S. Belshaw* 372

PREFACE

This is the second generation of a book that set out a dozen years ago to show how anthropology looked to the best American scholars still in their thirties. It was argued that:

> A "senior" member of a learned profession, with too rare exceptions, implements ideas created when he was a junior scholar. At that time his voice was drowned out in the fame of his teachers whose ideas, in turn, dated from still earlier years. To break the chain, it was necessary to identify a wide variety of the best specialists still in their thirties, and ask them to discuss what they thought interesting and significant.

Even the selection of the best young scholars was left to the young. The result was a fresh book that was an immediate and continuing success, so much so that the editor and publisher were at first hesitant to revise what had become something of a classic.

After ten years of continuing reprints of the original, during which the horizons of anthropology were surely changing, the compromise was achieved that is embodied in the present book. First, a younger anthropologist—one who was still a student when the first edition was put together—agreed to coedit a new edition; second, the authors of the original articles were asked to bring them up to date or to substitute new articles; and third, new authors for new horizons were selected from among the next generation.

The result reflects whatever mix of continuity and change has occurred in anthropology itself between 1964 and 1976. A dozen years of quantitative growth is reflected in the increase in the number of chapters from twenty-one to twenty-six. Of these, seventeen are revisions of the original papers and nine are completely new. Chapter One is a rethinking by the original editor of his introductory and concluding essays in the first edition.

Such an accounting is useful only to editors, publishers, and reviewers. Whether it is new wine in an old bottle or old wine decanted will not matter to those who come thirsty to anthropology. May they enjoy it and never lose their thirst.

SOL TAX
LESLIE G. FREEMAN

CONTRIBUTORS

ROBERT McC. ADAMS is Harold H. Swift Distinguished Service Professor at the University of Chicago in the Departments of Anthropology and Near Eastern Languages and Civilizations. His field work has taken him to the Middle East and Mexico, following his interests with historic urban civilizations.

CYRIL S. BELSHAW is Professor of Anthropology at the University of British Columbia and is Editor of *Current Anthropology*. Primarily, his field work has been in Melanesia and Canada. In recent years, he has written on economic anthropology, university affairs, and the relationship between anthropology and public policy, which he drew upon from his activities with international organizations.

PAUL J. BOHANNAN is Professor of Anthropology at the University of California, Santa Barbara. He has taught at Oxford University, Princeton University, and Northwestern University. His field work has brought him in contact with the Tiv of Nigeria, the Wanga of Kenya, and several econiches of American society. He has published several books and many articles.

EDWARD M. BRUNER is Professor of Anthropology and former head of the department at the University of Illinois. His field work has been among the American Indians and in Indonesia, specializing in cultural change. He has published many articles in professional journals.

SUSAN ERVIN-TRIPP is Professor of Psychology at the University of California, Berkeley. Her publications include research on children's reasoning and language and on bilingualism.

LLOYD A. FALLERS was, at the time of his death in 1974, an

Albert Michelson Distinguished Service Professor of Anthropology and Sociology, and Chairman of the Committee of the Comparative Study of New Nations at the University of Chicago.

RICHARD G. FOX is Professor of Anthropology at Duke University. His current research is on ethnicity in industrial society and he is the author of *Urban Anthropology: Cities in their Cultural Settings.*

LESLIE G. FREEMAN is Professor of Anthropology at the University of Chicago. His field work has taken him to Paleolithic sites in Spain and he published monographic reports on those excavations. He has published articles in edited collections and professional journals.

MORTON H. FRIED is Professor of Anthropology at Columbia University. He has conducted field work in China, British Guiana and Formosa, and his publications include books and articles on modern Chinese culture.

CLIFFORD GEERTZ is Professor of Social Science at the Institute for Advanced Study. He has worked extensively in North Africa and Southeast Asia and is the author of, among other books, *The Religion of Java, Agricultural Involution,* and *The Interpretation of Cultures.*

JAMES L. GIBBS, JR. is Professor of Anthropology at Stanford University. He has done field work among the Kpelle of Liberia, about whom he co-produced an ethnographic film and published several articles in professional journals.

RICHARD A. GOULD is Professor of Anthropology at the University of Hawaii, Honolulu. He has done field work among Australian Desert Aborigines and California Indians and has published many articles in professional journals. He also has planned anthropological exhibits for the American Museum of Natural History, New York, and the California Academy of Sciences, San Francisco.

F. CLARK HOWELL is Professor of Anthropology at the University of California, Berkeley. He has specialized in the study of early man and his evolution, and has conducted field work in Africa and Europe, most recently in Spain.

KLAUS-FRIEDRICH KOCH is Associate Professor of Anthropology at Northwestern University. He has done field research in New Guinea and on islands in Fiji and in the Ellice Group. His publications, based on this work, deal with conflict management, kinship, and social organization.

ALAN P. MERRIAM is Professor of Anthropology at Indiana University. He has carried out field work among North American Indians and in Africa, especially the Republic of Zaire. He is the author of many books and articles in professional journals.

LAURA NADER is Professor of Anthropology at the University of California, Berkeley. She has done field work among the Zapotec Indians of Mexico and the Shia Moslems of Lebanon. Her publications include comparative studies of conflict resolution and social organization as well as ethnographic studies.

MANNING NASH is Professor of Anthropology at the University of Chicago. He has done field work among the Maya in Guatemala, Burma, Malaysia, Indonesia, and Belice. He has published four monographs, three other books, and numerous articles in professional journals.

EDWARD NORBECK is Professor of Anthropology at Rice University. His interests in anthropology cover a wide range of subjects in addition to that of religion, and he is the author of several books and numerous shorter writings. His field research has been principally in Japan.

STEVEN POLGAR is Professor of Anthropology at the University of North Carolina, Chapel Hill. His field work includes research in Ghana and among Indians and Negroes in the United States. He is an action anthropologist specializing in public health and culture change.

DAVID PREMACK is Professor of Psychology at the University of Pennsylvania. He is interested in the nature and evolution of human intelligence, and has done research comparing chimpanzees and children on various aspects of intelligence including representational capacity, memory, intentionality, and language.

MARSHALL D. SAHLINS is Professor of Anthropology at the University of Chicago. His field work has been in Fiji, and his major theoretical concerns have dealt with problems of culture change and evolution.

MICHAEL SILVERSTEIN is Associate Professor of Anthropology, Linguistics, and Behavioral Sciences (Cognition and Communication) at the University of Chicago. He has been engaged in descriptive and historical research on languages and societies of northwestern North America and northwestern Australia, and is concerned with grammatical models and sociolinguistic theory.

SOL TAX is Professor of Anthropology at the University of Chicago. He was founding editor of *Current Anthropology* and is the editor of the *World Anthropology Series.* His field work among Middle and North American Indians has resulted in such books as *Penny Capitalism* and *Heritage of Conquest,* and in the development of what is now called "Action Anthropology." He has edited many books, including the three-volume symposium, *Evolution After Darwin.* He was President of the American Anthropological Association in 1958-59 and in 1962 received the Viking Fund Medal in Anthropology.

B. J. WILLIAMS is Professor of Anthropology at the University of California, Los Angeles. His research interests are behavioral and quantitative genetics and the population biology of hunter/gatherers.

ERIC R. WOLF is Distinguished Professor of Anthropology at Herbert H. Lehman College, City University of New York. He has done field work in Puerto Rico, Mexico, and the Italian Alps. His books on *Peasants* and *Peasant Wars of the Twentieth Century* exemplify his interest in the crosscultural study of peasant populations.

ARAM A. YENGOYAN is Professor of Anthropology at the University of Michigan, Ann Arbor. His major theoretical interests are primarily concerned with materialistic and structural explanations of cultural phenomena. He has done field work in central Australia and the Philippines.

1.

THE ANTHROPOLOGICAL TRADITION

Sol Tax

ONE CAN DEFINE anthropology as the study of the genus *Homo* from its beginnings, in all its manifestations and variations. Then subject matters called biological anthropology, paleoanthropology, prehistory, archeology, ethnohistory, ethnobotany, ethnozoology, folklore, cultural and social anthropology fall easily into the whole. Indeed there is infinite room for subclassifications in all fields; common specializations within cultural anthropology, for example, are psychological, political, legal, and economic anthropology. Conversely, the whole is by some scholars subsumed under primatology; and since all of our great human achievements—and problems—are part of the behavior of one zoological species, ethology also can make its claim.

Parts of so broad a field of study may have their beginnings in some dim prehistoric past beyond useful speculation. In times we can study, people have always been interested in studying themselves. Individual men or women spend their lives trying to understand themselves; a people provides itself with myths; nations write their histories. Therefore, it is futile to speak of a beginning of the study of man. We usually go back to the classical Greeks, but the study is worldwide—a philosopher can appear in any tribe—and it goes back anywhere that records carry us back. Yet there are times when a science gets a special impetus, crystallizes a new form, and forges ahead.

For the study of man, the great period in modern times

1

extended over the thirty years between about 1840 and 1870. One might almost call it a "thirty years' war"—a war between two words, *ethnology* and *anthropology*; a war between those who were historians and philosophers and those who were for science, particularly biology (wherever it might lead one); war between humanitarians whose science was related to their advocacy of a cause and pure scientists who would separate scientific truth from all other human concerns.

A good way to watch the thirty years' story unfold is to read the journals of the competing societies which sprang up. A quick and especially interesting summary is to be found in a paper by Paul Broca, the great French anthropologist. Broca founded the Anthropological Society of Paris in 1859. Ten years later, he delivered a Decennial Anniversary Address before the society which was published in its journal and also translated into English for publication by the Anthropological Institute of New York. Broca was himself an anatomist and human biologist, the descendant of a long line which included Blumenbach, Cuvier, and many others. Imbued with the spirit of exact science, he strongly opposed mixing science and sentiment, or science and politics, and his little history emphasizes the dangers.[1]

In Paris, in 1800 was founded the Society of the Observers of Man by a union of naturalists and of medical men to promote the study of natural history mainly by providing guidance to travellers and explorers of far places. The Society was deprived of new data by the long series of Napoleonic Wars which interrupted commerce and foreign travel, and turned its attention to questions of ethnology, historical and psychological. Natural history was neglected for philosophy, politics, and philanthropy.

This abortive experiment had been long forgotten when some English philanthropists founded in London, in 1838, the "Society for the Protection of Aborgines." Eminent scholars were among its members, but its aims were rather political and social than scientific. It was at this time that the question of slavery, already solved by England, began to occupy the attention of the French government. In the session of 1839, the Chamber of Deputies in Paris had appointed a commission to report upon this important subject; and

---

1. Adapted from the Address as published in the *Journal of the Anthropological Institute of New York* (New York: Westermann and Co., 1871–72).

the society in London, hoping that the pressure of public opinion might have a favorable influence on the decision of the Chamber, resolved to establish in France a society for the emancipation of the Negroes. One of its leading members, Mr. Hodgkin, came to Paris, and put himself in communication with several distinguished persons, and more particularly with the eminent naturalist and anthropologist Milne-Edwards. But an association of this kind was not at that time possible in France. Instead of a political association, Milne-Edwards and his friends resolved to found a scientific society, and thus sprang into existence the celebrated "Ethnological Society of Paris," authorized on the 20th August, 1839.

When the first volume of its *Memoirs* appeared, some English *savants* appreciated the usefulness of its work, and resolved to imitate it. Through their means, in May, 1844, a similar society was formed in London, and a short time subsequently a third society, founded in New York, adopted the same title.

In 1847, the meetings of the society, hitherto peaceful, were agitated by the question of slavery. The first thing was to determine the distinctive characteristics of the white and black races; but it was in vain that the naturalists and anatomists, too few in number, tried to restrain the discussion within the limits of natural history. The debate became more lively at each meeting; the outside world began to be interested and the public willingly believed that ethnology, of which it then heard for the first time, was not a science, but something between politics and philanthropy. This absorbing controversy lasted nearly a year when it was ended by the abolition of slavery. But the Ethnological Society had been so completely absorbed by this question that, deprived of it, its chief motive to action seemed no longer to exist.

The enfeebled society died—though weak sisters remained in London and New York.

In America, physical anthropology was making great progress. Then in 1851, the United States were agitated by the abolition question. By one of those confusions of ideas it was imagined that slavery was bound up with the polygenistic theory, while emancipation was inseparable from the monogenistic. A tremendous war absorbed for many years the resources of the country. Science was lost sight of amid the clash of arms, and when the victory of the North had solved the question of slavery, anthropology suffered a period of eclipse.

Meanwhile, in Europe anthropology was going ahead, but when facts ran counter to popularly conceived opinions, they were greeted with contempt. It was then that the founders of the

Anthropological Society of Paris determined to form a tribunal before which opposing views might obtain a hearing. After more than six months occupied in collecting subscriptions, and in obtaining, not without difficulty, authority to hold its meetings (under the control of the police), the new society met for the first time on the 19th of May, 1859, and began work on the 7th of July following.

In Germany, anthropologists in the many scattered cities were unable to meet frequently, so they established instead an annual Congress. The first session was held at Gottenburg, in the month of September, 1861. Circumstances interfered with well-laid plans, and the Congress never actually met again. But work continued through *The Germanic Archives of Anthropology,* founded in 1865, and the *Journal of Ethnology,* begun on January 1, 1869.

The Ethnological Society of London was quietly pursuing its labors when the perusal of our publications excited in its midst the desire to add modern anthropology to the old programme of ethnology. But the most influential members opposed the introduction of anatomy and natural history. On the 24th of February, 1863, the dissenting members founded, under the presidency of Dr. James Hunt, a new society, which took like ours, the name of the Anthropological Society. The Ethnological Society, weakened for a moment by this defection, increased its efforts, and soon saw the necessity of enlarging, in its turn, its own sphere. In 1862 Thomas Huxley was elected president. Nothing could be more significant than the choice of this gentleman, whose fame rests on his works on zoology, comparative anatomy, and craniology. From this time forward the Ethnological Society and the Anthropological Society differed only in name.

It was not only in France, Germany and England that anthropology was developing. Everywhere, from Sweden to Sicily; from the Volga to the Tagus; learned men were at work. In Moscow, in 1866, there was formed, in the "Society of the Friends of Nature," a special section of anthropology, which became quickly productive and successful.

At Madrid, a Society of Anthropology was founded in 1865. The Minister of Progress had been pleased to honor with his presence (the 5th of June, 1865) the ceremony of inauguration. It was only when the society wished to set to work that its difficulties began. The first question submitted for discussion was that of the aboriginal races of the peninsula—an inquiry offensive, imprudent, and savoring of heresy—for the very name of aborigines was pregnant with controversy. They stopped meeting until the Revolution of

September. Last 21st February they held their second inauguration.

In addition to the formation of national societies and of journals and periodicals, Broca could also report the founding of the International Congress of Anthropology and Prehistoric Archaeology and its first sessions, in 1866, 1867, and 1868, each in a different part of Europe. He could rightly entitle his address "The Progress of Anthropology."

Two years later, the rival English societies joined to become the Anthropological Institute of Great Britain and Ireland. In 1873, there was again a split, based on personalities, and a new London Anthropological Society was established with its journal *Anthropologia*, but it was shortlived. The sciences settled down to work. International communication, research, and publication made great strides. The names anthropology, ethnology, ethnography, archeology, prehistory, philology, and linguistics became firmly established, although they had different meanings from place to place and from time to time. In some places these branches of the science of man became more unified than in others, and everywhere each has its different history. But on the whole the hope of Broca was realized in the years which followed, that on the pivotal base of anatomy and biology, anthropology could "extract, by means of a rigorous synthesis, the ultimate ideas of *general anthropology* which sooner or later will be the crown and glory of our science."

The following thirty or forty years were a time of consolidation and development of theory, well described in 1904 by Franz Boas, a German-born geographer-turned-anthropologist, who settled in the United States in 1886 and until his death in 1942 was the leading figure in American anthropology. In a 1904 lecture on "The History of Anthropology," Boas suggests that by the middle of the nineteenth century theory had begun to develop from three points of view: the historical, the classificatory, and the geographical. Thus, geographical similarities among humans led both to theories of universal folk-psychology and to the notion of a single cultural evolution:

> This [latter] theory has been discussed most clearly by Edward B. Tylor, who finds proof for it in the sameness of customs and beliefs

the world over. The typical similarity and the occurrence of certain customs in definite combinations are explained by him as due to their belonging to a certain stage in the development of civilization. They do not disappear suddenly, but persist for a time in the form of survivals. These are, therefore, wherever they occur, a proof that a lower stage of culture, of which these customs are characteristic, has been passed through.[2]

Meanwhile classification of races, languages, and cultures led to other, including geographic, theories. And Boas summarized as follows the fundamental problems which gave to anthropology "its present character":

In the biological branch we have the problem of the morphological evolution of man and that of the development of varieties. Inseparable from these questions is also that of correlation between somatic and mental characters, which has a practical as well as a theoretical interest. In psychological anthropology the important questions are the discovery of a system of the evolution of culture, the study of the modifications of simple general traits under the influence of different geographical and social conditions, the question of transmission and spontaneous origin, and that of "folk-psychology" versus individual psychology.

Boas also described the fieldwork that by 1904 had become important in archeology, physical anthropology, and ethnology. He pointed out that the variety of methods being employed was such that it would soon be impossible for the general anthropologist to do more than set the problems for biologists, linguists, and ethnologists. He concludes:

Nevertheless we must always demand that the anthropologist who carries on field research must be familiar with the principles of these three methods . . . [and] have a prior grasp of the general results of the anthropological method as applied by various sciences.

The next thirty years of anthropology in the United States were so dominated by Franz Boas and his students that this caveat was also a prediction, and implementation rather than

2. In George Stocking, *The Shaping of American Anthropology, 1883–1911* (New York: Basic Books, 1974).

the development of new theory was the rule. In Europe, on the other hand, this was a period of increasing differentiation by national traditions and the separation of biological, linguistic, and ethnological studies. But in Europe beginning with Radcliffe-Brown and Malinowski, as in the United States with Boas, there was the beginning of deliberate fieldwork as the *sine qua non* of anthropology, which required also the professionalization of what had mainly been activities pursued by gentlemen and scholars in other fields.

If the first burst of anthropology was 1830 to 1870, the second was a hundred years later. The twenty-year-period, from 1948 to 1968, turns out to have been a climax at least in numbers, research, and publication. Perhaps more important, this was the beginning of a period of international communication and interchange among anthropologists, and of the entrance into the anthropological tradition of those who had been the subjects of study, with effects still to be seen. Although anthropology was born in a spirit of justice for all people, and a hundred years ago won its battle against racism, it nevertheless was involved heavily in the colonial system. On one side, we gave sympathetic support to the oppressed among whom we worked; on the other, we provided information of use to the oppressors. We maximized the first by acting when we could as advocates for our friends, but there was little we could do to change their situation. Meanwhile, to protect our friends and our own position, we tended to work on esoteric matters of our own invention rather than providing social-political-economic facts that—once free—they might have found useful.

In North America anthropology was at its least colonial, and its history here was a special case. With the American Indian one of the greatest mysteries of the Age of Exploration, it is little wonder that America should one day become a center of anthropological study. The English, French, Germans, and other Europeans provided the traditions of scholarship, the books, the theories, but America provided a laboratory close by. In the United States, for example, Thomas Jefferson is sometimes said to have been the first anthropologist. He not only developed empirical research in archeology but also studied carefully the data on living Indian tribes and was a pioneer in the study of Indian languages. As A. I. Hallowell[3] puts it:

> Jefferson emerges as a significant figure in early anthropological thinking in this country not only because of his enduring interest in the Indian, his personal investigations, and expressed opinions. Through his attitude of rational inquiry, his active association with learned men of his time, and his role in our national government, he personifies, in a sense, the distinctive historical context in which anthropology in the United States was nourished in its infancy . . . In a letter (1789) to Reverend Joseph Williard, the President of Harvard College, he said: "What a field have we at our doors to signalize ourselves in! The Botany of America is far from being exhausted, its Mineralogy is untouched, and its Natural History or Zoology, totally mistaken and misrepresented . . . It is for such institutions as that over which you preside so worthily, Sir, to do justice to our country, its productions and its genius. It is the work to which the young men, whom you are forming should lay their hands." While Jefferson does not mention any discipline explicitly devoted to the study of man in his letter, his own pioneer work in the collection of Indian vocabularies, his descriptive and statistical data on Indian tribal groups tabulated in the *Notes*, his excavation of a mound, and the memorandum he prepared for the Lewis and Clark expedition concretely demonstrate, in principle, the kind of inquiry that he thought could be profitably carried on in America. Thus, without an academic label, he himself and others of his circle set an example by accumulating new knowledge regarding "Homo sapiens Americanus." This was anthropology, without portfolio, pursued on our own frontiers.

Jefferson set the pattern of the nineteenth century, wherein statesmen-scholars investigated the American Indians for their own sake even as history was pushing them into isolated corners of the country. The long series of scholars of the American Indian, of which the best-known names are Gallatin, Cass, and Schoolcraft, culminated with Lewis Henry Morgan, one of the first men in the world to combine personal intensive fieldwork in a native culture with comparative work and

3. A. I. Hallowell, "The Beginnings of Anthropology in America," in Frederica de Laguna (ed.), *Selected Papers from the* American Anthropologist (Evanston, Ill.: Row, Peterson & Co., 1960).

general theory. Missionaries and others lived with Indians and occasionally published important observations. Morgan was the first of those who did firsthand observation who tried also to place his results in worldwide perspective. In doing so, he virtually founded one of the great branches of modern social anthropology—the comparative study of family and kinship structure.

Anthropology in America was thus never a simple offshoot of European thought; it was an independent center to which firsthand knowledge of a variety of cultures gave both special opportunities and a particular character. Brinton, Powell, Holmes, Putnam, Bandelier, and dozens of others were great names in the development of anthropology in the late nineteenth century. Europeans led in uncovering their own long prehistory; but they were required to go thousands of miles to experience non-European cultures in person. It was in America, then, that the theorists themselves also had close experience with a profusion of exotic languages, cultures, and peoples.

And it was the combination of European liberal traditions and American cross-cultural experience that may be responsible for what we think of as "cultural relativism." This phrase became associated with anthropology in the nineteen-twenties, when we recognized that Western man's judgment of what is right and wrong derive from our culture, and thus is not eternally valid for the species. A universal religion which says the contrary—that "Thou shalt not kill" is the commandment of a God standing above cultures—is itself part of the teaching of particular cultures. Since what is wrong for one culture is right for another, on principle anything is right; and for some the doctrine was destructive of the moral force of any particular culture. But the anthropological tradition—quite to the contrary—emphasized the positive value of the moral order which any particular culture had developed, and inveighed only against seeking to impose by force the value of one culture on the people of another.

For better or worse, most individuals are dependent for their wellbeing on the norms and values that are part of the culture into which they have become socialized. Anthropology therefore leads individuals to nurture their own cultural roots even as they insist on respect for the values of others. So we all carry with us the liberal tradition of the first authropologists. Humankind is one; we value all peoples and cultures; we abhor any kind of prejudice against peoples, and the use of power for the domination of one nation by another. We believe in the self-determination of free peoples. We particularly abhor the misuse by bigots or politicians of any of our knowledge. As scientists we never know all of the truth; we must grope and probe, and ever learn; but we know infinitely more than the glib racists.

We are equalitarians not because we can prove absolute equality, but because we know absolutely that whatever differences there may be between large populations have no significance for the policies of nations. This comes from our knowledge as anthropologists; but it also pleases us as citizens of the world.

The science of man marches on with vigor. In 1975 there were in the world at least six thousand professional anthropologists, spread unevenly but in every continent, who were trying hard to develop and maintain a community through a journal, *Current Anthropology*, and through international congresses. More and more scholars are trained; the methods of study improve every year; the exchange of ideas and knowledge increases rapidly; and the results of our labors accumulate at an ever-increasing rate. These results—some of the newest of which are recounted in these chapters—and the interesting discoveries just beyond the horizon, are sufficient justification for anthropology. The discovery of man and culture is one of the noblest endeavors of the human spirit. But we also live in a world beset with problems; thus it is a fair question whether anthropology also has something to offer to help to solve them.

Like other scientists, we anthropologists believe that our greatest service to mankind is in the pursuit of knowledge. This is why society trains us. If we stop being scientists and scholars, what are we? So, for the most part we pursue scientific problems, not practical or political or social problems. Paul Broca noted not only that anthropology in America had suffered a period of eclipse because we had become embroiled in the politics of the Civil War, but that there was the other side of the coin:

> We find fault, and justly, with the *savants* who, under the convenient pretense of concentrating their efforts on one pursuit, flatter themselves that they can remain indifferent to the great questions which agitate society. The very fact of the superiority of their accomplishments, so far from giving such a right, entails on those gentlemen the duty of taking part in political life, and of exercising a beneficial influence on those who surround them. Let them, then, interest themselves in the affairs of their country. They cannot do better than plunge eagerly, according to their several temperaments, into the philosophical, religious, social, or humanitarian problems which surround them.

It is as citizens—not as research specialists—that Broca asked us to participate in public affairs. He did not know that our experience as general anthropologists would in time give us a special niche in the world of public affairs. Each of us participates—as Broca says—according to his or her temperament. All of us tend to believe that what we have learned in anthropology is important for everybody in the world to know, and some of us find it difficult not to shout it from the housetops. But what is it that we shout or do?

One answer to this question is suggested by the phrase "applied anthropology." Engineering and medicine are professions which can be said to apply the knowledge gained by the physical and the biological sciences. After this pattern, some have awaited the development of a profession that would apply the findings of anthropology. Indeed, since 1941, we have had in the United States a Society for Applied Anthropology that has attempted to build such a profession. Although this society has encouraged the use of anthropological knowledge by government and private organizations, no profession of applied anthropologists has come into being, either in the United States or elsewhere. Anthropological knowledge is used by administrators and managers with the wit to use it. If they wish professional assistance, they must turn to anthropologists. Anthropologists, indeed, become involved in management and administration, as well as in social work, education, and public health.

These anthropologists are sometimes distinguished from others who work for museums, research institutions, and universities; but, in contrast to analogous medical scientists, they do not form a class of practitioners. Instead, almost all anthropologists conceive of themselves both as pursuing academic research and as putting their knowledge to social use. If outsiders seek anthropological counsel, they must search out a genuine anthropologist; anthropologists who give them counsel will not dissociate themselves from either the name or their academic pursuits.

Anthropologists study man. Each anthropologist pursues a particular special study—this is what we mean by research—but all are actively interested in the whole study. We are highly specialized as social anthropologists, or human paleontologists, or linguists, for example, but we are equally general anthropologists. As we learn and teach our specialties, we also learn from other specialists and we teach in a context that we share with them.

Here then we come to the second answer to the question. It is as teachers of the lessons of the whole of anthropology that we put our science to use, and we teach not only in the classroom, important as that is to most of us, but wherever we work and live. Anthropology has become for us a way of life, a set of values to pass on to whomever we touch: our parents and our children, our colleagues at work or play, our fellow citizens wherever they are.

What it is that we teach is implicit in this book. The first attraction of anthropology is the very breadth of our subject matter—the study of mankind as a whole—which brings and holds us together and gives us the special character we then pass on: man as an animal, as a population, as a species; man's behavior and culture, and the behavior of this culture; the origin, characteristics, and distribution of the varieties of man—language, social forms, ideas; man's genetics, prehistory, and history, and the laws of history, which explain all of these in all time over the whole earth; comparative anatomy, personality, religion and ethics, law, sociology, and science; national characteristics, acculturation, socialization. All of these and whatever else may become relevant is the grand problem which anthropologists have chosen to study.

The original anthropologists were anatomists, philologists, geographers, and antiquarians who met in Paris, in London, in Moscow, or in New York to listen each to the other. It was their interest in the all-inclusive problem that drew them together and that made papers on craniometry interesting to philologists and to students of customs and led the anatomists in turn to papers on chipped-stone industries, on grammar, and on folklore. Those first anthropologists surely contributed not only breadth but great tolerance for variety in subject matter and in techniques of study. They established these as values which anthropology ever since has tended to emphasize.

It is not surprising that anthropology should characteristically form a society of scholars open to new techniques, tools, ideas, and men. The tools acquired range from the geological "law of uniformity" to the psychological Freudian model and Carbon-14 dating from chemistry. We have freely adopted, reinterpreted, and made our own whatever has appeared useful to our varied problems. Sometimes whole new fields of study such as "culture and personality," are added, but, of course, all that is really added are new answers to the heterogeneous problems already there. Anthropology always has been as broad in conception as it is possible to be. In wandering correspondingly widely for its data and tools, it absorbs into the tradition of the discipline those new men and women with special ideas who accept the breadth of anthropology.

The breadth, eclectism, and openness of boundaries of our subject matter are associated not only with an unusual tolerance for a variety of subjects and tools, but also for surprising ambiguity. It is not possible to be (as we say) "holistic"—to take into account all aspects of a problem—if we also require a clear structure. Given a choice between fully understanding one piece of a whole out of context or only half understanding a larger whole, we generally prefer the second. This choice is related to our predilection for dealing with the real world. Unlike economists and others who deal with abstractions comfortably, we reflect our origins in natural history in feeling more comfortable the closer we are to nature and to substantive problems rather than to theoretical or methodological issues.

The original interest of anthropologists in "other people" is also related to our concern with the reality of man through all time and space. Knowing mankind is to know all varieties of mankind; knowing people means seeing them as people. This is one source of our "liberal" view of other peoples and cultures. When it is recalled that the original Ethnological Society of Paris was formed by members of the Society for the Protection of Aborigines, it is not surprising that anthropologists have generally taken the side of the oppressed. But it is not only tradition and the circumstance of our founding that lend us our character. Our tradition takes us out to study different peoples and cultures. Though we see them in the broadest context, it is living people whom we come to know. It is because we live with them and come to know them that we learn from them. We keep our liberal tradition because we are the pupils of other peoples. Even if the "other peoples" are only archeological remains (or even not "peoples" at all, but baboons or gorillas!), our point of reference is still other living peoples and cultures, whose accomplishments give us humility and perspective and make us, too, "other" people.

It is precisely our tradition of general anthropology that makes it possible not only to use specialized knowledge but also to recognize the relevance of new specialties. The question is not whether any piece of specialized knowledge is directly useful, but how the insights of general anthropology can be put to the service of society. Hence that second answer to the question posed: we serve by passing on to others the point of view and the understandings that we have ourselves gained. We have learned and we teach that peoples of other species are equally human and thus equally able to achieve what is great and what is base. We have learned and we teach that the different peoples have from the very beginning of time developed particular ways and particular values; it is part of being commonly human to differ not simply as individuals but systematically as communities of individuals. We teach our concept of culture and our tolerance of cultures. We have learned and we teach that a people values its identity and resists changes which threaten it; that nobody but the people itself can judge what is important in its values and what is threatening. Thus we teach the wisdom of discovering rather than assuming what other people want and fear, the more difficult and the more important as the culture difference is greater. These lessons we can teach in the classroom, on the lecture platform, in books; and we hope that they will become part of a liberal education, to be understood by many.

What else? When we are asked, we can go further specifically to influence programs that deal with other peoples. Now it becomes important to distinguish among the kinds of people in a nation and in a community. We have learned that at an operating level, we deal not with a culture at all but with many cultures, or rather with groups of people, who are influenced not only by their cultures but by their position and by their interests as they perceive them. The programs in which we become involved concern what are now called "new nations." A new nation characteristically has an elite that is perhaps less separated than we are from its tribes and its villagers, but with interests often opposed to theirs. Anthropologists generally see the problem from the village point of view, while the administrators of programs see it from that of the governing elite with whom they deal. The problem is now not one simply of teaching what we have learned; to be helpful means to become political, and at this point, most scientists properly leave the task to others.

Suppose, however, that we stay with the problem: even now—where there are differences of interest and perspectives to which education is not an effective answer—how can knowledge derived from the study of man be deliberately put to the service of man?

"The service of man" is a large phrase. If it could be limited to—say—the service of one's own country, the problem would be more manageable. The country—any country—is governed by people, by specific departments, bureaus, committees, administrators; scientists simply place their knowledge at the service of one of these, and their problems are resolved. They become technicians—instruments. Indeed, the capitals of nations are crowded with social scientists who do just this. They are not necessarily weak, immoral, dishonorable. Often they will press points of view to change the philosophy of the agency.

Anthropologists who put their knowledge to the service of their country need not, therefore, lose their integrity or their freedom of action, although they may well lose their patience. The difference between serving one's conscience and one's boss, one's boss and one's country, one's country and mankind in each case is neither clear nor absolute. It is easy to rationalize one's own behavior—whatever it may be—or to blame the next anthropologist.

It is characteristic of anthropologists that if they do continue their work of education into what is close to the political realm, they act as independent agents, taking upon themselves the ultimate responsibility for satisfying their consciences in terms of the obligations they feel toward their colleagues and fellow men. It may be because anthropologists cannot comfortably have clients or work for others that a class of applied anthropologists does not develop.

Let us then accept the independence of anthropologists. Supposing them to be research scientists serving only the one master and responsible only to their consciences and to their colleagues, give them this problem: What are the circumstances in which a community of people achieves its own goals or is, on the contrary, frustrated? Assuming that there is basic agreement on what is wanted, communities of people still fall short. This happens whether the community one has in mind is a modern city unable to keep itself clean and orderly or a nation unable to control the growth of a strangling bureaucracy or the faculty of a university unable to protect its academic freedom.

The problem is one for the tools of political science, economics, and sociology as well; but it is the sort of general problem which anthropologists characteristically tackle, borrowing what tools we need. We usually think of beginning our research in a small community of a culture different from our own, since this is our special method of objectifying the problem, but we would hope to end up with some general understanding of the processes involved. Should we succeed in learning how any community of people can better achieve its own goals, we would have put anthropology to important use.

To study such a problem requires helping the people of the community to discover their goals; but since there are competing goals and wants and forces in the society, this cannot be a simple educational process. (If it were so simple, there would be no problem to begin with.) So anthropologists take a special position in the society and become actors as well as observers. They help people try various ways of discovering their goals and the ways of achieving them which suit their own cultural norms and their own self-perceived interests.

One well-known example of this sort of research is Allen Holmberg's work at Vicos in Peru, where the researchers from Cornell University had to lease a plantation to become the *patron* of the serf-like Indian community in order to put the community in a position where it could act freely for itself. The community responded remarkably, and Holmberg's experiment proves an important point not only for anthropology but also for the people of Vicos and Peru, for all others in similar circumstances, and for the policymaking powers in the world. Similarly, the University of Chicago's experiment in helping a small community of North American Indians to resolve its problems has led to understandings not only about American Indian problems in general but also about those of other population enclaves, such as the Maori of New Zealand and tribal peoples in India or Africa. The general lesson—that they will adjust to the modern world when their identity and their own cultural values are not threatened—is important because such threats may not really be necessary. The understandings gained by this method of research by the anthropologists of Cornell and Chicago could probably not have come in any other way. The results are proving themselves in understanding of the problems of new nations, of North American cities, even of the organization of universities. The same understand ing may some day help the peoples of the world to achieve the common goal of peace.

This method of research, often called *action anthropology,* does not fit the distinction frequently made between pure and applied research. It requires the intellectual and the political independence that one associates with a pure researcher. It depends upon university and foundation connections and support rather than government connections. But it also requires that anthropologists leave their ivory towers and, without losing their objectivity, enter into some world of affairs which becomes for the time being their laboratory. Since we are ethical people, and our laboratory a community of people who are not to be sacrificed for our purposes or for science or even for some larger humanity, anthropologists who undertake such research must be willing and able to take on unusual burdens and risks.

Like physicians with their patients, they accept the problems of a whole community as their own problems. Since they can never be wholly successful, they must be prepared for disappointments and frustrations, without even the satisfaction of blaming others besides themselves. It is no wonder that this method of research has not become common, or indeed fully accepted as legitimate. The stakes are high and the game dangerous; but action anthropology is nevertheless quite in the tradition and spirit of general anthropology and promises to provide the best demonstration of its meaning and its use.

BIBLIOGRAPHICAL NOTE

Modern anthropology as crystallized in the nineteen-thirties is well represented by Alfred L. Kroeber, *Anthropology* (New York: Harcourt, Brace & Co., Inc., 1948), Ralph Linton, *The Study of Man: An Introduction* (New York: D. Appleton-Century Co., 1936), and Melville J. Herskovits, *Cultural Anthropology* (New York: Alfred A. Knopf, Inc., 1955), which can be read as well today as when first published, except where fossil and archeological finds and chemical dating have provided new information on evolution and prehistory. The 1952 Wenner-Gren international symposium discussion of the whole discipline to that date is published in Alfred A. Kroeber (ed.), *Anthropology Today* (Chicago: University of Chicago Press, 1953) and in Sol Tax *et al.* (eds.), *Appraisal of Anthropology Today* (Chicago: University of Chicago Press, 1953). Beyond these sources, the context of the changing discipline is best seen by perusing such journals as the *American Anthropologist*, the British *Man*, their equivalents in other countries and languages, and the international journal *Current Anthropology*.

The character and knowledge of the changing anthropological subdisciplines—biological, archeological, linguistic, cultural—are best seen through their own journals. Each has its own history and its relations with nonanthropological traditions in the humanities and in the biological and social sciences. The history of anthropology itself was until recently represented only by short sketches, Alfred C. Haddon, *History of Anthropology* (London: Watts & Co., 1910) and T. K. Penniman, *A Hundred Years of Anthropology* (New York: William Morrow & Co., Inc., 1974), among them. Robert H. Lowie's *History of Ethnological Theory* (New York: Henry Holt & Co., Inc., 1937) was the most substantial, supplemented by such specialized pieces as Sol Tax, "From Lafitau to Radcliffe-Brown," in Fred Eggan (ed.), *Social Anthropology of the North American Tribes* (2nd ed. Chicago: University of Chicago Press, 1955), and A. Irving Hallowell, "The Beginnings of Anthropology in America," in Frederica de Laguna (ed.), *Selected Papers from the American Anthropologist* (Evanston, Ill.: Row, Peterson & Co., 1960). Until the nineteen-sixties, indeed, the history of anthropology was largely a mythology developed casually among the in group by interested parties—for example, Tax's 1955 plea for the unity of the field. Beginning about 1960, professional historians joined us in interpreting our past: George W. Stocking, Jr., *Race, Culture and Evolution: Essays in the History of Anthropology* (New York: Free Press, 1968); "What's in a Name? The Royal Anthropological Institute: 1837–1871," *Man* 6:369–390 (1971); and *The Shaping of American Anthropology 1883–1911: A Franz Boas Reader* (New York: Basic Books, Inc., 1973). The most recent history is Annemarie De Waal Malefijt's *Images of Man: A History of Anthropological Thought* (New York: Alfred A. Knopf, Inc., 1974), which includes ideas about man in the ancient world and in Europe, with a good bibliography citing the two important earlier collections of such sources, Margaret T. Hodgen, *Early Anthropology in the Sixteenth and Seven-*

teenth Centuries (Philadelphia: University of Pennsylvania Press, 1964), and James Sydney Slotkin, *Readings in Early Anthropology* (Chicago: Aldine Publishing Co., 1965). Angel Palerm's *Historia de la Etnologia: los Precursores* (Mexico City: Centro de Investigaciones Superiores, Insituto Nacional de Antropologia e Historia, 1973) extends these horizons to include writings of early scholars in Asia and Latin America. Biographical and historical books continually increase in numbers abroad—for example, Ugo Bianchi, *Storia dell'etnologia* (Rome: Abete Press, 1965)—and in the United States—for example, Marvin Harris, *The Rise of Anthropological Theory: A History of Theories of Culture* (New York: Thomas Y. Crowell Co., 1968), and the biographical series of Columbia University Press.

The best view of how anthropology is used will come from perusal through the years of the journal *Human Organization* and two much-used casebooks, Edward M. Spicer's *Human Problems in Technological Change* (New York: Russell Sage Foundation, 1952) and Benjamin Paul's *Health, Culture and Community* (New York: Russell Sage Foundation, 1955). Two textbooks on applied anthropology are George M. Foster, *Applied Anthropology* (Boston: Little, Brown & Co., 1969) and James A. Clifton, *Applied Anthropology: Readings in the Uses of the Science of Man* (Boston: Houghton Mifflin Co., 1970). A more profound (and international) treatment by the late Roger Bastide entitled *Applied Anthropology* (New York: Harper & Row Publishers, Inc., 1974) has recently been translated from the French. Two well-known action anthropology programs— the University of Chicago's Fox project and Cornell's Vicos project—are described, respectively, in Frederick O. Gearing, *The Face of the Fox* (Chicago: Aldine Publishing Co., 1970), and Henry F. Dobyns *et al., Peasants, Power and Applied Social Change: Vicos as a Model* (Beverly Hills, Calif.: Sage Publications, Inc., 1971). The broadest perspective for anthropological input into national and international programs will come from the journal *Economic Development and Cultural Change* (University of Chicago Press).

2.

THE TRANSITION TO HUMANITY

Clifford Geertz

THE QUESTION OF THE relationship of man to the other animals has been a persisting one in the human sciences. Since Darwin, it has hardly been doubted that there is such a relationship. But concerning its nature, and particularly its closeness, there has been very much more debate, not all of it enlightening. Some students, especially those in the biological sciences—zoology, palaeontology, anatomy and physiology—have tended to stress the kinship between man and what we are pleased to call the lower animals. They see evolution as a relatively unbroken flow of biological process, and they tend to view man as but one of the more interesting forms life has taken, along with dinosaurs, white mice and dolphins. What strikes them is continuity, the pervasive unity of the organic world, the unconditioned generality of the principles in terms of which it is formed. However, students in the social sciences—psychologists, sociologists, political scientists—while not denying man's animal nature have tended to view him as unique, as being different, as they often put it, not just in "degree" but in "kind." Man is the toolmaking, the talking, the symbolizing animal. Only he laughs; only he knows that we will die; only he disdains to mate with his mother and sister; only he contrives those visions of other worlds to live in which Santayana called religions, or bakes those mudpies of the mind which Cyril Connolly called art. He has, the argument continues, not just mentality but consciousness, not just needs but values, not just fears but conscience, not just a past but a history. Only he, it concludes in grand summation, has culture.

The reconciliation of these two points of view has not been easy, particularly in a field such as anthropology, which, in the United States at least, has always had a foot in both camps. On the one hand, anthropologists have been the main students of human physical evolution, tracing the stages by which modern man emerged out of a general primate background. On the other, they have been the students par excellence of culture, even when they were not entirely certain what they meant by that term. Unlike some biological scientists, they could not ignore man's cultural life as belonging "over on the Arts side," beyond the confines of Science altogether. Unlike some social scientists, they could not dismiss his physical history as irrelevant to an understanding of his present condition. As a result, the problem of the origin of culture, no matter how often ignored as unimportant or derided as insoluble, has continually come pressing back to the center of our attention as, piece by piece, the story of the physical evolution of *Homo sapiens* has been put together. It is the peculiar genius of such an eclectic discipline as American anthropology that the triumphs of one branch of it expose the failures of the others; and in such a way the science is built.

For the past half century or so, the reigning solution of the origin-of-culture problem has been what might be called the "critical point" theory. This term, which I take from the onetime dean of American anthropology, Alfred Kroeber, postulates that the development of the capacity for acquiring culture was a sudden, all-or-none, quantum-leap type of occurrence in the phylogeny of the primates. At some specific moment in the history of hominidization—i.e., the "humanization" of one branch of the primate line—a portentous, but in genetic or anatomical terms probably quite minor, organic alteration took place. This change, presumably in cortical structure, enabled an animal whose parents had not been competent, in Kroeber's words, "to communicate, to learn and to teach, to generalize from the endless chain of discrete feelings and attitudes" to become competent. With him culture began and, once begun, set upon its own course so as to grow wholly independently of the further organic evolution of man. The whole process of the creation of modern man's capacity for producing and using culture was conceptualized as one of a marginal quantitative change giving rise to a radical qualitative difference. Kroeber used the simile of the freezing of water, which can be reduced degree by degree without any loss in fluidity until suddenly it solidifies at 0°C. Another anthropologist compared the process to that of a taxiing plane as it accelerates along the ground toward that tremulous instant when it is launched into flight. A physical anthropologist, critical of the notion, referred to it drily as the appointment-to-rank view of the appearance of man, "as if he had suddenly been promoted from colonel to brigadier general." Man's humanity, like the flare of a struck match, leaped into existence.

There were three major considerations which led to and supported this general view. First, there was the tremendous apparent gap between the mental abilities of man and his closest living relatives, the great apes. Man can talk, can symbolize, can fabricate tools, etc.; no other contemporary animal can even approximate such accomplishments. One primatologist couple even undertook the heroic experiment of raising a chimpanzee in their household as though it were an adopted sibling to their natural daughter, giving it, in a rough sort of way, the same care and education given to the human child. But though the chimp learned a good many rather unusual things for a chimp to learn—how to operate a spray gun, how to pry the lids off of tin cans with a screwdriver, and, at one glorious point, how to pull an imaginary toy around by an imaginary string—it never even began to learn to talk. And, unable to talk, it was soon left far behind by its less agile but more loquacious human sister, who proceeded onward, one presumes, to spin complicated theories about the uniqueness of the human condition.

Second, language, symbolization, abstraction, etc., seemed, on purely logical grounds, to be all-or-none, yes-or-no matters. One either spoke or did not; made tools or did not; imagined demons or did not. Half-religions, half-arts, half-languages did not seem even conceivable, for the essential process which lay behind them—i.e., the imposition of an arbitrary framework of symbolic meaning upon reality—was not the sort of activity of which there were partial versions. The progress from simple reflex activity, through conditioned responses and complex sign behavior, to symbolic thought was seen as a series of jumps, not an ascending continuum. Between the perception of the natural relationship of dark clouds to rain and the establishment of the arbitrary relationship of dark clouds to hopelessness there were, so it was thought, no intermediate stages.

And, third, there was the more delicate problem of what is usually called "the psychic unity of mankind." This has reference to the proposition—today not seriously questioned by any reputable anthropologist—which asserts that there are no important differences in the nature of the thought process among the various living races of mankind. If one assumes that culture appeared full-blown at some instant of time at a period before racial differentiation began, then this proposition becomes true virtually by deduction. To raise the question as to whether there might be historical differences in the ability to acquire culture among different species of hominids—i.e., among the various sorts of "men," living and extinct—seemed to raise it with respect to different races of modern men. And as the empirical evidence against such differences among the various groups of *Homo sapiens* was, and is, overwhelming, the hypothesis seemed disproved on the face of it. Thus comparative psychology, semantics, and ethnology converged to support the critical point theory of the origin of culture.

One branch of anthropology, however, did not so converge—human palaeontology, i.e., the study of human evolution by means of the discovery and analysis of fossil remains. Ever since that strange Dutch physician, Eugene DuBois, found the skull cap of *Pithecanthropus erectus,* the "erect ape-man," in a Javanese river bed in 1891, historical physical anthropology has been steadily piling up evidence that makes the drawing of a sharp line between man and non-man on an anatomical basis increasingly difficult. Despite some halfhearted attempts to establish a "cerebral Rubicon"—a critical brain size at which the ability to behave in a properly human manner springs full-grown into existence like Athena from the brow of Zeus—the findings of human palaeontologists have, bit by fossil bit, smoothed the curve of the descent of man to the point where flat assertions about what is human and what is not human have come to have a painfully arbitrary air about them. Whether or not human minds or souls come in degrees, human bodies most assuredly do.

The most disturbing fossil finds in this connection have been the various sorts of australopithecine "man-apes" which have been coming out of southern and eastern Africa since Raymond Dart dug the first one up out of the Transvaal in 1924. Certainly the most momentous discoveries in the history of human palaeontology, these fossils, which date anywhere from three-quarters of a million to three and three-quarter million years ago, show a striking mosaic of primitive and advanced morphological characteristics, in which the most outstanding features are a pelvis and leg formation strikingly similar to that of modern man and a cranial capacity hardly larger than that of living apes. The initial tendency was to regard this puzzling conjunction in one animal of a "manlike" bipedal locomotive system and an "apelike" brain as indicating that the australopithecines represented an aberrant and ill-fated line of development separate from both the human and the great ape lines—better to be a thorough-going ape than half a man, as Ernest Hooton once put it. But the present consensus is that they represent the oldest known forms in the evolutionary process which eventually produced modern man out of some generally simian stock. In these bizarre half-men our own full humanity is rooted.

F. Clark Howell discusses the significance of the australopithecines from the point of view of human phylogeny in his chapter; my interest in them here is in their implications for the critical point theory of the origin of culture. These more or less erect, small-brained proto-men, their hands freed from locomotion, manufactured tools and probably hunted small animals—or at least some of them did so. But that they could have had a developed culture comparable to that of, say, the Australian aborigine or possessed language in the modern sense of the term with a brain about a third the size of our own seems wholly unlikely. In the australopithecine we seem to have, therefore, a kind of "man" who evidently was capable of acquiring some elements of culture—simple toolmaking, sporadic hunting, and perhaps some system of communication more advanced than that of contemporary apes and less advanced than that of true speech—but not others, a state of affairs which casts something of a shadow on the critical point theory. What seemed presumptively unlikely, or even logically impossible, turns out to have been empirically true—like man himself, the capacity for culture emerged gradually, continuously, step by step, over a quite extended period of time.

But the situation is even more desperate. Because if the australopithecines had an elementary form of culture (what one anthropologist has called "proto-culture") with a brain one-third the size of that of modern man, then it follows that the greater part of human cortical expansion has followed, *not* preceded, the "beginning" of culture. In the critical point view man was considered more or less complete, neurologically at least, before the growth of culture commenced, because the biological capacity for culture was an all-or-none thing. Once achieved it was achieved entirely; all else was a mere adding on of new customs and developing of older ones. Organic evolution proceeded up to a certain point and then, the cerebral Rubicon crossed, cultural evolution took over, a process in itself autonomous and not dependent upon or productive of further nervous system alterations. The fact that this is apparently not the case, that cultural development was underway well before organic development ceased, is of fundamental significance for our view of the nature of man. He becomes, now, not just the producer of culture but, in a specifically biological sense, its product.

This is true because the pattern-of-selection pressures during the terminal phases of the evolution of the human animal was partly determined by the initial phases of human cultural development, not simply by natural environmental factors alone. A reliance upon tool manufacture, for example, puts a premium on both manual dexterity and on foresight. Within a population of australopithecines an individual somewhat better endowed with these characteristics would have had a selective advantage over an individual somewhat less well endowed. Hunting small animals with primitive weapons involves, among other things, great patience and persistence. The individual with more of these sober virtues would have an advantage over a flightier individual with less of them. All these various abilities, skills, dispositions, or whatever, are, of course, dependent in turn upon nervous system development. And so the introduction of tool manufacture and hunting must have acted to shift selection pressures so as to favor the rapid growth of the forebrain, as, in all likelihood, did the advances in social organization, communication, and more regulation which, there is reason to believe, also occurred during this period of overlap between cultural and biological change.

Much of the work in this area is, of course, still speculative, and we are just beginning to ask the questions rather than to answer them. The systematic study of primate behavior under natural conditions which is having such an impact on our interpretations of the social life of early man, is, save for a few isolated exceptions, scarcely a quarter of a century old, for example. The fossil record itself is now expanding at such a fantastic rate and dating procedures are becoming so rapidly refined that only the foolhardy would attempt to set out definitive opinions on particular matters. But, details, evidence, and specific hypotheses aside, the essential point is that the innate, generic constitution of modern man (what, in a simpler day, used to be called "human nature") now appears to be both a cultural and a biological product. "It is probably more correct," physical anthropologist Sherwood Washburn has written, "to think of much of our [physical] structure as a result of culture rather than to think of men anatomically like ourselves slowly discovering culture." The slogan "man makes himself" now comes to have a more literal meaning than originally supposed.

The ice age, with its rapid and radical variations in climate, land formations, and vegetation, has long been recognized to be a period in which conditions were ideal for the speedy and efficient evolutionary development of man. Now it seems also to have been a period in which a cultural environment increasingly supplemented the natural environment in the selection process so as to further accelerate the rate of human evolution to an unprecedented speed. It appears not to have been merely a time of receding brow ridges and shrinking jaws, but a time in which were forged nearly all those characteristics of man's existence which are most graphically human: his thoroughly encephalated nervous system, his incest-taboo-based social structure, and his capacity to create and use symbols. The fact these distinctive features of humanity emerged together in complex interaction with one another rather than serially, as for so long supposed, is a fact of exceptional importance in the interpretation of human mentality, because it suggests that man's nervous system does not merely enable him to acquire culture, it positively demands that he do so if it is going to function at all. Rather than culture acting only to supplement, develop, and extend organically based capacities genetically prior to it, it would seem to be ingredient to those capacities themselves. A cultureless human being would probably turn out to be not an intrinsically talented though unfulfilled ape, but a wholly mindless and consequently unworkable monstrosity. Like the cabbage it so much resembles, the *Homo sapiens* brain, having arisen within the framework of human culture, would not be viable outside of it.

The general implications of this revised view of the transition to humanity are many, only a few of which can be touched upon here. On the one hand, it has forced a reinvestigation and reformulation of the theoretical considerations which supported the critical point theory in the first place. The argument from comparative primate psychology, for example, it is now apparent, established not the uniqueness of modern man, but rather the distinctiveness of the whole five- to twenty-five-million year hominid line of which he is but the culminating and, it so happens, the only living representative, but which includes a large number of different kinds of extinct animals, all of them much "closer" to man than is any living ape. The fact that chimpanzees do not talk is both interesting and important, but to draw from that fact the conclusion that speech is an all-or-nothing phenomenon is rather like assuming that since the giraffe is the only living quadruped with such a long neck, he must have achieved it by a sort of quantum stretch. The great apes may be man's closest living relatives, but "close" is, to commit a pun, a relative term. Given a realistic time scale they are not actually so close at all, the last common ancestor being at the very least fifty thousand centuries back in what geologists call the Pliocene, and perhaps even further back than that.

As for the logical argument, that too has come to be questioned. The rapidly increasing interest in communication as a general process which has marked disciplines from engineering to ethology in the last decade or two has, on the one hand, reduced speech to but one—admittedly highly flexible and efficient—mechanism for the transmission of meanings among many, and, on the other hand, provided a theoretical framework in terms of which series of graded steps leading up to true speech can be conceived. This work cannot be reviewed here, but as an example one linguist has compared eight different systems of communication ranging from bee dancing, fish courtship, and bird singing through gibbon calls, instrumental music, and human language. Rather than pivoting his entire analysis around the simple, and by now somewhat overburdened, sign-*vs.*-symbol distinction, he distinguishes thirteen design features of language and attempts in terms of them to analyze the difference between human and subhuman communication more precisely and to construct a possible course from the gradual development of true speech out of proto-speech during the ice age. This kind of work, too, is only in its infancy. But the day seems to be coming to an end when the only thing that could usefully be said about the origins of language was that all humans equally possess it and all non-humans equally do not.

Finally, the established fact that there are no significant differences in innate mental capacity among the living races of man is not contradicted, but if anything supported and deepened, by the postulation of differences in the capacity to acquire culture among different forms of presapiens men. The physical divergence of the human races is, of course, a very recent matter, beginning perhaps only fifty thousand years or so ago, or, by the most conservative estimates, less than one hundredth of the length of the whole hominid, i.e., man-forming, line. Thus mankind has not only spent the overwhelming proportion of its history in an altogether common evolutionary process, but this period now seems to have been precisely the one during which the fundamental features of its humanity were forged. Modern races are just that: modern. They represent very late, and very secondary, adaptation in skin color, facial structure, etc.—probably mainly due to climatic differences—as *Homo sapiens* dispersed throughout the world toward the close of the glacial period. These adaptations are thus entirely subsequent to the basic formative processes of neural and anatomical development which occurred between the founding of the hominid line and the emergence, fifty to one hundred fifty millennia ago, of *Homo sapiens.* Mentally, man was made in the ice age, and the really decisive shaping force in producing his uniqueness—the interaction of the initial phases of cultural development and the culminating ones of biological transformation—is part of the common background of all modern races. Thus, the view that the capacity for carrying culture, rather than bursting into full flower at a single point, was hammered out in old stone age toolshops over an extended period of time, far from undermining the doctrine of psychic unity explains and specifies it. It gives it a realistic historical grounding it previously rather lacked.

But even more important than the revision of reinterpretation of older theories which the synchronous, rather than the sequential, view of the relationship between the evolution of human anatomy and the birth of human culture necessitates, is its implications for a novel way of thinking about culture itself. If man grew up, so to speak, within the context of a developing cultural environment, then that environment must needs be viewed not as a mere extrasomatic extension, a sort of artificial amplification, of already given innate capacities, but as ingredient to the existence of those capacities themselves. The apparent fact that the final stages of the biological evolution of man occurred after the initial stages of the growth of culture implies, as I have already noted, that "basic," "pure," or "unconditioned" human nature, in the sense of the innate constitution of man, is so functionally incomplete as to be unworkable. Tools, hunting, family organization, and later, art, religion, and a primitive form of "science," molded man somatically, and they are therefore necessary not merely to his survival but to his existential realization. It is true that without men there would be no cultural forms. But it is also true that without cultural forms there would be no men.

The symbolic network of belief, expression, and value within which we live provides for us the mechanisms for ordered behavior which in lower animals are genetically built into their bodies but which in ourselves are not. The uniqueness of man has often been expressed in terms of how much and how many different things he is capable of learning. And although chimpanzees who learn to play with imaginary toys may give us some pause, this is true enough. But what is of perhaps even more fundamental theoretical importance is how much there is for man to learn. Without the guiding patterns of human culture, man's intellectual life would be but the buzzing, blooming confusion that William James called it; cognition in man depends upon the existence of objective, external symbolic models of reality in a way no ape's does. Emotionally, the case is the same. Without the guidance of the public images of sentiment found in ritual, myth, and art we would, quite literally, not know how to feel. Like the expanded forebrain itself, ideas and emotions are cultural artifacts in man.

What this heralds, I think, is a fundamental revision in the theory of culture itself. We are going, in the next few decades, to look at culture patterns less and less in terms of the way in which they constrain human nature, and more and more in the way in which, for better or for worse, they actualize it; less and less as an accumulation of ingenious devices to extend pre-existing innate capacities, and more and more as part and parcel of those capacities themselves; less and less as a superorganic cake of custom, and more and more as, in a vivid phrase of the late Clyde Kluckhohn, designs for living. Man is the only living animal who needs such designs for he is the only living animal whose evolutionary history has been such that his physical being has been significantly shaped by their existence and is, therefore, irrevocably predicated upon them. As the full import of this fact becomes recognized, the tension between the view of man as but a talented animal and the view of him as an unaccountably unique one should evaporate, along with the theoretical misconceptions which gave rise to it.

BIBLIOGRAPHICAL NOTE

Alfred A. Kroeber's statement of the "critical point" theory is to be found in his *Anthropology* (New York: Harcourt, Brace & Co., Inc., 1948). A somewhat different, less cautious formulation of the theory, emphasizing the discontinuity between symbol using and other forms of thought, can be found in Leslie A. White's *The Science of Culture* (New York: Grove Press, Inc., 1949). For brief discussions of the australopithecine and their significance, see the selections by L. S. B. Leakey, "The Origins of the Genus Homo," and Sherwood Washburn and F. Clark Howell, "Human Evolution and Culture," both in Sol Tax (ed.), *Evolution after Darwin* (Chicago: University of Chicago Press, 1960). Some comments on australopithecine cultural achievements can be found in the chapter by Irving Hallowell in the same book. Irving Hallowell's "Behaviorial Evolution and the Emergence of Self," in Betty Meggers (ed.), *Evolution and Anthropology* (Washington, D. C.: Anthropological Society of Washington, 1959), is also valuable in this connection. A good popular summary of the theory of the relationship between tool using and neurological change can be found in an article by Sherwood Washburn in *Scientific American* (1960) and, in fact, the entire special issue on "The Human Species" is relevant. Finally, I have myself developed the above arguments at greater length and more technically in "The Growth of Culture and the Evolution of Mind," in Jordan Scher (ed.), *Theories of the Mind* (New York: Free Press, 1962), and have, in fact, adapted a number of passages from this paper into the above essay.

3.

THE STUDY OF EVOLUTION

Eric R. Wolf

EVEN TO THE CASUAL observer it will be apparent that the development of anthropological theory has been characterized by fits and starts rather than by orderly accretion and continuity. We shall need a sociologist of knowledge to tell us why this should have been so; but the fact is indisputable. The theoretical structure erected by the evolutionists of the nineteenth century fell under the axe of diffusionist criticism; but the pieces of the old house were not used in the construction of the new theoretical edifice. The diffusionists built anew, disregarding the problems and answers of their predecessors, only to suffer a similar fate at the hands of the functionalists.

The problems of the past were neither answered nor remembered; new problems and new answers simply replaced the old. Thus it is not surprising that the old problems should return now to concern us. In the recent past, American anthropologists have again become interested in the problems posed by the early evolutionists. Sometimes this interest is eclectic, seeing equal but separate "good" in evolutionism, diffusionism and functionalism; but there has also been a striving towards a new, integrated approach in which the theoretical contributions of the past would form a new and exciting synthesis.

The early evolutionists believed that the world in which they lived could be illuminated by the hypothesis that human culture had undergone progressive and cumulative growth; and they labored to show the lawful nature of this growth. The

33

categories they used in their demonstration proved unhappily clumsy, and their assumption that clusters of these categories, taken together, would serve to define unequivocal stages of cultural development, proved oversimplified and unwarranted. The diffusionists demonstrated the limitations of these categories when they showed that possession of the bow and arrow did not automatically raise the bushmen to the level of barbarism, while its absence did not condemn the Polynesians to a state of savagery. Concepts such as matriarchy or totemism, regarded as universal or near-universal, and therefore useful in building the evolutionary perspective, were dismembered into separate components which demonstrably did not always occur together.

Yet in performing their tasks of criticism and testing, the diffusionists did not return to the basic question that had exercised the minds of their antagonists. Rather they set aside altogether the problem of cumulation in culture, and sought instead greater knowledge of how the traits that made up a given culture had come together in one place at one time. There emerged a picture of culture as a congeries of unrelated, inherently separable components, "a thing of shreds and patches," a view which among American anthropologists was tempered only by the realization that in moving through space, culture traits, and the temporary aggregates of traits they called cultures, bore some relation to the nature of the physical environment and to the presence or absence of other neighboring societies. The first of these interests was to develop later into the culture-ecological approach of Julian Steward who came to inquire into the specific relationships of a particular technology to a particular environment, and into the resulting limitations on the borrowing of other traits; the other gave rise to the many interesting acculturation studies of the thirties and forties in which groups of Indians were seen in their multiple relationships to other cultural groups surrounding them.

Both of these approaches are now components of the new evolutionist perspective. But the diffusionists proper were in turn assailed by the functionalists who derided the diffusionist perspective of history as a Brownian movement of traits, and drew attention instead to the meshing of traits, their interrelationships and interpenetrations in real life as lived by Trobriand Islanders or Tallensi. We now know that they, too, overstressed the internal fit of traits and overplayed the analogy of culture to an organism in which every part contributes to the maintenance of every other. Their marvelously detailed studies of internal linkages in culture have led them to ascribe to their cultural bodies a "wisdom" *sui generis,* much as Walter Cannon, the physiologist, came to speak of the "wisdom of the body."

The new evolutionism that is arising in America wishes to make these various approaches relevant to each other, to synthesize their positive contributions and to supplement the shortcomings of one by using the insights of the other.

From the evolutionists of the nineteenth century, we take, first of all, the notion of cumulative development in human culture, its movement toward the maximization of certain values. This approach emphasizes quantitative differences and implies that cultures can be ranked along some scale ranging from small to large numbers. Such quantitative scaling is implied, for instance, in general propositions such as those made by Leslie White to the effect that "culture evolves as the amount of energy harnessed per capita per year is increased, or as the efficiency of the instrumental means of putting the energy to work is increased." In actuality, this measurement of energy conversion presents many problems, problems that engage the attention of anthropologists such as Richard Adams and Marvin Harris, and of sociologists such as Fred Cottrell and Alfred Ubbelohde. Another formulation holds that culture evolves as the ability to use different natural resources expands, or as culture is able to control more and different environments. A number of rough schemata for the classification of environments in relation to culture are now available, as for instance those developed by Chapple and Coon or Philip Wagner, but much greater refinement in scoring environmental variables is possible, for example, on the basis of the Köppen system of classification.

Another index of evolutionary cumulation in culture is the increase of population since the Palaeolithic, used by V. Gordon Childe to mark off major evolutionary advances; but here again greater refinement is possible through the techniques utilized by demographers to establish the comparative viability of populations. Raoull Narroll has used the number of people in the most populous building cluster of the ethnic unit studied as an index of social development, and has shown that this measure can be related systematically in a mathematical formula to the number of occupational specialties and to the number of organizational types. Morton Fried's study of the evolution of social stratification also implied two measures: a ratio between positions of prestige available for any given age-sex grade and the number of persons capable of filling them, on the one hand, and a ratio between strategic resources and persons possessing impeded or unimpeded access to them, on the other. Hornell Hart has drawn up logistic curves to demonstrate the ever increasing size of territorial and political units since palaeolithic times and has demonstrated the accelerated rate of growth in the development of these units. Various indices developed by Karl Deutsch to gauge the intensity of communication between social units await application to the measurement of cumulation in communication over the course of cultural evolution; and in a paper on folk medicine in Latin America, Charles Erasmus has related amounts and varieties of probable kinds of knowledge to the degree of specialization available to the society. It is furthermore not impossible that the movement toward componential analysis, such as Charles Frake's work on levels of terminological contrasts in the diagnosis of disease by a Philippine tribe, may ultimately yield a measure of the relative complexity of cognitive systems. Since environmental variables, energy conversion, division of labor, population, access to resources and prestige, intensity of communication and cognitive complexity appear to be mutually dependent, the possibility of establishing a master formula relating all or several of these terms seems within our grasp.

But evolution is not characterized merely by quantitative cumulation, it is also characterized by qualitative changes in organization. Such qualitative changes result in the emergence of new cultural components which subsume and integrate preexisting components in a new way. Thus the invention of the sailing ship represents the integration of the boat with a particular technique for harnessing wind power, together with the minimum tackle for holding the two components in the proper relationship. The state represents a coordination of specialized social groups through the development of an apparatus capable of wielding power. The emergence of new qualitative levels is often followed by further attempts to develop and integrate the component parts. The development of the sailing ship depended upon the ever greater improvement in the design of hull, sails and rigging, and their more careful integration. The development of the state depended upon the standardization and specialization of component units, and their ever more complete subordination of the governing authority.

It is possible to observe the emergence of new levels of organization in many series of culture growths, but one major qualitative change has engaged the attention of anthropologists since the beginning. This may be called the qualitative shift from unspecialized or totipotent cultures, to cultures which rely for their operation on the specialization of parts. Unspecialized cultures—and most early hunting-and-gathering cultures belong to this type—are totipotent in the sense that each group had at its command all the cultural components necessary to relate man to environment, man to man, and man to universe. Such groups were capable of replicating the entire gamut of components when fissioning into two or more separate units. Birdsell has indicated that the population of such groups could be expected to double each generation, and that fission was likely to occur when such a population rose to 60 to 80 percent of its carrying capacity. Such rapid fission and replication were therefore accompanied by an equally rapid movement into a wide variety of ecological niches, and a resulting adaptive differentiation of the various cultural sets to their different life situations.

This proliferation to totipotent units encountered a double limitation. First, differentiation and adaptation to different environmental variables favored a degree of complementary specialization and mutual interchange. Second, occupation of free niches by fissioning groups reduced the size of available territory to which their energy potential gave them access. With increased complementarity and limitations on free movement, there came increased interdependence and a correlative decline in the ability to fission freely. Social groups were ever less able to duplicate the entire range of needed cultural components in a new medium.

The characteristic bearer of such totipotent cultural sets was the kin group, ranging in forms from the nuclear family to the localized descent group embracing a number of nuclear families. The kin group, small or large, appears to be the ideal unspecialized unit, capable of providing all the services needed to sustain an individual while at the same time able to absorb maximal tensions and stresses which would sunder a more complex, specialized unit not similarly cemented together by the sexual division of labor and the bonds of emotional intimacy. Hence we witness throughout this stage, and indeed up to the very threshold of the industrial revolution, a proliferation of kin-based units, each oriented toward the maintenance of its particular membership, and hence often in opposition to other similar units or to the more specialized components of culture which characterize the next qualitative level of cultural evolution.

In the course of evolution, totipotent and specialized cultures have given way many times over to cultures which favor the growth of differentiation and specialization. In such cultures we witness the development of privileged positions, organized largely around the concentration of goods and labor from the different units and their subsequent redistribution. Such concentrations and distributions could be largely peaceful in character, as in the give-aways of Melanesians and British Columbian Indians, or in the intergroup exchanges of the Massim Island kula. But it could be based also on predatory activities in which the predators concentrated and distributed goods and labor originally produced by another group of people. Differentiation of roles between the pivotal position of chief, or war leader, or organizer of trade expeditions and the supporting positions of followers and applauding public polarized also the respective particularistic kin groups of these social actors. We witness not merely a differentiation in the power orbit of individuals, but a differentiation of their dependents into social classes. The result has been the emergence of social asymmetry in the place of equivalent, symmetrical relations. This asymmetry has grown steadily with the increase in surpluses made available by increased energy conversion and further specialization of labor.

Increasing social asymmetry in a more differentiated social order required the development of specialized machinery needed both to maintain and widen it, and thus prompted the emergence of the apparatus we call the state. It is important that the state emerged as a wide-ranging peak organization capable of maintaining order, of maximizing division of labor, and of concentrating and distributing surpluses produced, in competition with the particularistic kin groups of the past. To this day the success of any particular state depends on the respective competitive strength of its component units. Peak organizations may have to relinquish large areas of social control to such units, traditional or other, because their apparatus for maximizing administrative benefits is weak, or because the costs of administration stand in no relation to the benefits to be derived. Within these interstitial areas in the network of control, therefore, competitive units forever proliferate, especially when they offer their members goods and services not offered or delivered by the state. Anthropologists study such competitive relations when they examine the competition between the organization of the Chinese state and the kin groups of its gentry; the competitive orbits of particularistic caste and state-centered guild in India; the tug and pull of lineages in African kingdoms. Such problems are also studied by sociologists who appraise the bargaining power of organized sodalities such as businessmen's associations or trade unions, or the powers of organized crime, or the networks of personal influence (called *blat*) developed by Soviet industrial managers.

Implicit in the approach of the old-line evolutionists, though not spelled out in these terms, was also the notion that a given feature of culture possessed a certain potential or capacity. This concept, when applied to cultural components, implies not only a range of capabilities, but also a lower and an upper limit. The upper or lower limit may be established quantitatively, in terms of energy converted, numbers of people coordinated, or in terms of cognition yield. Further qualitative analysis will tell us whether it could be lower or higher; whether it possesses inherent limits, or whether its operation produces side-effects which inhibit its intended impact. Thus we can measure the relative capacity of a hoe made of the shoulder bone of a bison and a steel plow in the breaking of tough prairie soil. We can gauge the relative carrying capacity of a territory as exploited by slash-and-burn cultivation or irrigated agriculture. We can look at kinship systems, and take note of the fact that the Kariera system of Australia requires for its operation two intermarrying groups, the Arunta system four, the system of the Ambryms six. We may note that the mutual aid and security set involved in the Latin American *compadrazgo* relation, based on ceremonial sponsorship in life-crisis ceremonials, is limited in scope by the number of children available for sponsorship, while a savings-and-loan association in a Midwestern town can accommodate thousands of members. We are enabled to see how a Kachin chief attracts followers through the operations of the marriage system and the give-away, but how he cannot increase the exploitation of his sons-in-law without setting off a movement in the direction of egalitarian revolt. Nor can we see how the Melanesian big-man is forced to pile feast on feast to achieve and maintain prestige, but is prevented from maximizing his role by the danger of incurring the wrath of his overtaxed followers. We grow aware of how an ancestor cult builds the solidarity of men descended from a common ancestor, but simultaneously how such adherence splits society into a series of narrow-range descent groups, each set off by its own ancestors, while a universalistic religion such as Islam or Christianity possesses a wide range applicable to anyone wishing to enter the fold. The concept of capacity thus implies performance, but also limits and contradictions, a balance of gains and costs, to be used in a new kind of social cost accounting, both more important and more promising than the economic cost accounting with which we are already familiar from our own cultural experience.

Not all aspects of culture are, however, equally characterized by cumulative development towards a maximal value. It has long been realized that such cumulation is most characteristic of what has been called "the technical order," the energy converters of a society and the organization required by it. Harvey Moore has attempted to show why this should be so. According to Moore, only the technical order is capable of division of labor. Division of labor in turn involves specialization in skills and knowledge, and specialization in skills and knowledge renders more probable that increase in apparatus, skills, and know-how which results in the cumulative growth of the technical order.

In contrast, there are components of culture which are not cumulative in this sense. Their capacity is not measurable on a unidimensional scale, graded from low to high numbers; rather, they exhibit a capacity for multiple combinations. The technique for measuring this multivalence is the one first employed by E. B. Tylor (1889). It involves the application of the statistical method to ascertain the frequency of existing combinations, as well as the use of deductive reasoning to explain the resulting patterning of cases.

All attempts, for instance, to depict forms of descent reckoning as undergoing a progressive cumulation from primitive promiscuity through matriliny and patriliny to bilaterality have failed. Forms of filiation are not cumulative; they occur at very different levels of complexity in the technical order. Thus the horticultural Orokaiva of New Guinea are as patrilineal in form of descent reckoning as the pre-1946 Chinese, but both are clearly not at the same level of technical development. Forms of filiation and forms of marriage constitute some of the limited number of possible components through which groups of people can be related to the components of the technical order. Since their number is limited, they are recurrent rather than cumulative. No matter what the demands of the technical order, the forms of marriage will be limited still to polygyny, polyandry and monogamy.

Such recurrent components must be linked to the cumulative components of the technical order, but the linkage is often minimal and incomplete. "Perfect" combinations of matri-dominant division of labor, matrilineal kinship and matrilocal residence at marriage, for instance, have been shown to be rare among North American Indians, as have their patridominant opposite. Most groups show partial and incomplete combinations, due to a variety of interference in linkage. Similarly, there exist other sets in which apparently incompatible components are hooked together through the mediation of a third component which neutralizes the effects of their incompatibility. The Mundurucu of the South American tropical forest, for instance, are characterized by the apparently incompatible combination of patrilineal descent and movement to the wife's residential group upon marriage, a combination which brings together in one settlement a number of otherwise unrelated males, a difficult situation in a warlike society which demands continuous male coöperation. The required solidarity is here obtained through the introduction of a third component, the man's house, where the unrelated males sleep away from their wives and carry on in common their male-oriented tasks. Anthropological studies gain much of their importance precisely from the study of such unexpected third components that allow an otherwise unmanageable or poorly connected cultural set to operate and to survive.

Such third components also frequently govern the relation of a cultural set to conditions influencing it from outside. Here they act as regulators of cultural sets which would otherwise fall prey to disruption. Thus the potlatch, the great give-aways of the Northwest Coast Indians of British Columbia, regulated an otherwise incompatible relation between the native arrangements of kinship and status and the powerful flow of wealth emanating from the outside world as a result of the fur trade. Thus, too, in many Indian communities of Middle America enforced expenditures in religious ceremonial ensure an economic and social leveling that inhibits the growth of differential power within the community capable of delivering the community to its enemies.

Forms of marriage or descent are not cumulative; they may be substituted for each other or exist as alternative components in the same set. The same is true of other cultural components, for instance forms of burial, or magical beliefs, or ego-referent kinship terminology. The reason for this is probably that such components admit of no specialization, and that even in complex cultural sets they refer to the individual *qua* individual, the family *qua* family, the two least specialized groupings even in an industrial order. We have learned, for example, how magic—or religion akin to magic—persists on this level, even where science has made the behavior of statistical aggregates of people quite predictable and comprehensible. We may know how many people are struck down each year by cancer of the lung, or how many children are killed in automobile accidents. But the individual can take little comfort from this knowledge; for he must still come to terms with his unique personal fate if he discovers that he has cancer of the lung or if his child is run over by a car. Moreover, such existential realities and the responses to them remain remarkably similar among all human beings, no matter what their culture and the complexity of its specialized components. In this regard, there is little difference between the Dayak and the inhabitant of Kalamazoo.

The distinction between cumulative and noncumulative aspects of culture yields a new perspective in the study of particular cultures, a perspective which allows us to go beyond the organic models of culture postulated by the functionalists, and the mechanical models of culture possessed by the diffusionists, and yet make use of both. We are enabled to see any given culture as a set—an arrangement—of components coupled in a particular way, always located in an environment—a context—constituted by other cultural sets or arrangements. We recognize that cumulation in the technical order, actual or virtual, always poses an implicit or explicit threat to such a set. Put in another way, we can come to understand how a culture struggles against its past and toward its future. Similarly, any cultural set is forever under challenge from its neighbors, from the alternative components and alternative couplings of components present in its intercultural environment. In the end, we aim at an evaluation of how a cultural set maximizes the values we have selected as criteria for our linear scale and how it manages its internal and external schismogenesis to achieve this maximization; that is, we evaluate its capacity to contribute to cultural cumulation. In this evaluation, we are not debarred from considering, too, the existential values of the cultural set we are studying. Indeed, we need no longer shrink from the study of the particular and unique, for we have become aware that while our statistical treatments deal in frequencies and averages, in cultural evolution—as in other processes—it may be the unusual combination of components which can effect the transition to the next higher level of cultural cumulation.

BIBLIOGRAPHICAL NOTE

Significant statements of the renewed interest in evolutionism within American anthropology after the end of World War II are Leslie A. White, *The Science of Culture* (New York: Grove Press Inc., 1949), Julian Steward, *Theory of Culture Change* (Urbana, Ill.: University of Illinois Press, 1955), and Marshall D. Sahlins and Elman R. Service, *Evolution and Culture* (Ann Arbor: University of Michigan Press, 1960). These find further development in Morton H. Fried, *The Evolution of Political Society* (New York: Random House, Inc., 1968), Marvin Harris, *Culture, Man, and Nature: An Introduction to General Anthropology* (New York: Thomas Y. Crowell Co., 1971), Marshall D. Sahlins, *Stone Age Economics* (Chicago: Aldine-Atherton Publishing Co., 1972), and Elman R. Service, *Cultural Evolutionism: Theory in Practice* (New York: Holt, Rinehart & Winston, Inc., 1971). The distinction between cumulative and noncumulative aspects of culture is elegantly drawn by Harvey C. Moore, "Cumulation and Cultural Processes," *American Anthropologist* 56:347–57 (1954). Raoul Naroll, "A Preliminary Index of Social Development," *American Anthropologist,* 58:667–715 (1956), and Robert Carneiro, "Scale Analysis, Evolutionary Sequences, and the Rating of Cultures," in Raoul Naroll and R. Cohen (eds.), *A Handbook of Method in Cultural Anthropology* (Garden City, N.J.: Natural History Press, 1970), represent attempts to quantify aspects or evolutionary cumulation. C. J. Erasmus, "Changing Folk Beliefs and the Relativity of Empirical Knowledge," *Southwestern Journal of Anthropology,* 8:411–28 (1955), discusses evolutionary cumulation in knowledge; Robert N. Bellah,

"Religious Evolution," *American Sociological Review* 29:358–74 (1964), treats evolution in religion along lines foreshadowed by G. W. F. Hegel.

The distinctions used in this paper, between totipotent and specialized cultures and between symmetrical and asymmetrical social orders, are based on conceptual distinctions familiar to anthropologists. The concept of "capacity" of a given cultural component seems to me novel; it is illustrated in E. R. Leach's, *Political Systems of Highland Burma: A Study of Kachin Social Structure* (Atlantic Highlands, N. J.: Humanities Press, Inc., 1970) and in Marshall D. Sahlins's "Poor Man, Rich Man, Big-Man, Chief," *Comparative Studies in Society and History* 5:285–303 (1963). The technique for measuring the capacity of cultural components to combine with each other was first employed by E. B. Tylor, "On a Method of Investigating the Development of Institutions," *Journal of the Royal Anthropological Institute* 18:245–72 (1889) and forms the basis of the comparative work using the resources of the Human Relations Area File, which attempts to inventory and codify our knowledge of human cultures all over the world. A sophisticated example of how one may study the capacity of a cultural component, in this case matrilineal kinship, may be found in the contributions to David Schneider and Kathleen Gough (eds.), *Matrilineal Kinship* (Reprint. Berkeley: University of California Press, 1974).

4.

THE GENETIC BASIS OF BEHAVIOR

B. J. Williams

FROM THE BEGINNING OF this century to the present a major concern of American anthropology has been the relation between biology and behavior. The lead in this was taken by Franz Boas and by his students. The focus of this interest, until very recently, was highly specific and greatly limited. It was a period of debunking myths, mainly about the racial basis of behavior. If we ask: What are the major achievements of anthropology, the first must be the rejection of racial explanations of cultural advance. Not that racist statements will not be made in the future, but they no longer characterize any community of thinkers in the sciences or elsewhere.

The myth-debunking period is complete, and we can look forward to a more positive contribution toward understanding relationships between biology and behavior. Central to this large area of concern is the more specific concern with the genetic basis of behavior. Many behavioral differences are due, in some part, to differences in genotype. In behavioral traits where genetic variability is responsible for a significant portion of the behavioral variability, we can hardly hope to understand behavior without knowledge of the genetic differences involved. These differences we denote as the genetic basis of behavior.

We should be able to speak of the genetic basis of behavior differences between *Homo* and other primate species, as well as among individuals within our species, but we do not have very good methods for investigating differences between species. Most observed differences between species we assume to be genetic, but we can say little more than that. The classical techniques of genetic analysis require interbreeding. There are hybrid zones between a number of primate species on which a few investigators have recently begun work, but there are no hybrid zones involving *Homo sapiens.* In this sense we are one of the best of the Linnaean species, no biological fertility barriers within the species and absolute barriers without.

So until new approaches are developed we must look primarily at differences between individuals within the species. This area has come to be called behavioral genetics. It is largely quantitative genetics, as elaborated by R. A. Fisher in 1918, applied to behavioral traits. The application of these methods to man is recent, but within the past ten years a great deal has been done, more than can be surveyed here. Instead, I shall choose three or four items of general interest to illustrate the methods and findings of the past decade.

Much of the work in human behavior genetics continues to rely upon twin studies. Other degrees of relationship can be used but the analysis becomes more complicated. The largest number of studies being done today concerns behavioral pathology, including mental deficiency and personality disorders. These typically are conditions that have proven themselves rather intractable to environmental modification, appear to be familial in origin, and have, therefore, caused us to seek explanations in terms of genetic defect.

The most prevalent and the most studied of these disorders is schizophrenia. Since the nineteen-thirties a great variety of genetic hypotheses have been suggested to explain this disorder. These explanations continue to vie with a host of strictly environmental hypotheses, but within this seeming confusion there is progress.

The pioneering studies of Kallman in the United States and the population studies of Book in Sweden and Karlsson in Iceland brought a great deal of attention to genetic causes of schizophrenia. But, as was found, one of the major problems in fitting genetic models is the varying stringency of diagnostic criteria and the differences in sampling techniques used in different studies. Such variation between studies produces different rates of concordance between twins. Twins are considered concordant if both show the trait or if neither shows the trait. They are discordant if they differ in presence of absence of the trait. For example, if both members of a twin pair have schizophrenia, they are concordant for this trait. If neither has schizophrenia, they are concordant. If one has schizophrenia and the other does not, they are discordant. The proportion of pairs which are concordant is the concordance rate. Differences in concordance rates between identical twins and fraternal twins can provide an estimate of the degree of genetic influence on the expression of a trait.

Conventional comparisons between monozygous and dizygous twins have been followed by studies on the effects of foster homes. These provide strong evidence for a genetic etiology. Studies on adopted children have been carried out independently in the United States, Japan, Denmark, and Iceland. E. Inouye found that among monozygous twins separated before the age of five years, and where one of the twins is schizophrenic, the concordance rate in cotwins is the same as in such pairs raised together. L. L. Heston reports on children of schizophrenic mothers reared in foster homes. Approximately 11 percent of these individuals suffered schizophrenia as adults. There were no cases of schizophrenia in a control group raised in foster homes. The figure of 11 percent is comparable to the results of studies of the risk of schizophrenia in children of a schizophrenic parent raised in the home. Other studies have had similar results.

Heston also found many other behavioral differences within his experimental group of children of schizophrenic mothers. For example, he found "almost exclusively" within the experimental group exceptional musical ability (15 percent), unusually strong religious feeling (13 percent), and problem drinking (17 percent). Heston[1] says that the one-half of the children in the experimental sample:

> who exhibited no significant psycho-social impairment were not only successful adults but in comparison to the control group were

1. L. L. Heston, "Psychiatric Disorders in Foster Home Reared Children of Schizophrenic Mothers," *British Journal of Psychiatry*, 112:819–825.

more spontaneous when interviewed and had more colorful life histories. They held the more creative jobs: musician, teacher, house-designer; and followed the more imaginative hobbies: oil painting, music, antique aircraft.

All our stereotypes are uncomfortably well confirmed.

At present there are two major competing genetic theories of schizophrenia, neither of which can be rejected on present evidence. One is a single-locus model with several variants; the other is a polygenic model, which posits a threshold beyond which a person is diagnosed as schizophrenic. A single-locus mode of inheritance means that the appearance of the trait is controlled by variants of a gene at only one point on a chromosome. This is the simplest form of inheritance. A polygenic mode of inheritance is one in which alternate forms of genes affecting the trait occur at several places (loci) on a chromosome or on different chromosomes. Polygenic traits may be continuously variable as in the case of stature or there may be a threshold of effect giving rise to apparent discontinuities in the trait. The polygenic model of schizophrenia is the latter type.

As these models have evolved, investigators have come to think of themselves as dealing with a "liability" to schizophrenia, an inferred phenotype rather than the observed phenotype. This concept could use more critical scrutiny but seems to be quite useful in some new analytical approaches. The assumed liability to schizophrenia varies with the genetic model hypothesized, from 10 percent in some single-locus models to 73 percent in multilocus models.

The polygenic or multilocus models subsume single-locus models, so data confirming the polygenic model do not reject a single-locus possibility.

In many studies twins pairs are not ascertained (located) at random. For the sake of efficiency, an investigator often starts with the population of schizophrenics and asks who has a cotwin. So at least one of each pair will have schizophrenia. This individual through whom the pair was ascertained is termed the propositus. It has frequently been noted that if the propositus in the twin pair is severely affected, the cotwin is more likely to be affected than if the propositus has a milder form of schizophrenia. This has been taken as evidence for a polygenic etiology, but it may be an environmental effect. S. S. Kety and his associates found, like Heston, that children of schizophrenics were at as great a risk for schizophrenia whether reared at home or away and that those reared away showed a lower frequency of severe forms, supporting the suggestion that the severe forms have a large environmental component.

Single-locus hypotheses have also received considerable support, but again these studies do not reject a polygenic model. There is one approach which may. In 1950 A. M. Brues attempted to establish genetic linkage between discrete genetic traits and genes affecting a quantitative anthropometric trait. Roughly the idea is as follows: A trait may be too variable to exhibit a simple pattern of inheritance when traced through a pedigree. But particular genes for a discrete trait—the *ABO* blood groups, for example—can be traced through a line of descendants. If a single-locus contributes much of the variation in the variable trait (a major gene effect), and if this major gene is located close to the locus controlling the discrete trait, then it is possible to show that such genetic linkage exists by demonstrating an association within pedigrees between genes for the discrete trait and the trait being investigated.

Let us consider a hypothetical example of this procedure. Assume that we have data on *ABO* blood groups and stature in a number of pedigrees. Assume further that in one subset of pedigrees we find that everyone with the *B* allele is unusually short, in another subset of pedigrees everyone with the *A* allele is unusually short, and in a third subset everyone with the *O* allele is unusually short. This means that for the population overall there may be no association between an *ABO* allele and stature and that within pedigrees there is an association (linkage) between the *ABO* locus and an inherited factor affecting stature. An appealing feature of this approach is that there is no known environmental effect or any form of social inheritance that can mimic the genetic linkage found in such a manner.

R. C. Elston, E. Kringlen, and K. K. Namboodiri report evidence for the linkage of schizophrenia to the *Gm* and *Rh* antigen systems. The *Gm* and *Rh* systems are discrete phenotypes of known inheritance similar to the *ABO* system. There is a possibility, of course, that their finding could disappear with a larger sample. But if it does not, this is a very powerful argument for a single-locus controlling much of the genetic variation in the occurrence of schizophrenia.

Alcoholism is a form of deviant behavior that is much more common than schizophrenia and more costly to society. The overwhelming majority of investigators consider this condition to be entirely sociogenic. For this reason very few studies have been directed toward possible genetic factors. The strong proclivity to consider only external socioenvironmental variables in the etiology of this disease may provide us with an interesting case history of the relationship between ideology and science.

We have known for some years that, in laboratory rats, alcohol-preferring and alcohol-avoiding strains can be produced by selection. That such selection is effective implies the existence of genetic variability with respect to alcohol preference in the population to begin with. Indeed, selection experiments of this type are one way of estimating the heritability of any trait in experimental animals.

No selection experiment is possible with human populations, but there are data that bear on genetic factors in alcoholism. Methodologically, the data parallel the kinds of studies done on schizophrenia. Alcoholism tends to be familial. Twin studies show a higher concordance rate for monozygous twins than for like-sex dizygous twins. And, as in the case of schizophrenia, slightly different classification criteria make the different studies not quite comparable.

A 1971 study by M. A. Schukit, D. W. Goodwin, and G. Winokur presents rather strong evidence for a genetic basis of alcoholism. The investigators located one hundred and fifty half-siblings of a sample of alcoholics. From life histories they were able to show the following: the half-sibling was much more likely to be alcoholic if the common parent was alcoholic. Growing up in a household with an alcoholic parental figure who was not a progenitor was not associated with alcoholism in the half-siblings. Growing up with the alcoholic propositus was not associated with alcoholism in the half-siblings unless the common biological parent was alcoholic.

It can only be said, in view of such findings, that the relative neglect of possible genetic factors in the etiology of alcohol abuse cannot be justified.

The IQ score, like stature or ridge count in fingerprints, is a good example of quantitative inheritance. IQ scores within a population are continuously distributed, with both genetic and environmental effects involved in their differences. This is an interesting trait in that there has been as much data gathered on it in Western societies as on almost any anthropometric trait. Another feature of interest is that the IQ score has greater validity—in this case for predicting school performance—than most psychological tests and measures.

IQ scores are one of the first behavioral traits in man to have been analyzed by the methods of quantitative genetics. In 1928, based on a large study of adopted children, Barbara Burks estimated that 75 to 80 percent of IQ variances was due to genetic variation. There was a large intuitive leap involved in getting to this figure, so in 1931 Sewall Wright reanalyzed the data in a more rigorous schema and showed it to fit a heritability estimate that could be anywhere from 50 percent up to Burks' figure.

The many estimates of the heritability of IQ—of the proportion of the variation between individuals that is due to genetic variation—that have appeared since have changed these early estimates very little. The most thorough and exacting partition of IQ differences into various genetic and environmental components is that of J. L. Jinks and D. W. Fulker. By analysis of variance methods they found that 86 percent of the variation in IQ within their sample was due to genetic variation. The genetic variation they divided into additive and dominance components. Genes are said to be additive if heterozygotes are intermediate to the homozygotes in effect. On the other hand, a dominance effect is said to exist when the heterozygote is like one of the homozygotes.

If there were no environmental effects on a trait and all gene effects were additive, the value of the trait expected in the offspring would be exactly the average of the parents' values for this trait. This is not the case for genetic systems showing dominance. Any given polygenic trait may be influenced by both kinds of genetic systems, and it is of some interest to be able to estimate the relative importance of the additive effects versus the dominance effects on the total genetic variation.

In the case of IQ, Jinks and Fulker, again using analysis of variance techniques, found that 71 percent of the phenotypic variation was due to additive gene effects. The 15 percent remaining to the 86 percent genetic effect is the proportion ascribable to the dominance effect of genes.

Positive assortative mating (homogamy) means that parents will be more similar to one another than if spouses were a random draw from the total population. Increased similarity among parents increases the variance (through additive genes) among offspring in the total population of offspring. Jinks and Fulker found that homogamy accounted for 14 percent of the additive gene effects on IQ variance.

In terms of educational implications it is perhaps of more importance that they found no evidence of a genotype-environment correlation or a genotype-environment interaction. A genotype-environment correlation can occur when the genotype influences its own environment or seeks a particular environment. This should be distinguished from a genotype-environment interaction which occurs when one genotype benefits more from a change in environment than does another genotype under the same change.

The finding of no genotype-environment interaction may prove to be quite general. If so, it answers in the negative the long-standing question of whether or not some genotypes (less gifted versus more gifted) may be more sensitive to environmental stimulation or environmental deficit. Lack of a genotype-environment correlation in these data must be viewed with more caution. Although Jinks and Fulker were unable to demonstrate a significant genotype-environment correlation the test they used for this was not very sensitive to such an effect; in other words, a sizable genotype-environmental correlation could have been present but undetectable.

Our confidence in this kind of genetic model fitting is

increased by the finding that quantitative genetic models will not fit the IQ data without building in a sizable component of variation due to homogamy among parents. As L. J. Eaves found, the amount of homogamy estimated by the genetic analysis is, in fact, identical to the amount found in studies of the correlation in IQ between spouses, an independent source of data.

A strident political controversy concerning the genetics of IQ and school achievement was launched with an article written by Arthur Jensen in 1969. This was actually the resurrection of a very old controversy. Jensen, after reviewing standard material on quantitative genetics applied to IQ, suggested that the failure of compensatory education programs in the United States could be due to American Blacks' being genetically less capable than Whites of benefiting from standard education practices. This "could be" became stronger in subsequent publications. What has become known as the Jensen hypothesis is encapsulated in the statement that there are "various lines of evidence . . . which . . . make it a not unreasonable hypothesis that genetic factors are strongly implicated in the average Negro-white intelligence difference."

But a heritability score, the proportion of phenotypic variability—IQ in this case—due to genetic variability is population specific; it is relative both to the gene pool of the population and the environment of the population. To put the case in extreme form, a trait can have a heritability of 100 percent in each of two populations yet differences between the populations in this trait could be entirely environmental. Conversely, a trait could have a heritability of zero in each of two populations yet a difference between the populations in this trait could be entirely genetic in origin. Again a hypothetical example may help to clarify this point. Suppose we assign adults, at random with respect to height, to two islands designated A and B. They produce and raise offspring. If the samples were large to begin with, we can expect no genetic difference with respect to height between islands, though there will be genetic variation on each island. Now let us assume that the environment is controlled such that, at least with respect to growth in height, the environment is the same for all children on island *A* and the environment is the same for all children on island *B*. This means that all height variation on each island will be due entirely to genetic variation. The heritability of height on each island is 100 percent.

The children on island *A* are short and stunted in height; the children on island *B* are tall, due to a factor I have not mentioned. Neither had fish or vitamin D supplements in their diet and the children of island *A* received no ultraviolet radiation in sunlight. They are severely rachitic. To recall our point, the heritability of height is 100 percent on each island, yet there is a large difference in height between islands due entirely to environmental differences.

If we could identify the genes affecting height, we could exemplify the next point. By selecting identical genotypes for island *A* and identical genotypes for island *B*, we get offspring with no genetic variation within each island. The heritability of stature is zero on each island, and if the environment is again held constant (this time the same on both islands), there would be no variation in height on each island. But if the uniform genotypes of island *B* are not the uniform genotypes of island *A*, there can be large differences in height between islands even though the heritability of height on each island is zero.

Although hypothetical examples, these illustrate the general point that heritability estimates are relative both to the genotypes present in a population (the gene pool) and the environment of the population.

Although his statements were not entirely consistent on the point, Jensen recognized this problem and attempted to deal with environmental differences between ethnic groups. After reviewing the published studies, he concluded: "No one has yet produced any evidence based on a properly controlled study to show that representative samples of Negro and white children can be equalized in intellectual ability through statistical control of environment and education."

Such a study has now appeared. Jane Mercer and her associates studied the three major ethnic groups in Riverside, California: Anglos, Mexican-Americans, and Blacks. Differences in mean IQ were found, similar to national averages. A variety of cultural and socioeconomic variables were examined and found to be correlated with IQ differences. These variables were shown to "explain"—to be associated with—from 14 to 23 percent of the variation in IQ within the different ethnic groups. The remaining variation in each group, from 77 to 86 percent, would be the maximum explicable by genetic variation *within* each group. This is remarkably like the results of genetic approaches.

What about differences *between* the three ethnic groups? Ethnic identification itself was associated with IQ differences. But when the effects of the cultural and socioeconomic variables were removed, by partial correlation, from the between-group comparison, there was no variation left for ethnic identification to "explain." In other words, statistical control of the proper cultural and socioeconomic variables did, in fact, equalize the groups with respect to IQ.

As the situation now stands, IQ score constitutes a phenotype in which genetic differences account for much of the differences found within a group. The structure of this genetic component is rapidly being explored. At the same time, our best evidence indicates no mean genetic differences between groups within the limits of our ability to measure them.

I should note that the genetic basis of a behavioral trait can be explored in this fashion regardless of how the trait is defined and regardless of its importance or triviality. Fascination with the IQ measure stems from its demonstrated relation to success in a school class and the assumed relation of school success to some kinds of success later in life. The latter connection is very tenuous. Otis D. Duncan has shown that variation in IQ among school children explains a little over 5 percent of their variation in earnings at age twenty-five to thirty-four years. If earning power is an index of success, we must conclude that IQ tells us only a little about it.

It would be quite as easy to do a genetic analysis directly on a measure of success. If two persons would agree on such a measure, formal genetic analysis could be applied directly to it. The murky waters of the meaning of IQ would be avoided and—who knows—"success" may indeed have a heritable component to be further investigated.

Among normal cognitive abilities, spatial perception, or spatial visualizing ability, is easily tested and is clearly related to success in some occupations. For a number of years investigators have suggested that family data show sex-linked inheritance at one or more loci important in spatial perception. In 1973 R. D. Bock and D. Kolakowski presented a convincing summary of data on this question.

Sex-linked inheritance should produce a higher correlation between father and daughter than between father and son and, similarly, a higher correlation between mother and son than mother and daughter. Actual correlations depend on gene frequencies, degree of dominance, and heritability of the trait. Bock and Kolakowski showed results of spatial perception tests that fit the pattern of correlations quite well for a sex-linked recessive trait, in which a major gene, having a frequency of approximately 50 percent, contributes most of the genetic variance and this, in turn, constitutes 50 percent of the total variance found in spatial visualizing ability. A model of environmental factors which, alone, could produce this pattern of correlations seems a bit farfetched.

A sex-linked recessive trait will be expressed more often in males than in females. This can account for the significant mean difference in spatial visualization ability usually found between males and females. Care must be taken not to argue the inverse. Finding behavioral differences between males and females does not imply that sex-linked recessive genes are involved. Similarly, finding a sample in which males and females do not differ in spatial visualizing ability is not evidence against a sex-linked inheritance hypothesis.

In summary, it must be stressed that we have learned a great deal in the past few years about a number of questions concerning the genetic basis of behavior. The few examples discussed here illustrate the general trend: the rapidly increasing evidence that genetic variability within populations is important to the variability of many kinds of behaviors. And in some cases we can go further and say something about the structure of the genetic variables involved.

This trend of findings is only what might be expected. Social science, including anthropology, has had an ideological commitment for decades to exploration only of the cultural and environmental variables affecting human behavior, and an adequate explanatory system requires that all major sources of variation be accounted for. The research strategies necessary for this are known. Initial studies, such as those just cited, have been successful, and we look forward to an increasing pace of development in this area in the coming decade.

BIBLIOGRAPHICAL NOTE

A detailed account of some methods used in separating genetic and environmental influences on quantitative traits, behavioral or other, is provided in Douglas S. Falconer, *Introduction to Quantitative Genetics* (New York: Ronald Press, 1960) and in John L. Fuller and W. Robert Thompson, *Behavior Genetics* (New York: John Wiley & Sons, Inc., 1960). A selection of some studies of interest in anthropology has been provided in James N. Spuhler (ed.), *Genetic Diversity and Human Behavior* (Chicago: Aldine Publishing Co., 1967). General review of recent developments in behavior genetics in man and other animals is now provided in *Annual Reviews of Psychology.*

A. R. Jensen has amplified his views on the genetic basis of group differences in IQ in a recent major publication, "How Much Can We Boost IQ and Scholastic Achievement?" in *Environment, Heredity, and Intelligence,*" pp. 1–123, reprinted from *Harvard Educational Review* 39(1969). Opposing views are presented in C. L. Brace, G. R. Gamble, and J. T. Bond (eds.), *Race and Intelligence* (Washington, D.C.: American Anthropological Association, 1971), Richard C. Lewontin, "Race and Intelligence," *Bulletin Atomic Scientists,* March, pp. 2–26 (1970), and Frank Morris, *The Jensen Hypothesis: Social Science Research or Social Science Racism* (Monograph No. 2, Los Angeles: UCLA Center for Afro-American Studies, 1971).

5.

THE HOMINIZATION PROCESS

F. Clark Howell

MODERN PALEOANTHROPOLOGICAL STUDIES seek to understand, in both biological and cultural perspectives, those factors which effected the evolution of man. The biologically oriented anthropologist is especially concerned with the nature and adaptive significance of major anatomical and physiological transformations in the evolution of body and behavior from those of an apelike higher primate to those of the single variable species, *Homo sapiens.* Man must equally concern himself with the origin and evolution of distinctively human patterns of behavior, especially capabilities for culture and the manifestations of such capacities, and not only with their biological bases.

The fossil record of man and his higher primate relatives is still far from adequate. However, in the last several decades significant discoveries have been made which considerably expand our knowledge of ancient human and near-human populations. There is not now a single major range of Pleistocene time from which some one or more parts of the world has not at least yielded some hominid skeletal remains. The Pliocene, previously little known because its sediments were either poorly explored or inadequately dated, has now documented Hominidae as early as the Miocene-Pliocene boundary (about five million years ago); the fossil record between three and two million years is increasingly well substantiated. Hence, there is now some pertinent evidence to suggest the general sequence and relative order of those bodily transformations during this process of hominization. In this process major changes were effected at quite unequal rates in the locomotor skeleton, the teeth and their supporting facial structure, the size and proportions of the brain, and the enveloping skull bones. And there were equally significant and concomitant changes in behavior. In the course of the last decade the earlier phases of this process have received considerable investigation. Some significant aspects of that work are considered here.

Man is a primate, and within the order Primates man is most closely related to the living African anthropoid apes. This fact has been extensively and repeatedly demonstrated by over a century of comparative anatomical and related researches. In the past decade it has received solid confirmation from a diversity of biomolecular investigations. How immediate the relationship—or to put it another way, how far removed in time the point of common ancestry prior to divergence—is still unsettled. As there remains marked disagreement among investigators even in their own scientific specialities, this issue cannot as yet be satisfactorily resolved. An open, modest estimate is ten plus or minus four million years ago, but the estimate is more likely to be reduced—perhaps to nine plus or minus two million years—than elevated.

Except under special circumstances skeletal remains are not readily preserved in the acid soils of forested habitats; hence fossil remains of anthropoid apes from the requisite late Tertiary time range, some fifteen to a few million years ago, are uncommon, and when they are found, they are often inadequately preserved. Nevertheless, apelike higher primates are known to have had a widespread Eurasiatic distribution up until five to ten million years ago, by which time such creatures had disappeared from increasingly temperate Europe. They were presumably also common in parts of Africa, although fossiliferous beds of that age are still singularly rare in Africa. Fragmentary jaws and teeth of such creatures indicate their higher primate—indeed, specifically ape—affinities. They also suggest substantial diversity in anatomical structure as well as in overall size. The rare and fortunate occurrence of other skeletal parts (such as limb bones) convincingly indicates that some distinguishing characteristics of modern apes were later evolutionary "specializations" rather than the "primitive" ancestral condition. Several specimens of jaws and teeth, from regions as widely separate as northern India and eastern Africa, some ten to fourteen million years in age, show some hominid resemblances in their dentition, but other features are frankly pongid. Until more adequately preserved skeletal remains are recovered, these few provocative fragments will remain enigmatic. The antecedents of the hominids, the so-called protohominids, are still really unknown, and one can only speculate about the very early, formative phases in the process of hominid emergence. Over the past decade there has been a surfeit of such speculation, accompanied often by unnecessarily acrimonious debate in view of the hopelessly inadequate fossil record.

The anatomical-physiological basis of the radiation of the hominids is generally acknowledged to have been a major transformation in structure and function of the locomotor system. The lower limb skeleton and associated musculature were modified under selection pressures eventually to permit a fully erect posture and efficient, habitual bipedal gait. The changes effected in the lower limb were extensive and revolutionary. The characteristic curvature of the loins, the short, broad, and backwardly shifted hip bones and their displaced and strengthened articulation with the sacrum, their sinuous distortion to form a basin-like structure about the lower abdomen, as well as the shortened ischial region, were all part of a complex of largely interrelated modifications adaptive for terrestrial bipedalism. There were related changes in the musculature of the hip and thigh, in relative proportions and in structure and function of specific muscle groups, all to afford power to run and to step off in walking, to maintain the equilibrium of the upright trunk during the stride, and to extend fully and to stabilize the elongated lower limb at hip and knee—an impossible stance for any ape. The foot was fully inverted, with the lateral toes shortened and the hallux enlarged and immobilized, the rigidity of the tarsus enhanced through the angularity of joints and strengthened ligaments, with the development of prominent longitudinal and transverse arches, and the heel broadened to become fully weight-bearing.

The singularity of the erect posture was long ago recognized from comparative anatomical studies of man and the nonhuman primates. Its priority in the hominization process has been fully confirmed by the discovery in Africa of the earliest known hominids, the australopithecines (genus *Australopithecus*), creatures with small brains but with lower limbs adapted to erect posture and bipedal gait. Some evidence has been thought to suggest that full-fledged adaptation to bipedalism, which permitted leisurely and prolonged walking, was not yet wholly perfected. In fact, sufficient is now known of composite portions of the skeleton of *Australopithecus* from additional specimens recovered from South African sites, and especially from numerous remains recovered in the course of new field investigations in eastern Africa, to leave no doubt that the locomotor skeleton of these creatures was overall hominid, and not at all pongid, though the australopithecines demonstrate significant differences in structure, and hence perhaps also in functional capabilities, from that of the genus *Homo*. The hominid type of dental structure, with small incisor teeth, reduced and spatulate-shaped canines, and noninterlocking canines and anterior premolar teeth set in a parabolic dental arch, was also fully differentiated. Brain size, as estimated from skull capacities, was only about one-third to two-fifths that of the size range of anatomically modern man.

There are several distinct forms of the genus *Australopithecus*, surely distinct species (and, perhaps, valid subgenera). These appear to exhibit broad overall similarity in their postcranial anatomy, so far as that is known. However, there are fairly consistent differences in cranial and dental morphology. They appear to have overlapped in stature as well as in body weight. A smaller, more gracile form and a larger, more robust form are commonly distinguished.

Although restricted to Africa so far as we know, these earliest known hominids were nonetheless fairly widely distributed over substantial portions of that continent. Their ecological adjustments are now known in some measure and can even be paralleled among certain present-day African environments within the same regions. The belief that their paleoenvironmental circumstances and adjustments differed has been weakened by more intensive studies of the contexts of their find spots in South Africa, as well as by extensive studies of their locales in eastern Africa (especially at Olduvai Gorge, East Rudolf, and in the lower Omo valley). In southern Africa remains of these creatures, along with those of other animals, occur in caves in a limestone plateau landscape where caverns, fissures, and sink holes probably afforded fairly permanent sources of water, which was otherwise scarce. There, and also in eastern Africa, sites were in proximity to more wooded habitats fringing shallow water courses, or mantling the slopes of adjacent volcanic highlands, along the deltaic plains and floodplains of some major river systems. It is just such transitional zones, the *ecotones* of the ecologist, which afford the greatest abundance and diversity of animal and plant life.

The absolute age of some of these creatures can now be ascertained as a consequence of refinements in the measurement of radioactivity (potassium/argon or K/A) in some constituent minerals of volcanic rocks. Their temporal range extends back some five million years with one species at least apparently having persisted until less than a million years ago. The extensive application of such radiometric dating methods, and the investigation of remnant magnetization in associated sediments to determine patterns of past reversals of the earth's magnetic field, have revolutionized previous conceptions of the age of Hominidae and the tempo of human evolution. Their discovery has therefore tripled the time range previously known for the evolution of the hominids.

Culturally patterned behavior appears concurrently with these creatures. In several instances there is direct association with some of their skeletal remains. However, in most instances there is also skeletal evidence, at the same time and even the same place, for the presence of another hominid species. There is still uncertainty over the cultural capabilities of *Australopithecus* of whatever species. There are still no certain associations of artifacts with the small, gracile species. A number of occurrences of a robust *Australopithecus* together with skeletal remains of a hominid showing a number of resemblances to *Homo* are now known. Many, but not all, students of the problem are inclined to regard the latter as more culturally capable, but the evidence is still not conclusive.

The field investigation of undisturbed occupation places, maximizing the possibility for the recovery of evidence in an archeological context, has culminated in these significant discoveries. Traditional prehistoric archeologicical studies, on the other hand, were largely preoccupied with the sequential relationships of relics of past human endeavors, often in secondary contexts. The careful exposure of undisturbed occupation places has permitted wholly new inferences into the nature of past hominid adaptations and patterns of behavior. This work has broad implications, for it forces complete rejection of the traditional viewpoint of some anthropologists, which envisioned the sudden appearance of human behavior and culture at a "critical point" in man's phylogeny, a matter discussed in Chapter 2.

The complexity of the hominid condition shortly after two million years ago was suggested by discoveries at Olduvai Gorge in the early nineteen-sixties, and the attendant announcement of a new, ancient species of *Homo—Homo habilis*. The implications of these discoveries have been disputed ever since. However, discoveries elsewhere in eastern Africa, and particularly in the East Rudolf area in Kenya now confirm, at least in part, the coexistence of a robust australopithecine with another kind of hominid. On the basis of evidence of postcranial morphology and features of the cranium, face and dentition, the second hominid type is reasonably attributed to the genus *Homo*. The age of this taxon demonstrably exceeds that of the Olduvai occurrence—by how much is still unresolved, but by at least several hundred thousand years. Evidences of culturally patterned behavior are apparent also by this range of time, both at East Rudolf and in the Omo valley to the north, and probably extend back over a half million years earlier than the documentation afforded at Olduvai.

Very primitive cultural behavior is manifest in several ways. There was substantial ability to fashion simple tools and weapons from stone (and presumably in other media, although perishable materials are not preserved). These objects, the raw material of which was not infreqently brought from sources some distance away, include deliberately collected, sometimes fractured or battered natural stones or more substantially modified core (nodular) and flake pieces fashioned to produce chopping, cutting, or piercing edges. The oldest East Rudolf occurrences are fundamentally similar to those first well documented at Olduvai Gorge. The Omo occurrences, some of which may well be older by several hundred thousand years, appear for the most part to comprise the flake (waste) byproducts of lithic technology and we find only a minimal number of the presumed diversity of finished artifacts. In both instances, and in contrast to the Olduvai situations, the artifact densities are strikingly low, and undisturbed occupation places are still largely unknown.

Olduvai Gorge has revealed the fullest picture of the residues resulting from early hominid occupations and activities. Occupation sites, butchery sites, and even workshop sites at local raw material sources are represented. These occurrences afford unexpectedly rich evidence for tool manufacturing practices and artifact diversity, hunting and/or scavenging of meat, concentration at home bases or camps with attendant accumulation there of food remains, and, by inference, the practice of habitual food sharing. It was initially thought that only a narrow range of a broad spectrum of a rich savanna and woodland fauna was exploited. Such was surely not the case, for there are found in the sites invertebrates (gastropods, ostrocods) as well as a diversity of vertebrates, including fish, terrestrial and aquatic reptiles, many birds, and mammals. At least ten orders of mammals are represented including insectivores, bats, primates (prosimians and cercopithecoids as well as hominids), rodents (at least six families), lagomorphs, carnivores (at least five families), proboscideans, hyracoids, perissodactyls (three families), and a diversity of artiodactyls (hippos, suids, giraffids, and eight or more tribes of bovids). It is not yet easy to distinguish hominid prey from carnivore prey, or even the varied effects of natural agencies. At any rate, carnivorous behavior of these earliest hominids contrasts markedly with the essentially vegetarian proclivities of all recent apes (except chimpanzees) and monkeys (except some baboons).

Such food remains and associated stone artifacts are concentrated over occupation surfaces of restricted extent—in part at least seasonally exposed mud flats around ephemeral lakes adjacent to periodically active volcanoes at Olduvai, inland channels adjacent to levees at East Rudolf, and channels and backswamp situations in the Omo valley. These occupational concentrations have a nonuniform distribution over the occupation surfaces; there are dense central clusters of tools and much broken-up and crushed bones (crushed, one presumes, to extract the marrow), and periperally more sparse occurrences of natural or battered stones and different, largely unbroken skeletal parts of their prey. In one case at Olduvai a large ovoid-shaped pattern of concentrated and heaped-up stony rubble, with adjacent irregular piles of stone, suggests a structural feature on the occupation surface. These uniquely preserved sites in eastern Africa, sealed in quickly by primary falls of volcanic ash, afford some tantalizing glimpses into the activities of these primitive creatures. Such occupation places may well represent an ancient manifestation of the adjustment to a "home base" within the range, a unique development within the hominid adaptation.

We can now delineate some of the basic features of the early radiation of the hominids to include: (1) differentiation and reduction of the anterior dentition; (2) skeletal and muscular modifications to permit postural uprightness and erect cursorial bipedalism; (3) effective adjustment to, and exploitation of, a terrestrial habitat; (4) probably a relatively expanded brain; (5) extensive manipulation of natural objects and development of motor habits to facilitate toolmaking; and (6) carnivorous predation adding meat protein to a largely vegetal diet.

The adaptation was essentially that of erect bipedal higher primates adjusting to a predaceous-foraging existence. These adaptations permitted, or perhaps were conditioned by, the dispersal into a terrestrial environment and the exploitation of grassland or parkland habitats. The African apes (and also the Asiatic gibbon), especially juvenile individuals, show occasional though unsustained efforts at bipedalism; it is highly probable that this preadoptive tendency, which could have developed as a consequence of the overhand arboreal climbing adaptation of semierect apes, was pronounced in the still unknown protohominids of the Miocene. Wild champanzees are now recognized sometimes to eat meat from kills they have made, to manipulate inanimate objects, and even to use and occasionally to shape them for aid in the food quest. Even some troops of baboons are now known to be capable of persistent predatory behavior. This surely suggests that such tendencies were at least equally well developed among the closely related protohominids.

Terrestrial environments were, of course, successfully colonized long previously by other primates. These are certain cercopithecoid monkeys, the secondarily ground-dwelling quadrupedal patas monkeys and baboons of Africa and the macaques of Asia (and formerly Europe). Hence their adaptations, social behavior, and troop organization provide a useful analogy for inferences to the radiation of the protohominids. Comparative investigations of the nonhuman primates have substantially broadened our understanding of the primate background to human evolution. These studies serve to emphasize those particular uniquenesses of the human adaptation.

It is still unknown when hominids first dispersed outside the primary ecological zone exploited by the australopithecines. It is often presumed, but without any substantial evidence, that these hominids were restricted to the African continent. This appears to have been so for most of all of the Pliocene. By probably nearly a million years ago, at least, hominids were in the process of dispersal outside the primary ecological zone exploited by the australopithecines. In part, this dispersal can be understood only in respect to the opportunities for faunal exchange between the African and Eurasiatic continents and to the prevailing paleogeographic and paleoecological conditions of the Pliocene/Pleistocene. The diverse Saharan zone failed to constitute a barrier to this dispersal or to that of Pliocene and early Pleistocene mammal faunas, for that matter. Moreover the extensive seas of the Pliocene and earliest Pleistocene were sufficiently lowered, either due to continental uplift or, less likely, as a consequence of the incorporation of oceanic waters in extensive arctic-subarctic ice caps, so as to afford substantial intercontinental connections. And the Red Sea trough and Aden Rift had not yet come to form substantial barriers between a still persistent Afro-Arabian continent.

About one and one-half plus or minus one-half million years ago this dispersal occurred. There is no evidence to speak of to permit a greater precision, and this is surely a major untouched problem for paleoanthropological field research. Probably within a hundred thousand years, or less, representatives of the genus *Homo* were dispersed throughout most of the Eurasian subtropics and may have even penetrated northward well into temperate latitudes in both Europe and eastern Asia. This dispersal involved adjustment to a diverse new variety of habitats. Cultural and perhaps physiological adaptations permitted, for the first time, man's existence outside the tropics under new, more rigorous climatic conditions, characterized by enhanced temperate zone seasonality. However, this was still a far cry from the severe environmental circumstances to be imposed by the extensive alpine and continental glacial conditions of some three-quarters of a million years ago in those northerly latitudes. It was ultimately and unquestionably facilitated by anatomical-physiological modifications to produce the genus *Homo*, including prolongation of growth, delayed maturation, and behavioral changes favoring educability, communication, and an overall capability for culture.

The fully human pattern of locomotion was probably perfected by this time. These final transformations in the hip, thigh, and foot permitted a fully relaxed standing posture with the body at rest, as well as capabilities for sustained walking over long distances. The skeletal evidence is unfortunately still incomplete, but by at least a million years ago, and perhaps even earlier, the lower limb skeleton was quite unlike that of *Australopithecus*, and though it differs (particularly in the femur) from *Homo sapiens*, it is distinctly *Homo* in overall structure. By some four to six hundred thousand years ago the lower limb skeleton appears not to have differed in any important respect from that of anatomically modern man. Brain size, and especially the relative proportions of the temporal-parietal and frontal association areas, was notably increased to some one-half to two-thirds that of *Homo sapiens* (and to well within the range that permits normal behavior in the latter species). Some further reduction and simplification also occurred in the molar and premolar teeth and the supporting bony structures of the face and lower jaw.

Hunting was important as a basis for subsistence. Meateating doubtless formed a much increased and stable portion of the normal diet. Much of the mammalian faunal spectrum was exploited, and the prey included some or all of the largest of herbivorous species, including gregarious "herd" forms as well as more solitary species, and a variety of small mammals. Several occupation places of these early and primitive hunters, some of which are quite undisturbed, are preserved and have been excavated in eastern Africa and now also in Europe. These localities preserve prodigious quantities of skeletal remains of slaughtered and butchered mammals. The famous and enormous cave locality (Locality I) of Choukoutien (near Peking) in eastern Asia is a unique occurrence of occupation of a site of this type at such an early time. At Choukoutien, although other ungulate and carnivorous mammals are also present, about 70 percent of the seventy genera and some one hundred species are represented by only two species of deer. In Africa the impressive quarry included a number of gigantic herbivorous species, as well as other extinct forms. In two such occupation sites in eastern Africa, over a million years ago, the very abundant fauna included species of three simians, two carnivores, two rhinos, eight pigs, two to three elephants, sheep and buffalo, two hippos, three giraffids, a chalicothere, six horses, as well as numerous antelopes and gazelles, and other remains of small mammals (rodents), birds, and some reptiles (tortoises).

Preferential hunting of certain herd species is recognized at several younger occupation sites in Europe. At two sites in central Spain investigated by the author and associates a diversity of vertebrates is represented, including anurans, birds (four families), a monkey, rodents, lagomorphs, and canid and felid carnivores. However, these are all rare in comparison to the predominance of six large mammalian species—woodland elephant and wild horse being by far the most abundant, with infrequent wild oxen (aurochs), stag (red deer) and fallow deer, and very rare steppe rhinoceros. Although these sites are only a few kilometers apart, each differs in interesting and important ways from the other in respect to the nature, distribution, and frequency of occupation residues, artifactual and faunal, and the composition of artifactual assemblages including materials in stone, bone, and wood and in evidences of the use of fire. These differences must reflect at least a spectrum of activities and the social and cultural complexity of their ancient occupants. The number of individuals represented by the several dominant large mammal species is indeed unexpected and suggests a level of technological capability and social organization not heretofore envisioned.

Another ancient seaside hominid occupation place at Nice in southern France is approximately the same age as those in Spain. However, it shows distinctive differences in the nature and areal extent of the occupation surfaces, the presence of structures and hearths, the variety and composition of animal residues, which include reptiles, birds, a dozen or so mammals (but predominantly six large species, two of which are unrepresented in the lberian occurrences), and fish and marine invertebrates, and the composition and diversity of stone artifacts. Some indication of the level of cultural capability and adaptation, as well as the plasticity requisite for local ecological adjustment, is afforded by the diversity of game species which were exploited and the corresponding distinctions in occurrence, habitat preference, size of aggregation, species-specific patterns of behavior.

Toolmaking capabilities are notably improved along with the establishment of persistent habits of manufacture. These reflect, in part at least, more dexterous and effective control of manual skills. Corresponding evolutionary changes in the structure and function of the hand, especially development of the fully and powerfully opposable thumb, with expansion and complication of the corresponding sector of the cerebral motor cortex and interrelated association areas, were all effected under the action of natural selection.

Not only did the overall quantity and quality of the stone tools increase. New techniques were developed for the initial preparation as well as for the subsequent fashioning of diverse and selected sorts of stone into tools and weapons. New types of stone tools make their appearance, including in particular sharply pointed and cutting-edged tools of several sorts, seemingly most appropriate for butchery of tough-skinned game. Certain stones already of favorable form were deliberately trimmed into a spheroidal shape, it is thought, as offensive missiles. These and other forms of tools subsequently become remarkably standardized. This fact and the very broad pattern of their geographic distribution throughout Africa and southern and western Europe, and through western into southern Asia and the Indian subcontinent suggest also a sophisticated level of communication and conceivably even the capability of symbolization.

More perishable stuffs, such as wood and fiber, are unfortunately very rarely preserved. However, several early sites in Europe attest the utilization and working of wood, fashioned into elongate, pointed, and spatulate shapes. The discovery had doubtless been made of the thrusting spear, a major offensive weapon in the pursuit of large, thick-skinned mammals. Again, although traces of the use of fire are also rarely preserved, there is incontrovertible evidence of its discovery and utilization (whether for heat or cookery is uncertain) both in Europe and in eastern Asia.

The development of a hunting way of life, even at a very unsophisticated level of adaptation, it has been argued, set very different requirements on early human populations. It led to markedly altered selection pressures and was, in fact, responsible for profound changes in human biology and culture. Many workers regard this adaptation as a critical factor in the emergence of fundamentally human institutions. Some of those changes which represent the human (*Homo*) way of life would include: (1) greatly increased size of the home range with defense of territorial boundaries to prevent infringement upon food sources; (2) band organization of interdependent and affiliated human groups of variable but relatively small size; (3) (extended) family groupings with prolonged male-female relationships, incest prohibition, rules of exogamy for mates, and subgroups based on kinship; (4) sexual division of labor; (5) altruistic behavior with food-sharing, mutual aid, and cooperation; and (6) linguistic communities based on speech.

It may be impossible ever to obtain direct evidence of this sort from the fossil and archeological record. Yet an approach which combines the field and laboratory study of the behavior of living nonhuman primates with analysis of basic patterns of adaptation and behavior of human hunter-gatherer populations has enhanced enormously the kinds of inferences usually drawn from the imperfect evidence of paleoanthropological investigations. The favorable consequences of active cooperation between students concerned with the origin and evolution of human behavior, however diverse in background and orientation, are already evident and have considerably advanced understanding of the process of hominization. In the coming years they may be comparable with those advances in paleoanthropological studies effected through the fullest cooperation with colleagues in the natural sciences.

BIBLIOGRAPHICAL NOTE

The point of view expressed here was early discussed by Sherwood L. Washburn and F. Clark Howell, "Human Evolution and Culture," in Sol Tax (ed.), *Evolution after Darwin* (Chicago: University of Chicago Press, vol. 2, pp. 33–56, 1960) and some details were set out at greater length elsewhere by the author: F. Clark Howell, "Recent Advances in Human Evolutionary Studies," *Quarterly Review of Biology* 42:471–513 (1967), and "Recent Advances in Human Evolutionary Studies," in Sherwood L. Washburn and P. Dolhimow (eds.), *Perspectives on Human Evolution* (New York: Holt, Rinehart & Winston, Inc., vol. 2, pp. 51–128, 1972), where many pertinent references may be found. A colloquium volume (Colloques Internationaux 1958) with chapters by various authorities, provided the title for this essay; it is still rewarding reading for anyone seriously interested in the subject. Overviews of many aspects of the natural sciences and associated fields related to intensified paleoanthropological researches of the past decade or so, including the increasing concern with ecological matters, are represented in the volumes edited by F.

Clark Howell and Francois Bourliere (eds.), *African Ecology and Human Evolution* (Chicago: Aldine Publishing Co., 1963), Walter W. Bishop and J. Desmond Clark (eds.), *Background to Evolution in Africa* (Chicago: University of Chicago Press, 1967), and Walter W. Bishop and J. A. Miller (eds.), *Calibration of Hominid Evolution* (Toronto: University of Toronto Press, 1972).

The recent extensive field investigations in the Rudolf basin of Kenya and Ethiopia are treated in the volume edited by Y. Coppens, F. C. Howell, G. Ll. Isaac, and R. E. F. Leakey, *Earliest Man and Environments in the Rudolf Basin: Stratigraphy, Paleoecology and Evolution* (Chicago: University of Chicago Press, 1975). Overviews of much of the data relevant to the contexts, associations, age and paleobiology and taxonomy of early Hominidae are to be found in another symposium volume, edited by C. J. Jolly, *African Hominidae of the Plio-Pleistocene* (London: Duckworths, 1975). The Middle Pleistocene—its definition, correlation, faunal associations, and paleoanthropological evidence—is the subject of yet another recent symposium edited by Karl W. Butzer and G. Ll. Isaac, *After the Australopithecines* (The Hague: Mouton Press, 1974). All these symposia have been sponsored by the Wenner-Gren Foundation for Anthropological Research and have had a profound effect on the development and trajectory of paleoanthropological researches. G. Ll. Isaac, "The Diet of Early Man: Aspects of Archaeological Evidence from Lower and Middle Pleistocene Sites in Africa," *World Archaeology* 2:278–299 (1971), offers a splendid analysis of the evidence for the dietary and correlative behavioral adjustments of earlier Hominidae. Other important reviews of some of the newest data relevant to this subject are by B. G. Campbell, "Man for All Seasons," in B. G. Campbell (ed.), *Sexual Selection and the Descent of Man* (Chicago: Aldine, 1972), and "Conceptual Progress in Physical Anthropology: Fossil Man," *Annual Review of Anthropology* 1:27–54 (1972), and P. V. Tobias, "New Developments in Hominid Paleontology in South and East Africa," *Annual Review of Anthropology* 2:311–34 (1973), which serve also to indicate the diversity of opinion that prevails despite the increasing depth of paleoanthropological research in the field and in the laboratory. Finally, in addition to my own involvement with such studies for over twenty years many of my colleagues have shared with me their field experiences, basic data, and preliminary interpretations; to each of them I am deeply grateful.

6.

MAN, CULTURE, AND BIOLOGY

Aram A. Yengoyan

WE ARE FAR from a complete understanding of the interrelationships between culture and biology, but in the efforts of anthropologists to comprehend how man's biological evolution has influenced cultural institutions and behavior, and vice versa, many interesting ideas have been developed. To understand what has occurred over the past million years in the evolutionary process, anthropologists must use data from the fossil record, from our general knowledge of evolutionary forces such as selection, migration, mutation, and random genetic drift, and from how early forms of *Homo sapiens* lived in different environmental conditions. Evidence of this kind is limited, and in many cases anthropologists have analyzed contemporary nonliterate societies in order to extrapolate backward into time. Thus simple hunting and gathering cultures such as the Eskimo, the bushmen of South Africa, and the Australian aborigines provide us with clues about how early man lived, what his cultural and social institutions were, and how they were influenced by biological forces.

The first section of this chapter deals with cultural and biological interconnections as they are manifested over time, in the diachronic dimension that embraces human cultural and biological evolution. From this viewpoint, many cultural institutions can be interpreted as *instrumentalities*, in the sense that their appearance was a result of human need based on the imperatives of biological survival. The second section suggests how biological and cultural forces interact synchronically, in any one period of time. Here we will present a number of examples from advanced societies and from *primitive* cultures to demonstrate how and why this interaction occurs and what it means. The distinction between the diachronic and the synchronic approaches is artificial, but it is a convenient device for organizing some of the ideas I hope to convey.

When anthropologists discuss biological influences on culture, social institutions, and behavior, they commonly start from two kinds of interconnections. In one case the biological realm is seen as directly influencing or even determining certain cultural practices. An example of this interrelationship is found in the types of marriage systems among human populations. In almost all cases, marriage rules encourage one to marry into social categories of individuals who are distantly related, such as first or second cousins or more distant relatives. One possible explanation for this custom is that human populations are helped to survive by maximizing the number of relatives within the total social network. Thus by marrying out of a direct family line one increases the number of kinship relations, and it is this large network that provides assistance during periods of physical and environmental stress. The argument here implies that there is a direct connection between biological needs and social practice.

A second kind of linkage between culture and biology involves the contention that biological forces not only determine particular cultural and social institutions but also provide the entire arena or range within which culture operates. All of culture is based on the underlying biological parameters of our species, and it is these parameters that directly or indirectly determine what culture must do and, in some cases, how culture must do it. Both kinds of interconnections hold to the premise that culture, either as practice in terms of behavior or as a set of mental relationships, is fundamentally a result of biological imperatives that have conditioned and determined what man is all about.

In recent years, *biological determinism* has surfaced in the field of ethology, which is primarily concerned with the biological basis of behavior both in human and nonhuman populations. From their study of other forms of animal life, ethologists are attempting to determine if man similarly acts out biological imperatives. The extreme ethological position argues that behavior is coded in the genetic structure of individuals and thus what is manifest on the overt behavioral level is a result of what is inherent in the biological constitution of the species. The next step in this line of thought is that behavior can be altered or modified if we know how the biology of the species works by changing the genetic code.

Ethologists, though varying in their interests and theoretical positions, generally contend that certain kinds of human behavior are a result of biology and not of particular forms of cultural development. The best example of this concern is the search for the causes of aggression, hostility, and war as universal cultural phenomena. Ethologists such as Konrad Lorenz argue that all species—human and nonhuman—are characterized by aggression, and war is thus a result of the very nature of life itself.

However, when this proposition is examined in terms of human behavior, the results are not so clear. For one thing, war and warfare are *not* universal among humans; there are many societies whose members may engage regularly in feuds but in which war as a consciously motivated cultural practice is absent. The Semai of the Malayan uplands and the Australian aborigines are examples, and there are many more supportive cases. Furthermore, to claim that aggression is universal due to a shared biological potential is also to argue that there are no qualitative differences among the different kinds of aggression—that the holocaust of World War II, the ritualized (and harmless) feuds of the Tsembaga, and the behavior of barroom drunks are all expressions of identical causes and needs. To explain such qualitative differences, the ethologists would have to demonstrate how they exist in the biological realm. On both counts, ethologists have not substantiated their position.

The most extreme of these statements, as set forth by "popularizers" of ethological research, would argue that World War II and the Vietnam War resulted from some complex component of human genetic inheritance. But the wars of global imperialism during the nineteenth century cannot be dismissed simply as a result of genes and chromosomes, for, in fact, they are a consequence of political evolution, multinational business combines, and power politics. Wars conducted by advanced societies are markedly different from the armed conflict and feuding manifested in so-called primitive societies. Their causes, their means, and their results are entirely different, and in neither case can we attribute these differences to our genetic constitution.

The ethologists' claim that all species have a sense of space and territory which they defend against intrusion is probably valid, and the evidence from many studies does support this line of thought. But to extrapolate from a universal sense of spatial possessiveness to organized warfare as the logical outcome of our genetics is scientifically unsound and politically dangerous.

The Diachronic Dimension

A million or so years ago, before the advent of food production, all human beings lived in small population clusters, which were the most appropriate forms of social organization for securing a livelihood by collecting and gathering plant foods and hunting game. The precise size of these clusters or bands is difficult to determine, but there is evidence that the range was from four to five families up to larger units of sixty to eighty individuals. The size of particular groups presumably depended on specific environmental conditions and the kinds of animal foods that were pursued. Of the evolutionary forces operating on these populations, selection and random genetic drift were most important, although migration and mutation were also present. Selection operates directly on human populations in two ways. First, individuals who were unfit to sustain themselves probably died at early ages and seldom reached the point where they could reproduce. Thus a man with poor eyesight or with arm defects simply could not hunt with the competence required to sustain himself and his family. Food was consumed quickly and storage was impossible, so sustenance was a daily process, and if individuals failed to feed themselves adequately, the odds in favor of their survival were poor. The social group did not possess enough resources to maintain individuals who could not carry their own weight.

Selection also works on the group as well as on the individual. Each population had a defined area of economic exploitation, and the total population size was regulated by the carrying capacity of the environment. The idea of carrying capacity is tricky, since it involves not only the total amount of food resources in a given area but also the extractive efficiency of a given technology. In a hunting technology, the carrying capacity of particular areas was quite low. Exactly what these figures were is unknown, but from our knowledge of contemporary hunters and gatherers, we can guess that the average was about one person per ten square miles. In extremely adverse cases such as central Australia the carrying capacity was and is one person per thirty to fifty square miles.

The critical point is that human populations tend to expand at a rate greater than a particular carrying capacity can support. Human societies must find a way to limit their size to what the prevalent economic conditions can provide with a margin of safety. (You will note that this applies to societies today much as in the Pleistocene, although modern technology has increased the carrying capacity in many parts of the world.) There are at least three ways in which a population can check its numbers to regulate its balance with what a particular environment can support: (1) through reduction of the population by war and other aggressive activities, (2) through outmigration into unoccupied areas; and (3) through control of the number and spacing of children by utilizing infanticide as a conscious cultural practice.

We can assume that the human species in the Pleistocene, as in many hunting and gathering societies today, had a high mortality rate, which operated on the population structure with differing intensities. Data collected in 1966 and 1967 and during 1970 from the Pitjantjatjara, a hunting and collecting society in the great western desert of Australia, indicates that over twelve years the average infant death rate was 186.9 per 1,000 from one settlement and that over five years it was 290.2 for another settlement. The crude death rates for the entire population of both settlements were 16.16 and 28.7, respectively, per 1,000. The infant death rate as well as the overall death rate are markedly high in comparison to advanced societies' ratios, but such figures for hunting and gathering societies are quite normal. The astonishing fact is that in the same population the rate of natural increase was 48.64 per 1,000 in one settlement and 22.6 in the other. This indicates that although mortality took a high toll, the overall fertility was still high enough to produce significant increases in the population.

Outmigration is also a means of keeping balance between population and resources. In the evolution of man and the gradual expansion throughout the world of hunters and gatherers, migration must have been important. Joseph B. Birdsell has detailed the processes by which man migrated from southern and central Africa to the Middle East and gradually into Asia, southeast Asia, and Australia. When groups move into new areas, if they do not contact other forms of *Homo sapiens*, they normally can be expected to increase their numbers to the upper limits of the carrying capacity for a given level of technology. Throughout the Pleistocene this budding-off process followed by population increase occurred again and again until most of the major land masses in the Old World were filled. Migration is still an important national and international process, but with the emergence of national boundaries and governmental policies toward immigration, the rate of migration varies greatly over time and space. It remains clear that in the evolution of man, migration provided a critical "safety valve" as carrying capacities approached their upper limits.

For equilibrium to develop at a particular carrying capacity, each generation has to reproduce itself, with each mating pair adding two persons to the next generation. But the evidence we have about human fertility indicates no population has ever reached this low a level. During the Pleistocene, fertility generally outstripped mortality, so other means, such as infanticide, had to evolve to keep the population in check.

The practice of infanticide is linked to the spacing of offspring and the duration of breastfeeding. Due to the absence of suitable foods such as mush and palatable grains in hunting and gathering societies, children are nursed for two or three years. Females can best insure the survival of their offspring by breastfeeding only one child at a time, and it is therefore necessary to prevent any disturbance in this pattern. If twins are born, usually one is killed. In some cases both are killed. If a female gives birth eighteen months or less after an earlier child, the new infant is often killed regardless of its sex. Infanticide occurs among all hunting and gathering populations, as well as in some more advanced horticultural societies, as one of the most effective means of population control.

Infanticide as a cultural practice is a result of human needs, which are in part determined by biological imperatives. In the long evolutionary process a number of cultural forms emerged which can be shown to depend on what human beings had to do to survive. Thus, infanticide, certain forms of marriage systems, types of household composition, and population clustering are either directly or indirectly based on biological survival. These sociocultural institutions are called *instrumentalities* since they are a result of need and function.

But we cannot assume that all cultural practices of early societies were of this type. Art, language, and supernatural beliefs all existed throughout the late Pleistocene, and it would be ridiculous to argue simplistically that these practices and symbolic forms were also based on the requirements of survival. The most interesting aspects of culture are those that are not a result of our biology, but it is important to note that the biological paradigm, along with language, was the most critical element in the development of culture until culture itself took control of ourselves.

The Synchronic Dimension

With the rapid evolution of culture in the past fifteen thousand years, human beings are now primarily controlled by the very forces that they have created. Culture, in terms of both its conceptual and its behavioral aspects, has become the critical element in determining how biological forces work on us. This does not mean that evolutionary forces are not operative, since all human populations are still susceptible to biological processes. But culture is now the critical and creative force in determining how these forces work themselves out in a given population.

One basic example will demonstrate this point. Natural selection operates on both the individual and the population but at varying intensities depending on the particular circumstances of a particular human group. In simple cultures, selection is direct and tends to eliminate those phenotypes that are unfit. But as culture evolves, many unfit phenotypes survive because they are less at the mercy of evolutionary forces. Vision is a case in point. Most advanced societies possess culturally developed means of improving eyesight through the use of glasses, contact lenses, and surgery; the same defects in simple societies would have meant an early death.

Thus the quality and content of human culture can no longer be regarded as simply a response to biological forces. All cultures studied by anthropologists are truly creative, in that each of them is composed of a set of detailed yet abstract configurations of elaborate symbols. Our ability to devise vast and complex cosmologies, the intricacy of our mythologies, the aesthetic qualities of art, music, and literature, and our creative use of language in metaphor and rhetoric attest to the creativity and richness of the human mind and human cultures. Such qualities cannot be converted to and explained by a *biological logic* which stresses the existence of cultural forms due to survival, need, and function. All societies and cultures contain more than what is biologically imperative, and all cultural elaborations must be considered as autonomous products of a distinctive symbolic logic whose locus is in the human mind. It is this particular human quality which I define as the *mental logic*.

One contemporary example will demonstrate the changed relationships between culture and biology. All cultures have a set of beliefs which are linked to the concept of "handedness." Anthropologists such as Robert Hertz and Rodney Needham have noted differences in cognition toward left and right handedness, and more recently psychologists and physiologists have shown that these conceptions are related to the two hemispheres of the brain. In general, left-handedness is associated with evil, sinister behavior, darkness, activities that are profane. In some cases, it is given female attributes. Yet at the same time and in the same cultures one who is left-handed is also regarded as creative, insightful but odd, imaginative but erratic. Thus we have two linked conceptions, one being sinister, wrong, and evil, the other being creative, odd, and unpredictable.

The right, on the other hand, is regarded as logical, correct, good: it is associated with light and male. In most societies, right-handedness is thought of as normal and proper, and in many ways the virtues that are desired are commonly associated with the right. In French, the term for right is *droit*, and *droit* also means the study of jurisprudence, which in French culture is considered the highest and noblest profession that can be pursued. *Gauche* means left, and it also is used for awkwardness, wrong, devious, clumsy, and oblique.

This contrast also occurs in non-European languages. In Tagalog, one of the major languages in the Philippines, *kanan* means right and *kaliwa* means left; a left-handed person is referred to as *kaliwete*. *Kaliwa* is also the root word for *naŋaŋaliwa*, which is used for adulterous behavior and other kinds of dishonest and sinister behavior involving one's spouse. In Mandarin Chinese the contrast of left and right occurs in varying forms of *tso* (meaning left, useless plan, cantankerous, heresy, to degrade) and *yu* (meaning right, honorable family, peerless, and so on).

Left-handedness ranges from 8 to 13 percent in most populations. What would happen if the percentage of left-handedness in a human population were significantly above the 10 percent mark? Would the language reflect this proportion by an increase in the number of words that refer to handedness? These questions assume that this particular phenomenon would have an effect on the way people speak and presumably also on the way they think about themselves and others.

In American English we have few distinctive terms for either right or left-handedness. "Southpaw" and "portsider" are the only terms which denote the left other than such terms as "leftie," which only describe the condition. In British English, however, the number of words for left-handedness is considerable. Terms such as "ker-handit," "carry-handed," "carry-pawed" are used for the left, while "car-sham-ye" is a common term of abuse referring to left-handed shinty players. All of these phrases derive from the surname Kerr, which is Scottish in origin, or Carr in its anglicized form. This surname is historically associated with left-handedness, and through time its folklore has spread over the British Isles, giving rise to numerous slang forms that refer to the left.

In 1974 data presented by the Royal College of General Practitioners showed that left-handedness among bearers of the Kerr surname was nearly twice as great as among other surnames, and ambidexterity was also more prevalent. Out of two hundred cases with Kerr surnames, 29.5 percent were left-handed or ambidexterous, compared to only 11 percent among two hundred cases with other surnames. The study was further confirmed by data from Kerrs residing in North America. According to the Oxford English Dictionary, the surname Kerr is derived from "caerr" (Gaelic), which means awkward. Here again, the symbolic association of left-handedness with undersirable attributes is apparent.

The Kerrs and Carrs have lived in the border areas of Scotland and England at least since the early fifteenth century, and from other evidence it appears that a high degree of left-handedness was present among them even during their early days. How was cultural practice and content influenced by their higher-than-normal degree of left-handedness? Interesting evidence comes from the castles which the Kerrs built in defense of their lands. The Royal College's report summarizes as follows: "In those [castles] which survive, some spiral staircases are built with an anti-clock-wise spiral, to be defended, no doubt, by the 'carry-pawed' members of the family whose swordmanship would be impaired were the stairways to turn in the more usual direction." While most adjacent castles belonging to other surname groups had stairwells that were clockwise in direction, the stairwells of the Kerr castles were opposite.

This is a nice example of how cultural adaptations are made on the microlevel in response to minute yet significant biological differences in particular populations. What appears on the surface as a difference in castle architecture with no apparent significance can be explained as the result of the degree of left-handedness, and we can see how such differences may bring forth a set of adaptive processes.

Conclusion

Human evolutionary growth, biological and cultural, consists of a series of complex interactions in which the career of the species was shaped in form and function. Until the past fifteen or twenty thousand years, biological evolution occurred sometimes by drastic and rapid revolution and sometimes in a more gradual form. The changes in human brain size from about 500 cc. to the present average figure of 1,450 cc. seems to have been a slow growth. In other aspects, evolutionary changes seem to have occurred much more quickly. For example, I believe that human language is partly the result of certain brain developments, but that language probably developed in relation to the growing capacity of the brain for conceptualization and abstraction. When humans combined events and experiences into meaningful categories that could explain other activities and events, the brain had reached a threshold beyond which man was released from the narrow limits of circumstances and situations. Language might have evolved only after the human ability for abstraction and conceptualization had occurred. Language arbitrarily assigns symbols and meanings to categories and other abstractions; thus the function of communication in language emerged only after symbols and meanings were linked as part of conventional thought.

Within the past twenty thousand years, human cultural evolution has come to dominate the continuing biological changes of the species. Sociocultural development has taken us from simple band existence to complex metropolitan centers so congested that the phenomena man has created may destroy the creator. The growth of civilization has not produced the ultimate paradise. Many biological ills in contemporary Western societies, such as heart disease, diabetes, and tuberculosis, are themselves the result of social and cultural evolution and the emergence of activities that are deterimental to the physical condition of human beings.

Man must seek a convergence which will gradually restore mutualism and compatibility between cultural growth and biological change, for mankind's fate is dependent on how we control the very developments which made humans human.

BIBLIOGRAPHICAL NOTE

Interest in relationships between behavior and biology in man has been a dominant focus in anthropology; however, systematic work on this problem has been undertaken only during the last fifteeen or twenty years. Some of the most interesting work has been done by James N. Spuhler, *The Evolution of Man's Capacity for Culture* (Detroit: Wayne State University Press, 1959) and *Genetic Diversity and Human Behavior* (Chicago: Aldine Publishing Co., 1967), and J. B. Birdsell, *Human Evolution: An Introduction to the New Physical Anthropology* (2nd ed. Chicago: Rand McNally Co., 1975), both of whom explore the interconnections through genetic, demographic, and evolutionary approaches. The recent textbook by Birdsell (1975) provides a iscussion of biological-cultural relationships with examples from particular ethnographic sources. Alexander Alland, *Evolution and Human Behavior* (New York: Natural History Press, 1967), has written a small book in which he approaches the problem as a cultural anthropologist interested in establishing the determinants of behavior. One of the better works is Anthony Barnett's *The Human Species* (London: Penguin Press, 1961), which explores the range of human similarity and diversity while attempting to account for evolutionary processes through demographic, nutritional, and environmental analysis. Though the book needs revision because of recent findings, Barnett does provide an interesting, highly sophisticated, and readable approach.

Recent studies stressing the biological basis of behavior and culture are found in the field of genetics. The following is only a partial listing of some major works that should be consulted: Cold Spring Harbor Symposia in Quantitative Biology (1950,

1957); Theodosius Dobzhansky, *Mankind Evolving* (New Haven, Conn.: Yale University Press, 1962); Jerry Hirsch (ed.), *Behavior-Genetic Analysis* (New York: McGraw-Hill Book Co., 1967); Frank B. Livingstone, "Anthropological Implication of Sickle Cell Distribution in West Africa," *American Anthropologist* 60:533–62 (1958), Ashley Montagu (ed.), *Culture and the Evolution of Man* (New York: Oxford University Press, 1962); and Anne Roe and G. G. Simpson (eds.), *Behavior and Evolution* (New Haven, Conn.: Yale University Press, 1958). Focus on the evolutionary aspects of cultural development are found in the numerous publications of Sherwood Washburn, *Social Life of Early Man* (Chicago: Aldine Publishing Co., 1962), and in a collection of papers on evolutionary anthropology edited by Sol Tax, *Evolution after Darwin* (3 vols. Chicago: University of Chicago Press, 1960).

The ethological approach to biology and behavior has been popularized by the numerous works of Konrad Lorenz, who stresses the role of aggression as a social phenomenon, Robert Audrey, who focuses on the role of territory and property in group formation, and Desmond Morris. One of the best compendiums on the transition of natural species to social species is Edward O. Wilson's *Sociobiology: The New Synthesis* (Cambridge, Mass.: Harvard University Press, 1975).

7.

LANGUAGE AND THOUGHT

Susan M. Ervin-Tripp

LANGUAGE HAS LONG been viewed as the chief differentiator of human from beast. Yet there has been increasing evidence that other species than humans have both highly developed intelligence and systems of communication. Do humans alone have language? The question is a tantalizing one, for we find many features of human language in other species. Bees can give information about distant food sources to other bees. Other primates can warn about hazards, gesture to induce action in their fellows, develop new sounds in new situations. But here we must hesitate, for as far as we know, neither bees nor primates nor any species but humans discusses kinship, or justice, or emotion recalled in tranquillity.

Human language is unique not in its particular features, but in its combination of them. Three of these features of human language are paramount: (1) it combines and recombines limited elements; (2) it creates arbitrary meanings for combinations, conventional in a social group; and (3) it refers to distant objects and events and to intangible concepts. The first property, the creation of new combinations, makes human language flexible and expandable in form. We can always invent new sentences which can be immediately understood. The other properties make it expandable in meaning. We can eventually talk about space exploration and the United Nations in any human language. There are a few who expect to find that chimpanzee language has equal versatility, but as far as we now know, human language is indeed unique.

Primates in the wild have remarkably rich social and emotional communication systems, which appear to be progenitors of human gestural and vocal emotional communication. But in these primate systems, we have so far found no antecedents for human referential language, for grammar, for phonetic structure. Even if nonhuman primates did not invent a referential language, can they learn one?

To some extent, they can. Like the dating of the original human fossil or the establishment of athletic records, we have not yet pushed chimpanzee learning to its limits. In the laboratory, chimpanzees can reject sentences as ungrammatical. They can respond correctly to questions and directions which contain quantifiers (such as *some* and *all*) and conditionals. When child language acquisition conditions are simulated, they can learn the deaf sign language, to which chimpanzees are better adapted than to vocal language. They appear to know as much semantically, functionally, and grammatically as many children; they produce and understand simple sentences, respond correctly to different information questions, and generalize semantically. But it remains a question whether they can use a grammar in which the grammatical classes are not also semantic classes, or talk about propositions as if they were objects. These features of language are present in the third year in humans. These are necessary features if language is to serve its many abstract functions.

We do not know when the various features of human language emerged. The fact that we see, in the chimpanzee and child studies, that earlier and simpler forms of human language exist suggests that language evolution, like physical evolution, was gradual. Language itself and many of its effects are nonmaterial and leave no clues for the archeologist. We can see the associated skull and vocal tract evidence, but these tell us nothing about language functions or structure, within broad limits. What, so far as we can tell, were the consequences of the development of abstract language? Much of what we call human culture—religion and oral literature, for instance—consists in largely verbal products. Further, it is clear that language must have made possible a more flexible and complex social organization. If you have ever arrived alone in a foreign country with no knowledge of its language, you can understand how powerless a creature is when reduced to the use of gesture and force.

Social organization is certainly possible without language, just as culture can be transmitted without language. We are not driven back to instinct or even to learning anew all the experience of our elders if we are mute. Any animal which imitates by instinct or by learning can also learn the use of tools, appropriate reactions to danger, and social responses to fellow animals. In fact, it is still true of humans that we acquire most of our face-to-face social skills and our physical and manipulatory skills this way. What does language add? It adds efficiency in time and space. It is hard to conceive of large political systems without language. Even today writing and radio transmission continue to alter political possibilities. Language also adds the possibility of certain complex categories of social organization regardless of technological level. Even in the isolated village where transmission through time and space is restricted, social organization may include such units as the paternal uncle, a unit difficult or impossible to convey without speech.

To view language as a tool or as a channel like a telephone wire designed for transmission is too simple. Our utterances are only in part influenced by what we know and feel. The point to be examined more thoroughly is that what we know and feel may be influenced by what we say. Here we glimpse an unexpected and pervasive effect of language.

The idea that language is formative as well as formed is not a new one. Wilhelm Von Humboldt and, more recently, Edward Sapir and B. L. Whorf have expressed this notion forcefully. Since they wrote, there has appeared a variety of experimental evidence on the place of verbal skills in human behavior, which puts the problem they defined into a different perspective.

In its most extreme form, this view states that humans can think only what they can say, that the categories of their language provide the categories of their perception, memory, metaphor, and imagination. This view implies that the categories of language make humans radically different from other species in their intellectual processes and make the child different from the infant. This view would lead to the conclusion that speakers of different languages cannot think alike since there is a difference in categories and modes of thought which no translation can bridge.

Of course, there is some truth in all these statements. But are the differences we see due to language? Perhaps it is impossible to isolate the effects of language from all the other sources of different behavior. Species differ in thousands of ways besides language, both in structure and in experience; a child inevitably has learned more than an infant; speakers from different language communities vary in social organization, values, and cultural traditions. None of these comparisons can answer the question we have asked—what is the effect of a contrast in language itself, when everything else remains the same?

Let us go to the simplest of actions—comparison. Species differ a good deal in their sensitivity to fine contrast in various physical dimensions. Speech has given humans no superiority to dogs in discriminating odors or to owls in detecting objects in the dark. We can compare people from various linguistic communities with differing detail in their systems of labeling colors, and we find that they can all match and compare colors equally well, whether their labels are refined or crude. For example, Zuni Indians have a single term for the hues that English speakers call "yellow" and "orange." This does not lead them to confuse the two colors—they can still see the differences.

There is one dimension, however, that we know is affected by training in a language. That is the discrimination of speech sounds themselves. We hear best those differences our own language employs. That is one reason we have trouble learning to pronounce the words in a new language. Why does language improve our hearing of speech sounds but not our sensitivity to colors? We discriminate colors all day, in judging distances, picking out objects by their contours, and so on, but we employ speech sounds only in hearing speech. In our transactions with the physical world, we learn to make discriminations whether or not our language provides categories to talk about them.

Judgments about the physical world are often probabilistic because neither humans nor animals can test all the dimensions of concern to them. They learn that it is economical to make use of the correlations in the physical world—for instance, that what is large tends also to be heavy. There is evidence that some fundamental dimensions—in this case a dimension of size, strength, and weight—permeate the judgments made by various people, regardless of language. Children, in fact, only gradually learn to distinguish these logically distinct but empirically correlated dimensions. In a large program of cross-cultural studies, Charles Osgood and associates have found that dimensions based on these natural correlations underlie many systems of metaphor. Anyone who judges the United States to be large is also likely to judge it to be heavy though it has never been weighed. While these correlations show up in verbal reports, they seem usually not to be caused by them but rather to reflect direct experience. It is possible that similar probabilistic judgments would be made by other species if appropriate tests were devised.

In any ordinary situation, a great many things are present at once. What determines what we notice first? Experience, of course. We are likely to notice the unfamiliar, and we are likely to notice those things that have been helpful in the past, if we must act. Does language and its categories influence us? Evidently, yes. Let me describe a relevant experiment.

The largest tribe of American Indians in the United States is the Navaho tribe, living on and near an area in Arizona reserved for its use. The typical occupations there are sheepherding and a little agriculture. The Navaho often live in isolated clusters of dwellings, speaking little or no English. It is possible to find Navaho children varying in their degree of knowledge of Navaho or English but living in similar circumstances. The Navaho language has an interesting set of verb categories. In many European languages, if I say, "Hand it to me," I must specify the gender of the object. But the gender, for inanimate objects, may be arbitrary. In Navaho, the verb categories are also different according to the object whenever I say, "Hand it to me." But the categories are semantically consistent and predictable. All flat, flexible objects such as paper and rugs require the same category, and long, rigid objects—pencils and sticks—a different category. There are about eleven of these categories. The Navaho child must learn the categories very early, since they apply to all verbs concerning handling of objects. It may be expected that children who speak Navaho learn to notice the physical form of objects especially early.

In an experiment, two groups of Indian children, one speaking primarily Navaho and the other English, were compared. The children were shown a painted block and asked to pick another like it. The choice they were given was between a block similar only in color and one similar only in form. In fact, the English-speaking children matched the blocks by color and the Navaho-speaking children by form.

Thus we might conclude that language has determined what the children noticed. However, in another experiment, the Indian children were compared to Boston nursery school children with very different surroundings and training. These children, like the Navaho-speaking children, matched by form, though they did not speak Navaho. Why? Perhaps because they had used form-board puzzles or any of the numerous commercial toys in the United States requiring choices according to form. At any rate, we can see here that language can indeed be the determining factor in leading to the saliency of certain physical dimensions. But when other living conditions change, other factors can also change which aspects of the situation seem dominant. Language is thus not the only determinant and appears important only when other factors are carefully controlled.

There is another point to be observed in this experiment. The children did not say anything. The differences in their choices were based on past emphasis on observing the features of their environment. The effects may occur whether or not people speak or even think verbally.

The evidence presented so far may be summarized in this way: language has little importance where direct comparison of simple sensory dimensions is involved; it begins to matter when more complicated choices are required.

There have been many attempts to compare species in

complex problem solving. Any differences between humans and other species might of course be based on other factors, such as greater intelligence, and not merely on verbal skill. The great variety of differences between species makes interpretations of behavioral contrasts difficult. Some of the procedures used with animals have been tried with children. In this case, verbal training could be used experimentally, to see if verbal habits alter problem solutions.

Delayed-response experiments have been used for many years. They require that the subject watch the experimenter hide a reward—often food—and then wait before responding. Duration of delays before successful responding differs in various species. For some, the longest possible delay is only a few seconds. It has been found that some children who have been taught verbal descriptions of the various alternatives rehearsed the description of the correct cue during the delay. Thus they were able to bridge the time gap. But rehearsal is a special skill that children do not have when they are young and that some children do not spontaneously develop and use. Of course, we know that adult humans can retain information over very long periods of time, but it is still a puzzle how they do this without constant verbal rehearsal. At any rate, it does seem that verbal skills aid in the delay of response.

In another type of experiment, an animal might be required to choose the left-hand side twice, the right-hand side twice, and so on. (The rules are always stated in terms of number.) We know that primates perform better than rats in this procedure, and that in humans, performance is related to mental age. Before deaf children have learned to count, this procedure is more difficult for them than for normal children.

Suppose a child has to behave differently toward different people. This is a common social fact. Perhaps he or she must be more polite to some than to others: stand up to greet them, use a special greeting, use special request forms, be especially quiet. It has been found that children who were taught labels for the classes to which distinctive behavior was necessary learn that behavior faster than children not so taught. The category, of course, was established in learning the names. The rest was easy. Perhaps the child says the name to remember the correct behavior or, on the other hand, that the learning of the name suffices to establish the cues for the distinctive behavior.

Another case when verbal learning most clearly aids in a difficult problem is in a procedure in which the rules are shifted after a solution is learned. For example, suppose you are given four blocks differing both in size and in color. You learn first that you are correct whenever you choose the black one. Then the rules shift. There are two shifts possible. One might be that the white one is correct, the black is always wrong. The other simply is a shift to the size dimension, ignoring color. It is quite clear that rats and people differ in this problem. For rats, the shift to a different dimension is easier than reversing the rules. For people, this is not so. It seems clear to an adult that he or she would simple note that "black is right" becomes "black is wrong" or "white is right." Opposites are always close verbal associates. But what happens with children? Before they are fluent verbally, they behave like rats in this experiment. But if they are taught to mention the color when choosing, the reversal of the rule becomes easier for them than switching to a new dimension. This experiment is a good one because it has shown clearly that it is verbal training and nothing else which makes for differences in performance.

In this group of problem-solving experiments, the benefits from verbal skill derive from what may be called verbal mediation. During exposure to the materials, the subject may talk—or think about them verbally—and the categories available in his or her language are appropriate to the behavior that he or she must perform subsequently. In all of these experiments, there are some interspecies difference and an advantage to verbal training that is small but consistent. The ability to delay choices while retaining the relevant information, the ability to generalize new behavior to a category defined by a label, the ability to solve more complex problems by using labels, all have practical implications both for human technology and social organization.

The evolution of covert responses which help performance has actually been observed in young children. At ages one and two, children do not use language as an aid in choosing between actions. Speech serves more as a trigger than as a differential aid. For young children one word in a given situation may be as good as another. Soon we find that children who must press a button twice can do better if they count, "One, two," than if they say, "Press two times." Eventually, they do not have to speak aloud. Here we see the self-directive role of language in the evolution process in children. At first, it comes from outside as a communicated direction; then, it is spoken aloud by children (and by chimpanzees, too) as self-direction; and, finally, it becomes silent thought. Presumably, further abbreviations occur with training as the quick and efficient mental processes of the adult are developed.

Is it always more efficient to have verbal training? No. In some forms of activity language gets in the way. In aiming at a target, in the manipulation of tools, in solving mechanical puzzles, in learning physical skills, practice may be of more use than talk. Occasionally, if it distracts or misdirects observation, speech may hinder learning.

For the retention of information, the evidence suggests, language is important, since it supplies ready categories. The price of efficient codification, however, is some distortion. Suppose you are shown a color chip. If you are asked to select it again a few minutes later from a large assortment, performance will be good. But if a longer lapse in time occurs, your performance will deteriorate and will come to depend increasingly on the appropriateness of the categories for color which your language supplies. Suppose you labeled the color: "Blue." If, in fact, the color was the one you most often call blue, you may choose it again, but if it was a pale lavender blue, you will probably select a hue that is bluer than the original. Many experiments with more complex materials than color show that memory can be distorted by the categories available.

Speech and verbal thought imply codification of the complex and infinitely varying stimuli of experience into the finite categories supplied by the grammar and vocabulary of a particular language.

Codification simplifies greatly the task of organizing and retaining information. A scholar in a new field knows that he or she retains more information as a consistent framework of categories is developed. The codifications made possible by language permit humans to solve many problems more easily than other species and to generalize to other problems which are similar only in the most abstract way, and to solve them quickly, too.

It would be a mistake to suppose that other species are completely incapable of solving any of the complex problems it has been reasonable to try with them. With clever training, primates have solved some astonishingly complicated problems and such experiments clearly show that language is not necessary for all kinds of complicated thinking. They have also shown that verbal responses do shorten training time and hasten certain solutions. What we do not know is the point where it is possible to draw a sharp, qualitative line beyond which it is impossible for an animal without language to go. For example, we do not know what mathematical processes are not possible for some primates.

Thus far only cognitive organization has been considered. We can only speculate about the role of language in the internalization of social categories and values. Humans can label their own behavior and react to it as if it occurred in others. They can compare their own acts to those of others and to an idealized norm and thereby make moral judgments about themselves. This objectivity about the self can be compared to a change in logical thinking. Jean Piaget, the great Swiss psychologist, has studied the growth of logical and moral thinking in children. As they grow older in a socially stimulating surrounding, children's judgments of the world take on a changed perspective, away from the self. They can then even recognize the state of ignorance of the blindfolded person or someone on the opposite side of the room from an examined object. Modern astronomy is the extreme in the evolution away from a self-centered view. While the labels of language may be, and often are, applied differently to others and to the self, to outsiders and to insiders, they are potentially neutral. G. H. Mead, a philosopher-sociologist, has said that language helps one to "take the role of the other," to place one's self, one's social position, and one's behavior in the same perspective as others'. Piaget has implied a parallel evolution in children's concepts of natural science. But as yet we do not have experimental evidence of the role that language actually plays in this evolution.

The effects discussed earlier depend on the provision of categories by languages for classification and evaluation of experience, but languages differ. Children who learn a language learn a system of categories—those categories signaled by the grammar of that language and those codified by its vocabulary. In addition, they learn the probabilities of what different things will be said in that language. Normal individuals know what the listener expects, though they may not always say just that. For example, the French talk more often about verbal disputation than Americans and the Japanese more often about filial duty. These are differences in the actual usage of speech which reflect contrasts in values. Anyone brought up in a society learns not only the language but what its speakers are likely to say. Both the language and the rules of its use enforce attention to particular dimensions of social relationships, such as sex and status and age, just as they may force attention to form. Consequently, as has been demonstrated, bilinguals shift language and content together. This does not mean that speakers of different languages are not *able* to say the same things. It is simply that languages differ in what it is easy to talk about. Psychiatrists have found that under special conditions people will say things they have never said before. The fact that they do not ordinarily say them is of more interest than the fact that they can say them under special conditions. Societies differ in the aspects of culture which they transmit by verbal means rather than by other methods of direct reward or imitation. In some societies the voice of conscience may not be a voice at all.

We may conclude that the existence of a formalized and conventional system of symbols in humans has had important consequences. It affects not only what we ordinarily consider social life but also the processes of thought, memory, and feeling which we ordinarily consider private. The importance of a symbol system increases the further the situation is from direct sensory or motor experience. Those activities which involve comparing simple stimuli, aiming at a target, and manipulating tools show least dependence on symbolic behavior. But if complex choices and observations are necessary or if much information must be processed and retained through time, the codification made possible by language has more pronounced effects. It often makes humans more flexible and efficient than other species, and it helps make people from different language communities different in their nonverbal behavior. While we need more evidence on this point, it may be that the development of certain kinds of thinking in the domain of logic, morality, and social organization are so difficult as to be virtually impossible without language.

Today, scientists do not all agree that the development of language necessarily has affected the inner experience of humans as profoundly as it has changed their social and cultural behavior. It still remains an open issue what the limits of these effects may be.

BIBLIOGRAPHICAL NOTE

A collection of papers on primate problem-solving appears in Allan M. Schrier and Fred Stollnitz (eds.), *Behavior of Nonhuman Primates* (New York: Academic Press, 1971). Descriptions of specific animal communication systems and discussions of comparisons between them have appeared in Thomas A. Sebeok (ed.), *Animal Communication: Techniques of Study and Results of Research* (Bloomington, Ind.: University of Indiana Press, 1968); W. E. Lanyon and W. N. Tavolga (eds.), *Animal Sounds and Communication* (Washington, D.C.: American Institute of Biological Sciences, 1960); and Phyllis C. Jay (ed.), *Primates: Studies in Adaptation and Variability* (New York: Holt, Rinehart & Winston, Inc., 1968). Studies of the capacity of chimpanzees to acquire human language have been done in the laboratory by David Premack, "Language in Chimpanzee?" *Science* 172:808–22 (1971) and by naturalistic immersion in communication by B. T. and R. A. Gardner, "Comparing the Early Utterances of Child and Chimpanzee," in Anne Pick (ed.), *Minnesota Symposium on Child Psychology* (Minneapolis: University of Minnesota Press, 1973). The results of the Gardners's work has been compared to child language development by Roger Brown, *A First Language:*

The Early Stages (Cambridge, Mass.: Harvard University Press, 1973).

The thesis that language and thought are related to each other was developed by Edward Sapir, whose *Language, An Introduction to the Study of Speech* (Reprint. New York: Harcourt, Brace & Co., Inc., 1921) has become a classic. A widely read elaboration of this idea with many examples appears in B. L. Whorf's writings, *Language, Thought and Reality* (New York: John Wiley & Sons, 1956). J. B. Carroll and J. B. Casagrande, "The Function of Language Classifications in Behavior," in Eleanor E. Maccoby, T. M. Newcomb, and E. L. Hartley (eds.), *Readings in Social Psychology* (3rd ed. New York: Holt, Rinehart & Winston, Inc., 1958), then conducted confirmatory research. The field has recently been critically reviewed by E. Rosch, "Linguistic Relativity," in A. Silverstein (ed.), *Human Communication: Theoretical Perspectives* (Potomac, Md.: Lawrence Erlbaum, Assoc., 1974). Related Soviet research on language and thought is reported by A. R. Luria, *The Role of Speech in the Regulation of Normal and Abnormal Behavior* (New York: Liveright Publishing, Inc., 1961). A philosophical view of the role of language in social development is provided by G. H. Mead, *Mind, Self and Society: From the Standpoint of a Social Behaviorist* (Chicago: University of Chicago Press, 1934) and has led to a school of sociology which bases social structure on verbal interaction, D. Sudnow (ed.), *Studies in Human Interaction* (New York: Free Press, 1972), and to studies of the relation of language to social organization, J. H. Gumperz and D. Hymes (eds.), *Directions in Sociolinguistics: The Ethnography of Communication* (New York: Holt, Rinehart & Winston, Inc., 1972).

8.

SYMBOLS AND LANGUAGE

David Premack

LANGUAGE IS THE MOST evident difference between man and other species. Granted that man is the only species with natural language, the question still remains: Can language or any part of language be taught to another species? To answer that question we must first decide what to accept as evidence for language. The basic evidence consists of reference relations or words, on the one hand, and of a sentence-generating capacity, on the other. This chapter concerns only words, not because sentences are unimportant, but simply because they presuppose words.

In man, reference relations include the names of objects, agents, actions, and properties. These are the basic categories of human ontology, the classes of items in terms of which we perceive the world and, not surprisingly, the classes of items which we name. Even more important than the range of lexical items is the psychological nature of the referent relation itself. The classical phrase "power of the word" celebrates, I think, the ability of the human word to substitute vigorously for its referent. This substitutibility of word for referent is well displayed in match-to-sample tests; with such tests we can observe the human subject match components and features of an object to the name of the object no less well than to the object itself. Thus, the basic evidence for reference relations is expressed by two factors: (1) arbitrary items (words) can serve as information retrieval devices, in the limiting case providing as much information about their associated referent as is contained in the referent itself, and (2) in the human case, words can serve as information retrieval devices for agents, objects, actions, and properties.

At least six chimpanzees have now been taught some degree of language by human tutelage. In all cases the language is nonvocal and syntactically simple, decidedly more like that of young children than of adults. In one approach, the language vehicle was hand signs, the training was naturalistic, and the syntax achieved was slight, for example, "gimme banana gimme." The main basis for the language claim in this case is spontaneous constructions: sequences of two or more signs different from those exhibited by the trainers and generated by the animal itself in more or less semantically appropriate circumstances. In another approach, the language vehicle was pieces of metal-backed plastic that adhere to a magnetized slate. Each plastic piece is wordlike in function, and sentences consist of sequences of plastic pieces arrayed on the vertical. The training in this case was more rigorous and the syntax achieved more complex, including both compound and complex sentences, such as, "Sarah insert apple (in) red dish, banana (in) green dish." In both procedures, the animals produced and comprehended new combinations of old words, that is, sentences not previously taught them.

On the basis of what evidence shall we decide whether or not an item is used as a symbol? In the context of our artificial language, the main question translates to: When is a piece of plastic a word? The standard answer is that a piece of plastic is a word when it is used as a word. An item is a word when it is used in grammatically appropriate ways on semantically appropriate occasions. For example, we agree that a small blue triangular piece of plastic is the name for apple if (1) it is used consistently when the subject requests apple—for example, "Mary give Sarah apple" and (2) it is the answer given when the experimenter points to an apple and asks: "What is the name of that?" In addition, we can obtain a second kind of evidence, corroborative of the first, by giving the subject only the putative word and asking it to describe the referent of the word. For example, we have given Sarah and more recently Elizabeth and Peony (new chimpanzee language trainees) a small blue triangle and asked them to match it to one member in each such pair of alternatives as: red vs. green, round vs. square, square-with-a-stem vs. square-without-a-stem, and so on. On these tests they consistently assigned to the word all the features they independently assigned to the referent.

A special set of tests was held using painted plastic fruit. A plastic apple, banana, orange, grape, cherry, and lemon—all familiar to the subjects from other tests—were painted white. Both a nonverbal and a verbal form of the test was done, with colored cards as samples in the first case and names of colors as samples in the second case. Names of colors were achromatic pieces of plastic—either white, black, or gray—and thus were no more iconic than names of the fruits. The alternatives in both cases were the painted fruit. The matching could not be done on a perceptual basis in either the nonverbal or the verbal form of the tests. For instance, to match a white apple to red, whether red was a colored card or the word "red," the subject would have to know or have stored in memory the fact that apple is red. In addition, the subject had to be able to recognize the fruit in its color-distorted form. When shown, say, a white lemon, one could conclude either that (1) this is a lemon painted white, or (2) this white fruitlike item is a new fruit with which I am unfamiliar. Only the first conclusion would make matching possible.

The results for these tests were comparable to those for other verbal tests. Names of the colors could be substituted for the colored cards without loss of accuracy. There is only one way in which a subject could match, say, a white cherry to the gray piece of plastic meaning red. That is by both knowing that the cherry is red and by having associated with the word "red" some actual representation of the color. The association of a representation of the color with the name of the color should come as no surprise, however. In principle, it is no different from the association of a fruit symbol with the name of a fruit.

Words were used to request fruits, describe actions applied to fruits, and to answer questions about them. Attributes of the fruit were never used in these ways. For instance, the animals did not put aside a stem, peel, or seed and then use it as a kind of self-initiated icon to request the whole fruit or an edible part of it. Although the attributes were more intimately associated with the fruit than with the pieces of plastic, the attributes were never used as linguistic devices. For most subjects, the attributes did not have the retrieval power of the word. Most subjects could reconstruct more about the fruit from the arbitrary piece of plastic that stood for fruit than from an actual part of the fruit. Thus a major consequence of giving an arbitrary object various linguistic prerogatives is to transfer to the object some or all of the information contained in the associated referent.

Under what circumstances does this transfer of information take place? Does it occur only after the piece of plastic has been used in a wordlike way, say, to request or describe the referent some number of times? That would be the most tenable hypothesis if the only way to produce names was by repeatedly associating them with their referents in one linguistic context or another. But we already know that this procedure can be short circuited. Names can be generated by instructions of the form " X is the name of Y," where X is so far an unused piece of plastic and Y is so far an unnamed object. This suggests that the effect of instructions such as "X is the name of Y" is to transfer to X some or all of the information the subject has stored in its memory about Y. This fact clarifies some of the power of language and at the same time suggests the kind of intelligence a species must have in order to acquire language.

To qualify for language a species must have at least two capacities. First, the species must be capable of storing a rich representation of Y. If not, the information transferred to X would be "weak" and the name would be a poor substitute for the referent. That is, if the mnemonic capacity of the species were limited, then information associated with names would be commensurately limited; and names could not then be substituted for their referents in match-to-sample tests without loss of accuracy, as in fact we have seen can be the case with chimpanzees. Secondly, instructions of the form "X is the name of Y" must have the force of transferring to X some—ideally all—of the information which the subject has stored about Y. These are not the only capacities a species must have in order to qualify for language, but these two are basic.

Visual Representation

Chimpanzees scribble but do not draw representational pictures, and in this failure they differ from man no less profoundly than in the case of language. Man is never found without reproduction or transformation of the visual world, any more than man is found without language.

Attempting to account for the ape's lack of visual production revives all of the questions raised by its lack of language. Is the deficiency motor, cognitive, motivational, or some combination of the three? To address these questions we devised a form of visual production which reduced motor demands to a minimum. Then an inability to draw or otherwise fashion visual products would not obscure a possible mental capacity for such tasks.

An example of the simple visual device is shown in Figure 1. An enlarged photograph of a chimpanzee's head (Peony's, to be exact), with the face blanked out, was mounted on stiff material. The eyes, nose, and mouth were cut out from another identical photograph and mounted on stiff material. Each piece was large enough to be easily handled by the chimpanzee. We used two sets of facial elements, one that preserved normal size relations, another in which all elements were of the same size, as shown in the upper and lower panels, respectively.

Sarah appeared to make faces or transforms thereof and differed from the other subjects which did not make faces either in a canonical or transformed sense. The data were characterized statistically by defining an ideal face in terms of grid positions and the elements occupying those positions, and then by measuring the distance between observed constructions and the ideal face in terms of two parameters: (1) the number of exchanges necessary to move the pieces from their observed to the ideal positions, and (2) the number of pieces outside the blanked-out or facial area.

Children's constructions with the same material displayed a number of regularities that simplified interpretation of the chimpanzee data. However, to enjoy the benefit of these simplifying regularities, it was necessary to use children of

FIGURE 1.

appropriate age. When the children were too young, their constructions resembled those of the chimpanzees, Peony, Elizabeth, and Walnut; they were apparently unable to reconstruct the face. When they were too old, they did *nothing but* reconstruct the face. It was only children at an intermediate age (5.2–7.0 years) and only a minority of them who both reconstructed the face and transformed it—and in so orderly a fashion that transformation was not an inference but an observable act.

Several of the children's transformations were sexual improvisations, either an arm or leg placed in the pubic region and explicitly labeled by the child as "penis" or "wiener." When given puzzles that consisted of themselves, no child carried out a sexual transform on itself; two did so when given a puzzle that consisted of a friend. The transformation of this kind shown in Figure 2 was selected because of the nice way in which a 7.2-year-old child solved the major problem posed by transformations in the context of *nonsurplus resources*. The objective of a transformation is, I assume, not simply to make a change but to do so while at the same time preserving the identity of the original figure.

By a bit of good fortune, we obtained some semantically interpretable transformations from Sarah. On the day preceding a test of the chimpanzee-face puzzle, Sarah spent part of

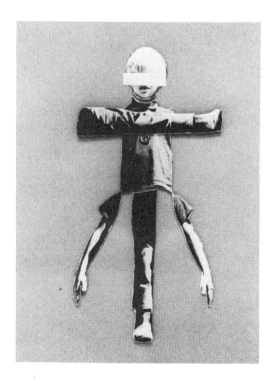

FIGURE 2.

the morning with the trainer trying on women's hats and viewing herself wearing the hats in a mirror. Approximately thirty-six hours after Sarah had viewed herself wearing a hat, she was given a standard session with the chimpanzee-face puzzle. On the fourth trial of that session, she produced the construction shown in Figure 3. The mouth has been turned over and placed in a hatlike position on the head. Is this a coincidence or can we attribute to the chimpanzee the same dispositions we attributed to the children? We said that the child used the leg (or arm) to represent a "penis." Can we say that the chimpanzee used the mouth to represent a "hat"?

Since the first apparent hatlike transformation was a chance observation, we undertook to replicate the outcome in a controlled way. We eliminated the morning hat sessions and gave Sarah the chimp-face puzzle on two daily sessions, four trials a session; reinstated the hat sessions on two daily sessions giving Sarah the chimp-face puzzle on the same two days; and then returned to the original or base conditions.

FIGURE 3.

Sarah did not produce any hatlike transformations in either the pretreatment or posttreatment phases. During the treatment phase, when hat and puzzle sessions occurred in the same time period, she made two constructions different from any she had made before. Both are shown in Figure 4. In the first of these, not only the mouth but also the nose were inverted and placed in a hatlike position, the nose on top of the mouth. She made this construction in the puzzle session that was immediately

FIGURE 4.

preceded by the hat session. In the second case, she added a banana peel, which was often available to her in the cage along with an orange peel and occasional candy wrappers, in a hatlike position on the head.

Sarah's transformations appear to be a form of natural or untrained symbol use and make her success with arbitrary symbols more understandable. To sustain this argument, however, we must establish a more rigorous equivalence between symbols in language and out of language than we have hitherto. A symbol is any item used to stand for an item other than itself. Without doubt the word is the most familiar form of a symbol. For example, we say that the word "hat" stands for *hat*. We also say, in the context of Sarah's visual play, that the mouth, when inverted and placed on the head, stands for *hat*. We use the same key phrase *stands for* in the linguistic and nonlinguistic case: "hat" stands for *hat*, and "mouth" (when appropriately operated upon) stands for *hat*. Does "stands for" have the same meaning in the two cases? It must if we are to consider that symobls when used inside and outside of language reflect the same psychological process.

Earlier we presented two criteria that can be used to evaluate claims of symbolization. First, an item is a word when it is used in grammatically proper locations on semantically appropriate occasions. Second, an item is a word, if, in the presence of the word alone, the subject can give a description of the referent of the word. In terms of these criteria all four subjects used the pieces of plastic as symbols or words.

However, we have only to attempt to apply these criteria outside of language to discover that they are inapplicable. For example, can we say of an item used in play that it either is or is not used in a proper position in a sequence of items and is used on semantically appropriate occasions? A judgment of this kind presupposes (1) a syntax of play and (2) that the main function of play is or can be the same as that of language— communication of nonlinguistic states of affairs. One need not deny the possibility of a grammar of play or visual transformations generally in order to reject the burden of working it out. Yet it is clear that nothing short of this will serve. The criteria that serve to identify symbols in language can be applied outside language—in play, dreams, myth, and ritual—only if the apparatus which the criteria presuppose—grammar and semantic functions—also is found outside of language.

The second criterion depends on the fact that words and referents are not alike—any more than a blue triangle is like an apple. But when applied outside language, the criterion loses its force, for there symbols are heavily iconic. When symbols and their referents are physically alike, the ability to describe one given the other is inconsequential. In brief, neither of the criteria that serve well in language has any force outside language.

From this difficulty we can draw either of two conclusions: (1) symbols used in a linguistic and nonlinguistic context could not reflect the same psychological process or the criteria applicable to one would be applicable to the other; or (2) the criteria considered are not the only ones possible. We need other criteria that can be applied to both cases in order to evaluate the possible relation between the two cases. In the rest of this chapter, I consider two other criteria that can be applied to both language and nonlanguage symbolic processes. They have the interesting feature of attacking the difference between language and nonlanguage symbols from opposite directions. The first one denies to language a would-be unique function, showing that the function can be found outside language. The second one gives to language a function normally reserved for nonlinguistic processes. The net effect of subtracting a difference and adding a similarity is to reduce substantially the difference between symbolic processes inside and outside language.

The main function ascribed to language is the communication of information. The information can be of any kind; it can concern the speaker's state, the world outside the speaker, or both. For years the psychoanalyst has sought to use symbolic play in children as a substitute for language, primarily to learn about the speaker's state but also to learn about conditions external to the speaker. For example, a child may say, "My mother and father had a fight," or the child might act out the scene of one "parentlike" doll hitting another "parentlike" doll. There is no question but that the verbal statement is the preferred form of evidence. However, legitimate inferences can be drawn from symbolic play, and such play can be a source of information just like the verbal statement. Therefore, it becomes important for us to understand just what makes the verbal statement the better source.

We confront several kinds of difficulties in attempting to infer states or conditions from play or nonverbal symbolic acts generally. The most serious is the lack of a general theory of nonverbal symbolic acts. However, the lack of such a theory should not lead us to suppose that we have an exhaustive one in the case of verbal statements. Language emerges as an excellent system—at least when compared to our other alternatives—and does so despite the fact that we cannot give a detailed account of how the system works. Fortunately for us its efficiency is not dependent upon our theoretical under-standing of it. However, the case is not likely to be the same with nonverbal symbolic acts. They "work" less well than verbal statements and, so far as I can see, are not likely to work any better until we can improve upon our theoretical account of them.

Here are two major competing views of nonverbal symbolic acts between which it is not yet possible to decide. (1) In play, children carry out acts which they desire, but are prevented from doing so directly. This might be because they lack the physical resources—for example, they cannot ride a horse because they do not have one—or because they are also afraid of the consequences—for example, if they hit their broth-er they will be punished. (2) Children carry out in play acts which they have experienced in some other form—thought, dreams, watching television or movies, reading about it in a book, drawing pictures of it, and so on. The child's behavior is an instance of this principle: every salient experience seeks its expression in some other form. This alternative is likely to seem vacuous or bizarre until we have a chance to flesh it out with some predictions and to show how it works.

A child who was observed striking a doll resembling his or her brother would be said to do so because (1) he or she would like to hit his or her brother but is afraid to do so; or (2) he or she has thought about hitting his or her brother, seen other children hit their brothers, read stories about such acts, or in any case experienced the act in some other form on many occasions. On this alternative, the child carries out in play a persistent or salient experience that he or she has had in one or more other forms.

By and large forbidden or otherwise unrealizable desires will be experienced in some form, if only as the content of thought, and therefore the two interpretations will often lead to the same predictions. There is, however, a simple diagnostic case. If the subject is first allowed to fulfill its desires and still engages in symbolic play, it would be difficult to maintain the first interpretation. The outcome would be entirely compatible with the second interpretation, however, for it does not draw categorical distinctions between the various forms which experience can take. This also differentiates it from the first position, for the former definitely links fulfillment to real action and gives a shadowy character to all other forms of experience. The second interpretation, though it may distinguish between the several forms of experience with regard to the parameter of salience, does not otherwise distinguish one form of experience from the other. Thus if the experience in question were a real act, the principle would still apply and the subject would seek to carry out the real act in some other form, for example, draw a picture, tell a story, and so on.

In a sense, we tested these alternatives inadvertently when we gave Sarah the chimpanzee-face puzzle immediately after giving her an opportunity to watch herself trying on hats. Within minutes of having returned the hats for lack of further interest in them she made a hatlike transformation on the veridically reconstructed face of the chimpanzee. If one did not know all the facts, which the analyst seldom does, and subscribed to the first theory, Sarah's symbolic act would almost certainly be interpreted incorrectly, as a request for a hat. Ethical considerations preclude doing the corresponding experiment with children. But if the hostile child were allowed actually to attack his or her brother, from the results with Sarah we would predict that he or she would subsequently attack a doll resembling the brother. If so, it would be incorrect to interpret the symbolic act as expressing a desire to beat up the brother; that desire would already have been fulfilled.

If the second position were verified, not only in one test but in many, it would not necessarily negate all interpretations based on the first position. On the contrary, there could be many cases in which the reason the subject thought persistently about an act—and thus experienced it in one or more forms—was because the act represents a deeply held but unrealized desire. The research needed on this topic has only begun, and for now there are more questions than answers.

Even if we had a satisfactory general theory of nonverbal symbolic acts, their interpretation is almost certain to remain ambiguous in some respects. Since symbols outside language are perhaps always iconic, certain kinds of features are not likely to be coded for, simply because they do not lend themselves to iconic coding. Time is perhaps the single most important feature not coded for in symbolic play; nor is it evident how to code for time in an iconic system. When the child is observed hitting one doll with another, there is no feature in the play itself that distinguishes between such interpretations as: My parents fought last night, last month, will fight, never fought but I wish they would, and so on. To draw these distinctions requires additional information, external to the play episode itself. This suggests another way in which to compare the efficiency of verbal and nonverbal symbols. How much auxiliary information is needed to interpret them accurately? It would be a mistake to assume that verbal statements are self-contained, interpretable without external information, yet the dependence is less acute in the verbal case, in part simply because the verbal system codes for features for which the nonverbal one does not.

The second criterion is actually a continuation of the first, for though it does not concern information or communication, it returns to a generic topic opened but not closed by the first criterion. This concerns the fact that experience can take multiple forms. What is the relation among those forms? Tradition has set a premium on motor action, which it calls real experience, and distinguishes from lesser representations, such as talking about an act, representing an act pictorially, carrying out a play version of an act, and so on. The allocation of a superior position to real action makes sense if one adopts the customary biological view. Organisms can live only by eating and species survive only by copulation; real acts are necessary in both cases. But suppose we reject the biological view and consider instead that the purpose of an organism is not simply to stay alive and reproduce its kind but, rather, loosely speaking, to figure out the nature of the world. Then staying alive and reproducing one's kind are secondary, of interest only insofar as they contribute to the first purpose. And from the point of view of the first purpose, real action need have no priority. There may be occasions on which it could contribute more to figuring out the nature of the world and other occasions on which talking or thinking about an act could contribute more. This viewpoint leads one to suspect that there may be a higher order of substitutability between the several forms of experience than is customarily proposed.

One experimental paradigm that can be used to measure substitutability is based upon the habituation function and involves two steps: (1) determining the effect of X upon itself and Y upon itself, and (2) determining the effect of each upon the other. There seems little question that any act, linguistic as well as nonlinguistic, will affect itself, initially perhaps incrementally—appetizer effect—in the long run decrementally. The only real question—and one of theoretical interest—is the effect of "unlike" acts upon each other, specifically linguistic acts upon designated real acts, and vice versa.

The argument is completed by raising the same question of substitutability with regard to two nonlinguistic acts that bear an iconic relation to one another, such as putting an object into a circle and putting oneself into a circle, both of which are found in the chimpanzee. Can these acts substitute for each other? Suppose substitutability is shown to hold between iconically related real acts on the one hand and between linguistic acts and their designated real acts on the other. Then it would seem reasonable to hold that the phrase "X stands for Y" has a significant overlap in meaning when applied inside and outside language.

The whole relation between speaking, reading, or thinking about an act and the act itself needs clarification. The common sense understanding of that relation certainly does not suggest that one can be substituted for the other and thus does not suggest that the habituation model is the appropriate one to use in attempting to decide whether or not X is a symbol of Y. For example, no one proposes to solve even temporary hunger by speaking, reading, or thinking about food. Likewise, one is not advised to solve sexual deprivation by symbolic means. In fact, it is usually supposed that engaging in the symbolic version of an act will have a facilitative effect, not a decremental one.

Yet the very fact that participation in the symbolic version of X may have a concupiscent effect upon X is itself highly suspicious and, as such, not incompatible with the habituation model. Many habituation functions have an initial ascending arm. The first bite or even first few bites of food increase rather than decrease the probability of subsequent eating. Likewise, the frequency-probability function for sex is not a simple decreasing one. There is an ascending arm there, too, early members of a series of sexual bouts increasing the probability of later members. Ultimately, the functions for eating, sex, and presumably all acts, is a decreasing arm, the outcome we have in mind when speaking of habituation. But the initial facilitative effect of an act upon subsequent occurrences of the same act is apparently no less genuine, though it is less widely reported.

Now it may be possible to interpret the facilitative effect of symbolic acts upon real acts as an instance of the ascending arm of the curve—and to argue that if symbolic participation were carried out long enough, the effect would become decremental. Then, taking common-sense evidence seriously—for it suggests that the effect is always concupiscent—it becomes a matter of explaining why the symbolic participation is always brief, never long enough to produce a decremental effect.

Notice that typically we do not engage in symbolic participation for "long" intervals. There are several reasons for this. First, when we find ourselves made hungry by a symbolic act and are in an unrestricted environment, we are likely to put down the book and return with an apple or sandwich. We do not read the passage over and over until the effect may become decremental but quit the symbolic version to participate in the direct one. Second, the amount of material of a constant thematic kind put into a book or movie is calculated not to produce a decremental effect. True, the decremental effect the writer seeks to avoid is not that of the reader's participation in the direct version of the acts in question, but that of a decrement in the reader's likelihood of continuing the book. Nevertheless, in carefully attempting to ward off the first effect, writers may indirectly prevent the second effect, that is, never permit an amount of material sufficient to produce a decremental effect in the real act.

The thrust of the argument is thus twofold. In any symbolic act two processes go on concurrently. The first is the effect of the symbolic act upon itself; the second is its effect upon the real or nonsymbolic version of the act. Why do symbolic acts tend to have a concupiscent rather than soporific effect upon real acts? Because, even though the ultimate effect of a symbolic act upon a real one may be negative, the symbolic act habituates before occurring in sufficient amount to have a negative effect.

I raise these speculations deliberately so the reader may see the area is in an unsettled state. Old views about the differences between man and other animals are false. But it is not clear what new truths should replace the old falsehoods. This should come as no surprise; our knowledge of man is perilously slight, so slight that everything reported here is, I think, best interpreted in this light—not as showing that man and ape are closer than was supposed, but rather as showing that we know so little about man that we can simulate in an ape most, if not all, of the few processes we understand about man.

BIBLIOGRAPHICAL NOTE

The human use of nonlanguage symbols is traditionally discussed in three domains: dreams, ritual and myth, and symbolic play in children. References for each of these include Sigmund Freud's classic *Theory of Dreams and the Unconscious*, Nancy Munn's *Walbiri Iconography: Graphic Representation and Cultural Symbolism in a Central Australian Society* (Ithaca, N. Y.: Cornell University Press, 1973), and the many works of Jean Piaget, Erik Erikson, and others. More difficult to find are theories of symbol that are sufficiently operational as to have testable consequences. This problem is addressed to some extent in Grace A. DeLaguna's *Speech: Its Function and Development* (Bloomington, Ind.: Indiana University Press, 1963), C. W. Morris's *Signs, Symbols and Language* (New York: George Braziller, Inc., 1955), and B. F. Skinner's *Verbal Behavior* (New York: Appleton-Century-Crofts), 1957.

Accounts of the language man has taught chimpanzees can be found in B. T. Gardner and R. A. Gardner, "Teaching Sign Language to a Chimpanzee," *Science* 165:664–72 (1969); David Premack, "Language in Chimpanzee?" *Science,* 172:808–22 (1971); Ann Premack and David Premack, "Teaching Language to an Ape," *Scientific American* 227:14:92–99 (1972); and Volume 3 of Allan M. Schrier and Fred Stollnitz (eds.), *Behavior of Nonhuman Primates* (New York: Academic Press, 1971). Data in the present article were taken from my book *Intelligence in Ape and Man*, which struggles with the relation between symbols inside and outside of language.

9.

LANGUAGE AS A PART OF CULTURE*

Michael Silverstein

. . . there is nothing more dangerous than to imagine that language is a process running parallel and exactly corresponding to mental process, and that the function of language is to reflect or to duplicate the mental reality of man in a secondary flow of verbal equivalents.

The fact is that the main function of language is not to express thought, not to duplicate mental processes, but rather to play an active pragmatic part in human behaviour. Thus in its primary function it is one of the chief cultural forces and an adjunct to bodily activities. Indeed, it is an indispensable ingredient of all concerted human action.[1]

. . . it is well to observe that whether or not thought necessitates symbolism, that is speech, the flow of language itself is not always indicative of thought. We have seen that the typical linguistic element labels a concept. It does not follow from this that the use to which language is put is always or even mainly conceptual. We are not in ordinary life so much concerned with concepts as such as with concrete particularities and specific relations . . . It is somewhat as though a dynamo capable of generating enough power to run an elevator were operated almost exclusively to feed an electric doorbell.[2]

*Adapted from the English version of "Linguistik und Anthropologie," in Th. Vennemann and R. Bartsch (eds.), *Linguistik und Nachbarwissenschaften* (Skriptor Verlag, 1973), sections of which are here amended and reproduced with permission of the publisher.

1. Bronislaw Malinowski, *Coral Gardens and Their Magic* (London: G. Allen and Unwin, 1935), p. 7.

2. Edward Sapir, *Language: An Introduction to the Study of Speech* (Reprint. New York: Harcourt, Brace & Co., Inc., 1921), p. 14.

It is important to see that Malinowski, the social anthropologist, and Sapir, the linguist, agree to a large extent on the actual
function of speech in human behavior. Our own folk wisdom
about language and the traditional linguistics that has evolved
from it are based on the recognition of a single use or function
for language, making referential propositions, that is, describing things or telling about them. However, facts about other
functions of language have been accumulating, especially
from the study of "exotic," non-European speech in anthropological investigation, and even from our own language. Such
distinct uses of speech ultimately show that the structure of
language as it emerges from the assumption of propositionality
is only one way of looking at the phenomenon of speech,
though, in our own society, it is the way dictated by our
intellectual tradition. When linguistic function itself becomes
the problem for investigation, then the true realm of the
anthropology of language is entered.

Functions of speech overlap in any given behavioral event of
speaking. In this chapter, we will gradually build up a notion
of how there is a systematic overlap of functions, which even
the most strictly linguistic approaches must deal with through an
attempt at a full specification of the meaning of forms. Along
with acts of reference or describing, speech consists of concomitant acts of "indexing" or marking and creating the very
boundaries of the communication itself, without describing
them necessarily in the referential way: the roles of speaker,
hearer, audience, and so on; the socially recognized attributes
of persons; the time, place, and occasion of communication;
the goal of the speech event itself; and many other factors.

All of these aspects of the meaningfulness of speech behavior are missed by the traditional kind of analysis—the kind of
analysis that, for example, goes into our usual language textbooks. It is only in recent years that the uniqueness of
language in its referential functions and the fundamentally
"cultural" nature of uses of language have become clear
enough to attempt a systematic anthropological formulation.
Let us then begin with some characterizations of professed
goals before moving on to the substantive analysis.

To explain social behavior, anthropologists speak in terms of a conceptual system called "culture"; to explain linguistic behavior in particular, linguists speak in terms of a conceptual system called "grammar." It follows that a grammar is a part of a culture. We should add immediately that there must be a psychological basis for both of these conceptual systems, though we cannot yet specify the nature of the mental processes in detail. We should also add that both grammar and culture are manifested only in society, that is, only where we find organized groups of people.

On the one hand, then, the pursuit of anthropological studies without the use and investigation of the native language of the people being studied is unthinkable in theory, although all too frequently the case in practice. On the other hand, the pursuit of grammatical studies without understanding the function or uses of the speech forms being studied is actually impossible in theory, although again linguists have simply assumed that this is the correct and necessary approach.

To demonstrate why the above contentions are true, let me explain the importance of the two observations I quoted above. Malinowski and Sapir are in effect contrasting two approaches to the first goal of anthropological research—to understand "meaning." In terms of language, meaning is what is communicated each time one member of society speaks to another (a "speech event"). In terms of social behavior, meaning is what is communicated each time one member of society behaves in certain ways toward someone (a "cultural event"). For example, think of all the ways, linguistic and nonlinguistic, in which the meaning of "deference" is communicated by one person to another.

One approach, which has dominated linguistics and gives certain kinds of results, explains only the fact that speech behavior communicates describing or referential meanings. This approach hypothesizes that a grammar is a closed, abstract conceptual device. Such a grammar associates propositional meaning (akin to logical propositions) with an abstract grammatical form (a sentence) in such a way that there is a direct relationship presumed between abstract sentence and speech behavior. This is what is meant by Malinowski in talking of duplicating mental reality (propositions about, or descriptions of, the world) by verbal equivalents (the sentences underlying speech). So also Sapir talks to the "typical linguistic element" (part of an abstract sentence) representing a concept (an element in a mental proposition). Obviously, Sapir, in the tradition of linguistics, feels that this is the highest form of linguistic behavior, since he compares this marvelous and powerful device for reasoning to a great dynamo. We have called this the approach to "propositionality" in language.

The other approach, which is more strictly justified by what we now know about speech behavior, sees that it is impossible to attribute exactly propositionality to the vast majority of utterances in everyday social interaction. (Let us say that utterances are propositional when their directly related sentences produced by the grammar are propositional.) Speech behavior which may even be formally indistinguishable from fully propositional utterances intergrades with all other forms of behavior and communicates native facts about society that are presupposed and brought into relief by the very event of speaking. This is what Malinowski means by the pragmatic part of speech behavior and why he calls it one of the chief cultural forces. Social behavior in general communicates native facts about society realized in the actual circumstances of the events at hand. This is what Sapir means to include in the concrete particularities of the speech event; that they require the mental amperage of a doorbell, in his metaphor, is true only because they are usually unrecognized by native speakers at a conscious level.

The rules by which a speech act presupposes or creates certain elements of the native system of cultural concepts characterize the "function" of speech. Malinowski's assertion, then, is that the function of speech is not primarily propositional: the very behavior of speaking (as opposed to the closed, abstract grammatical system) contributes its own "meaning" to the sentences underlying utterances. This seeming paradox can be resolved only by broadening our view of what a "grammar" is, for to study speech only for its sentential and, hence, propositional value—which we overtly recognize as unique in our European tradition—is to appreciate only a fraction of the meaning of speech behavior.

This is what I mean by saying that anthropological linguistics studies the function of speech behavior in society. Sapir says that "ideation reigns supreme in language" and that for this ideation "the sentence . . . is the linguistic expression of a proposition." Yet he spent the rest of his career gradually uncovering all the ways in which this was not true.

Malinowski on his part admits that "the sentence is at times a self-contained linguistic unit," though "the real linguistic fact is the full utterance within its context of situation." Yet he never could come to grips with a rigorous linguistic analysis made on the basis of assumed propositionality, heuristically always our starting point. Clearly we must keep function fixed as referential in order to study propositionality by itself; but equally clearly the linguistic analysis is never complete until we can describe the relationship of linguistic form to total meaning, including the pragmatic function of which Malinowski spoke.

Contemporary linguistic theory now recognizes the equivalent of what I have called, along with Malinowski, "function" in language; however, its methodology is firmly linked to the assumption of propositionality independent of context. It cannot really deal with "function" because this depends on speech behaviors being culturally meaningful in an anthropologically observable and describable speech situation. Obviously, either the covert assumption must be made explicit, and linguistics must become a branch of philosophical logic, or function must be included in linguistic investigation, with the necessary consequence that linguistics become explicitly a branch of anthropological investigation. There is no principled middle ground.

What kinds of facts motivate this conclusion? What kinds of observed regularities become explainable once the function of speech behavior is recognized? What, then, is the relationship developing between grammar and culture, between linguistics and anthropology more generally? I can mention some of the number of things and the solutions one can now see emerging. However, the reader should remember that contemporary theoretical linguistics has completely ignored the long tradition of which both Malinowski and Sapir were part and that so-called anthropological linguistics has, paradoxically, built up this tradition with an implicit theory which assumed that for practical purposes the functions of all languages were the same as those recognized by us. To the extent that this traditional anthropological linguistics has succeeded, we have data to be explained about functional universals of language, not data that can be assumed to be irrelevant to linguistics.

Consider now a speech situation in which person A is speaking with person B. In the speech situation, the *speaker* utters a *message* to the *hearer* which corresponds in some direct fashion, let us hypothesize, to a *sentence* which is to be characterized by a grammar. Consider the two sentences in English represented by the written forms *He went away happy* and *I went away happy*. If A utters the message corresponding to the first of these sentences to B, then a part of the meaning of this utterance, different from the meaning had A uttered the second message to B, is that it is not A or B who went away happy. If B utters the message corresponding to the first sentence to A, then it is clear that the meaning of the message is the same to this degree, that again it is not A or B who went away happy. The meaning of the first sentence, then, must incorporate no information about who is speaking to whom.

Contrast with this a speech situation which is the same except that A utters the message corresponding to the second sentence to B. The meaning of this message incorporates some indication that it is the person who is speaking, A, who went away happy. Again, if B utters this to A, then the meaning must incorporate some indication that it is the person who is speaking, B, who went away happy. Both of these messages correspond to the second sentence, and in order to give an account of the meaning of the second sentence, we must incorporate some indication that the meaning changes systematically so that whoever utters the second message is referring to himself as the one who went away happy.

The meaning of the first sentence is formulable without any indication of who utters its message form except in a negative way. The meaning of the second sentence is not so formulable. Here is an example of our inability in certain cases to formulate a description of the meaning of a *sentence* without knowledge about the speech situation (Malinowski's "context of situation") in which its corresponding *messages* are uttered. We might say that any simple sentence which includes the linguistic unit *I* posits a proposition about the individual who is uttering the message corresponding to it. Every language has such words, called "personal pronouns."

Pronominal meaning must be stated in the form of rules that point to the individuals in the social roles of speaker and hearer in the context of situation. These words *shift* their reference depending on who is speaking to whom. We might say that the class of objects to which they refer can be defined only with some specific knowledge about the context of the situation. True pronouns refer or describe someone—in one mode of speech function—only by presupposing the socially defined boundaries of the very speech event—another mode of function. The class of linguistic items to which they belong has been called "shifters," "indexical signs or indices," "referential particulars," and so forth. They are "duplex signs" because they function in two modes, one referential, one not. No linguistic theory currently in vogue has satisfactorily dealt with them.

But why should I bring up this phenomenon of English, which seems to be remote from the problems of linguistic "function" in a broad anthropological sense?

The relevance of these little words (which occur in all languages) to anthropological approaches to the phenomenon of language is that in principle all "functions" of language can be reduced to a similar kind of statement: to describe the meaning of a sentence we must have some kind of data about the relations of the messages that correspond to it and the context of situation. To the extent that the message form and sentence meaning are linked to the context of situation, we can say that the purely abstract propositional function, the "ideation" of Sapir, gives way to other, context-defining functions of language. Note then that the only truly unpredictable sentences are those which have no part determined by the context of situation of their messages. It is basically to this latter set of sentences that Chomsky's linguistic theory and the theories of all those that follow a similar methodology, are directed.

To take our own analysis further, consider now the English

sentence written as *You went away happy*. English uses the messages corresponding to this sentence in situations where the going away of the hearer at least, and perhaps of someone else as well, is to be predicated. We say that the English pronoun *you* means that the speaker using it is referring with it to the person or persons to whom he or she is uttering the message containing the pronoun. It does not distinguish between one hearer and the hearer along with other persons.

Contrast the same kind of sentence in another language, for example, French. How do we say the equivalent proposition? *Vous vous en êtes allé content* and *tu t'en es allé content* are both ways of saying this, given only the information contained in the analysis of the English sentence. The second of these French sentences can be used only for a unique hearer, never for more than one, and there are other ways in which it contrasts with the first of these sentences.

In fact, there are various kinds of cultural facts, such as whether or not the speaker and the hearer are of the same kin group, are of the same age, have the same status, have intertwined personal histories, and so forth, that determine which of the two forms of this proposition is the sentence underlying the correct utterance under the circumstances. In other words, we must know several things about the relationships between natively analyzed values of age, kin status, and so on, for speaker *A* and hearer *B* in French society, before we can determine if the sentences underlying the messages represent true or false propositions. The meaning of the sentences depends not only on the identity of the hearer in the speech situation as the person referred to in the proposition but also on the various relationships that hold—to a member of French society—between speaker and hearer. Exactly the same may be said of the German usage of sentences with *Du* vs. *Ihr* and *Sie* and of the Russian *ty* vs. *vy*.

There are thus sentences the meanings of which can be formulated only by reference to correct use of corresponding messages, determined by the values of social variables represented in the speech situation. These social variables are recognized (explicitly or implicitly) in the society of people who speak with these forms. Such sentences contain social indexes, which code the facts of the social world into features of form (words, grammatical categories, turns of phrase, pronunciation, stress, and intonation) that mesh with the features we can characterize with abstract propositional meaning.

We can formulate the dependency as *rules of (message) use of indexical signs,* relating such factors of the speech situation as roles of speaker and hearer, relative status or sex, and so forth, to the indexical elements of message form, as a contribution to speech distinct from rules relating underlying propositional characteristics to nonindexical referential elements. Thus, with a notion of rules of use that determine the meaning of such indexical elements of sentences, there is no way we can still maintain the fiction of the closed, bounded nature of the "grammar" or abstract linguistic device, without appeal to cultural factors. Speech as a flow of messages is a complex of nonindexical referential signs, indexical referential signs, and nonreferential indexical signs, at the very least.

The examples of rules of use most obvious to a native speaker of a language involve categories such as personal pronouns and syntactic markers of style (for example, the use of *who* vs. *whom* in English speech levels), or alternate sets of vocabulary items (for example, obscene vs. nonobscene reference to body parts and functions). These all have in common the properties of being "segmental"—isolable stretches of speech—and "referential," that is, they make up part of propositions at the same time as they index social variables of the speech situation. Native speakers can frequently give accurate evidence about the use of these kinds of indexes. But there are other kinds of indexical devices—among them a particular "accent" that identifies a certain regional upbringing or social class of the speaker, or certain intonation patterns individuals use that identify their social class or the particular role in terms of which they are interacting with us by means of speech (for example, delivering a sermon). These subtle *phonological indexes* are just as amenable to description within this general framework as the categories just mentioned. That they are part of the sound system of a language usually puts them out of the realm of features on which we can secure accurate testimony from native participants. People can perhaps duplicate a phonological "style," but they find it difficult to characterize accurately both the phonetic effects (the *form*) and the precise conditions of use (the *function*). These indexes, which are "nonsegmental" and "nonreferential," are particularly hard for a native speaker to give accurate information about. But the anthropological linguist investigates all such indexes that associate ways of speaking with cultural factors, trying to give a total meaning to sentences and their messages.

To see how profoundly this kind of linguistic device, the pure cultural index, differs from the usual sort of conditions for denotation of the philosopher or the usual sort of meaning that enters into the propositional analysis of sentences of most contemporary linguistic theories, we should observe so-called male and female forms of speech. Recall from the discussion of personal pronouns that the essence of meaning of these forms is that their proper reference depended on (or "presupposed") culturally imparted knowledge such as role structure, relative status of the participants in those roles, and so on. Since these conditions are expressed by a linguistic element that refers to one of the participants of the speech act (the hearer, for example, in T–V forms), these indexes accomplish two functions, the one referential to the specific role, the other deferential to the asymmetry of statuses. If one did not have a functional perspective, and were limited to studying reference only, one might easily confuse these cultural conditions on the use of pronouns with further referential conditions on the set of objects denoted. That is, one might miss the duality of function formulable with respect to the speech situation. These cultural conditions are conditions on the use of messages, however, not general conditions on the class of objects to which abstract elements of a sentence can refer. To see this more clearly, we turn to the male vs. female forms that have no referential function.

In simple male vs. female speech forms, certain messages are systematically used by sociological (not biological) males, and certain referentially equivalent messages that systematically differ in form are used by females. That is to say, the message form depends on the sex of the speaker, socially recognized. In a complicated case, in Yana, a California Indian language, it is essential to know the relative social sex of both speaker and hearer (male speaking to male, and so on) as the conditioning factor of the difference of message form.

From the formal point of view, we can examine how the functional indexing is achieved. In several Muskogean languages of the American southeast, for example, the distinction between male and female speaker is manifested in the forms of the verb in a sentence: if the female form ends in an unaccented vowel, then the male form is the same; if the female form ends in anything else, then a suffix -*s* is added to the verb for a male speaker and a series of phonological changes, for which regular, though complex, rules can be stated, takes place. It does not matter whether or not the speaker or hearer is referred to in the sentence by any of the words. The phonological changes that take place depend only on the sex of the actual speaker of the message or of the original speaker in a quoted message. At the level of propositional content of the sentence, the function of referential speech, there is exact equivalence of everything said in one form or in the other. At the level of cultural behavior, manifested in message form, there is a profound difference.

These specific rules of the grammar implemented in constructing proper sex-role forms must depend on the facts of the speech situation. We might say that the rules of the grammar specifying the formal features of sentences consist partly of rules of use of the language, specifying the function(s) of messages corresponding to sentences. Certain rules of grammar in this wider sense are appropriate under certain conditions of discourse, other rules of grammar under other conditions. A total *"functional"* grammar of a language, then, the goal of the anthropological linguist, consists of many overlapping partial grammars, which are *functional subgrammars* of rules that are context-dependent.

The claim being made here can, in fact, be reformulated as follows. The context-independent propositionality of the sentence underlying a message with indexical features cannot be properly analyzed until we have properly described the function of the sentence and its messages in terms of rules of use. This means that the study of "grammar" cannot *in principle* be carried on in an adequate way until we tackle the ethnographic description of the canons of use of the messages corresponding to sentences. Reformulating this result, we may say that grammar is open-ended, not closed, and a part of the statement of the total meaning of a sentence is a statement of the rules of use that determine the indexical—or "pragmatic"—effect of the message features. This means, again, that if we call the "function" of a sentence the way in which the corresponding message depends on the context of situation, then the determination of the function of the sentence, independent of its propositional value, is a necessary step in any linguistic analysis.

Thus, a theory of rules of use, in terms of social variables of the speech situation and dependent message form, is an integral part of the grammatical description of the abstract sentences underlying them. Rules of use depend on ethnographic description, that is, on analysis of cultural behavior of people in a society. Thus, at one level, we can analyze *sentences* as the embodiment of propositions, or of "semantic" meanings more narrowly; at another level, which is always implied in any valid grammatical description, we must analyze *messages* as linguistic behavior, embodying cultural meaning more broadly.

So the relationship between grammar (language) and culture is not a kind of mirror effect, whereby there is only structural analogy (isomorphism) between these two objects of scientific description (the position, apparently, of such theorists as the influential social anthropologist Lévi-Strauss). The relationship is rather one of part-to-whole: a valid description of a language by (functional) grammar demands description of the rules of use in speech situations that structure, and are structured by, the variables of culture. Thus could Malinowski assert, and Sapir agree, that speech behavior is part and parcel of cultural behavior more generally.

BIBLIOGRAPHICAL NOTE

The viewpoint of this paper is developed in greater technical detail in M. Silverstein, "Shifters, Linguistic Categories, and

Cultural Description," in K. Basso and H. Selby (eds.), *Meaning in Anthropology* (Albuquerque: University of New Mexico Press, 1976). The basic bibliography of linguistic anthropology to about 1960 is contained in D. Hymes (ed.), *Language in Culture and Society* (New York: Harper & Row Publishers, Inc., 1964), along with some of the most important contributions to shaping the field. Also see Hymes' development of a viewpoint close to my own in his *Foundations in Sociolinguistics: An Ethnographic Approach* (Philadelphia: University of Pennsylvania Press, 1974). The papers in J. Gumperz and D. Hymes (eds.), *Directions in Sociolinguistics: The Ethnography Communication* (New York: Holt, Rinehart & Winston, Inc., 1972), and Joshua A. Fishman (ed.), *Advances in the Sociology of Language*, Vols. 1 and 2 (Atlantic Highlands, N.J.: Humanities Press, Inc., 1971–72), present specific analyses which can be seen in light of the overall theory sketched here, along with up-to-date bibliography. For lively topical discussions and reviews of important works, one should look to the issues of the new journal *Language in Society* (Cambridge University Press).

To get a sense of recent discussion of the "meaning" of language, on which all else rests, see the many treatments—philosophical, linguistic, psychological—in D. Steinberg and L. Jakobovits (eds.), *Semantics* (New York: Cambridge University Press, 1974), most of which are distinctly traditional in outlook.

10.

ANTHROPOLOGY WITHOUT INFORMANTS

Leslie G. Freeman

Anthropology and the Several Archeologies

ANTHROPOLOGY IS UNIQUE AMONG the disciplines which study mankind in the breadth and diversity of its approaches. This multiplicity of perspectives is its major strength, lending it a flexibility and adaptability few fields can rival. Ideally, continued feedback among its subfields should ensure that each periodically may come to new insights about the nature of our species. For that ideal to be realized, communication between the subfields must be kept easy and open.

Just a few years ago, ease of communication could be guaranteed by exposing students in depth to all branches of anthropology. Then, anthropologists shared a basic vocabulary and a common set of referents. With the tremendous increase in quantity of anthropological data that has accumulated in the last twenty years, anthropological subfields have tended to multiply, specialize, and diversify, developing unique interests and multiplying esoteric jargon. As a result of this fission, some anthropological subdisciplines have begun to lose sight of one another. The increased complexity of our field makes it ever more difficult for the individual to become a competent anthropological generalist.

Although the changes that have taken place make it considerably harder for individuals to learn each other's specialties, they are by no means to be regretted, as some seem to think.

132

Such changes always accompany the development of any discipline; they are a sign of the increasing maturity of anthropology. If we devote more attention to the growing differences between subfields in the process of individualization and force ourselves to be more fully aware of the uniqueness of each specialty, we shall eventually see the way to a new and more realistic synthesis. Only when we appreciate what each field has to offer will we be able to draw from the strengths of each what it is best equipped to contribute to the study of man.

These remarks apply fully to the archeological subfields. Although nonspecialists still regard archeology as one kind of beast fit to carry one kind of burden, its branches have become intriguingly diverse. Their evolution has been so rapid that different kinds of archeologists have begun to misunderstand one another and sometimes to hold very narrowly circumscribed views of the nature of archeology as a whole.

This essay attempts to provide a clearer picture of one emerging anthropological subfield—*paleoanthropology*, a relatively recent development fusing aspects of physical anthropology and prehistoric archeology. In particular, it examines the part of paleoanthropology which studies the evolution of human behavior.

The field has always excited its share of public and professional interest, and rightly so. The immense majority of the story of humanity unfolds in the remote past and is known only from archeological remains. Paleoanthropology offers the only direct means of attaining any idea of the range of possible variation in the human condition, or of the prehistoric antecedents of its present state. To give a better idea of the nature and limits of the field, we may as well begin by explaining what paleoanthropology is *not.*

There are several kinds of archeology, not one. The only attribute all archeologists share is a reliance on the enduring material evidence of past human behavior. The largest distinction between archeological specialties, which will probably be familiar to most readers, sets the family of historical archeology off from the group of prehistoric archeologies. But that distinction is not the only one which must be made. Each family, in fact, encompasses a distinctive set of disciplines which are quite idiosyncratic, regardless of the general attributes they share.

Since all the historical archeologies deal with the very recent past, all may utilize documents written by contemporaries of the relics they study, whenever such documents are available. Nevertheless, the family is internally diverse. Its subfields may be very narrowly specialized by interest in a certain region (U.S. colonial archeology, Mesopotamian archeology), linguistic group (Slavic or Celtic archeology), or time period (medieval archeology) or focus on a specific aspect of economic life (nautical archeology, industrial archeology). Unlike the other subgroups, some of the specialized historical archeologies do not rely primarily on excavation as a data–gathering technique.

The various branches of historical archeology offer fascinating prospects when they can rely on eyewitness documents about their data. As a whole, they are finely focused "personal" kinds of archeology with the potential to capture remarkably specific details and to weave them into a surprisingly full and compelling fabric. If that potential for bringing the past to life is seldom realized, it is because the written records are themselves often inadequate. The documents that survive mostly concern important personages: the few leading inventors, traders, statesmen, courtiers, soldiers, and churchmen of the day. Too often, historical archeology becomes the archeology of the historic, concerned with the pompous and monumental. Preserved documents tend to be incomplete, or biased, or simply unconcerned about the problems of greatest interest to us. But given a sufficient number of suitable texts to place a well-dated, closely spaced sequence of events in the context of their times, the historical archeologists have the greatest potential for the study of innovation, acculturation, and cultural process.

The research workers who have no contemporary written texts to draw on are usually called prehistoric archeologists. Paradoxically, however, some branches of the field have better documentation to rely on than the historical archeologists. In North America, Australia, parts of Asia, and the Pacific Islands, writing was unknown for millennia after other parts of the world had become literate. So, at the time they were first contacted by literate peoples, the inhabitants of those regions were "prehistoric" in a perfectly legitimate sense. But that contact took place only a few generations ago. A few of the peoples in question have been able to keep crucial portions of their ancestral beliefs and customs relatively intact, and these exceptionally conservative groups have now been well studied by ethnologists and social anthropologists, whose monographs are far better sources of anthropological data than historical documents or traveler's tales of any antiquity. In other cases, the prehistoric societies themselves have vanished, but living individuals learned about the traditional lifeways from their grandparents, who may even have lived in the very settlements now being excavated and analyzed by prehistoric archeologists. The paradox is obvious: this is a *prehistory* with the benefit of living informants.

As it happens, North American anthropologists pretty generally think of this very anomalous kind of archeology as prehistory *par excellence*, without recognizing just how unusual it is. That is to some extent understandable, since American ethnology and New World archeology grew up together, each contributing substantially to the development of the other. New World archeology eventually gave ethnology the chronological frame essential to rescue it from the tail-chasing of pseudohistorical reconstruction, but, in exchange, the theories and methods of American archeology have gained immeasurably because its conclusions have consistently had to be tested against hard ethnographic fact.

It is no accident that New World archeology has erected its sturdiest and most elegant structures in those areas where it has been able to rely on living informants or good ethnographic studies. Such sources provide it with much information about all aspects of culture, including those which leave the fewest durable material traces: the symbolic content of behavior or its material products, the social contexts in which those products were used, and the shape of the networks of social relations. Without informants or documentation, some of these aspects could not be inferred directly from archeological materials. With such evidence as a basis, reconstructions can, with caution, be pushed back in time on the order of several centuries without losing their general validity. Since the total time depth of New World prehistory is extremely shallow, amounting to less than 1 percent of the hominid story, and since, as far as we know, all the prehistoric inhabitants of the New World are members of our own subspecies, *Homo sapiens sapiens*, there may even be justification for assuming broad behavioral continuities between any of them and living people.

In some well-studied regions of the New World, the density of excavated or decently tested sites occupied during the last millennium is impressively high: sometimes there are a score or more sites per century. Coupling the thickness of the archeological record with the density of the ethnographic detail available, late New World archeology and its analogues elsewhere in the world can provide more insight into relevant aspects of social and cultural change—long-range cultural process—and more specific evidence about the enduring corporate fabric of social relations among ordinary men than any of the historical archeologies. Nevertheless, the very factors which give this paradoxical "prehistory" its robustness for the testing of method and the development of theory often make it hard to apply its findings outside its home area.

In the Old World true prehistorians leave to others the study of the shadowy "protohistoric" zone where "prehistory" gives way to "history." Normally they are concerned with nothing more recent than the local Neolithic. Ordinarily, those who study Paleolithic and Mesolithic remains are considered to have the only unblemished claim to the title "prehistorian." Of course, New World archeologists who analyze Paleo-Indian or Archaic remains and those who work on the early archeology of preagricultural peoples anywhere in the world should have an equal right to the title, but the use of the single, unqualified term "prehistory" for what are really very different studies is awkward, at best. So, a few professionals have adopted the designation "paleoanthropology" specifically for the study of early man (especially fossil man) in the Old World, including the examination of skeletal remains as well as the study of behavioral residues. That usage seems to me to have much to recommend it: it designates a kind of prehistory with unusual characteristics, limits, and potentials.

The Quality of Paleoanthropological Data

Paleoanthropology is an unique kind of prehistory because the things it studies are so old and odd, scarce and scattered. The paleoanthropologist's world, as we now see it, begins four million years ago or somewhat more and lasts through the appearance of the earliest true modern human beings. There is some haziness at both boundaries, but most of what we study is at least thirty thousand years old and we almost never treat anything less than ten thousand years old. For more than 90 percent of that remote time, we are dealing with the products of fossil men whose skeletons were so different from ours that it would be foolish to assume extensive behavioral continuities between them and us. (In fact, there is some reason to think that early *Homo sapiens sapiens* was probably quite unlike us behaviorally.)

It is no accident that archeologists working with more recent material can sometimes make very penetrating guesses about the behavior of their human subjects, based on a shrewd appreciation of human nature. There is much empirical evidence suggesting that, in some general ways, all living human beings are pretty much alike, even though the specifics of their behavior differ tremendously. Such observations are the basis for the doctrine of the *psychic unity of mankind,* which is especially fundamental to structuralist anthropology today. But man attained his modern physical structure gradually, and all evidence indicates that his present psychic unity is a recent phenomenon. Thus paleoanthropologists cannot assume that extinct populations thought like living men, or that long-vanished cultural systems are simply stochastic transformations of modern ones. Other archeologists, even some prehistorians, may fill gaps in the archeological record with guesswork or direct ethnographic analogy, with some chance of success. Paleoanthropologists cannot make use of these tools except to formulate hypotheses susceptible to evaluation, verification, or rejection on the basis of the hard evidence they find in the ground.

The oddness of paleoanthropological data is manifest in another fundamental way. Over the millennia, the present world landscapes, vegetation patterns, and animal communities to which cultural systems are adapted have gradually evolved from earlier states. Those states were so different that it requires the collaboration of a great number of specialized natural scientists to reconstruct them. Without specialist cooperation to recreate past natural settings, meaningful paleoanthropological research is impossible.

Because it must wring the maximum information from rare material archeological remains, paleoanthropology has turned increasingly to quantification to make analysis more rigorous. Most professionals were not adequately prepared for this development, and as a result there has been much trial-and-error learning, involving many mistakes. Still, despite the fumbling, we can now define problems more concisely and approach their solution with an order and precision impossible before quantification.

The scarce and scattered nature of paleoanthropological data has other important implications for research. Since immense periods of time are involved, we usually find far less perishable material than our colleagues in the other archeological specialties. More important, ages of action of normal geological processes have swept away most sites and disturbed most of those that remain. For the first three million years of the hominid story, we have only a few score undisturbed sites in all. The later Paleolithic record has fewer gaps, but it is still incomplete. As a result, we are usually faced with the task of reconstructing an extinct sociocultural system from the materials produced by only part of its members operating in only one or a very few of the many modes the system could assume. For example, in Spain during the whole of the mid-Pleistocene we have only Acheulean hunting and butchering camps: not one contemporary "base camp" has ever been recovered. So far, we cannot generate one verifiable reconstruction of the total subsistence and settlement system of a single Paleolithic society, let alone discuss sensibly any cultural system which left less tangible evidence.

The natural forces which destroy sites do not operate uniformly over the whole land surface. For millennia, there may be sporadic sites in Africa only. Then, suddenly, the African record gives out, while a clump of five or six later sites will be found in Asia or Europe. There are vast temporal gaps where we have not yet found any sites at all. Where we do have a record it is always skewed. Sometimes all the undisturbed sites are in river valleys; at other times all may be on seacoasts or lakeshores. Since there are so few sites in any case, these erratic geographic shifts of the archeological record through time make it impossible to follow the continuous development of any prehistoric cultural system in any of its functional modes for more than a very brief period. If prehistorians are supposed to produce a kind of history of cultures—to delineate connected sequences of events in the past—then there is a sense in which one can reasonably maintain that paleoanthropologists are not prehistorians at all, for the history of any past sociocultural system eludes them.

Paleoanthropology and Process

One popular school of thought has it that archeology's major potential for anthropological theory is its unique perspective on the long-term operation of "cultural process." According to this view, social anthropologists see only relatively static, instantaneous slices through the constantly changing spectrum of behavior. On the other hand, the much greater time depth afforded by the archeological record shows the striking results of long continued action of forces of cultural change and thus permits a special facility for understanding those forces.

One kind of "cultural process" is certainly accessible to the prehistorian. Process is sometimes defined as the set of dynamic relationships which characterize the operation of one of the system's functional modes, or which integrate those modes, without causing noticeable permanent change in the structure or functioning of the system as a whole. For example, the sequence of events and behavior characteristic of a religious ceremony, the context and meaning of that particular ceremony and the purpose it is meant to achieve, the organization of the participants and the effect of the ceremony on their status, all are processual in this sense. I grant that paleoanthropologists may study aspects of process so defined. However, the cultural anthropologist who observes the dynamics of the living system can do a better job. I am less confident of the paleoanthropologist's ability to study process defined as those dynamic operations which bring about a permanent alteration of one or more parts of the system and, consequently, change the functioning of the system as a whole, despite the vast time depth accessible to us. After all, if we do not produce a kind of history, how can we study cultural change?

Perhaps nothing seems more logical than that great differences between prehistoric assemblages of distinct ages are "caused by" age difference—that they result from cultural change over the interim. But even the greatest differences need not indicate this kind of change. Difference between archeological assemblages can also be due to sampling error, the influence of raw materials, variations in performance by individuals, stylistic boundaries between societies or their segments, or the suitability of distinct toolkits for the performance of specific tasks. Unless we can evaluate the contribution of each of these factors, something which has not to my knowledge been done in past, our conclusions about "cultural change" are bound to be unwarranted and misleading. The revisions made in the supposedly well-established sequences of European Paleolithic industrial evolution during the past twenty-five years clearly illustrate the insecurity of our reconstructions of "cultural change." In fact, it is the paleoanthropologist, not the ethnographer, who observes frozen, instantaneous slices of behavior. Our great time depth will not restore fossilized data to life so that we may watch the system change. There is no guarantee that the few available, widely spaced windows on the remote past illuminate episodes from the same unfolding drama. Regardless of assertions to the contrary, our contribution to the study of cultural process consists mostly of a series of untestable speculations and unanswered (and perhaps unanswerable) questions.

To those who believe that paleoanthropologists must write history, because that is *all* they can hope to do, this view will seem pessimistic. I think that judgment is wrong. No doubt, some branches of anthropology do attempt historical reconstruction above all, but that is not the overriding aim of most of the field. Many social and cultural anthropologists, physical anthropologists, and linguists are not mostly or even peripherally concerned with historical reconstruction. I think archeologists sometimes let the looming presence of time blind them to more important aspects of their data. Certainly some archeologists (especially those who deal with abundantly documented recent products of fully modern man) can make and have made important additions to our knowledge of culture history, but not all archeologists should necessarily try to. Paleoanthropology is one of the fields whose primary potential lies in other directions.

Reasoning from Garbage to Culture

Having presented these negative observations, I must now indicate where the productive dimensions of paleoanthropological research may, in fact, be found. For this exposition, certain general assumptions about the relationship between functioning sociocultural systems and the archeological record must be stipulated. First, cultures are systemic: their elements are inextricably interrelated, so that change in any element must bring about a concomitant change in at least some of the others. (There is abundant proof of this assertion in the ethnographic literature on technological change and its effects on other aspects of culture.) Second, sociocultural systems are adaptive. It is not necessary to stipulate that all elements have a direct and immediate relationship to the survival of the society, just that some elements do function to adapt the personnel to each other, to the natural setting, and to other human groups nearby.

Next, culture is manifest in shared and observable behavior patterns. Since we are forced to deal with material residues of behavior, the currently popular definition of culture as models in people's heads is inappropriate. In fact, it is naive. Even the cultural anthropologists who subscribe to this view cannot observe ideas in their informants' heads until they come out of those heads and into concrete words and behavior. For paleo-anthropologists, ideas which are never manifest in behavior are irrelevant. Most ideas are, in fact, frequently expressed in some aspect of behavior, and most have multiple behavioral manifestations. Last, by studying patterned occurrences of material residues in relatively undisturbed sites, we must assume that paleoanthropologists can identify significant aspects of the behavior which produced those residues. There are certainly limits beyond which their reconstructions cannot be pushed. While we do not yet know exactly where these limits lie, we do know that these limits permit them far more interpretive scope than we suspected ten years ago.

As we are all aware, human beings live today in organized groups (societies), and each modern society has a distinctive set of shared behavior patterns, beliefs, and values which it communicates to new members by the socialization process. These shared behavior patterns and attitudes enable group members to deal effectively with their natural and social environments: they provide sets of routine and predictable responses to recurrent situations, even for situations which recur only rarely and seldom to the same individuals. Living societies have relatively large and complex behavioral inventories. Some of these are more appropriate to some members than others (that is, sex roles and roles that require especial strength, wisdom, or maturity), and all societies simplify the learning task by apportioning different sets of specialized behavior patterns (roles) to those defined as especially suited to those patterns. This provides for adequate performance of essential tasks with a minimum of duplicated effort and without requiring every individual to learn the whole cultural repertoire.

The inventory of learned beliefs and behavior may be broken down into convenient analytical units in more than one way. When one is interested in the patterns assigned to the several positions in a society which an individual may occupy, "roles" are the most appropriate behavioral sets. If, on the other hand, one focuses on the purposes of the behavior, individual performers and their positions are less pertinent than the patterns themselves, and the behavioral categories of greatest relevance are sets of responses culturally defined as appropriate to identifiable and recurrent situations. These sets of responses may be called the "functional modes" of a social group. Curing, dancing, mourning, hunting, toolmaking, fighting, trading, feasting, burying, butchering, housekeeping, and gossiping are examples of functional modes of behavior. The concept of the functional mode is deliberately flexible; no attempt is made to stipulate its minimal or maximal scope. Gossip as a functional mode is a subset of the more inclusive functional mode of "social control." Any attempt to refine the concept further runs counter to the fact that neither living human behavior nor patterned archeological residues are ever packaged in minimal, nonoverlapping sets.

In any society, some functional modes are manifest in the behavioral usages of lone individuals; other require cooperation by several persons; and some may involve participation by all members of society. The personnel who participate in some functional modes (such as hunting) may form loosely consti-tuted, temporary groups which dissolve as the purpose of action is accomplished or as they fail. Other functional modes require participation by more rigidly structured, long-enduring corporate bodies (such as lineages). Several function-al modes may simultaneously be manifest in the behavior of a single individual or group.

Each functional mode has a cultural apparatus, consisting in the total range of permissible behavioral alternatives open to the performers, the attitudes and values which guide perform-ance, and (only sometimes) a set of physical equipment used by the performers, which we may call the *matériel*. A single type of artifact may be part of the matériel of several functional modes. The behavior actually produced by the performers from the larger culturally defined inventory of appropriate alternatives may be called the set of activities generated (on that occasion) by the social unit operating in the specific functional mode. Even in cases where the functional mode of behavior requires no durable matériel, its activities often alter the natural surroundings in lasting and recognizable ways.

The paleoanthropologist, excavating undisturbed occupation layers, recovers durable artifacts in association with particular contextual material, such as fungal spores, chemical traces, isotopes, phytoliths, animal and plant remains, sediments, and information about the location and the relative position and abundance of each category of recovered evidence. A quantitative search for significant, patterned relationships between artifactual and contextual data can optimally define related constellations of material which vary together, independent of other sets. These represent the matériel and byproducts of activities associated with distinct functional modes of behavior: some are toolkits and products of extractive processes or technological activities; others mostly reflect organizational or ideological elements.

Because of idiosyncracies in individual behavior, the artifacts and byproducts produced by different performers may be expected to exhibit recognizable differences, and the matériel used by one team may vary stylistically from that used by others engaged in the same activities. A careful analysis of the durable residues of behavior may therefore give information about the composition of teams and about overlap in team membership. When sufficient overlap in characteristics can be discerned in the residues of activities specific to several different functional modes, we may be able to demonstrate the presence of enduring, multipurpose social units. Once we have recognized specific and recurrent functional modes, we can proceed to make reliable comparisons between the matériel appropriate to a particular functional mode through time. Where a sufficient number of contemporary occupations exists in a small region, stylistic similarities in the matériel of distinct functional modes may permit the recognition that all those modes are aspects of a single cultural system, and the spatial and temporal extent of the system may be delineated.

I have no desire to give the reader the impression that this sort of analysis is easy in practice, but neither is it an unattainable dream. A few prehistoric occupations have begun to be studied in this way, and with improvements in technique suggested by our struggles with these cases such analyses will become increasingly feasible and their results more reliable in the future. By the diligent application of such techniques we may hope to squeeze the maximum information about past lifeways out of archeological materials.

Shifts in Perspective

Due to its new interests, paleoanthropology needs to supersede some analytic practices that are customary among other kinds of prehistorians. In the last few decades, Old World prehistory abandoned an earlier concern with the geographic and temporal spread of a few supposedly diagnostic "guide fossils"; it has turned to the comparison of whole artifact assemblages to delineate chronological and "cultural" relationships. To recognize basic similarities between tools used at different times and places, certain peculiarities of the tools are ignored so that assemblages from all over the Paleolithic world may be discussed in the same terms. The key to maximizing the points of comparison between assemblages has been the development of a generally applicable scheme for assemblage classification consisting of a clearly defined set of nonoverlapping formal categories into which any Paleolithic artifacts may be sorted and a set of rules for the objective and systematic comparison of the relative abundance of each tool type in different assemblages. Prehistorians interested in describing past lifeways commonly speak of the whole occupation level or the whole site as the smallest spatial unit of practical relevance for analysis. Productive as these developments have been, they must themselves now yield to more refined approaches.

Paleoanthropologists, too, are concerned with artifacts, and, to communicate with other prehistorians, they will undoubtedly have to continue to use the current classificatory schemes up to a point. However, they are more interested in determining just what types of artifacts were significant in the cultural systems of the prehistoric occupants of a single horizon and in defining the characteristic attributes of functionally equivalent artifacts made by different individuals, groups, and societies. Typologies which were designed to be universally applicable and to maximize the recognition of similarities between assemblages must necessarily be insensitive to the sorts of distinctions paleoanthropologists wish to make. As a result, for paleoanthropologists' own particular purposes they must first develop a separate classification for each occupation based solely on artifacts from that level. As it becomes pertinent to compare different occupations, the statistical descriptions of the individual assemblages are pooled, building out from the specific case to greater generalizations. This is the inverse of the practice most Old World prehistorians accept: they begin with a set of preestablished general categories and add specific detail to describe the peculiarities of real tools which do not conform exactly to the "ideal" types. (The results of the two processes are distinct and should prove complementary.)

The minimal spatial unit of interest to paleoanthropologists must logically become the smallest space in which distinct functional modes were manifest: activity-specific areas within a single occupation level rather than the undivided level as a whole. So far, new techniques for artifact classification and the analysis of spatial distributions are still in the developmental stages, but there have been encouraging preliminary results.

The Present and Future of the Study of the Past

Studies of the behavior of early humans have already produced data which other anthropologists find relevant and interesting, but paleoanthropology is such a young field that most of present knowledge is based on the findings of more traditional prehistorians. While specific details are always being added so that the picture of past adaptations changes, some general conclusions seem firmly established.

It is often said that tools made our species, and while that is broadly true, tools did not make us what we are today all at once. The ability to manufacture rudimentary stone tools does not indicate that the toolmakers had attained a fully efficient cultural means of adaptation. The first stone tools are not much more consistently patterned than the termiting sticks and sponges used by living chimps, but they are more durable and thus they strike our attention in the archeological record.

The "cultural" gulf between the first toolmaking hominids and some living apes was apparently not great. Had stone tools immediately conveyed an overwhelming competitive advantage on their makers, the first stone-chippers should have radiated with extreme rapidity over much of the temperate and tropical world, and they apparently did not. Had tools been the most crucial means of adaptation, one would also expect that the record would show a rapid increase in consistent patterning of stone artifacts, and an immediate selective advantage for control, perfection, and diversification of the artifact forms produced. That did not happen either. If stone tools were so efficient, the first species of hominid to make them should have displaced the rest virtually overnight. Yet for a million years after the first stone tools were chipped, several different kinds of hominids survived in Africa and no one of them got the upper adaptive hand. Taken all together, this evidence suggests that the advantage stone tools conveyed was not what one would expect if they signaled the appearance of fully effective cultural systems as we know them today. Several hominid groups may have experimented with stone toolmaking, and only eventually did other factors, probably involving increased efficiency of communication and more effective social organization, begin the kind of feedback between tools, the brain, society, and culture that started one species down the long track toward the modern human condition.

For a long time, the processes of socialization and communication must have been much different from their present counterparts. For millions of years, the variability tolerated in the manufacture of any particular kind of tool to a pattern was very great, and there was little evident stylistic difference in the products of distinct societies. Mostly the study of the earliest tools shows the latitude permitted in performance.

Lithic artifacts give little indication by themselves of the kinds of complex, controlled behavior that would require articulate speech. That is probably so because flaked stone is inherently limited as an indicator of behavioral complexity. When total systems of artifact and context are examined, however, the earliest European Acheulean sites provide evidence of intricate kinds of organization, planning, and programming of activities which seem highly unlikely without well-developed systems of articulate speech.

The behavioral complexity and functional specialization

manifest in modern cultural systems—the number of recogniz-
ably different functional modes—have increased through time
and continue to increase at present. Many still maintain that
the behavioral gulf between nonhuman primates and modern
industrial humanity was bridged by a series of quantum
jumps; the invention of fire, the "blade-and-burin revolution,"
and the agricultural revolution are examples. As we learn more
about the past, these revolutions seem more likely to have been
long, gradual sequences of almost imperceptible adaptive
readjustments rather than cataclysmic changes.

It was formerly suggested that revolutionary advances accompanied the appearance of new forms of hominids and that
the advent of the *Homo erectus* grade or the spread of *Homo
sapiens sapiens* was correlated with marked progress in behavior. Now it seems that was not the case. Mid-Pleistocene *Homo
erectus* is found associated with both chopper-chopping tool
complexes and Acheulean industries. The authors of Mousteri-
an assemblages were sometimes Neanderthals, sometimes anatomically modern people. The significant behavioral innovations we can define do not coincide with the appearance of new
hominid forms, and, as a corollary, we may affirm that there
was no necessary connection between body form and cultural
type or behavioral sophistication in the remote past, any more
than there is a necessary connection between race and culture
today. Interestingly, there is no convincing evidence that
Pleistocene hominids of either the same or different species
were ever particularly hostile toward their neighbors. The
comparative lack of evidence for interpersonal violence contrasts rather markedly with some later situations and contradicts popular misconceptions about man's inborn aggressive-
ness.

In this brief outline, I have presented conclusions about
past behavior of direct relevance to social anthropologists, physical anthropologists, and linguists. Many other similarly interesting observations could have been discussed. For example,
future investigations of the constitution and functions of
temporary, goal-oriented social groups will be pertinent to
social anthropologists studying the characteristics of hunting
parties, trapping teams, boating crews, and similar groups

based on flexible bonds of partnership. Certainly our intensive analyses of the specifics of cultural adaptations to a variety of natural settings will be relevant to all other anthropologists.

Paleanthropology's goal, which it is showing it can attain, is the reconstruction of vanished lifeways from durable archeological residues. The universe of behavior of fossil hominids has many aspects which are unrepresented among living societies. Paleoanthropologists can study variations in behavioral complexes that today are invariant. That is their major strength. Paleoanthropology need not justify its research by claiming to contribute to the definition of universal laws governing cultural behavior. Whether we eventually learn that such universal laws do or do not exist, the description of the vast spectrum of cultural variation is a worthwhile end in and of itself. As Clifford Geertz[1] so aptly put it:

> If we want to discover what man amounts to, we can only find it in what men are: and what men are, above all other things, is various. It is in understanding that variousness—its range, its nature, its basis and its implications—that we shall come to reconstruct a concept of human nature that, more than a statistical shadow and less than a primitivist dream, has both substance and truth.

It is in contributing to that understanding that paleoanthropology achieves full partnership with the other sciences of mankind.

BIBLIOGRAPHICAL NOTE

Some other kinds of archeological investigation are described by A. Franzen in *The Warship Vasa* (Stockholm: Norstedt and Bonnier, 1960), Tom Jones in *Paths to the Ancient Past* (New York: Free Press, 1967), A. Raistrick in *Industrial Archeology* (Frogmore, St. Albans: Paladin Books, 1973), and L. Wooley in *Digging up the Past* (Baltimore: Penguin Books, 1960). Alternative views of prehistory are presented by James Deetz in *An Invitation to Archeology* (New York: Natural History Press,

1. Clifford Geertz, *The Interpretation of Cultures* (New York: Basic Books, Inc., 1973).

1967) and by D. de Sonneville-Bordes in *L'Age de la Pierre* (Paris: Presses Universitaires de France, 1970). Among some of the best surveys of what prehistorians do are Grahame Clark's *Archaeology and Society* (Cambridge, Mass.: Harvard University Press, 1957) and F. Hole's and R. Heizer's *An Introduction to Prehistoric Archeology* (New York: Holt, Rinehart & Winston, Inc., 1973).

The role of natural scientists in prehistoric research is brilliantly discussed by Karl W. Butzer in *Environment and Archeology: An Ecological Approach to Prehistory* (2nd ed. Chicago: Aldine-Atherton Press, 1971).

The place of ethnographic analogy in archeological interpretation has been discussed by Robert Ascher in "Analogy in Archaeological Interpretation," *Southwestern Journal of Anthropology* 17:317–25 (1961), Lewis R. Binford, "Methodological Considerations of the Archeological Use of Ethnographic Data," and L. G. Freeman, "A Theoretical Framework for Interpreting Archeological Materials," in both Richard Lee and Irven DeVore (eds.), *Man the Hunter* (Chicago: Aldine Publishing Co., 1968), and by B. Orme in "Twentieth-Century Prehistorians and the Idea of Ethnographic Parallels," *Man* 9:199–212 (1974).

Several works by social anthropologists and ethnologists have influenced the writer's thinking about the place of paleoanthropology and its potential contribution to the broader study of man. Specific works which have conditioned this presentation include Homer Barnett, *Innovation: The Basis of Cultural Change* (New York: McGraw-Hill Book Co., 1963), Clifford Geertz, *The Interpretation of Cultures* (New York: Basic Books, Inc., 1973), Claude Lévi-Strauss, *Structural Anthropology* (New York: Basic Books, Inc., 1963), and V. Turner, *The Forest of Symbols: Aspects of Ndembu Ritual* (Ithaca, N.Y.: Cornell University Press, 1967).

My discussion of functional modes is based in part on a permutation of Frederick O. Gearing's concept of the structural pose, which can be found in *Priests and Warriors* (Memoir 93, Washington, D.C.: American Anthropological Association, 1962).

11.

THE ARCHEOLOGIST AS ETHNOGRAPHER

Richard A. Gould

HOW DOES AN ARCHEOLOGIST go about the task of reconstructing human behavior in an ancient, prehistoric society? When the more or less mechanical tasks of site excavation, mapping, and cataloging are finished, something more is needed. Since the beginnings of archeology as a discipline, excavators have turned to ethnographic sources for guidance in their cultural interpretations. This has been mainly true of archeologists dealing with prehistoric or nonliterate societies, where written documents are lacking for such interpretations. This has been done so much, in fact, that at times archeologists are scarcely aware that they are making interpretations. The function of the stone arrowhead, for example, is so well known from historic societies in different parts of the world that its recognition in archeological sites seems commonplace.

Yet even this simple case illustrates the principal pitfall of this approach. In using ethnographic sources in archeological interpretation there is always the danger of assuming the very things one is trying to find out. For years, archeologists and individual collectors in North America had been finding chipped stone points of varying sizes with a longitudinal flake removed from one or both sides. The smaller of these "fluted" points were labeled as arrowheads in museum collections and publications. The discovery in 1926 of fluted points in direct association with the bones of extinct *Bison antiquus* at a site near Folsom, New Mexico, led to the awareness that man had been in the New World at least ten thousand years and that these fluted points were part of this ancient Indian culture. Further work made it clear that the bow and arrow appeared much later in North America, and today the generally accepted view is that fluted points were actually the tips for thrusting and/or throwing spears. The great antiquity of the Folsom find meant the assumption that these distinctive points were arrowheads was no longer possible, and archeologists had to search the ethnographic literature for alternative explanations which would fit the new archeological facts.

After considering the case of Folsom fluted points, one is led to ask: Why were the alternative possibilities not considered earlier? And how many more assumptions of this kind do archeologists continue to make? Archeologists who turn to ethnographic sources for interpretations must do more than search for analogies to the tools, settlements, and other remains they have discovered. They must be willing to approach their ethnographic data with an awareness of the alternatives they present in human behavior, and they must then attempt systematically to relate these alternatives to the archeological evidence from particular sites.

It is easy to point out the obstacles archeologists face in making their reconstructions. The survival of organic materials such as wood, hide, fiber, and basketry in archeological sites is chancy, and most of the material culture of a prehistoric society is likely to vanish unless exceptional conditions of dryness, water-saturation, or cold prevail. Often, too, the archeological record is ambiguous about less tangible aspects of behavior (for example, religious beliefs, social organization, values, and so on). These are problems every archeologist must cope with. While such problems limit the extent of the cultural reconstructions at archeological sites, archeologists continue to look for ways to extract the maximum of information from minimal and often intractable data. Archeologists are scientific opportunists, and their use of ethnography can be a tool enabling them to make a fuller reconstruction of past human behavior at each site as they find it. This paper is concerned with finding some ways archeologists can do ethnographic field studies which will be of value in their archeological research.

The focus for the archeologist's efforts is always the site. Two American archeologists, Gordon R. Willey and P. Phillips,[1] comment:

> A *site* is the smallest unit of space dealt with by the archaeologist and the most difficult to define. Its physical limits, which may vary from a few square yards to as many square miles, are often impossible to fix. About the only requirement ordinarily demanded of the site is that it be fairly continuously covered by remains of former occupation, and the general idea is that these pertain to a single unit of settlement, which may be anything from a small camp to a large city. Upon excavation, of course, it rarely turns out to be that simple. The site is the basic unit for stratigraphic studies; it is an almost certain assumption that cultural changes here can only be the result of the passage of time.

Any regional studies undertaken by the archeologist must depend on comparisons of an array of sites. The use of ethnography as an archeological tool should begin at the level of the "single unit of settlement" ideally represented at the site before it is extended to the wider sphere of whole regions and societies. Thus the use of ethnography by archeologists must necessarily be applied at several levels, starting with the single site and expanding to broader levels of generalization. Unlike ethnographers who may study whole institutions within a culture, archeologists must find ways to relate the behavior they observe to the site they excavate. *Archeologists as ethnographers are distinguished from other ethnographers primarily by their "site-oriented" approach.*

Case Studies

These points are best demonstrated with specific case studies. The two case studies described in this paper happen to deal with hunting-and-gathering societies, but the general approach, of course, is applicable in many parts of the world and to cultures on every level of technological and economic complexity. These examples should serve to clarify the nature

1. Gordon R. Willey and P. Phillips, *Method and Theory in American Archaeology* (Chicago: University of Chicago Press, 1958), p. 18.

of this approach as well as show the inferences about particular human behavior that can be gained by it.

One of these case studies is from the coast of northwest California; the other is from the Western Desert of Australia— two dissimilar environments. In the Western Desert of Australia the average rainfall is less than eight inches per year, tending to be distributed erratically both from year to year and from place to place. In northwest California, however, there is abundant rainfall (on the order of ten to twenty inches per month from about early November through the middle of May), which occurs regularly each year. In the Australian desert there are no abundantly "harvestable" wild plant or animal foods; in northwest California a variety of these resources were (and to some extent still are) available in large amounts at specific times each year. These included two species of sea lion, the most common being the Steller sea lion *(Eumetopias jubata)*, two species of salmon, acorns from two species of oak and the so-called tanbark oak, eels, smelt, cormorants, and several species of shellfish. In California these resources occur close together, with fresh water always available nearby. In Australia the food resources (mainly a wide variety of plant foods along with small game such as lizards, bandicoots, and, in recent times, rabbits, and an occasional emu or kangaroo) are widely dispersed, as are the relatively few reliable sources of fresh water.

The basic differences in these environments are reflected by differing population densities of the ethnographic and historic inhabitants. M. A. Baumhoff recently estimated the population density of the Tolowa Indians of the northwest California coast at 2.51 persons per square mile, whereas in the arid Western and Central Deserts of Australia population densities among the Aborigines are estimated by M. J. Meggitt to fall off to around one person per thirty-five to forty square miles. There are also important contrasts in the movements of these different people, owing to their climates and natural resources. Most of the Tolowa Indians moved in a regular seasonal cycle, from semipermanent coastal villages with redwood-plank houses to the smelting beaches in late summer, then, about a month later, to the interior to collect acorns and fish for salmon, and finally back to their coastal villages around October or and finally back to their coastal villages around October or November, where they remained until the next smelting season. This movement was accomplished within about a ten-mile radius. The Ngatatjara and other desert Aborigines followed a much less regular pattern over a much wider area. In drought periods the tendency was for Aboriginal families to disperse to more or less permanent waterholes and come together in places where heavy local rains had occurred. Group size for the aborigines was extremely fluid, varying between the extremes of an individual extended family of ten to twenty people to temporary gatherings of from one hundred to two hundred fifty persons. Under these conditions families might move as much as three hundred miles following strings of waterholes and looking for areas where food and water were locally abundant.

The Point St. George Site and the Tolowa Indians

A check of published and unpublished sources on Tolowa Indian ethnography and interviews with Tolowa informants revealed the presence of an important village at the westernmost tip of Point St. George, a windswept, grassy headland near the present Oregon stateline with rocky cliffs, shoals, and offshore islets and bordered by long sandy beaches to the north and south. Although the Tolowa no longer live as they did before white contact, a remarkable amount of traditional knowledge had been retained by the remaining few Indians, including details about the long-abandoned village. These traditional accounts stated that the village had been abandoned before the arrival of whites. George Vancouver, the first European to observe Point St. George (in April 1792), failed to see any Indians living there.

The Indian informants were able to describe the general layout of coastal villages, including the one at Point St. George. Each village site had three distinct parts: a habitation area (the segment to which the village name was applied) with a midden; a "workshop" locality for rough flint-chipping, working antler and bone, heavy butchering, woodworking, cleaning fish, and so on; and a cemetery. At many villages, they said, these three parts were widely separated, and this was the case at Point St. George. In each case they were able to point out the precise spots where these different areas had been and even indicated exactly where they had been told individual houses once stood. There were no housepits on the surface to show this, however, so it remained for excavations to test the accuracy of their oral traditions about the site.

Excavations were carried out in the summer of 1964, while the Indians periodically visited the site and commented on what we should expect to find. Their predictions proved remarkably accurate. In the part they indicated as a habitation area were found the midden and remains nearby of a redwood-plank house. In an area over four hundred yards away from the habitation area, on the northwest side of the point, were found remains indicative of the workshop activities described earlier by the Indians: (1) an unusually high ratio of stone waste flakes to stone artifacts compared with the habitation area; (2) an abundance of antler wedges used for splitting wood; (3) large concentrations of sea lion, cormorant, and fish bone; and (4) large numbers of partly finished tools of antler, bone, and ground stone.

These remains pertained to the protohistoric Tolowa occupation of the site, which has been designated Point St. George II. No historic materials (for example, glass beads, metal objects, bones of cows, sheep, or other domesticates, and so on) were found at the site, so the archeology tended to confirm the traditional and historical evidence that the village was abandoned before white contact. However, an earlier cultural assemblage was found to underlie the protohistoric occupation at the site, and this earlier period of occupation was termed Point St. George I. Radiocarbon samples from the lower part of this occupation-level indicate that the Point St. George I people first arrived at least 2,260 years ago. These people, evidently the first Indians to visit Point St. George, occupied only part of the area later to become the workshop of the Point St. George II people. No habitations were found for this earlier group, but part of a stone-chipping station was found in the fill atop an exposed knoll. At present, the best hypothesis is that these first arrivals visited Point St. George mainly for the large quantities of agate and cobbles of cherty material on the shore of the point. The absence of shells and sea mammal bones in the lower levels of the site suggests that they did not attempt to exploit the natural resources of the locale but made irregular visits (perhaps collecting expeditions) to the point for workable lithic material.

There are strong elements of continuity between the stone artifacts of the Point St. George I and II people, but in general the ethnographic evidence did not offer much help in reconstructing the Point St. George I occupation. However, for the Point St. George II occupation the Indians' traditional knowledge added greatly to the detailed reconstruction of important features at the site. A few of these are worth noting.

THE "LIVING" HOUSE

It took three weeks to excavate the house in the habitation area at the site. As the plan and dimensions became clearer, it was apparent that we were dealing with a "living" house of a type described by the Tolowa informants. Most of these informants had lived in houses such as this in their youth. A Tolowa man (with the help of relatives) built one of these houses for his wife (or wives) and children, although he would reside separately with other men and older boys of the village in a fully subterranean sweathouse.

The Indians anticipated our discoveries by describing several features before we found them, including the rock-lined hearth near the center, the floor-covering of blue clay, and the rock grinding-slab. Horizontal and vertical profiles were obtained of the housepit, and the remains of twenty-five upright redwood planks were found in positions indicating their use in both the inner and outer walls. Although set into a slope, the floor of the housepit was level. But there still remained the question of which side the entrance was on and how the building had been oriented.

The Indians had said that sometimes there were smooth rocks set near the entrance to houses as part of the threshold to make it easier to crawl in and out. We found only one such rock in the building, along the southwest side and set into the platform between the outer wall and the edge of the housepit. Was this part of the entrance?

The principal evidence to support this idea was presented by the Indians in their description of the ways in which houses were oriented with respect to wind. They stated that in siting a house one important factor to be considered was the direction of the prevailing wind, so the house could receive the best possible ventilation. For the wind-boards and smokehole to be effective, the longitudinal axis of the roof ridge had to be at right angles to the wind. The strongest prevailing winds at Point St. George are from the northwest, though spoken of colloquially by Indians and others as the "north wind." Any houses on the point would have to be longitudinally oriented NE–SW to get the full ventilation from these winds. That, in fact, is the orientation of the excavated house. Since the entrance had to be at one end of the longitudinal axis, and since the Indian informants said that on the houses they knew the entrance was on the downhill end (to facilitate drainage), it is likely that the smooth rock at the southwest end of the building was part of the entrance.

THE FISHPITS

Among the materials collected from the Point St. George II occupation in the workshop area of the site were several large samples of fish remains, mainly vertebrae and facial bones. These were extracted from a series of pits which had apparently been dug by the inhabitants of the site as dumps for fishbones. The samples were sent to W. I. Follett, an icthyologist at the California Academy of Sciences in San Francisco, for identification. Follett made a preliminary examination and wrote a brief report:

> The presence of remains of the turkey-red rockfish (*Sebastodes ruberimus*) and of the vermilion rockfish (*S. miniatus*) is noteworthy. These species occur in water 30 fathoms or more in depth, over rocky bottom. Such conditions are found in the vicinity of Northwest Seal Rock (see U.S. Coast and Geodetic Chart 5895, St. George Reef), some 6½ miles off Point St. George. The Chinook salmon, the Pacific hake, and the Pacific halibut were probably caught from a boat, as were the fairly large individuals of soupfin shark, bocaccio, yellow tail rockfish, lingcod, and cabezon. The black rockfish and cabezon could have been taken either from a boat or from shore.

The cultural interpretation of this is plain: the Point St. George II Indians were venturing into rough, open seas to catch some of these fish. There are no places this deep between the Seal Rocks and the Point. Thus, to get out this far, they must have had boats and nautical skills sufficient to the task. Further interviewing revealed that seagoing dugout canoes around forty feet long had been used by the historic Tolowa for offshore fishing and sea lion hunting—a fact not previously reported in the literature. This inference is supported, too, by the discovery of numerous notched stone net-sinkers, chipped stone harpoon-points, and carved bone harpoon-toggles in the excavations associated with other Point St. George II material. By combining the information from the fishpits and what the Indians could tell us, it was learned that seagoing canoes were in use by the Indians before white contact came in northwestern California.

HARPOON-TIPS AND ARROWHEADS

The chipped stone projectile points recovered from the Point St. George II levels of the site were by any standards exceptionally well made. Their symmetry and regularity of pressure-flaking place them among the finest examples of stone chipping in North America. The Tolowa informants we interviewed had never made such stone tools themselves, but they had seen them being made and used when they were youngsters, and they understood their basic classification.

Archeologists frequently classify stone artifacts by their shape. Two major shape categories of stone projectile points were present—hollow-base points and tanged points. The hollow-base variety ranged continuously in size from tiny points less than one inch long to large examples of about two inches in length. The tanged points were all approximately the same size as the smallest hollow-base points. What differences in function and terminology did these variations in size and shape represent?

The Indian informants were asked separately to sort the chipped stone points recovered from the excavations and from surface collections in this region into whatever groupings they thought were significant. The results of these interviews were remarkably consistent and show the characteristics of the native classification. The largest hollow-base points were identified as harpoon-tips. These were set into a groove at the end of a carved bone harpoon-toggle used, they said, mainly for hunting sea lions. As independent confirmation of this statement, many of the large hollow-base points were found embedded among the butchered sea lion bones at the site, sometimes with broken harpoon-toggles nearby.

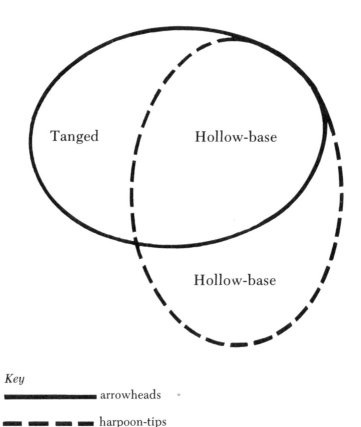

Key

———————————— arrowheads

▬ ▬ ▬ ▬ harpoon-tips

FIGURE 1   *Diagrammed relationship of protohistoric stone projectile points from Point St. George excavations and adjacent surface collections.*

The small hollow-base points and tanged points were classed together as arrowheads. The Tolowa classified their stone projectile points by function, with size, not shape, as the main criterion. Thus the category based on size and function crosscuts any which might be based on shape. This relationship is diagrammed in Figure 1. Would the archeologist have classified these stone projectile points in the same way without the aid of native informants? Such examples demonstrate the need for archeologists to compare their systems of classification with those of native peoples whenever possible.

The Puntutjarpa Rockshelter Site and the Ngatatjara Aborigines

In August 1967 during the course of an anthropological study of the Ngatatjara Aborigines of the Warburton Range region of Western Australia, I was taken to a small native site called Puntutjarpa. It lies in and around a small rockshelter at the base of a twenty-five-foot-high escarpment on the north side of a long, low ridge called the Brown Range. This locality is part of the totemic *ngintaka* (*Varanus giganteus*, or "perentie" lizard) myth, a minor Aboriginal sacred tradition of the Warburton region.

Nowadays the site is visited infrequently and only for short periods of time. Occasionally men visit the site to paint designs on the walls of the rockshelter and on the rocks outside. I was told, too, that people sometimes went into the rockshelter to get out of the rain (though uncommon, rains here can sometimes be torrentially heavy) and at times used the place as a game trap. The men built fires along the south slope of the Brown Range, driving kangaroos, wallabies, and other game over the edge of the escarpment. A few men would be posted at the bottom of the escarpment with spears and clubs to finish off wounded animals. During these hunts the game was usually cooked in earth-ovens on the natural sandy terrace in front of the escarpment. The site is also visited around October and November for wild figs (*Ficus sp.*), which grow on trees along the escarpment, and in July and August for quandong fruits (*Santalum acuminatum*), another staple food which grows nearby. Today, there is no reliable source of water within two miles of the site, so the Aborigines do not camp there.

The surface of the site was littered with stone tools, including several kinds known to be quite ancient in other parts of Australia. During the course of a subsequent test excavation a large number of stone tools was found along with hearths, two of which, occurring about two-thirds of the way down in the deposit, were radiocarbon dated to 4700 B.C. The stratigraphic evidence revealed that there were no interruptions in the cultural sequence at Puntutjarpa. A brief description of these preliminary findings was published in 1968, and plans were made then to begin the second phase of the program.

Intensive excavations were carried out at Puntutjarpa. The site was laid out in a grid of three-feet-by-three-feet squares and was excavated by a combination of natural levels and three-inch arbitrary levels. All excavated soil was put through one-quarter-inch mesh sifter screens, and samples of the sifted soil were subjected to flotation to extract carbonized vegetal and seed remains. PH testing and fossil pollen sampling were also carried out. Except when heavy rocks had to be removed, excavation was done entirely with trowels and brushes.

In terms of stone artifact and waste materials this is one of the richest sites yet excavated in Australia. Up to 1,553 stone flakes and tools have been recovered from a single three inches deep three-feet-by-three-feet level, and densities of this magnitude were not unusual. The site was also rich in faunal remains and such features as hearths and living surfaces. Perhaps the most important and distinctive stratigraphic features of the site were two rockfall layers within the site fill. The lower one, composed mainly of small rocks over a fairly limited area of the cave, rested between two and three inches above the cave floor and appeared to have fallen as a single event. The upper rockfall was made up of massive boulders with layers of soil between the rocks, indicating that they fell in at least two phases. This rockfall layer covered the entire excavated area in the main cave including the trench dug in 1967.

In the latest series of radiocarbon dates from Puntutjarpa a date of 8220±230 B.C. has been obtained from a hearth within the layer of soil sandwiched between the lower rockfall and the rock floor of the cave. Associated artifact and faunal material was abundant at this level. From hearths in a living surface situated in the soil layer between two sequential units of the upper rockfall layer we have a radiocarbon date of 435±90 years ago. This latter sample came from a depth of seventeen to nineteen inches below the surface. In all now there is a total of eight radiocarbon dates from different levels within the excavated fill of the main cave. These point to a continuous sequential occupation of the rockshelter from at least ten thousand years ago to the present.

CLEARED LIVING-SURFACES

The entire lower rockfall was mapped and photographed *in situ*, and within it two oval-shaped clearings eight and twelve feet in maximum diameter were discovered at the back of the cave. These rock-free areas contained hearths, stone tools and flakes, and butchered bones—all typical camp debris. The two rock-free areas measured 38.5 square feet and 56.7 square feet in area, respectively, and compare closely with the mean area of 44.97 square feet obtained for a sample of 41 ethnographic Aboriginal camps mapped and measured during these studies. Thus in terms of shape, size, and associated artifacts and debris there are compelling reasons to regard these two oval-shaped cleared areas as ancient Aboriginal campsites dating to sometime between ten thousand and seven thousand years ago. Another, similar living-surface was cleared and mapped in the soil layer within the upper rockfall (the one dated to around 435 years ago). This one had an area of 38.5 square feet—again comparing closely with ethnographic campsite figures—and its shape and associated hearths, butchered bones, stone tools (including several grinding-slab fragments), and debitage all support the interpretation of this as an Aboriginal camp similar to those used today in the Western Desert.

STONE ADZES AND ADZE-SLUGS

Small and obviously hafted stone scrapers, which are being termed micro-adzes, occurred in the earliest levels and continued throughout most of the sequence, and slightly above these stratigraphically there occurred larger discoidal stone adze-flakes, similar to the micro-adzes in shape and use-wear but larger in size. These continued in use throughout the sequence and are made and used by the Western Desert Aborigines today. They are currently hafted to the handles of spear-throwers or clubs and used as woodworking scrapers. After successive resharpenings and reuse they become worn down to slugs which are too narrow to be held any longer by the haft, at which point they are discarded. Worn adze-slugs constitute the most distinctive class of stone tools that one finds at ethnographic camps, and they occur continuously back almost to the earliest occupation at Puntutjarpa. Along with the micro-adzes there also occur numerous micro-adze slugs, similar in every way but size. Micro-adzes and adzes at Puntutjarpa represent an early documented appearance of hafted, chipped stone tools in Australia and form part of what is being referred to now as the Australian small-tool tradition. Later, around four-thousand years ago by stratigraphic and radiocarbon estimates, there occurred the first appearance of backed blades at Puntutjarpa, in forms similar to those seen throughout the Old World. Lunates and asymmetrical lunates abounded then but faded from use within the last four hundred years.

LARGE FLAKE-TOOLS AND CORES

Side by side with this small-tool tradition throughout the sequence at Puntutjarpa there also occurred a wide variety of large stone flake tools and cores which Australian archeologists have recently termed the Australian core, tool, and scraper tradition. Examples of these items, which were discovered at the Lake Mungo site in western New South Wales, date back to around thirty thousand years ago. They are the earliest evidence of human habitation in Australia to date, and the Mungo tools are virtually indistinguishable from the core and flake tools found at Puntutjarpa. In this tradition the most distinctive item is the "horsehoof" core, a core which has a single striking platform and shows deep undercutting. These continued in use at Puntutjarpa until within the last four hundred years. Along with the "horsehoofs" there occurred various other large, polyhedral cores with multiple striking platforms of a type similar to those currently manufactured by the Western Desert Aborigines and large flake scrapers and

spokeshaves in a wide variety of shapes which persist throughout the excavated sequence and continue in use today.

To sum up: Certain stone tools at Puntutjarpa show signs of
changes, but these changes must be considered in terms of
even stronger evidence for overall continuity. Perhaps the most
important thing to note is that the modern desert Aborigines'
toolkit is made up of both hafted and unhafted types of tools
which can all, without any exceptions, be traced back continuously through at least ten thousand years of prehistory at
Puntutjarpa Rockshelter.

THE WEST CAVE PIT

About twenty-five feet west of the main cave and habitation
area, there is a small cave, which contained relatively few stone
tools or flakes and little in the way of animal bones or teeth. At
a depth of fifteen inches a large pit was encountered, filling
most of the cave interior. Its internal stratigraphy was complex,
with many lenses of soil and thin layers of ash and charcoal, all
dipping inward toward the center. It is worth noting that the
only rain which fell during the field season came in December,
when there was a downpour of just under a half inch. Excavation of this pit did not begin until a month later, so it came as
something of a surprise when the excavators encountered
moist soil within the pit as they dug downward, level by level.
The water had percolated down through fissures in the rock,
eventually emerging from the back wall of the cave, where it
remained despite a month of intense summer heat outside the
cave. It was this clue which first suggested that the pit may
have been part of an ancient water catchment, much along the
lines of the "native wells" used by the present-day Aborigines.
The Aborigines use wooden digging-bowls or just their hands
to dig down to the water in these places. Frequently, during
intervals between visits, large amounts of tumble grass, weeds,
and thorns accumulate within the pit, and the sides of the pit
may slump. Upon revisiting such a place the first step is
generally to set fire to the brush within the pit—by far the
easiest way to clear it—and the next step is to dig back down to
the water table. I suggest that behavior of this kind furnishes

the best available explanation for the shape, size, and internal features of the pit in the West Cave at Puntutjarpa. It would have been by far the most readily accessible source of fresh water for the ancient inhabitants of the site. There is evidence in the form of a radiocarbon date from a hearth that overlies one side of the pit that this presumed native well went out of use around three thousand eight hundred years ago. After then the inhabitants would have had to look farther afield for water or else occupied the site only after heavy rains, when Hughes Creek, about one thousand five hundred feet away, contained water.

Considering the tremendous quantities of bone and the extent to which these bones were smashed and charred, it is apparent that hunting, butchering, and consumption of game were principal activities of the cave's ancient occupants. So far the faunal analysis has revealed only modern desert species as being present through the sequence. While the evidence is still preliminary, it does suggest that little climatic change has occurred in the Warburton Range area during the past ten thousand years. It is also worth noting that stone seed-grinders identical to those used ethnographically occurred back stratigraphically to a point somewhere between seven thousand and ten thousand years ago. Thus there is indirect evidence to show that plant foods, probably staples, were collected and processed during most of this time, and when the carbonized plant remains obtained by flotation are eventually identified, there may be some direct evidence bearing on this point as well.

SUMMARY OF THE PUNTUTJARPA SEQUENCE: THE
"AUSTRALIAN DESERT CULTURE"

To sum up: There are no sharp breaks in the Puntutjarpa sequence. There were no interruptions and no changes which transformed the culture. The earliest inhabitants arrived about ten thousand years ago under post-Pleistocene conditions apparently not too much different from conditions in the Western Desert today. They settled on a thin layer of sand almost directly upon the cave floor, depositing stone tools which included micro-adzes as well as "horsehoof" and other large stone cores and a variety of large flake scrapers.

They hafted the small tools and used them for woodworking. Their occupation of the case was intermittent. During one of their absences the lower rockfall occured. Before long they reoccupied the cave and cleared the two oval spaces at the back for campsites. Other camps may have been established on the terrace outside the cave, although no excavation was attempted there. A period of continued intermittent habitation followed, with the greatest densities of lithic material appearing around six thousand years ago. The site was clearly an important stone-chipping station then in addition to an important base for hunting and consuming game. By three-thousand eight hundred years ago the native well in the West Cave had dried up, but visits to the site continued. Some time prior to four hundred years ago the first part of the upper rockfall fell. Backed blades achieved their greatest popularity around this time. A further reoccupation of the site occurred during the brief interval before the next phase of the upper rockfall, leaving behind a well-defined campsite. The cave was again reoccupied after the upper rockfall and continued in use to the present day, although it is now not a habitation but merely a focus for brief visits. This basically unchanging adaptation to post-Pleistocene desert conditions is here being termed the Australian desert culture, along lines proposed originally by Jesse D. Jennings in his archeological studies at Danger Cave, Utah. Present evidence suggests that in terms of both stability through time and uniformity in space this Australian case even surpasses the original example from the Great Basin of North America.

Conclusions

The cases of the Point St. George Site and Puntutjarpa Rockshelter demonstrate that ethnographic knowledge can be brought to bear on at least three levels of archeology. First, there is the *practical level*, where, for example, Tolowa Indians and Ngatatjara Aborigines were able to direct the archeologist to useful sites and to describe the current or recent uses of these sites. Assistance of this kind can increase the efficiency and scope of archeological survey. Second, there is the level of

specific interpretation. Examples of this are seen in the reconstruction of the "living" house, the analysis of materials from
the fish-pits, and the interpretation of the stone projectile
points from the Point St. George Site. The analysis of the
hafted stone adze and other stone tools, ancient living surfaces,
and the West Cave pit in the Puntutjarpa excavations can also
be included in this category. In each case the interpretation
was directed at solving a specific archeological problem within
the context of the individual site. Finally, there is the level of
general interpretation, where broad syntheses of cultural adop-
tation are attempted. These appear as hypotheses of varying
completeness and detail, such as the idea introduced here of an
Australian desert culture. Like any hypothesis this one can and
should be tested and refined by further work. Its main value is
the guidance it affords in planning a strategy for further
archeological research. This final level of interpretation carries
the archeologist beyond the individual site to wider generalizations, but always, it will be remembered, by starting at
the individual site and extending outward.

The case studies mentioned here show that ethnography
works best for the archeologist when it is "site-oriented." The
most reliable interpretations are those in which a direct historical connection can be drawn archeologically between the
particular ethnographic and prehistoric cultures concerned. It
does not matter particularly if the historic connection is
short-range (as is presumed to be the case with the Point St.
George II culture) or long-range (such as the sequence at
Puntutjarpa) so long as the continuity of the sequence can be
shown. By combining archeology and ethnography into a
holistic site-oriented approach one can avoid the temptation to
draw improbable analogies or make premature assumptions
about prehistoric human behavior. In this way ethnographic
knowledge may serve as a guide to the archeologist instead of a
trap, as in the case of the Folsom "arrowhead."

BIBLIOGRAPHICAL NOTE

Recent interest in relating ethnographic observations to archeological patterning has led to a varied and rapidly growing

body of literature. A good place to begin is with Robert Ascher's "Analogy in Archaeological Interpretation," *Southwestern Journal of Anthropology* 17:317–25 (1961), since his ideas about analogy in archeological interpretation are often referred to by archeologists such as Lewis Binford, "Smudge Pits and Hide Smoking: The Use of Analogy in Archaeological Reasoning," *American Antiquity* 32:1-12 (1967), who question the use of ethnographic analogy in archeology. Further cautionary views are presented by Karl Heider, "Archaeological Assumptions and Ethnographic Facts: A Cautionary Tale from New Guinea," in *Southwestern Journal of Anthropology* 23:52–64 (1967), Richard B. Lee, "Kalahari–1: A Site Report," in *The Study of Man* (Anthropology Curriculum Study Project, 1966), Nicolas Peterson, "Open Sites and the Ethnographic Approach to the Archaeology of Hunters-Gatherers," in D. J. Mulvaney *et al.* (eds.), *Aboriginal Man and Environment in Australia* (Canberra: Australian National University Press, 1971), and Robson Bonnichsen, "Millie's Camp: An Experiment in Archaeology," *World Archaeology* 4:277–91 (1973). More positive views concerning the applicability of ethnographic interpretation of archeological evidence may be found in Richard A. Gould, "Archaeology of the Point St. George Site, and Tolowa Prehistory," *University of California Publications in Anthropology* 4:1–153 (1966), "Living Archaeology: The Ngatatjara of Western Australia," *Southwestern Journal of Anthropology* 24:101–22 (1968), and "The Archaeologist as Ethnographer: A Case from the Western Desert of Australia," *World Archaeology* 3:143–77 (1971), Michael B. Stanislawski, "What Good is a Broken Pot? An Experiment in Hopi-Tewa Ethno-Archaeology," *Southwestern Lore* 35:11–18 (1969), and Carmel White and Nicolas Peterson, "Ethnographic Interpretations of the Prehistory of Western Arnhem Land," *Southwestern Journal of Anthropology* 25:45–67 (1969). In addition to these ethnographic studies, which cover a broad range of cultural behavior, there are also studies which deal with specific aspects of technology in particular societies and their relevance to archeology. Among these are Michael B. Stanislawski, "The Ethno-Archaeology of Hopi Pottery Making," *Plateau* 42:27–33 (1969), Carmel White's research on New Guinea stone tools, in David H. Thomas (ed.), *Predicting the Past*

(New York: Holt, Rinehart & Winston, Inc., 1974), and an account of the lithic assemblage of the Australian desert Aborigines by Richard A. Gould, Dorothy A. Koster, and Ann H. L. Sontz, "The Lithic Assemblage of the Western Desert Aborigines of Australia," *American Antiquity* 36:149–69 (1971).

12.

THE ORIGINS OF AGRICULTURE

Robert McC. Adams

THE IMPORTANCE OF AGRICULTURE for all that we know of a full and secure life hardly needs to be described. Great as are the cultural differences between peoples today who are dependent upon agriculture for subsistence, all of them have more in common than they share with the few surviving groups of independent hunters and collectors. Man's shift to a primary reliance on domesticated plants and animals, first occurring in some areas not long after the end of the Pleistocene ice age, accordingly has long been recognized as a great turning point or "revolution," perhaps comparable in importance only with the Industrial Revolution in which we are still engaged. Yet the direct, empirical study of this great transformation is still very young, hardly antedating World War II.

Not surprisingly, our understanding of the origins and early spread of agriculture is still very insecure and fragmentary. In fact, there is no area of the world for which the transition to food production can be traced step-by-step in adequate detail. But if general formulations about agricultural origins are thus somewhat hazardous, there is a corresponding advantage in discussing them here. The study of the rise of food production has been able to flourish only as a consequence of new conditions—the "explosion" of scientific manpower and research support which the postwar years have brought. Hence this problem perhaps can exemplify at least some of the anthropological work which these new conditions make possible, above all the crystallization of a group of major problems upon which the interests of many scholars, and even many disciplines, are focused intensively.

The problem of the early development of agriculture is rooted in the environmental and cultural conditions obtaining at the end of the Pleistocene, and we may begin by summarizing these very briefly. By this time, people whose skeletal remains were anatomically modern in type had made their appearance, and it can only be assumed that they were essentially modern in their capacities for cultural innovation as well. Although little survives other than material equipment devoted to the food quest, purposive human burials attended by a modicum of ritual hint at customs and preoccupations extending well beyond the realm of immediate subsistence requirements. Moreover, although most of the astonishing cave art of France and Spain during this period depicts animals to whom the hunt was devoted, both the technical quality of these paintings and the circumstances surrounding their execution clearly indicate that they were meant to symbolize and convey a world of conventionalized belief outside the practical requirements of the small bands who were responsible for them.

Relative at least to their predecessors in the Lower and Middle Pleistocene, these hunter-collectors during the last few millennia of the ice age were more specialized and better equipped, more numerous and widely distributed. In Western Europe, where the sequence is best known, groups not only successfully hunted great herds of reindeer, wild horse, and bison but also harpooned salmon and caught rabbits and grouse with snares. Caves and rock-shelters in many cases seem to have been occupied fairly continuously over long periods. The finding of bone needles, together with suggestions of skin costumes, in the Magdalenian art implies that sewn clothing had been evolved which was well adapted to the cold climate. Hunters in Eastern Europe displayed comparable efficiency in the pursuit of the mammoth, and had developed semisubterranean dwellings in the absence of caves.

Increasingly able to adapt through cultural specialization to such challenges as the harsh subarctic environment around the fringes of the great European glaciers, man was able to increase the range of his occupation enormously. His first entrance into the New World, probably having occurred from twenty to thirty thousand years ago, was one apparent consequence since it must have involved exposure to comparable climatic conditions in the crossing of a now-submerged land bridge from eastern Siberia to Alaska. Australia, too, first may have been occupied during the terminal phases of the Pleistocene, possibly involving at least modest and accidental marine crossings by raft.

The end of the Pleistocene, marked by the gradual but somewhat irregular onset of modern climatic conditions, is usually agreed to have occurred about eleven thousand years ago. While the causes for the shrinkage and disappearance of the enormous ice sheets covering Europe and North America are still disputed, at least there is full agreement that the effects were dramatic. The concentric zones of treeless arctic tundra, boreal forest, and deciduous forest, successively more distant from the ice, marched north in the wake of the retreating glaciers, while the melting of the great weight of ice induced complementary changes in land and sea levels which substantially altered the continental margins. With the northward progression of climatic and floral zones came new fauna— generally smaller, less gregarious, less migratory animals— appropriate to the dense forests which now began to extend well into the northern latitudes. But even where open plains remained, as in western North America and large parts of Eurasia, many of the larger Pleistocene species failed to survive. Among those which disappeared altogether were the mammoth, the mastodon, and the American camel, horse, and sloth—all within a relatively short time, and all under circumstances which leave little doubt that man's increasing proficiency as a hunter was a major contributing cause. This very proficiency may have served, in other words, to exterminate major resources of game and thus to help pave the way for radically changed patterns of subsistence.

As a general account of the end of the Pleistocene, what has just been said is incomplete or misleading in two respects. Firstly, most of the world open to human occupation lay at great distances from the main glaciated regions centering on the poles, and the climatic changes associated with the end of the Pleistocene in more equatorial latitudes involved decreases in precipitation more prominently than increases in temperature. Moreover, the whole problem of whether or not climatic changes in all latitudes took place closely in phase with one another is still not fully resolved. Secondly, the Pleistocene as a whole was a time not of continuous glaciation but rather of almost continuous climatic changes, changes whose sequence and correlations long have been a major theme of research. Shifting climatic, floral, and faunal boundaries at the end of the Pleistocene thus were not a new phenomenon but one which had gone on repeatedly through all of man's biological evolution as a separate species. What was new was neither the fact of an ameliorating environment nor the consequent enlargement of life zones favorable for man's existence. Rather it was the increased exploitative efficiency and adaptability with which he took advantage of these conditions.

Comparatively less is known of the new subsistence patterns which emerged at around the end of the Pleistocene in regions other than Europe and the United States. Much recent work is redressing the balance in the Near East and Middle America, however, where the wild progenitors of many of our major domestic plants and animals flourished. To generalize from the more northern areas, perhaps the dominant character of the post-Pleistocene response was its diversity. Faced with habitats whose differences were amplified as the ice receded, and with the extinction of many species of great herbivores upon which he formerly had relied heavily, man rapidly worked out a whole series of specialized adaptations based on a bewildering variety of new local resources. We find groups such as the Tardenoisans, Azilians, and Maglemosians in Western Europe, for example, coexisting within short distances of one another and yet utilizing entirely different types of habitat. There is evidence that nuts, seeds, and wild fruits were relied on more heavily as sources of food than they had been in Pleistocene times, and that this increased emphasis on the gathering or collecting of vegetal products also was characteristic of roughly contemporary assemblages in Mexico and the western United States. Of course, this shift required the development of ground stone tools for pounding or milling in order to remove husks and render the tough kernels digestible—tools which later would be necessary for the processing of domesticated grains.

The increasingly intensive and localized, even semi-sedentary, character of these post-Pleistocene subsistence patterns is evident also in the faunal resources they sought to exploit. The bow and arrow came into use in Northern Europe, and, perhaps as a consequence, much greater numbers and varieties of bird bones turn up in refuse deposits than previously. Especially rapid technological developments took place in fishing, with gorges, nets, fish-spears, weirs, and even boats and paddles, all employed already in preagricultural times. Among land animals, most of the common smaller species of the forest were hunted or snared, implying less reliance on collective drives and greater stress on the individual stalking of prey within a restricted territory. Here the dog played a crucial role, perhaps first becoming a scavenger around the hunting camps but before long being fully domesticated. Particularly along the rivers and sea coasts, where land marine resources supplemented one another, relatively permanent settlements made their appearance upon great heaps of discarded shellfish. These characterizations apply first and most directly to Europe, but by 3000 or 4000 B.C. they also become applicable to subsistence trends in North America.

The potentialities of an agricultural mode of subsistence for transforming man's way of life do not remove the origins of agriculture from this early postglacial milieu that I have sketched; nor do they establish the appearance of agriculture as an inexplicable historical "accident." Instead, we have here a series of broad cultural and environment trends, alongside which the introduction of agriculture in certain favored areas seems a consistent and harmonious development. The widespread diversification of food resources after the Pleistocene, the numerous corresponding elaborations in technology, the increasing sedentarism—these are circumstances which alone can explain the tide of still largely unknown innovations which led to the domestication of plants and animals.

The bulk of present evidence suggests that the earliest

agricultural hearth lay in the Near East, possibly extending into Southeastern Europe as well. There are obvious difficulties in identifying the ranges of the wild progenitors of the later domesticates within that huge and diverse region, whether from modern distributions that may have been displaced by many intervening millennia of intensive land use or from still-sparse archeological findings. But it is certain that most of the potential domesticates, like other naturally occurring organisms, were geographically restricted by altitudinal, climatic, soil, and other factors. Only a few species at most, therefore, would have been accessible to any particular, localized human group. Hence it is no surprise to find that morphologically identifiable domesticates do not appear simultaneously among all species but only over an extended period. Recent studies suggest the domestication of the sheep by perhaps as early as 9000 B.C. While the age of domestication of the goat is somewhat more obscure, it is probably of comparable antiquity. Domestic pigs, on the other hand, do not appear in the archeological record, as it is available at present, until around two thousand years later, while the earliest domestic cattle yet known are somewhat later still. Meanwhile, the domestic cereals, at first principally emmer wheat, einkorn, and two-row barley, can be firmly traced to at least 7000 B.C.; increases in cereal pollen suggest that they may have been in use considerably earlier.

While the material now available from which to generalize is admittedly fragmentary, we may infer from the long span suggested by these dates that the development of even a rudimentary subsistence agriculture probably did not take place as a single chain of events in a single small region. Instead it seems to have been a complex process which involved a prolonged period and consisted of many episodes not always closely dependent upon one another. The same conclusion emerges from a comparison of the substantially different life zones in which our earliest known agricultural sequences occur.

One such zone is represented by the lowland Palestinian valley in which biblical Jericho later was situated, an oasis where man and his potential domesticates gradually may have

evolved a set of symbiotic relationships under hot, arid conditions. By not long after 8000 B.C., the spring at Jericho and
other neighboring Natufian sites had been occupied by small
groups of hunter-collectors who also may have practiced some
cultivation. At any rate, the presence of stone hoes and flint
sickle-blades polished with use suggests that cereals were
being reaped if not necessarily sown. Such are the accidents of
archeological discovery and preservation that this ambiguity as
to the presence of purposeful agriculture at Jericho continues
until much later. Before 7000 B.C. a substantial walled village
apparently had grown up on the site, but even from these levels
domestic plants and animals have not been surely identified.

By way of contrast with Jericho, the site of Sarab in a cool
Persian mountain valley near Kermanshah possibly was only
the summer encampment of herdsmen-cultivators who had
adapted their own patterns of winter and summer movement to
those of the flocks of wild sheep and goats which they must
have domesticated by the early seventh millennium, if not
earlier. And between the environmental extremes of Jericho
and Sarab at opposite ends of the Fertile Crescent, we find
roughly contemporary sequences of relatively transitory encampments followed by permanent villages at sites ranging
from the Anatolian plateau and Zagros intermontane valleys to
the arid steppes of southwestern Iran and southern Jordan.

In not a few of these sites, sedentism and considerable
population growth may initially have been based on favorable
combinations of primarily wild resources. Indeed, it has been
plausibly argued that the decisive steps toward agriculture are
more likely to have taken place instead in the less naturally
productive zones into which later settlers were forced as a
consequence of population growth. But in any event, village
life seems to have been fully established on an agricultural
basis by about 7000 B.C., settlements having sprung up on the
Anatolian plateau and all along the foothills of the Zagros,
Taurus, Lebanon, and Anti-Lebanon mountains wherever
local circumstances were favorable. However, just as in the
early postglacial cultural adaptations of Northern and Western
Europe, the most impressive features of these early agricultural manifestations are an apparently considerable degree of

cultural isolation from one another (in spite of the unifying link of long distance trade in obsidian) and the diversity of their responses to differing local resources and opportunities.

The picture which emerges from recent research in the New World is broadly similar. While debate continues over possible individual exceptions, there is little doubt that most of the food crops upon which the Indians of the Americas relied prior to European colonization had been independently domesticated from wild forms native in the western hemisphere. Maize, by far the most widespread and most important crop, was derived from a wild progenitor which had flourished in Mexico and perhaps Central America. On present archeological evidence its domestication probably occurred during the fifth millennium B.C., but preserved specimens from cave deposits as late as the mid-third millennium were still so small that maize must have furnished only a very limited contribution to the diet. Even the earliest maize yet found, it may be noted, appears to have been derived from wild forms already divergently adapted to the pronounced regional differences in soils and climate which make Middle America what has been called "a geographical, cultural, and ecological mosaic." And this same observation applies to the even more numerous varieties of beans and melons or squashes (Cucurbita), the other members of a trinity of food plants which eventually provided the basis for a nutritionally adequate diet even without meat or dairy products from domesticated animals. Beans and the Cucurbita are also thought to have been of Middle American origin, first having been domesticated by 6000 B.C. or even earlier. Yet a fully developed agricultural regime in which the cultivation of maize, beans, and squash provided a sufficiently assured level of subsistence to support the formation of settled villages apparently does not antedate 2000 B.C. anywhere in the New World, and may even have been considerably later.

The domestication of these crops reflects, in other words, the same kind of prolonged, independent experimentation in many diverse centers as for the Old World cereals. Moreover, the same process of many divergent, local derivations of food crops probably could be documented elsewhere in the New World. For example, the potato-oca-quinoa complex began in, and always was restricted to, the high plateaus of the central Andean region of South America. We still await a concentration of archeological attention on those areas and time-ranges of the prehistoric past in southern and eastern Asia and sub-Saharan Africa which will similarly illuminate the rise of food production in those vast regions where parallel courses of development may have begun at an equivalently early time.

Thus the formation of settled village communities relying mainly on agriculture probably had taken place by 7000 B.C. in the Near East and then, largely if not wholly independently, five thousand or more years later in Middle America. While the process of selecting suitable domesticates and developing the techniques for their cultivation and consumption had extended over several thousand years in both cases, the consequences of the new mode of subsistence were profound. To begin with, it permitted a substantial enlargement of the residence group which could be sustained by a given area of land. With the introduction of storage facilities for agricultural products (here the invention of pottery played a vital role), it also gave far greater assurance of secure, continuous occupation than was possible with the fluctuating returns from hunting and collecting. Further, agriculture created new opportunities for trade and for the growth of specialized craft skills, for it demanded the farmer's labor only during periods of sowing, weeding, and harvesting and left unprecedentedly long periods free for activities not directly concerned with subsistence. It must have stimulated population growth not only by expanding food resources but also by creating a new economic importance for children, who became productively employed at an earlier age than was possible in hunting. Finally, the agricultural cycle itself, the yearly renewal of the plants and herds, furnished a stronger, more integrative focus of group belief than ever had existed previously. Perhaps for this reason small shrines or temples appear very early in the archeological record of agricultural villages in all of the great nuclear areas of the Old and New Worlds. These temples, gradually evolving from small cults into great specialized hierarchies, in turn played a central organizing role in the subsequent growth of larger, progressively more complex and stratified societies that became the earliest urban civilizations. But our emerging understanding of that further evolution is another story and cannot be dealt with here.

From what I have tried to outline of present knowledge as it emerges from ongoing research, the study of the origins of food production is a preeminently interdisciplinary problem. Yet at the same time it also remains a problem in which the role of the anthropologist is central. The first of these interrelated points is evident from the kinds of empirical work which have proved to be necessary. They include, for example, the laboratory analysis of soils and refuse from archeological excavations in order to reconstruct the environmental milieu in which early steps toward agriculture took place. This may involve a botanist in the identification of woody flora from lumps of charcoal or a soil chemist concerned with the climatic implications of ancient leaching. Another line of approach begins with carefully plotted present distributions of wild species thought to be antecedent to the early domesticates. From a comparison of these with the zones of archeological incidence of the same species, a plant ecologist then may seek to infer differences in climate or other natural conditions between the original period of domestication and the present. Still a third type of inquiry involves the quantitative study of the changing morphology of archeological remains of early domesticated plants and animals in the attempt to understand the process of domestication itself. Turning from the domain of the natural sciences, studies of contemporary agricultural technology, village organization, or modes of land use by ethnologists have furnished useful leads to the interpretation of archeological findings from the same areas. Or again, the historical geographer working with documentary materials sometimes can help in assessing the importance of long-continued activities, such as overgrazing or deforestation, which make extrapolation from present conditions back to the past more difficult. Finally, the determination of the rate and time of different aspects of the process of domestication depends increasingly on a wide range of new physical and chemical techniques, of which radiocarbon dating is the best-known example.

From these examples it is clear that geologists, zoologists, botanists, and representatives of other disciplines frequently assume essential roles in the investigation of early food production, roles often at least as important as that of the archeologist in the collection of primary data. Herein lies the interdisciplinary aspect of research on the problem. But the role of the anthropologically oriented archeologist still remains a crucial one. In the first place, data from excavations or distributional studies do not provide a direct and accurate description of an ancient environment or even of a particular mode of prehistoric subsistence. Instead, they are the very incomplete remains of an extinct culture which maintained certain patterned relations with its wider ecological setting, and it requires an interpreter who is cognizant of cultural problems to determine what these patterns probably were. Furthermore, the rise of food production as a new mode of subsistence is an episode only in the human career, involving the transformation of specifically human institutions and behavior. Not surprisingly then, it generally falls to an anthropologically oriented archeologist to direct, coordinate, and synthesize the various lines of research into the nature of this episode so that they converge on what is a preeminently anthropological problem.

To generalize further, the emergence of the food-producing revolution as an important focus of research exemplifies a shift that is underway in archeology toward the delineation of processes of change. Of course, what sometimes is called "space-time systematics"—the formulation of archeological time-units and the determination of their geographical extent and interconnections—continues as an essential component of research. But even the working out of such sequences and correlations is seen more and more as merely preliminary to intensive studies of the causes and content of particular cultural transitions. Moreover, these processes of transition or transformation increasingly tend to be viewed as affecting an interrelated system of cultural and environmental variables rather than as detached typological trends which can be studied and understood in isolation.

With this newer approach, slight differences in local adaptations at a given period in the prehistoric past cease to be minor details and become the basic source for understanding how cultural and environmental variables interact with one another. In fact, much of the effort of specialists on the flora and fauna is devoted precisely to the fuller analysis of what local variations may signify. This implies that a progressively larger and more complex basis of local observation is required for the common effort on agricultural origins to go forward, and that explanations can be drawn from other regions or modern conditions only after the degree of comparability has been carefully assessed and explicitly stated. More important still, it implies a concentration of archeological attention on demonstrable basic trends, above all in the subsistence economy, instead of on intuitive reconstructions of ancient cultures as wholes.

Finally, as the tide of research advances in these new ways, broad shifts occur in the character of the questions that are asked. The claims of rival "hearths of domestication," localized (or at least potentially localizable) in time and space, become less valid and interesting to substantiate than the highly adaptive processes that all represent: the onset of conscious practices of selective breeding, modification of the habits and life cycle, and conservation, intensively directed toward a few potential domesticates that formerly were only a small part of the spectrum of food resources that human groups were utilizing in any area. At least some of such practices, it is increasingly recognized, may have an immensely greater time depth back into the Pleistocene than can yet (or perhaps ever) be directly detected in the vestiges of plant and animal anatomy that the archeologist can recover. But the test of husbandry is only secondarily that its new selective pressures sooner or later led to the modification of a species. Our concern is instead for a new and unfolding symbiotic relationship that *man* entered into. Hence attention is turning to where it has always properly belonged, to the detection and interpretation of developing patterns of husbanding behavior on the part of human communities.

The research finding that some very early Near Eastern villages apparently lacked agriculture, at first a genuine surprise to most, if not all, investigators, coincides with and reinforces this intensified scrutiny of ancient patterns of activity and forms of organization that were socially mediated. Degree of community nucleation and permanence, that is, the appearance of "village" life, is seen to be analytically separable from reliance on domesticated plants or animals. Attention thus is turned toward identifying new and subtler variables whose impact was on the social unit: contrasting patterns of resource selectivity, cyclical annual movements and social aggregation and disaggregation that were imposed by variations in the food supply, and homeostatic mechanisms that might have acted to maintain human populations well below the optimal sustaining capacity of a given ecosystem.

Thinking no longer of archeological assemblages but of ancient social units, we are led ineluctably to inquire as to what the conditions were that disposed groups toward sedentary village life. Agriculture alone, it seems clear, was neither a necessary nor a sufficient condition. With little risk, the question may be rephrased: What induced bands, for whom the cornerstone of life is always thought to have been generalized reciprocity, to give way to extended kin groups that were characterized both by a more developed sense of territoriality and by greater stress on the solidarity and continuity of the nuclear family? This has been a classic anthropological question ever since the days of Lewis Henry Morgan, and my assumption, like his, would be that the transition must be linked fundamentally with the emergence of genuine "property"—ownership or at least lengthy periods of socially recognized control of productive resources. A tilled field or a flock generally has come to represent such an asset, but so also, we are now reminded, might a preagricultural bed of mussels or a grove of pistachio trees or a spring around which all life had to congregate during the dry season. What is more important than any specific findings, therefore, is our rediscovery of the underlying unity of anthropological themes—from present to remote prehistoric past, from social anthropologist and ethnologist to archeologist.

In one relatively small area of research, then, this is the consequence that the great postwar increases in foundation support and scientific manpower have brought. Groups of specialists now collaborate much more frequently and effectively, across both disciplinary and institutional lines. Differences tend to emerge between the accepted limits of academic fields, on the one hand, and the more rapidly shifting problems generated by this evolving team approach, on the other. As a result, the overall structure of research is more fluid, the pace is more rapid, and the emphasis on a rigorous and preferably quantifiable mode of analysis is more pronounced. A conscious structure of theory emerges, at once growing out of research findings that only the new conditions have made possible and seeking to direct, sharpen, and explain those findings from the perspectives of ecological and population biology, general systems theory, and above all the broad tide of anthropological work devoted to the immensely richer and less ambiguous data of the "ethnographic present." To argue, as I have done earlier, that this is a time when processes of change or transformation have become the central focus of study is only part of the story. The other, and perhaps ultimately more important, part is that the structure of our discipline and our methods of study are themselves undergoing rapid transformation. The end to this process is not yet in sight.

BIBLIOGRAPHICAL NOTE

Two major symposiums, held at the Institute of Archaeology in the University of London, provide a comprehensive and authoritative overview of contemporary thought on this subject. The more recent—Peter J. Ucko, R. Tringham, and W. Dimbleby, *Man, Settlement and Urbanism* (Cambridge, Mass.: Schenkman Publishing Co., Inc., 1972)—while concerned primarily with the later transition to urban life, contains a number of important papers dealing with the beginnings of agriculture from the viewpoint of settlement patterning. Its predecessor—Peter J. Ucko and G. W. Dimbleby (eds.), *The Domestication and Exploitation of Plants and Animals* (Chicago: Aldine Publishing Co., 1969)—although now occasionally superseded in detail because of the rapid progress of the field, brings together a quite unprecedented mass of primary data and scientific viewpoints on all aspects of domestication that are relevant to the problem of agricultural origins. Still a third volume—Stuart Struever, (ed.), *Prehistoric Agriculture* (Garden City, N.Y.: Free Press, 1972)—provides ready access to many papers that contributed significantly to the development of thought on the subject over the past two decades or so, but that are widely scattered and often difficult to obtain in their original publications.

As suggested in this article, the dominant trend in recent work has been one articulated in a fourth important collection of papers—E.D. Higgs (ed.), *Papers in Economic Prehistory* (Cambridge, Mass.: Cambridge University Press, 1972)—as a preference for the study of the development of agriculture "not essentially as an invention or a series of inventions designed to control man's environment, but as a continuously developing natural process of great selective value." Except in the case of a very few scholars (notably Kent V. Flannery), this research paradigm tends to minimize or exclude culture and human consciousness as important factors and to cast the introduction of agriculture largely in terms of the biological processes of natural selection and adaptation. This has proved to be a very powerful and productive research paradigm and undoubtedly will remain so. Nevertheless, one may venture to predict that its limitations also will become progressively more apparent. Adequate explanations of the course of cultural evolution, of which the development of the subsistence economy is inextricably a part, surely will require greater sensitivity to sociopolitical and even symbolic dimensions of culture that cannot be accounted for by narrow attention to the food quest. On the theme of research paradigms attending the study of agricultural origins, reference may be made to G. A. Wright's survey of the ideas that have been associated with the subject, which is useful well beyond its self-imposed limitation to the Near East, in "Origins of Food Production in Southwestern Asia: A Survey of Ideas," *Current Anthropology* 12:447–78 (1971).

The bulk of research attention remains concentrated on two classic "hearths" of domestication, the Near East and Middle America and the vigorous and, it seems, closely related but not subordinate developments tending in a similar direction in ancient Europe and North America. There is an excellent, regionally oriented survey, unfortunately now somewhat out of date, of what is known of the transition from food gathering to food production in other world regions as well as these: Robert Braidwood and Gordon Willey (eds.), *Courses Toward Urban Life: Archeological Considerations of Some Cultural Alternates* (Chicago: Aldine Publishing Co., 1962). African domestication has been the theme of a recent Wenner-Gren symposium awaiting publication. Reports of recent fieldwork in southeast Asia clearly presage important advances in our understanding there, although controversy still ·attends the initial claims of very early, independent sequences: C. Gorman, "Hoabinhian: A Pebble-Tool Complex with Early Plant Association in Southeast Asia," *Science* 163:671–72 (1969); J. R. Harlan, "Agricultural Origins: Centers and Noncenters," *Science* 174:468–74 (1971). Attention must also be devoted, of course, to interregional agricultural dispersals as well as to multiregional, essentially independent origins. Much evidence is brought together on this, although its interpretation tends less toward dispassionate appraisal than toward frank and comprehensive diffusionism, in another recent volume of papers concerned with Old World–New World relationships: C. J. Riley, J. C. Kelley, C. W. Pennington, and R. L. Rands, *Man across the Sea: Problems of Pre-Columbian Contacts* (Austin: University of Texas Press, 1971). The complex problems of interpretation that arise in dealing with this subject have been briefly adumbrated by J. R. Harlan and J. M. J. de Wet in "On the Quality of Evidence for Origin and Dispersal of Cultivated Plants," *Current Anthropology* 14:51–55 (1973).

13.
PERSPECTIVES GAINED FROM FIELDWORK

Laura Nader

AS PART OF THEIR training, professionals in every discipline develop a particular way of looking at the world—especially that part of the world which is the subject of their study. This essay is about how anthropologists look at human societies.

It is no exaggeration to say that nearly everybody, at one time or another, exhibits an interest in the language, physical type, and customs of other groups, whether they be foreign nationalities or minority groups at home. This was true of the Egyptians, of the Greeks, and even more of the Arabs who touched on most modern anthropological interests in their philosophical explorations. However, it has been only during the past century that Western scholars have really grappled with the problem of understanding *all* the cultures of the world, from those of the Germans and Chinese to those of the Eskimos and Australian aborigines. This development in scholarship came after Europeans had been traveling to distant corners of the globe for about four hundred years. Ever since the age of Columbus, explorers have been voyaging to all parts of the globe, sometimes repelled by, but always reacting to, the diverse customs of the people with whom they visited, traded, and lived.

These early explorers were soon followed by missionaries, traders, and government officials. Some of these wrote reports of what they had seen, and these reports pointed out to other Europeans that human life was much more varied than anyone had before supposed. The field reporters of that day were, first and foremost, nineteenth-century Europeans, so it was only natural that the things which impressed them most about non-European cultures were exactly the customs that were unknown to European civilization—customs such as cannibalism and plurality of wives. It was only natural, too, that societies with habits so strange to the Europeans should be regarded by them as somehow less advanced in the total history of mankind.

When some of the earlier explorers came to the New World, they found Indians belonging to tribes in which no one seemed able to tell the difference between uncles and cousins (this was because the Indians used one term for what Europeans thought of as two distinct categories). In the same way, early explorers believed that primitive people, who often spoke in proverbs, did not know how to think properly. The problem was that Europeans saw everything in terms of the values, attitudes, and ideas that they had learned from being a part of European civilization. Their thinking was circumscribed by a lack of self-awareness. Regardless of their biases, however, it is interesting that these early observers did think that their observations were worth recording. The information that they made available stimulated the minds of many, and by the nineteenth century anthropologists were reading these detailed collections of facts and trying to find some sort of order in the great potpourri of data.

After this initial period of anthropology—the study of human societies primarily based on the accounts of travelers, missionaries, and government men—a new practice developed: the firsthand, systematic exploration of the variety of cultures by anthropologists themselves. This foray into the field was the exciting step which was to force a twentieth-century revolution in thinking about the many questions raised by the nineteenth-century anthropologists. The very fact that the anthropologist abandoned the comfortable armchair for the rigors of life in the field was destined to expand the field of factual knowledge upon which theories of human behavior are built. It functioned also to affect radically anthropologists' image of themselves as scientists and humanists.

In the early days of fieldwork, which began in widescale form at the turn of the century, anthropologists went to live with a group of aborigines, either accompanied by several other scientists or alone. When they proceeded alone, they were isolated from their family, from their friends, from their whole cultural setting. They found themselves among a people whose culture was often quite alien to their own, though as they learned something about it, they realized that it was not totally alien.

The early fieldworkers—people much as Rivers, Boas, Malinowski, and Radcliffe-Brown and later Benedict and Mead—began, in a sense, to find new identities by learning about the people among whom they found themselves living. What they learned, they painstakingly recorded. Their notebooks were filled with details of what they saw and heard, and their resultant monographs attempted to record their experiences intelligibly in terms, not of Western European culture, but of the native culture itself.

Early fieldworkers, somewhat like people shipwrecked upon a desert island, found it necessary to do a bit of everything. They were alone, and a division of labor was impossible, even if it had been desirable. And so it was that one person alone recorded the economic, the ritual, the technological, the political, and the kinship aspects of a single society. In fact, they found they could only achieve an understanding of some of the more strange and exotic customs by this sort of overview of the whole culture. The fabric of native life seemed to be so intricately woven that Malinowski, for example, could only perceive the meaning of certain fishing patterns among the Trobianders when he had understood certain magical notions. Or, in the case of the Andaman Islanders, it was only after Radcliffe-Brown had analyzed their rituals that he could begin to understand the bonds that hold these men together. These early fieldworkers were trying to understand how all the parts fit together to make a working "whole" society—a society which had adapted to and was adapting to a local environment for the purpose of life.

The functionalist approach—the view of culture as an interwoven whole—was not new. Armchair anthropologists of an earlier time, such as Maine and Fustel de Coulanges, had this same view of culture. What was new was the act of going out with this viewpoint and collecting raw data. The results were not just more data on the variety of cultures in the world but a different sort of data from that picked up by traders and government officials. It was now more than an interest in exotic minutiae torn out of context. These field studies were explorations in the commonplace and familiar, as well as in the strikingly different. Customs which had previously been conceived of as strange or unusual were described as parts of the general design of living.

Since the time of the early fieldworkers, the detailed and often tedious process of recording the social and cultural life of a people has been replicated by anthropologists in a variety of cultures the world over. The range of societies covered is great—from hunting-and-gathering groups such as the American Shoshone and South African bushmen to large-scale civilizations such as those in Japan and India; from the study of nomadic societies such as the Bedouin to an industrial American town such as Yankee City. And the topics upon which anthropologists focus are equally diverse—child-rearing practices, technology, language, law, politics, music, and religion. As a result of this unprecedented ethnographic activity, we are now beginning to document in detail the range of variation in human societies. We are now beginning to realize what men have been capable of in social and cultural creations.

The anthropologist has two different kinds of tasks. Anthropologists in the field record data by observation and interview. In all of their studies, they investigate patterns of behavior, and much of this work is descriptive. Beyond this, however, there is the analytic part of the science—that part which seeks to relate direct observations to a logical framework of concepts and to a body of general statements about human culture. Anthropologists have to keep both the particular and the general in mind at the same time. Their experience with cultures through time and space stimulates them to work at the complementary tasks of recording unique historical events *as well as* generalizing about such events.

The special perspective of anthropologists requires them to be aware of time events; for example, the development and diffusion of certain ideas and material objects, such as tobacco or the alphabet. We also have to be aware of what we might call timeless events—the fact that certain cultural phenomena recur in the same way under special circumstances. For example, in many societies in the world people practice a custom we refer to as the postpartum sex taboo. It is taboo for a husband and wife to have intercourse for a specified period after their child is born. John Whiting and his associates have suggested that in societies where this taboo extends into many months or even years, it is quite likely that we will find another customary practice, namely, that of plural marriage.

Another custom which has worldwide distribution is that of male initiation rites, and again the anthropologist is curious as to why some societies have male initiations and wonders what may be associated with them. Whiting and his associates also looked into this question and came up with the intriguing hypothesis that in patrilineal, male-dominated societies, where the mother nurses her son for a very long period, we are likely to find very severe male initiation rites. It is important, in male-dominated societies, to have men that are *men*, and the purpose of male initiation rites is to emphasize this. These rites are designed to make a man out of a boy who has had for so many years of his life a much closer identification with his mother than with his father.

In every culture, however simple or complex, we find some kind of family, some kind of political and economic organization, religious beliefs, ways of settling grievances and punishing crimes, ways of aesthetic and recreative expression, material culture, and so on. I have indicated that we study a wide range of societies in order to understand the universal features of human societies, as well as to understand the particular nature of any idea or institution in a society. At this point, I would like to mention some observations that have been made about culturally patterned aggression and conflict.

Conflict between husbands and wives occurs, in different degrees, in all societies. Sometimes such conflict ends in what we call "divorce"; but again this varies with the culture.

Working with two societies in Africa, Max Gluckman noticed that among the Zulu of Natal there was a very low incidence of "divorce" and that among the Lozi of northern Rhodesia there was a high incidence of "divorce"—and he wondered why it should be that some societies are characterized by brittle and others by long-enduring marriage partnerships. He puts forth an interesting hypothesis, namely, that "divorce" rates vary with the type of descent system. A high divorce rate would be expected to occur in matrilineal societies, a low divorce rate in patrilineal societies, and bilateral societies such as ours would be expected to fall somewhere between the highest and the lowest rate.

Another anthropologist, Lloyd Fallers, worked with an African group which was patrilineal in descent but not characterized by stable marriage, as Gluckman would have predicted. Fallers[1] reformulated the original hypothesis as follows:

> Where a woman, either through the complete transfer of her childbearing properties, or by other means, is socially absorbed into her husband's lineage, patriliny tends to stabilize marriage: where a wife is not so absorbed (into her husband's lineage group) and thus remains a member of the lineage into which she was born, patriliny tends to divide marriage by dividing the loyalties of the spouses.

While such theories do not take cognizance of the total range of variables relevant to marriage stability, they do center our attention on a very pertinent point, namely, that an understanding of the context of marriage is crucial to an analysis of marital stability.

There are certain conditions where the prognostication for a lasting marriage is not good. We tend to approach the problem of divorce in Western society by looking at case histories of particular couples in conflict, but we would profit by looking also at the relation between the couple and the larger kin and nonkin groups in society. As Gluckman states: "Social factors and not only personal disharmonies may control divorce rates in Western society." Regardless of whether one is interested in the Zulu or the Lozi, the theories formulated to explain

---

1. Lloyd A. Fallers, *Law Without Precedent: Legal Ideas in Action in the Courts of Colonial Busoga* (Chicago: University of Chicago Press. 1969).

specific aspects of these and other particular societies will be useful as points of comparison for viewing marriage stability in our own society. The study of divorce is a study in the conflicts between a man's and a woman's interests and allegiances—a study which has broad implications for society, above and beyond an interest in the elementary family.

The anthropologist also argues that the functions of conflict are multiple. Using African data, for example, Gluckman examined the cohesive effects of conflicts of interests. Referring to the Nuer of East Africa, he describes a situation where an individual is linked with a group of people through the bonds of kinship, on the one hand and, on the other hand, to another group, who may be enemies of the first, through bonds of residence. Gluckman concludes, "If there are sufficient conflicts of loyalties at work, settlement will be achieved and law and social order maintained." Such a theory does not, of course, make a case for the cohesive effects of strife or contentious behavior but rather suggests that conflicts of interest may bring people together.

Conflict may also be a way of maintaining order. Let us take the study of the feud, for instance. The feud as an institution has often been described by ethnographers as an important mechanism of social control in societies which lack formal governmental institutions and officers. A classical case is the Ifugao of the Philippines. Another would be the Scottish Highlanders, among when the feud has historically been viewed as a "lawless" institution. But is it a lawless institution? A close analysis of the feud in context illustrates that in a very real sense the feud was a "legal" institution, the function of which was to punish serious transgressions and act as a brake to prevent aggression. Among the Nuer of Africa we could say that the feud was a valuable institution, necessary for maintaining and integrating social groups in a society where the principle of opposition is basic to the social structure. It is interesting that much of this perspective on the cohesive functions of conflict was developed in the colonial period, in a context of cultural pluralism, when African indigenes were subordinate to European rulers, and between whom there was a great deal of disruptive conflict. It is an observation on the mind-set problems that all scientists have that the analysis of the conflict of interest between colonial powers and indigenes only began to flourish after independence was accomplished.

Research on conflict and aggressive behavior bears serious thought because the implications are so important to the modern world and the dilemma of war. We know that destructive behavior is not a necessity for human life, for there have been enough cases recorded of the constructive channeling of human behavior to conclude that warfare was not necessary. Evidence indicates that warfare was unknown during the earlier part of the Neolithic period in Europe and the Orient. Organized warfare was unknown in aboriginal Australia and in certain parts of the New World. What we have been able to establish is that different types of culture carry with them varying degrees of propensity for war. Groups such as the Pueblo Indians of the American southwest for many centuries rarely engaged in offensive warfare. On the other hand, among the Tupinamba of Brazil warfare was a major activity. We need to look into such cases. The suggestion that severe inhibition of aggression within a society such as the Tupinamba "encourages" outlets for aggression by means of warfare is not to be taken lightly; nor should we take lightly the escalating consequences of modern technology on contemporary warfare.

All the examples previously mentioned of marital conflict, feuds, and war have in the main been concerned with the impact of such behavior on the society at large. Other anthropologists have been concerned with the ways in which a society inculcates in its children certain ideas about aggression—attitudes about aggression are taught to children in all societies. Clyde Kluckhohn and J.W.M. Whiting and I. Child have explored the general question of what happens when aggression is severely inhibited in early childhood—that is, when children are taught never to express anger by aggressive behavior toward their fellow men. Preliminary findings suggest that if such feelings cannot be expressed between people, there will be a high degree of fantasy projection of such feelings onto sorcerers and witches. And this hypothesis, when followed through, leads us into the generally fascinating problem of why some societies practice witchcraft and others do not.

Thus far, I have talked principally about findings and hypotheses derived from fieldwork in preliterate societies. Anthropologists, however, have not found it difficult to shift their focus from the small preliterate society to the modern world, and today this is evidenced in the kinds of research they are doing. We find anthropologists not only in the university but also in government, in industry, and in hospitals, and their research is not so different in general method and approach from that of their colleagues engaged in field trips in preliterate societies. Gregory Bateson and his colleagues, for example, found themselves, as anthropologists, working with schizophrenic patients. Some thirty years ago Ernest Beaglehole noted that there were strong tendencies among certain Pacific Island groups to particular kinds of mental illness. The Filipinos, for example, tended toward catatonic schizophrenia; among the Hawaiians there was a predominance of paranoia; and manic and depressive states were common among Japanese patients. All these patterns suggest the influence of cultural factors, although there is some evidence that this remains to be clarified. Urban ecologists have found that certain types of mental illness characterize the center of a metropolitan area, whereas others are usually found on the periphery. These findings again suggest the importance of environment.

New questions being raised by anthropologists require different methods. We observe that fewer and fewer people are responsible for the lives of more and more people, yet access to the large-scale organizations by means of which such control is possible is difficult due to secrecy and confidentiality patterns. Anthropologists who wish to study such large-scale institutions will need to develop a competence beyond the traditional anthropological techniques of participant observation, and we must not allow traditional methods to determine whether we can study pollution, insurance, fertility, social security, the military, or the Atomic Energy Commission.

We are only on the edge of studying the mental health of institutions or professions such as those who are responsible for major policies, as in the area of energy. We are only now on the verge of studying the assumptions, the sub-culture, of professionals managing institution-based health care. For example, Edgerton reports on his studies of a hospital for mentally retarded people and in the process raises questions having to do with the use of intelligence testing—a major concept in tracking classes in United States society.

The main point to remember in all these examples is that what we learn about one culture can tell us something about another. Margaret Mead gained insight into American problems of adolescence by investigating the lives of young Samoans. Political movements such as Zionism can best be understood if compared with a variety of similar nativistic movements that have been recorded through time. Similarly, the deterrent effects of capital punishment can be evaluated by the study of societies where capital punishment is not used. What we discover in the study of an institution such as the family in any one society makes more intelligible the nature of the family in our own culture, while the comparative view enables us to see mankind as a whole.

The phrase "viewing culture as a whole" is often repeated in anthropology, and it is often repeated because it has led to some valuable insights. Statements such as "people drink too much" may be relatively meaningless unless they are supported by a detailed description of drinking in a particular context. In my own work among the Zapotec Indians of Mexico I recorded the various settings in which drinking took place. In each context drinking meant something in particular. It was considered bad for a man to drink alone; good to drink in company; courteous to drink in courts of law; improper to drink in the presence of ritual kinsmen, unless invited; and so on.

In 1943, Donald Horton demonstrated that the higher the level of anxiety in a society, the greater the frequency of alcoholism. Now the interesting question arises: In what settings does alcoholism increase and with what kinds of anxieties? When I left the Zapotec there was a generally worried atmosphere about what was going to happen to them since the rapidly expanding Mexican system of roadways now had put them in closer contact with modern Mexican national culture. They were worried as to how this contact with the non-Zapotec world would affect their mores and customs. Merchants would now be able to come in from the state capital. There was already an increase in the production of cash crops, and many of them realized that their economy no longer would depend solely upon the fluctuations of climatic conditions but would also be affected by price conditions of the nation and the world. These people are facing new crises and new anxieties, and alcoholism is on the increase. Will they increase their consumption of alcohol by drinking in groups, or will there be an increase in solitary drinking—drinking which is not traditionally sanctioned—and why, with what consequences.

The anthropologist realizes—painfully at times—that few problems involving humans can be defined and solved within the confines of a narrow analysis. Any kind of anthropological research itself is a multilevel investigation. We are aware that cultures which appear to be quite similar in many basic features may nevertheless show striking behavioral dissimilarities, and it is necessary for the anthropologist to investigate simultaneously form, content, and the various levels of culture—what people do, what they think they do, and what they feel they ought to do. It has been pointed out by anthropologists working in industry, for example, that you cannot always find out what will motivate efficient work production simply by asking people what will motivate them. The reason you often cannot is because so much of culture is out of the range of the conscious. This is why an anthropologist doing research in a factory not only interviews workers but also spends hours working and observing in the production room. The emphasis placed upon participant observation cannot be overstressed.

On the other hand, it takes something more than participant observation to analyze something such as lawlessness in the ghetto. It takes a perspective that relates the ghetto to the world outside the ghetto, where it is a known fact of law that the ghetto itself is a result of breaking the law. Slums are illegal and symbols of landlords who violate building code laws. It takes more than participant observation to notice that the ghetto is indeed lawless, without law, without courts that process the legal problems of the poor, cheaply and efficiently, without a police force dedicated to protect ghetto dwellers from victimization. When studying island societies anthropologists had access to all the strata; we have to realize that lack of access to upper classes in stratified societies can lead to distortion of the scientific data. The horizontal perspective must be supplemented by the "vertical slice," whereby we study "up" as well as "down."

Several themes have been underlined in this description of anthropological exploration: How anthropologists view culture as a whole; how their description of particular societies permits them to generalize for mankind; how anthropological techniques may be extended to apply to modern societies; and how perspectives gained in other societies enable us to view our own with some measure of detachment. Participant observation and more recent techniques developed as part of the quantitative ethnoscientific inquiry should allow anthropologists to discover both conscious and out-of-conscious levels of culture not easily reported by informants or observed by the anthropologist. Much has been accomplished in less than a century of fieldwork, but we have yet only a glimmer of the possibilities for anthropology, the study of human variation and universals through time and space.

14.

ANTHROPOLOGY'S URBAN PROGRESS

Richard G. Fox

AS PEASANTS COME TO market day in the city, so social anthropologists have entered the study of the urban world. Attracted and yet bedevilled by the city's great size, its complex and heterogeneous social patterns, both peasants and anthropologists nevertheless realize that this realm of social interaction, political authority, and economic activity cannot be avoided. Warily, anthropologists have initiated urban studies, unsure whether methodology derived from the tribal world will prove adequate for urban complexities, fearful that the city may strip away their special scholarly identity and leave them outcasts, shadow sociologists or historians. As the peasant fears the greed of the city merchant, so the anthropologist wonders what scholarly price must be paid for dealing with urban environments.

Paths To The City

Entering the city for research is for many anthropologists a pilgrim's progress to a wider definition of their discipline and to an increasing relevance for its formulations. The all-but-final demise of the pristine primitive world has propelled anthropologists in new directions over the last generation. The growing numbers of community studies in rural India, Latin America, or Alpine Europe, where supposedly no "natives" live, have helped destroy the common conception of anthropology as the study of (exotic) primitives. Anthropology's

199

recent urban path confirms for its practioners as well as, one hopes, for the general intellectual community the discipline's ability to encompass human social organization and analyze human social behavior at a sophisticated level.

Some scholars see the rewards of anthropology's urban progress in an increasingly close relationship of scientific research to society's blights and social ills. To show an excessive scholarly concern with the few remnant nonliterate societies of the contemporary world would be for anthropology consciously to turn away from the reality of the world in which it exists. The monumental urban problems which beset both the industrial and industrializing nations have elicited scholarly response from many disciplines. Anthropologists have joined together with the geographers and sociologists in this pursuit of knowledge to be reached through research on the city.

These several objectives of anthropology's urban progress as well as the complexity of urban experience mean that the term *urban anthropology* collapses into a single reference category what are in fact many different goals, methodologies, and viewpoints in the anthropology of cities. The belief that cities are possible and important research locales for anthropology is perhaps the only and certainly the most significant common understanding within this would-be urban anthropology. Even this agreement remains a presumption of hope and expectation rather than an outgrowth of established and incontrovertible reality.

Beyond this seeming commonplace understanding, the real significance of which is that it finally puts to rest the hackneyed definition of anthropology as the study of primitive peoples, lies a scholarly no-man's-land of many different urban anthropologies—or perhaps more correctly, of many different "urbans" in anthropology. Anthropologists approach the urban locale in so varied a manner and with such distinctive goals that the city becomes different and divergent things according to the observer's sensibilities. For some scholars, the urban in urban anthropology consists of ghettos with a culture of poverty; for others, it is composed of cultural and intellectual centers with great traditions; and for still others, it denotes shanty towns or "native" locations filled with people newly come to the city. To talk of a single urban anthropology at present is to give a false impression of conceptual uniformity (and clarity) in a situation in which the only common ground is the desire to interweave the city in anthropology's design. The following pages discuss the different reasons why anthropologists have entered urban research, the different ways they have pursued this progress into the city, and the prospects for the future course of their endeavors.

New Paths and Old Ways

Some anthropologists come to urban research because the city represents a stage of human evolution or level of cultural complexity possessing distinctive social properties and organization; other anthropologists enter the city because its ghetto misery and discontent reverberate throughout the general society; and still others approach the city in the wake of urbanizing peasants and tribals who are no longer only to be studied in village, community, or tribal compound. The research methodologies and conceptual orientations of these urban anthropologists chart distinctive and often conflicting destinations for scholarship in the city.

Conceiving the city as a stage in human social evolution or as a highly complex cultural institution has brought anthropologists such as Robert Redfield, Milton Singer, Horace Miner, and Conrad Arensberg to an interest in those qualities of urban life and social institutions which differentiate it from tribal societies and peasant communities. Relying conceptually on the image of urban life projected by the Chicago school of urban sociology and practically on his own research in rural and urban Yucatan, Redfield proposed a folk-urban continuum as a first step along this particular anthropological path to the city. Redfield's notion was that as folk communities evolved into urban societies, they changed from small, self-contained, isolated, highly personalized, religious, and traditional social locales into large, heterogeneous, impersonal, secular, and innovative social milieus. Redfield's implicit acceptance of industrial urbanism as a universal urban model

has been effectively invalidated by Gideon Sjoberg's distinction between "preindustrial" and "industrial" cities, wherein
the former do not share the characteristics of impersonality,
secularism, and great size assumed in the folk-urban hypothesis. In a different vein, Oscar Lewis found that migrants to
Mexico City did not suffer the family breakdown by which
Redfield typified urban existence. English urban working-class
life, as studied by Michael Young, Peter Wilmott, and Elizabeth Bott, exhibits a similar pattern of strong kin cooperation
and extended family ties.

Although the specific image of urbanism utilized in the
folk-urban continuum was too heavily pinned to Western
industrial cities, as Redfield himself shortly realized, his
concern with the city as an emergent level of cultural evolution
or social complexity mapped one route of investigation for
anthropologists in the city. Their scholary involvement with
the special qualities of urbanism leads these urban anthropologists to a macrostructural view of what cities are and how
urban centers are linked to the societies in which they occur.
They investigate the cultural roles of cities and cross-culturally
analyze cities with distinctive physical forms and internal
social organization. Thus, in correcting the initial folk-urban
formulation, Redfield and Singer delineated two cultural roles
for cities which all urban places performed, although with
varying degrees of intensity and elaboration. Cities with predominantly *orthogenetic* functions serve as centers for the
construction and codification of the society's traditions. In
such urban locales, cadres of literati rationalize a great tradition of cultural performance and ideology for the society at
large. The cultural message emanating from Varanasi, Bang-
kok, Peking and other cities with heavily orthogenetic functions is to safeguard, sophisticate, and elaborate cultural tradition and stability. Cities with predominantly *heterogenetic*
functions are centers of technical or economic change, and
their cultural role depends on the creation and introduction of
new ideas, cosmologies, and social procedures into the greater
society. In cities such as London, Marseilles, and New York,
the intelligentsia challenge old methods, question established
traditions, and help make such cities the innovative centers of
their societies.

For Redfield and others with similar approaches, the city does not stand isolated from the surrounding society. Its intelligentsia promotes wide social change, its literati codifies a great tradition for the entire society, its sacred geography serves as both physical marker and ideological product of the larger society's values, its changing conditions alter the content of traditional practice without necessarily destroying it. In this approach, cities appear as realms of social life inextricably bound—either as receptor or generator—to the institutions and values of the society in which they are set.

Urban anthropologists who approach the city in this direction enjoy a strong conceptual framework for research and utilize a historical and cross-cultural orientation which entertains the great varieties of urbanism and urban dwellers. This viewpoint is weakest, however, in visualizing the city as a congeries of desperate groups, neighborhoods, ethnic elements, economic classes, and associations, some of which are highly assimilated to the urban pattern and others of which are not. The holism which leads investigators to analyze the sacred geography or the political pattern of the urban center in relation to the values or power blocks of the larger society rests on (the assumption of) an urban homogeneity that discounts ghettos, noncitified urbanites, ethnic conflicts, and all the other behavioral and ideological disparities which define an urban center. The intimate knowledge of a small and sharply demarcated social group or community, so often the anthropologist's trademark in tribal and peasant societies, is lost. Similarly, urban methodology and research procedure are another weak point of this approach to the city. The question remains how the traditional intensive and small-scale research technique of the anthropologist in the field, at best a perception of a very limited urban segment, can be generated into an analysis of the urban whole.

The opposite problem of methodological exactness at the expense of conceptual inclusiveness besets another path to the city taken by anthropologists. Study of ghetto populations and, by extension, urban ethnic subcultures and poverty-induced urban social adaptations allows the traditional intensive and small-scale methods of tribal or peasant anthropology to be redefined in a city context. The poor in Puerto Rico and New

York, urban alcoholic nomads along Skid Row in Seattle, streetcorner blacks in Washington, D.C., and Amerindians throughout the United States have all been subjects for this anthropology, which sees the city reflected through the ghetto and views urban life mirrored in the customs of the poor. The appeal of the ghetto approach to urban anthropology has been very great, not only because it promises methodological continuity with anthropology's traditional disciplinary style, but also because it offers a direct confrontation of the (activist) scholarly investigator with the sore spots of American, or contemporary, urbanism. This approach takes the city as a separate realm with its own dynamic within the larger society—specifically, those ghetto ethnics or urban alcoholics who are said to live out a skewed and twisted version of the society's goals or whose lifestyles are at the furthest cultural remove from the mainstream world.

Both because it emphasizes small, relatively closed urban social groups and urban lives under adverse social and economic conditions, the urban anthropology which hopes to reach the city via the ghetto often never moves beyond the poverty or ethnic enclave. The social intricacies of ghetto life, the ideological framework of poverty existence, the nature of disfranchised and outcast populations whose residence happens to be urban generally assume larger scope than the city as such. Charles Valentine and others have suggested that full comprehension of the poor emerges not from study in the ghetto alone but from research among the rich and politically powerful as well. Similarly, to talk of the cultural roles of cities, to put cities in cross-cultural perspective, to treat them diachronically as subject to fundamental change and variation presumes a magnitude of insight and a degree of generalization beyond and outside the urban anthropology which perceives the city from the urban canyons of its disesteemed and unvalued.

The theoretical propositions of this urban anthropology thus concentrate more heavily on poverty and ethnicity than on the nature of urbanism. Many of its hypotheses serve to vindicate the anthropologist's concentration on the ghetto innards of the city. If ghetto inhabitants can be shown to be radically distinct from the urban mainstream, then they warrant the singular attention of the anthropologist, much as did the self-contained societies of the Trobriand Islanders, the Kwakiutl, or the Nuer. Oscar Lewis believed that the urban poor lived within a "culture of poverty" which existed (somewhat) autonomously from their economic and political deprivation and which conditioned familial organization, belief patterns, and work behavior antithetical to the larger society's values. The urban culture of poverty was to be the anthropologist's entrée into the many disparate groups and activities which made the city impossible to study in a holistic fashion. Lewis's conjecture has been attacked on many levels: it substantially alters the anthropological notion of culture, it contradicts many qualities of ghetto life, it takes as codified and enculturated behavior in the ghetto what may only be a transitory adaptation to the harsh conditions of deprived urban existence, it comprehends only a small proportion of the urban poor. At best, the concept is tied to contemporary societies and their urban patterns; at worst, it has become a poorly reasoned catch phrase promoting political passivity toward the poor.

Other anthropologists of the ghetto have also explored the conceptual framework which orients life among the urban poor or destitute. Although he, too, speaks of a "culture-" of urban nomads, James Spradley's work on alcoholics indicates the different environmental references and life code developed by inhabitants of skid row. Ulf Hannerz also follows this interest in an analysis of "soul" among Washington blacks, and in an investigation of the adaptive strategies of urban ethnic groups striving for mobility in contemporary American society. The latter approach promises to make what the anthropologist discerns in the ethnic ghetto relevant to comprehension of the society as a whole, but through a study of acculturation rather than urbanism. By striking deeply into the lifeways of the industrial city's downtrodden, these urban anthropologists, if they do not encompass the nature of urbanism, develop intensive and insightful studies of bypassed or economically deprived peoples and their lifeways, which is traditionally anthropology's path.

Another urban anthropology comes from the contemporary

large-scale physical movement of rural peoples to cities and
the adaptations of these immigrant populations to the new
urban environment. In the wake of these urbanizing peasants
and tribals follow anthropologists, thereby traveling the scholarly path from village to city. Urban anthropology, seen as the
process of urbanization, is especially strongly developed in
African research (undertaken mainly by British anthropologists) and in Latin American studies (pursued by American
scholars). In this urban anthropology, the city represents a
distinct arena of social arrangements and lifestyles to which
immigrants must accommodate at least as long as they interact
within the urban sphere. The anthropology of urbanization
emphasizes the altered social structure, interpersonal ties,
associational life, and ethnic or tribal identity which develop
as tribal or peasant becomes urbanite. Because the approach is
microanalytic, specific aspects of the heterogeneous city—
those related to its most recent immigrants—can be specified in
great detail, often as a sharp corrective to accepted notions of
the typical urbanizing experience. The notion that urban
residence inevitably leads to nuclear family patterns has been
seriously challenged in several world regions. Tribal identities
and associations (in altered form) appear not as useless ascrip-
tive barriers for the new urban dweller but as important
channels through which individuals newly come to the city
find their place within it. Retribalization, quasi-ascriptive
voluntary associations, and rituals from rural life resurrected
in the city promote acculturation or at least adaptation to city
ways.

Urbanization as a path to the city often continues most
exactly the nature of anthropology's traditional methods and
units of study. The city as such does not appear in the
investigation or directly as the goal of research. Interest centers
on a process—urbanization—and its consequences for human
social existence rather than an involvement with a form—
urbanism—and its relations to human society and culture. The
characteristic form of the urban locale—its cultural roles in
society, its demography, class organization, or government—
stands as an unanalyzed or assumed backdrop for the more
focused attentions of the anthropologist on urbanizing tribals

and peasants. Anthropology's involvement with tribal society or peasant community has simply been transferred to urban locations as anthropologists follow their informants from their rural homes to the city. Since the continuities of methodology are very great, urbanization anthropologists perhaps feel less departure from traditional scholarly models within their disciplines (and less distance from their colleagues) than either of the previous urban anthropologies. Indeed, students of urbanization have often further refined investigative techniques originally used in tribal and peasant studies for application in urban environments. *Network analysis,* which traces the many-stranded links between urbanites, and *situational analysis,* which charts the social adaptations of the newly urbanized, have more fully rationalized for the city context methodologies which ultimately derive from the small-scale and intensive field methods of the tribal world.

The difficulties which beset urbanization anthropology emerge from the very methodological continuities with past anthropology which make it the shortest path to the city. The nature of cities cross-culturally and in historical perspective is difficult to see when the scholar deals with recently urbanized populations and *their* accommodation to the urban locale (rather than, as Anthony Leeds critically notes, the accommodation of the urban locale to them). Fieldwork undertaken in "native locations" or shanty towns also leads to a perspective which only sees the city by looking in from its very margins. Although a convenient research unit for the anthropologist, these locales are not the effective boundary of social relations for recent migrants to the city. Urbanization studies try to avoid this myopic view by dealing with a "field of social relations" which may transcend the residential communities of newly urbanized people. But it is extremely difficult to build the complexities of the city and urban existence out of the multitudes of social networks in any urban center, and impossible to fit these into some larger view of the city in a diachronic and cross-cultural framework. Like the anthropology of the ghetto, therefore, urbanization anthropology is heavily dependent both in conception and in field technique on a particular kind of urbanism—in this case, cities as colonial outposts or in developing nations—with a specific pattern of rural-urban relationships.

These three paths to the city have taken anthropologists to very different urban quarters in very different ways. The city as evolutionary level, as ghetto community, or as urbanization zone—each path is traversed with different amounts of theoretical and methodological baggage brought from research on tribals and peasants. Each path requires relative degrees of scholarly flexibility and innovation in attaining the city. Variations in anthropology's urban directions undoubtedly reflect the complexity of urban phenomena; they also mirror different orientations in preurban anthropology; and above all, they highlight the great disciplinary transformation and struggle required by anthropology en route to the city. The challenge has led some urban anthropologists to resist change and others to enhance it, in either case too often with little sense of what should be preserved and what discarded, only sure of how much about the city remains to be conceived and understood.

Urban Ways

Perhaps in the enthusiasm of discovering a "new" anthropological frontier with unlimited research possibilities, perhaps in reaction to the sheer magnitude of the urban world, anthropologists working in cities have generally set aside discussion of the basic definitions and conceptual directions which should orient their scholarly enterprise. Like neighbors in the proverbial city apartment building who hardly know each other, the three urban anthropologies follow their own separate courses with little argument about proper direction and yet with little agreement about the ultimate goal.

Very basic things go unsaid, perhaps unthought. Nowhere have anthropologists really indicated what special contribution they can make to urban studies (apart from poverty and ethnicity, which are neither inherently urban nor necessarily anthropological). To be called an "urban anthropologist" at this moment specifies more clearly *where* one locates for research rather than *what* conceptual goals lie behind this choice of location. Anthropologists have occupied the city in a physical sense before they have captured it conceptually, and the danger is that they will regard mere physical occupation as sufficient.

Just as anthropologists have analyzed the kula ring of the Trobriands, the potlatch of the northwest U.S. coast, the Jajmani system of northern India, so they must comprehend the city as yet another institution within their framework of knowledge about human society and culture. The distinctive approach which anthropology has developed to the study of social institutions should make it ask novel questions about urban life as its specific contribution to the general view of the city toward which many scholarly disciplines labor. Yet absent from urban research in anthropology so far is any guiding definition of the city or urbanism or even specification of the constituents of such a definition. Conceptualizing the city from an anthropological perspective would orient presently scattered urban research in method and theory and would make what is done in the city relevant to the anthropology of primitive and peasant peoples.

This disarray of urban anthropology has made its acceptance within the larger discipline problematic. Desire for urban anthropology abounds among students, faculties, administrations, publishers, and government agencies. These strong outside pressures have often brought anthropologists to the city more quickly than the disposition of their discipline would have suggested. Yet all except perhaps government agencies hesitate and hedge, unsure whether their interest is more than passing scholarly or political fad. A discipline so heavily committed to the exotic and nonwestern, so traditionally defined by the primitive and nonliterate would expectably hesitate at any movement which ruptured its scholarly past. The often *sotto voce* judgments of "poor" or "opportunistic" against urban research, the dearth of urban courses in undergraduate and graduate curricula, and the absence of introductory texts to chart the field indicate that city research in anthropology has not reached its majority. The fear of many anthropologists is that if its present course continues, urban anthropology may never mature into a sophisticated approach which informs both nonurban anthropologists and nonanthropological urbanists.

For what, after all, have the several urban anthropologies told us? Have the supposedly defining qualities of urbanism helped us understand how cities develop and the range of cultural roles performed by urban areas? Do we know why shanty towns emerge, and how they differ according to the composition of particular cities or the values and economics of particular societies? Can we generalize about urbanization behavior in any society, and can we place the urbanization process today in Africa along side what occurred in fifteenth-century England or eighteenth-century America? Have urbanization and ghetto anthropologies escaped the charge of scholarly ethnocentrism leveled by Gideon Sjoberg against an urban sociology defined in the image of industrial cities? And can they critically evaluate the concept of "preindustrial city" which Sjoberg proposes as cure? Do urban studies as presently constituted speak to the problems of city development advanced by archeologists, geographers, and historians interested in the organization of the earliest urban communities or in the validity of such cross-cultural distinctions as Weber's "oriental vs. occidental" urbanism? Properly answering "no" to these questions, urban anthropologists indicate the scholarly vacuum in which they often work, a thinness induced to some extent by the novelty of their research but brought about in part by absent conceptual orientations. The difficult scholarly journey to the city thus provides anthropology with an immense challenge, and a major aspect of the excitement (and variety of perspectives) surrounding urban anthropology concerns the proper response to this challenge. What is being entertained is no less than a reordering of anthropology to comprehend the urban milieux in which most of the world's population lives or will live.

Future Courses

Urban anthropology's future course is already guaranteed by numerous research projects, books, and articles in progress, covering many hitherto unsurveyed cities, ghettos, shanty towns, and "native locations." In terms of growing maturity of conception and orientation, however, such a future merely continues the present. The various disarticulated approaches to the city remain; the uncertanties about what is sought within the urban locale or even when it is reached go unresolved. Anthropology's urban progress may simply stop and retrench into numerically escalating but conceptionally stationary studies which merely duplicate the urban society, ghetto, and shanty town research which has gone before.

A real future course for urban anthropology will only come by recognizing its present deficiencies and varieties and by probing ways to overcome or collate them. This appraisal will undoubtedly conclude that the insights and techniques which anthropology brings to the city invaluably comprehend the urban experience over time and across cultures. But whether affirmative or negative, the appraisal would at least move us away from the present inadequate situation where anthropologist's physical presence in the urban environment (or some part of it) is sufficient proof of their having attained the city in a scholarly sense. We must recognize that anthropology's progress into the urban world has just begun. The current difficulties and deficiencies in urban research only remind us of how much journey yet remains and challenge us to proceed further and with greater speed. The next step in anthropology's urban progress is to clarify what precisely it has entered in coming to the city, why in scholarly terms the entrance has been valuable, and how the new urban research follows and yet continues further along the road already traveled in anthropology's past.

BIBLIOGRAPHICAL NOTE

The anthropology of urbanism is the first conceptual path followed by anthropologists in their passage to the city. Robert Redfield's *The Folk Culture of Yucatan* (Chicago: University of Chicago Press, 1941) stipulated the city as a proper locale for anthropological research and defined the folk-urban continuum as a model for its investigation. This approach was further developed by Redfield in "The Social Organization of Tradition," *Far Eastern Quarterly* 15 (1955), and *The Primitive World and Its Transformation* (Ithaca, N.Y.: Cornell University Press, 1967), applied to the city of Timbuktu by

Horace Miner in *The Primitive City of Timbuctoo* (Rev. ed. Garden City, N.Y.: Anchor Press, 1965), challenged in Mexico City by Oscar Lewis, "Urbanization Without Breakdown," *Scientific Monthly* 75:31–41 (1952), corrected and expanded by Robert Redfield and Milton Singer, "The Cultural Role of Cities," *Economic Development and Cultural Change* 3 (1954), and followed with major modification and different insights in recent work by McKim Marriott, *Village India: Studies in the Little Community* (Chicago: University of Chicago Press, 1955), Richard G. Fox, *From Zaminder to Ballot Box: Community Change in a North Indian Market Town* (Ithaca, N.Y.: Cornell University Press, 1969), and Clifford Geertz, *The Social History of an Indonesian Town* (Cambridge, Mass.: M.I.T. Press, 1965).

The anthropology of the ghetto has its beginnings in case studies undertaken by sociologists of the Chicago human ecology school, such as Nels Anderson, *The Hobo: The Sociology of the Homeless Man* (Reprint. Chicago: University of Chicago Press, 1975), Harvey Zorbaugh, *The Gold Coast and the Slum* (Chicago: University of Chicago Press, 1929), and Paul Cressey, *The Taxi-Dance Hall* (Reprint. New York: AMS Press, Inc., 1972). Oscar Lewis, "Further Observations on the Folk-Urban Continuum and Urbanization with Special Reference to Mexico City," In Philip M. Hauser and Leo Schnore (eds.), *The Study of Urbanization* (New York: John Wiley & Sons, Inc., 1965) and *La Vida: A Puerto Rican Family in the Culture of Poverty—San Juan and New York* (New York: Random House, Inc., 1966), with his concept of the "culture of poverty," is the major figure to define this interest in anthropology. His viewpoint is followed by James Spradley, *You Owe Yourself a Drunk: An Ethnography of Urban Nomads* (Boston: Little, Brown & Co., 1970), in a study of urban alcoholics, and it is criticized by Ulf Hannerz, *Soulside: Inquiries into Ghetto Culture and Community* (New York: Columbia University Press, 1969), and Elliot Liebow, *Tally's Corner: A Study of Negro Streetcorner Men* (Boston: Little, Brown & Co., 1967), in their research on urban blacks. Charles Valentine, *Culture and Poverty: Critique and Counter-Proposals* (Chicago: University of Chicago Press, 1969), is especially critical of the "culture of poverty" concept in a major review of this literature. Gerald Suttles, *The Social Order of the Slum* (Revised ed. Chicago: University of Chicago Press, 1968), Lincoln Keiser, *The Vice Lords: Warriors of the Street* (New York: Holt, Rinehart, & Winston, Inc., 1969), and Jack Waddell and O. Michael Watson (eds.), *The American Indian in Urban Society* (Boston: Little, Brown & Co., 1971), have added measurably to our understanding of interethnic accommodations in a Chicago slum, gang behavior in Chicago, and American Indian adaptations to American cities, respectively.

Urbanization anthropology in Africa, what it is and what it ought be, is set out by A. L. Epstein, "Urbanization and Social Change in Africa," *Current Anthropology* 8:275–96 (1967), and J. Clyde Mitchell, "Theoretical Orientations in African Urban Studies," in M. Banton (ed.), *The Social Anthropology of Complex Societies* (London: Tavistock Press, 1966). Major ethnographic studies include J. Clyde Mitchell, *The Kalela Dance*, Rhodes-Livingston Papers Number 27 (Manchester, England: Manchester University Press, 1956), A. L. Epstein, *Politics in an Urban African Community* (Manchester, England: Manchester University Press, 1958), Abner Cohen, *Custom and Politics in Urban Africa: A Study of Hausa Migrants in Yoruba Towns* (Berkeley: University of California Press, 1969), and the various studies reported in J. Clyde Mitchell, *Social Networks in Urban Situations* (Manchester, England: Manchester University Press, 1969). Urbanization and shanty town settlement in Latin America (and elsewhere) are surveyed in William Mangin (ed.), *Peasants in Cities: Readings in the Anthropology of Urbanism* (Boston: Houghton Mifflin Co., 1970), and modeled in Anthony Leeds, "The Significant Variables Determining the Character of Squatter Settlements," *America Latina* 12:44–86 (1969).

Several recent volumes of collected papers take a broad view of urban anthropology. The books edited by Elizabeth Eddy, *Urban Anthropology: Research Perspectives and Strategies* (Athens, Georgia: University of Georgia Press, 1968), and Aidan Southall, *Urban Anthropology: Cross-Cultural Studies of Urbanization* (New York: Oxford University Press, 1973), are addressed to other scholars working in cities and contain a wide variety of ethnographic materials and viewpoints. Horace Miner's *The City in Modern Africa* (New York: Praeger Publishing, 1967) concentrates on African urbanism and brings together contributions from scholars of other disciplines besides anthropology. An important source for understanding the rigors of ethnographic fieldwork in urban places is George Foster and Robert Kemper (eds.), *Anthropologists in Cities* (Boston: Little, Brown & Co., 1974).

John Gulick provides an overview of urban anthropology, its accomplishments, deficiencies, and disagreements in "Urban Anthropology," in John J. Honigmann (ed.), *Handbook of Social and Cultural Anthropology* (Chicago: Rand McNally & Co., 1974). Since 1972, a journal devoted to the anthropology of urban places, *Urban Anthropology*, has been published at the State University of New York—Brockport under the editorship of Jack R. Rollwagen.

15.

CULTURE AND ENVIRONMENT:
THE STUDY OF
CULTURAL ECOLOGY

Marshall D. Sahlins

"THE STERILITY OF THE soil in Attica," wrote Montesquieu, "established a popular government there, and the
fertility of Lacedaemon an aristocratic one." We are not
convinced. Yet the statement is characteristic of a main intellectual legacy in the ecological study of culture, environmental
determinism, that ancient idea of "a mechanical action of
natural forces upon a purely receptive humanity." From more
recent forebears, notably including American field anthropologists of this century, we are heir to an opposed position,
environmental possibilism, which holds that cultures act se-
lectively, if not capriciously, upon their environments, exploiting some possibilities while ignoring others; that it is environment that is passive, an inert configuration of possibilities
and limits to development, the deciding forces of which lie in
culture itself and in the history of culture.

Another outlook appears. At first it was only as an offhand
remark, a critical argument. Now it informs some of the best
work in American archaeology and ethnology: It is an idea of
reciprocity, of a dialogue between cultures and their environments. The truism that cultures are *ways of life*, taken in a new
light, is the ground premise—cultures are human *adaptations*.
Culture, as a design for society's continuity, stipulates its
environment. By its mode of production, by the material
requirements of its social structure, in its standardized percep-
tions, a culture assigns relevance to particular external conditions. Even its historic movement is movement along the eco-

215

logic seam it is organized to exploit. Yet a culture is shaped by these, its own, commitments: it molds itself to significant external conditions to maximize the life chances. There is an interchange between culture and environment, perhaps continuous dialectic interchange, if in adapting the culture transforms its landscape and so must respond anew to changes that it had set in motion. I think the best answer to the received controversy over which is the determinant, culture or environment, should be this: both—the answer lies at both extremes.

The significance of given environmental features, as well as their weight upon a culture, is contingent on that culture. Here is a politically developed Asiatic society relying upon intensive, double-crop agriculture. Subjected to a shortening of summer seasons by five days, it may be under critical selection. A certain isotherm becomes a threshold beyond which the system as constituted cannot be maintained. Yet the same climatic shift means little or nothing to a fishing tribe; its niche is governed by the conditions that directly concern the fishing. Similarly, coal is a relevant resource of an industrial technology, and its distribution in the ground affects the design, the external relations, even the historic fate of an industrial nation. But to a hunting-and-gathering people, to Australian aborigines, say, coal is completely irrelevant: in the ground or no, it is not part of their environment; it has no selective impact on them, unless

Australian Aborigines Hit It Rich
Special to the *Detroit News*

CANBERRA, April 17 (1963)—One of the world's most primitive people—scientists say they are just passing through their stone age—will get a multimillion dollar rake-off from a big Australian mine project.

They are the aborigines on the Arnhemland Peninsula of northern Australia. They are sitting (squatting?) on one of the biggest bauxite lodes, the ore of aluminum, ever found in the country.

Because the effects of natural circumstances are thus conditional, one cannot read, with geographical determinists, from the configuration of an environment to a configuration of culture. On the other hand, the equally simple-minded textbook rebuttal to the effect that different cultures may emerge in similar environments—standard example: Manhattan Island 1962 *vs.* Manhattan Island 1492—does not dispose of environmental influence. The environment-culture relation need not be one-to-one, but environment is never, thereby, a powerless term. Natural resources, when relevant to prevailing production, govern dispositions of technologies and populations; a line of rainfall, no matter that the precise line is determined from within, is, as such, a cultural boundary; topographical features are so many barriers to or routes of communication, sites for settlement, or strategic positions of defense.

The circumstances with which most peoples have to deal, moreover, are of two distinct kinds; relations are developed with two environments. Societies are typically set in fields of *cultural influence* as well as fields of *natural influence*. They are subjected to both. They adapt to both. Indeed, terms of the relation to nature may be set by intercultural relations—as when avenues of trade govern avenues of production—and terms of intercultural relations may be set by relations to nature—as when avenues of production govern avenues of trade. It is all so obvious. But until recently the discipline of cultural ecology has operated myopically as if it were biological ecology, without reference to intercultural adaptation. We have, mistakenly in my view, limited the notion of environment and the concern for selection to the geography and biology of a milieu. Research into relations between cultures has been carried on as a thing apart, mostly under the traditional head of "acculturation," and thus not so much from the perspective of adaptation as from that of assimilation. A widespread recognition that cultures act as selective forces upon one another, and with it the realization that culture contact creates complementarity, not merely similarity in structure, seems imminent. Cultural ecology has an untapped potential to provoke useful thoughts about militarism, nationalism, the orientation of production, trade, and many other specialized developments which, if they are not "acculturation" in the conventional sense, still come out of the interaction of cultures.

The dual quality of "environment" is sometimes brought home by actions of nature and of outside cultures from different directions, setting off change in different sectors of an affected culture. Just for this point, let me use the "architectural" or "layer-cake" model of a culture-system that has been popularized in evolutionist writings. The model holds that economic and material elements—"mode of production" or, in another view, "technology"—are basic, the decisive foundation of the cultural order, and that polity and ideology are "superstructure," resting upon and systematically reflecting material foundations. Now ordinarily the imprint of nature may be traced upward through the cultural order—but external cultural influences may very well impress themselves from the top down. Natural circumstances directly affect technical deployment, productivity, the cycle of employments, settlement patterns, and so forth; from these points the systematic relations of base to superstructure relay impulses to the higher political and ideological spheres. The material base adapts to nature and the superstructure to the material base. Grant that—even though it is mechanical and oversimplified. A culture, on the other hand, may come to terms with its social milieu in the first place by ideological and political adjustments—the outside cultural pressure itself is often ideological and political in the main and at first. Such has been the classic course of adaptation in primitive and underdeveloped societies opened to Western dominance. The initial revisions appear in ideology, as in conversion to Christianity, and in social-political sectors, by virtue of incorporation in a colonial realm, with radical economic change setting in derivatively or afterward. Hence the characteristic crisis of the postcolonial period, the "inverse cultural lag" compounded of advanced political norms harnessed to an underdeveloped economy.

For decades, centuries now, intellectual battle has been given over which sector of culture is the decisive one for change. Many have entered the lists under banners diverse. Curiously, few seem to fall. Leslie White champions technological growth as the sector most responsible for cultural evolution; Julian Huxley, with many others, sees "man's view of destiny" as the deciding force; the mode of production and the class struggle are still very much in contention. Different as they are, these positions agree in one respect, that the impulse to development is generated from within. The system by one means or another is self-sustaining, self-developing. The case for internal causes of development may be bolstered by pointing to a mechanism, such as the Hegelian dialectic, or it may rest more insecurely on an argument from logic, which is usually coupled with indifference to the source of change in the presumed critical sector. In any event, an unreal and vulnerable assumption is always there, that cultures are closed systems. Cultures are abstracted from their influential contexts, detached from fields of forces in which they are embedded. It is precisely on this point that cultural ecology offers a new perspective, a counterpoise to conventional evolutionary arguments. For it shifts attention to the relation between inside and outside; it envisions as the mainspring of the evolutionary movement the interchange between culture and environment. Now which view shall prevail is not to be decided on a sheet of paper; the test as always is long-term utility. But if adaptation wins over inner dynamism, it will be for certain intrinsic and obvious strengths. Adaptation is real, naturalistic, anchored to those historic contexts of cultures that inner dynamism ignores. Perhaps it even helps explain why no agreement has ever been had on which aspect of culture takes the lead in development. The various inner dynamisms, though contradictory, have each and all been supportable because, in fact, different sectors, from the mode of production to the view of destiny, at different times are decisive—depending on the point of impact of the selective field.

The trial of the ecological perspective must, and will, be in the empirical arena. The decision rests on its success in handling the facts of this case and that, and indeed an impressive list of accomplishments, headed by the researches of Julian Steward, can already be proclaimed. And it begins to be possible to reflect upon the empirical encounter, to generalize, tentatively, about the adaptive behavior of cultures. The remainder of my remarks are in this vein.

Adaptation implies maximizing the social life chances. But maximization is almost always a compromise, a vector of the internal structure of culture and the external pressure of environment. Every culture carries the penalty of a past within the frame of which, barring total disorganization, it must work out its future. Things get functionally arranged. The present American industrial system runs on an agrarian seasonal cycle. The American educational process, legislative process, a whole host of critical activities virtually cease in summer, as if there was pressing work to be done, the harvest to be taken in. And now that in fact 90 percent of the population has no such obligation, the summer becomes a holiday, and industrial output is accordingly adjusted to demands of a travel and sports-minded market.

There is more to this adaptive compromise than mere contradiction between received cultural order and new conditions of existence. We see different selective pressures working at cross purposes, evoking insoluble contradictions within a culture itself. We see too that adaptive responses can have disadvantageous side effects, as the modification of one constellation of customs sets off untoward consequences elsewhere in the system. To adapt then is not to do perfectly from some objective standpoint, or even necessarily to improve performance; it is to do as well as possible under the circumstances, which may not turn out very well at all. In one of the tropical islands of Fiji, if I may draw upon personal observations, there is a great demand at present for houses of timber with galvanized iron roofs, houses that Fijians are pleased to call "European," an allegation that curiously outvalues the fact that these dwellings retain the heat and are otherwise unsuited to the native climate and mode of life. At the same time, the number of punts—the most feasible type of boat for Fijians at present and also, one might note, "European"—declines steadily in this island, which means the decline of a rare opportunity for getting some needed protein through fishing. The rise in tin-roof demand is directly related to the decline in boats: the materials for both must be purchased and carpenters rewarded, so it is a question of allocation of scarce finances. Yet, at an obvious cost in personal comfort, and possibly in health too, this peculiar pattern of desires does neutralize an adaptive dilemma. On one side, the native kinship organization with its strong ethics of mutual aid has been very much kept going in Fiji. It is still effective—no, necessary—in the subsistence sector of their lives. On the other side, the usual tendencies of individual acquisitiveness have been touched off by their involvement in copra production and world trade. Now, while the traditional norm of share-alike keeps people alive, it also weakens the producer's hand in movable things that he has purchased. Boats may just be taken outright by kinsmen in need, or, being scarce, they are frequently borrowed, and the owners saddled with maintenance costs. A tin-roof house becomes desirable, and I suspect it is singularly identified with the dominant European (i.e., British) order, because it is, in the cultural nature of things, inalienable—one can neither take it home nor decently throw a relative out of his own house. So the Fijian produces copra, continues to have many relatives, fishes less than he needs to, and swelters. An adaptive perspective, goes the moral, must not presume that whatever is there is good, rational, useful, or advantageous. Lots of things people do are truly stupid, if understandable, and many cultures have gone to the wall.

In fact a culture's downfall is the most probable outcome of its successes. The accomplished, well-adapted culture is biased. Its design has been refined in a special direction, its environment narrowly specified, how it shall operate definitively stated. The more adapted a culture, the less therefore it is adaptable. Its specialization subtracts from its potential, from the capacity of alternate response, from tolerance of change in the world. It becomes vulnerable in proportion to its accomplishments. Alterations of the milieu are less than likely to be opportunities, more than likely disturbances. By its commitment to an external *status quo* it assigns the negative (negative selection) to environmental change.

Unfortunately, all this is probably convincing in the same measure as it is abstract. How shall we describe in detail the meaning of a cultural specialization, state precisely the mechanisms of its self-defense, assess accurately its adaptive potential? We are in thrall at the moment to organic notions of culture, like the evolutionist "layer cake" model I used before. A beginning on the critical questions can be made by capitaliz-

ing that central idea of the organic outlook: "functional interdependence." It should be possible, for example, to uncover
chains of interdependent customs that terminate in components directly joined with the environment: an ancestral cult
that sanctifies the patrilineal principle, small-scale lineages
acting as social proprietors, permanent but limited neolithic
agriculture-that kind of thing. Professor Wolf remarks in his
chapter that properties of the elements within such circuits set
restrictions on what may be coupled in, and prevailing relations between elements will bear just so much modification in
any one of them. Yet what seems truly striking about a mature
culture is not so much the organic logic of it as the idiocies of
its functional connections, the irrelevancies of its structure.
Things bear upon one another that, in the nature of these
things, need not do so.

I am saying that there are two kinds of functional couplings
in culture, logical and idiosyncratic, and that specialized
cultures may be distinguished by an overburden of the latter.
The coexistence of a centralized Asiatic bureaucracy and
intensive irrigation agriculture is, for an example, logically
consistent, in the nature of imperatives. Bureaucracy and
irrigation perform necessary services for each other. Each fits
within the complementary requirements of the other. But what
are we to make of this fact, so painfully familiar in American
television: that the style of drama is constrained by the
requirements of selling soap or underarm deodorants? The
constraint, incidentally, is no less compelling for its idiocy, but
it is clearly of a different order from functional relations of the
irrigation-bureaucracy sort. Irrelevancy is the penalty of a
particular past, the structural anomaly of a specialized culture.
It is only understandable, and only tolerable, in the context of
its own history and the circumstances that have made history.
Outside of that context, any mature culture is a monstrosity.

In the past, before World War II, American anthropologists
worked from a different model of culture. It was a model of
"mechanical solidarity" rather than "organic solidarity," the
idea that customs of a society are more importantly alike than
they are complementary. Ruth Benedict, in *Patterns of Culture*,
unfolded the idea; since then many intellectual descendants

and cousins of it have appeared—cultural style, cultural ethos, cultural configuration, and others. "Culture pattern" means design and Gestalt, but more, it means a common alignment of the diverse pieces of culture. It has to do with the singular and pervasive genius of a people. So among the militarist tribes of the American Plains the Dionysian element appears again and again in many different areas of culture: in their vision quests and guardian spirit beliefs, in super-machismo definition of the male role and a corollary acceptance of transvestism among those who could not live up to it, in military qualifications of leadership, suicidal pledges of revenge, in Spartan childhood training. We are confronting a cultural orientation, and although Benedict saw it artistically as a people's selection from the great arc of human-temperamental possibilities, in the harder view it looks to be selection of a different kind. The internal orientation of Plains culture was cast from the forge of ecological selection: the Dionysian pattern was hammered out in intertribal battle over access to trade posts and trade goods, horses and hunting grounds. I think that the Benedictian models ought to be revived, to be reconsidered in the light of new interests. We know already, as Benedict had observed, that an integrated pattern cuts down the capacity for change—in current usage, the adaptive potential. Innovations are either given the prevailing polarity or, if they do not lend themselves to it, are rejected.

However cultural specialization be ultimately perceived, in configurational, organic, or some other terms, many of the little devices that insulate peoples against cultural alternatives are already apparent. Among them are negatively charged ideas about conditions and customs in neighboring societies. These are well known under the head "ethnocentrism," but they have been more despised as unenlightened attitudes than they have studied as ideological defenses. For they are "ideology" in the strict sociological sense of beliefs that prevent people from knowing what is going on in the world. One species of ethnocentric idea is specially important for this discussion, the peculiar notions that societies put out about the environments of their neighbors. The species could be called "great wall ideology," for like the Chinese wall these beliefs divide the terrain in which the received way of life is effective from the terrain in which it cannot survive, and by fantastic allegations of an outer darkness they keep people within the wall, and so committed to the traditional order. Consider, for example, the warnings solicitously tendered by Pathans of Swat State (Pakistan) to an anthropologist who was contemplating a visit to the neighboring Kohistani people: "Full of terrible mountains," they said of Kohistani territory, "covered by many-colored snow and emitting poisonous gases causing head and stomach pains when you cross the high passes, inhabited by robbers and snakes that coil up and leap ten feet into the air; with no villages, only scattered houses on the mountain tops." The noteworthy difference the anthropologist discovered between Kohistani and Pathan territories was seasonal temperatures somewhat lower in the former, a small enough matter in itself but sufficient to keep Pathan political economy from operating effectively beyond its proper border.

Adapted and specialized, mature cultures are conservative, their reactions to the world defensive. They accommodate new environmental conditions to their structures more than their structures to new conditions, absorbing fluctuations of their milieus within the prevailing order of things, so that the more they change the more they remain the same. They compensate rather than revise. And new relations to the world suggested from within remain stillborn. These are manifest tendencies of primitive and modern societies alike, dramatically manifest in successful attempts to preserve the old social regime by letting slip new economic opportunities. It is organizational sabotage. It is the essence of Kwakiutl potlatch extravagances during the fur trade, as it is also of the planned obsolescence that saves industries by wasting their productive capabilities. It is the "creeping socialism" that prevents large sectors of private enterprise from falling to prices. Anthropologists record the herculean technical efforts of the Yakut, an inner Asian pastoral people pushed into the Siberian forest, to keep horse nomadism alive out of its element rather than switch over to a more functional economy—the Yakut went so far as to develop irrigation, but mostly to grow more winter fodder. From New Guinea comes word of an inland people moved to the coast under missionary aegis who, for forty years, have refused to learn to fish, swim, or handle canoes.

In the final defensive phases of its history, a specialized culture may reach yet greater heights of dysfunction. As normal technical and political competences fail, supernatural reserves are engaged. This foxhole propensity of man and culture we have known for some time, at least since Malinowski's famous observation that the involvement of ritual in Trobriand Island fishing increases with the hazards of the enterprise—just as in America religious ikons have been enshrined on the dashboards of automobiles since the advent of overpowered engines and overcrowded highways. The same escapism comes over cultures as wholes when faced by pressures beyond practical control: preservation becomes a supernatural business and what is threatened becomes holy. Just so with some famous millennial movements, such as the American Indian Ghost Dances of the later eighteen hundreds that looked to a magical restoration of the buffalo, the land, dead customs, and dead Indians. (Perhaps modern, overdeveloped nations are showing symptoms of defensive sanctification. Social critics in America, especially the daily syndicated viewers-with-alarum, despair that our healthy respect for the past is sometimes translated into reverent superstition, our historic legacy into the tyranny of an ancestral cult. However that may be, it has been deemed advisable to insert "this nation under God" into the pledge of allegiance to the flag, and a fine contrast this makes to the old saw about pioneer days: "Well, parson, maybe I did hew this fine farm out of the wilderness with God's help—but you should have seen it when He had it alone!" God help those who cannot help themselves!)

Yet then the question is posed: If highly specialized peoples are conservative, where do the breakthroughs occur? Our theory seems to predict that evolution should grind to a halt, which it certainly does not do. Speculation turns to the idea of "generalized cultures," those with good adaptive possibilities. We find them sometimes on frontiers, among pioneering fringes that of necessity have simplified a heritage of little use at the present juncture. Or, from the analogy of genetic drift in species, we find them among peoples suddenly reduced to small remnants by large catastrophes, a condition that might favor the rapid spread of innovations. Yet these circumstances are too rare, on the whole too insignificant, to bear the grand movement of evolutionary variation.

We know—we take it as premise sometimes—that competition has a salutary effect on development. Even the seeming tragedy of conquest and defeat may have its phoenix aftermath. Perhaps there is room in ecological theory for some such concept as the "Hamburg effect," referring to the remarkable service performed for German industry by Allied bombers in the last war whose obliteration of entrenched handicraft business in that city finally put production on an all-out military line. The conflict created by expanding, dominant cultures seems specially critical for the creation of evolutionary potential. Throughout history, advanced cultures have displayed a special gift for generating further advance, but not so much in their developed centers as on their ethnic borders.

For the advanced societies, in displacing backward peoples or harnessing them to their own progress, become agents of a disruption that frees the backward region from the dead hand of its own past. "To make scrambled eggs, one must first crack the eggs." But hinterlands are not merely disorganized by dominant cultures, they become committed to main streams of progress as tributaries of it. Thus they are first, involved in development, and second, set politically against its historic agent. They could become, therefore, revolutionary cultures, prepared at the same time to overthrow the old order and overtop the one presently on their backs. Look closely at the so-called nativistic movements along the Melanesian and African peripheries of modern civilization; ostensibly symptoms of cultural bankruptcy, on examination they reveal themselves as capitalizations of advance. Although at certain early phases a Melanesian cargo cult has its inclinations toward a native restoration, in its jealousy of "way belong white man" and its goal of "coming inside" it turns irreversibly from tradition, and its rebellious organization of heretofore autonomous communities is, in the understanding of the most acute observers, the germ of nationalism.

In other words, advanced and dominant cultures create the

circumstances for their own eclipse. On one hand, they themselves become specialized. Their development on a particular line commits them to it: they are mortgaged to structures accumulated along the way, burdened, in Veblen's phrase, with the penalty of taking the lead. On the other hand, they restore adaptability to previously stable and backward peoples within their spheres of influence. These underdeveloped orders, rudely jolted from historyless equilibrium, may now seize "the privilege of historic backwardness" and overturn their submission by taking over the latest developments of advanced cultures and pushing on from there. How many great civilizations have lived with, and finally died from, the menace of border barbarians? Of course, as is made obvious today by the struggles of new nations, it is not easy for the "barbarians," if only because progress in the hinterland is rarely to the interest of dominant civilizations. Yet no matter how often underdeveloped peoples fail to gain evolutionary momentum, history shows that progress is not so much nourished in the strategic heights as in the fertile valleys of the cultural terrain.

Cultural progress then is an outcome of adaptation and selection. Progress, moreover, is itself adaptive, or at least the complex cultures have the greatest "all round adaptability" in Julian Huxley's words. So progress will be selected for from time to time.

Advanced cultures are distinguished by superior means of coping with the world. The improvements in productive technology that have occurred through prehistory and history, especially the several revolutions from the development of agriculture to the development of nuclear power, are the best known, but they are not alone. There have been very important improvements in the technology of mobilization, that is, in means for delivery of power, goods, persons, and messages. These particularly give advantage in intercultural relations, making it increasingly possible to base an advance on the exploitation of surrounding societies through trade, conquest, or colonial rule. The existence of one set of cultures, especially rich ones effectively exploiting their several environments, creates a niche as it were for the cultural predator that can adapt itself to the adaptations of others. (Perhaps overly impressed with the consequences of the Western Industrial Revolution, anthropologists have been wont to locate the basis of progress in breakthroughs of production, forgetting that the development of Rome, Greece, and many other civilizations had no such ground.) Finally, there have occurred improvements in still another realm, that of protective technology: the advances in shelter, clothing, or medical techniques, for instance, that defend society against natural hazards; and those in armament that subdue cultural hazards.

It is often said that highly developed cultures are comparatively free from environmental control. But environmental influences are not really put in abeyance by cultural advance. It is rather that advance cannot be put in abeyance by environmental features. The performance of the highest cultures is least constrained by natural conditions. In a way, culture acts to repeal for humans the famous biological law of the minimum. In recent millennia especially, progressive cultures have shown great capacity to wheel and deal in the face of local natural deficiencies. On top of Mt. Everest, Westerners have lived despite the natural lack of oxygen; they have maintained themselves in outer space despite the absence of gravity. What has happened in the long habitable regions of this earth, however, is more important—for the moment. The advanced peoples have sustained imperialist probes of various kinds far beyond their traditional home base, if necessary by provisioning these outposts by the exploitation of the home base. And they maintain high levels of order and complexity at the home base by drawing in resources over long distances. The advanced cultural type is not as confined as the less advanced. It is distributed over greater ranges of rainfall, topography, soil type, whatnot, and it is engaged too with a greater external cultural diversity. A higher culture has more environment than a lower one.

Thus the rise in the first place of dominant cultures. Deploying power and personnel in a variety of zones, advanced cultures often compete successfully with the indigenous occupants of these zones for resources that have become indispensable to the developed peoples. The higher orders typically displace less developed ones in regions similar to, and available to, centers of progress. Societies more distant, and those exploiting other natural settings, are harnessed to the centers of development and thereby are partly acculturated. This closes a circle: we had seen that dominance can initiate progress; we see now that progress sets off dominance. I suggest that the Hegelian interplay of these main adaptive processes provides the momentum by which culture continuously transcends itself.

Anthropology was conceived in the first place out of the dominant power of high civilization. In those "new worlds given to the world" by the European expansion were peoples and customs that could not fail to provoke an anthropological curiosity. One hopes that anthropology and its sister human sciences will keep pace now with the accumulating consequences of dominance. To do so, the development of the ecological perspective is a first requisite. The era of world history has begun. The scale of functional dependence between societies expands, drawing together the histories of different parts of the planet. The several cultures of mankind become subcultures, subsystems, differentiated parts of a larger complex of cultural relations. Cultures cannot any longer be understood by contemplation of their navels. None is intelligible in isolation, apart from its adaptation to others in the world-cultural net. As each society's history so becomes the history of every other society, and each society becomes an environment of every other, it becomes for us common sense and necessity to learn how to interpret cultures as much from the outside, from their environmental contexts, as from their inner values.

BIBLIOGRAPHICAL NOTE

The tradition of environmental determinism is discussed at length and in detail by Lucien Febvre and Lionel Bataillon, *A Geographical Introduction to History* (Reprint. Westport, Conn.: Greenwood Press, Inc., 1975). The characterization of environmental determinism and the quote from Montesquieu in the introductory passage of the present essay have been cribbed from Febvre. His work is also a useful introduction to possibilism.

Anthropological interest in the relation between culture and

230   MARSHALL D. SAHLINS

nature—mostly from a possibilist vantage—developed markedly in America in connection with the culture-area approach:
Clark Wissler, *The Relations of Nature to Man in Aboriginal
North America* (Stanford: Stanford University Press, 1969),
and Alfred L. Kroeber, *Cultural and Natural Areas of Native
North America* (Berkeley: University of California Press,
1939). It was Julian Steward, however, who self-consciously
initiated the study of cultural ecology and placed the question
in an evolutionary framework. *Theory of Culture Change*
(Urbana, Ill.: University of Illinois Press, 1955) expounds
Steward's view of ecology and the conclusions of his concrete
ecological research.

   Among the many contributors to current ecological thought,
Frederik Barth deserves special recognition, not simply for
artful brilliance in handling ethnographic data but also for his
explicit inclusion of external cultural influence within the
concept of environment; for examples, see Barth, "Ecological
Relationships of Ethnic Groups in Swat, North Pakistan,"
American Anthropologist 58:1079–89 (1956), "The Land Use
Pattern of Migratory Tribes of South Persia," *Norsk Geogra-
fisk Tidsskrift*, 8:1–11 (1959), and *Nomads of South Persia:
The Baseri Tribe of the Khamseh Confederacy* (Boston: Little,
Brown & Co., 1968). I have drawn heavily from Barth's work;
the citation concerning Pathan views of Kohistani territory is
from Barth (1956). Owen Lattimore's *Inner Asian Frontiers of
China* (New York: American Geographical Society, 1951) is a
classic study of historic interplay between culture and environment. The greatest single contribution to the adaptive or
ecological perspective (in my opinion), it raised and speaks
directly to all the critical theoretical issues.

   At the risk of making invidious distinctions, a few more
empirical analyses of note might be listed: Karl A. Wittfogel,
Oriental Despotism (New Haven, Conn.: Yale University
Press, 1957); Wayne Suttles, "Affinal Ties, Subsistence and
Prestige Among the Coast Salish," *American Anthropologist*
62:296–305 (1960); Morton H. Fried, "Land Tenure, Geography and Ecology in the Contact of Cultures," *American
Journal of Economics and Sociology* 11:391-417 (1952); Lawrence Krader, "Ecology of Central Asian Pastoralism," *South-*

western Journal of Anthropology 2:301–26 (1955); Max Gluckman, *The Economy of the Central Barotse Plains* (Livingstone, Northern Rhodesia: Rhodes-Livingstone Institute, 1941); Angel Palerm and Eric R. Wolf, "Ecological Potential and Cultural Development in Meso-America," in *Studies in Human Ecology*, Social Science Monograph No. 3 (Washington, D.C.: Pan American Union, 1957); and Harold Conklin's contribution in *Transactions of the New York Academy of Sciences*, Series 2, 17:133–42. June Helm, "The Ecological Approach in Anthropology," *American Journal of Sociology* 67:630:39 (1962), has reviewed the anthropological study of ecology, and her paper ought to be consulted for further bibliography.

The discussion of dominance, progress, and evolutionary potential in the latter part of my essay has its basis in Marshall D. Sahlins and Elman R. Service (eds.), *Evolution and Culture* (Ann Arbor: University of Michigan Press, 1960).

16.

THE ORGANIZATION OF ECONOMIC LIFE

Manning Nash

ALL MEN AND WOMEN have rough ideas of what economic acts are and intuitive notions of when they are engaged in economic acts. The variety of economic activities and organization over time and space challenges not only common sense but theoretical ingenuity. In a northwest coast potlatch a man destroys a copper, his most valuable possession, in order to shame a rival for status. In the New Hebrides Islands men raise pigs, exchange pigs, lend out pigs at interest, and finally in a large ceremonial feast destroy the pig holdings of a lifetime. Among the Siane every member of a patrilineage when asked who owns the land he and his lineage mates will respond: "I do." In the Kula ring of the Solomons there are elaborate exchange systems with token shells moving in one direction and goods moving in a counter-direction. There are unlimited examples of economic activities and organization that defy, on the surface, understanding, explanation, and incorporation into a coherent system.

As its first task, *economic anthropology* is concerned with the development of economic ideas, classifications of economic systems, and the explanation of the operations and changes of these economic systems in the ethnological record by a set of ideas which transcend ethnocentric or single-culture-based systems. To these ends some ideas are borrowed from existing academic economics and others are invented by anthropologists as they confront the refractory realities they are attempting to account for.

232

As in all anthropological work, the primary data are the activities of the people of the society and the meanings they attribute to those socially recurrent patterns of behavior. Economizing is a sort of strategy of matching limited means with alternate uses to a hierachy of ends by the rule of getting the most out of the available resources. When the people of a society habitually strive to activate this strategy, we have economic behavior: all the acts of exchange—production, consumption, and distribution—predominately using this strategy form an empirically identifiable domain of the economy.

Take the exchange of women. Is it or is it not an economic activity? First ask the actors; then observe them. If the exchanges are made for kinship alliances in the service of extending the area of peace settlements, no. If the exchanges of women are based on the amount of cows or dowry they command, yes. So in the real world we have economic activities *and* activities that have an economic aspect. When a temple dancer in Bali dances, that is not economic, but when she gets a gift or payment for the act of dancing, the dancer has an economic aspect. Economic activities and economic aspects of non-economic activity together form the economic system, the object of analysis for economic anthropology.

For about the last four decades anthropologists have worked chiefly in the small-scale economies of nonwestern societies, usually labeled peasant and primitive economic systems. But by method and principle they are not limited to these societies. Further, the march of events as the poorer nations struggle for economic development and modernization has forced anthropological attention to shift from the isolated local economy to the interactions of peasants and primitives with developing national and even international economies. Where once anthropologists delighted in saying that every economic mechanism known to industrial society existed somewhere in the simpler world of peasants and primitives, it is now possible to say that all forms of exchange, production, distribution, and consumption that exist in primitive and peasant economies have their counterparts in industrial society. The economic life of man forms a continuum with only two or three major quantum jumps into qualitatively different economic organizations. For example, the distribution of product in peasant and primitive societies is usually governed by rules of group membership and social status. A Siane has a claim on food because he or she belongs to a certain clan grouping, not because he or she is a horticulturalist, good or bad. In the contemporary United States the distribution of product by entitlement (based on mere membership in some political unit and not on economic performance) is a rapidly growing trend, with perhaps the so-called war on poverty the best example.

Since anthropologists are concerned with whole societies and cultures, with macrostructures and patterns, they habitually seek to relate the economic subsystem of a society to the other subsystems (for example, family and kinship, law and politics, religion, and so on) to learn about their mutual determination and interactions. Hence, ironically, economic anthropology, as a branch of social and cultural anthropology, is the current seedbed for the rebirth of the political economy, the grand laws of motion of social systems, while academic economics goes about the mathematical refinement of its limited successes.

In abstracting the distinctive features, a basis is laid for classifying the variety of human economic organization, and a beginning is made on the functional analysis of that variety. The distinguishing features of peasant and primitive economic systems fall along four axes.

The first is *technological complexity and the division of labor.* In three ways, these societies are relatively simple: (1) tools to make tools are few; (2) the number of different tasks in any productive act are few; and (3) the energy conversion potential of the technology is small. Usually it is the skill of a single producer or a few producers which carries production from beginning to end. Many primitive and peasant technologies are ingenious, marvelously fitted to a particular environment requiring high levels of skill and performance but still very simple. The Bemba of Rhodesia wrest a living from poor soil with uncertain water supply by an intricate method of cultivation. With good rain and luck they harvest their crop of finger millet. Malaysian fishermen on the east coast of Kelantan set out to fish led by an expert diver who is skilled in locating the schools of fish. The Eskimo toggle harpoon, slit bone sunshade, and blubber lamps are clever devices for survival in a rigorous environment.

In these systems the task structure is simple and the tools involved require only human energy to operate. The specialized operations involved do not require interrelated webs of occupations. The division of labor follows the natural lines of sex, age, and prowess. It is a social division of labor more striking than an economic division of labor, with high interchangeability among persons in the proper social categories. The occupation list in a peasant or primitive society is neither long nor complex. Persons tend to learn their productive skills in the ordinary business of growing up, as an aspect of socialization. Work and tasks are apportioned to the socially appropriate persons, by sets of cultural rules without much regard to differences in skill or productivity. The technology also sets the limits on the size of combined working parties. Except at peak periods—planting, harvesting, and transplanting in agricultural communities, an organized hunt at the height of the animal-running season—large working parties are not found. Effort and work are closely tied to a pattern fitted to the annual and ceremonial cycles, not to the continuous demands of a highly organized economy with a wide technical or economic division of labor.

The second feature of peasant and primitive economy is the *structure and membership of productive units.* The unit of production, the social organization carrying out the making of goods, is dependent on and derived from other forms of social life. Peasant and primitive economies do not have organizations whose only tasks are those of production, and there are no durable social units based solely on productive activities. The bonds of kinship which structure families, clans, and kindreds are often the bonds used to organize economic activities. Territorial bonds may serve to create local production units. And the political structure, especially in societies with hereditary nobilities, is often used as a mechanism for forming productive units. For example, a religious elite may found a temple economy, as in ancient Assyria. This dependence of economic units on prior kinds of social relations has a typical series of consequences. Productive units tend to be multipurposed. Their economic activities are only one aspect. The economic activities of a family, a local group, or a compound composed of patrons and clients are just one area where the maintenance needs of the group are being met. Therefore, in these societies there tend to be many productive units, similarly structured, all doing the same sort of work. These productive units are limited in the type of personnel recruited, the capital they are able to command, and the ways in which they may distribute their product. Labor or capital markets do not exist; neither does a distribution system. A striking example of productive units based on relations derived from the organization of social groups only partially oriented to economic activity is the Indian pottery-making community in southeastern Mexico. This community is composed of 278 households. Each household is engaged in the production of pottery for sale, with virtually the same technology. Every household looks like every other in its productive organization. Or again, from Mexico, among the people of Tepoztlan, many make their living by the sale of services at a wage. Yet people must be sought out for employment, and hiring a fellow member of the community is a delicate social job. The transaction cannot appear as a strictly economic one.

The third distinguishing feature of peasant and primitive economies is *the systems and media of exchange.* In a simple technological economy with multipurposed productive units often derived from other forms of social organization and with a division of labor based chiefly on sex and age, a close calculation of the costs of doing one thing or another is often impossible or merely irrelevant. The advantages of a change in the use of time, resources, and personnel are arrived at through the logic of social structure, through a calculus of relative values, not in terms of the increase of a single magnitude such as productivity. This inability to estimate closely the costs and benefits of alternate forms of economic activity is aggravated by the absence of money as the medium of exchange. Most of the world now has some familiarity with the use of money, defined as tokens of exchange with generalized command over a range of goods and services. In fact, some societies developed highly generalized monetary systems prior to contact with the industrial and commercial West. And many societies have standards of exchange such as the Polynesian shell currencies, the tusked pigs of Melanesia, the cocoa beans of the Aztecs, and the salt currency of the horn of Africa. These currencies tend to be more restricted than money, which is not confined to a particular sphere of exchange. But all societies have goods and services of high value, and that value depends precisely on the social fact that they cannot be obtained for money (the Congressional Medal of Honor, election to a national honorary society, and so on). Currencies confined to a particular circuit of exchange, as among the Siane of New Guinea, can only be exchanged for specific classes of goods. Some goods may be exchanged only for subsistence items, others only for luxury items, and others only for items which confer status and prestige. The Tiv of Nigeria have a similar multicentered exchange system with media appropriate to each sphere of exchange. Food is exchanged for food and can be exchanged for brass rods; brass rods can be exchanged for the highest valued goods, women, and slaves. A reverse or downward movement of exchange items was severely resisted and considered illogical and unfortunate among the Tiv.

The media of exchange and the circuits of exchange are set into various kinds of systems of exchange. The most common exchange systems are markets, redistributive systems, reciprocal exchanges, and mobilizations exchanges. The major systems are not exclusive, and all four may be simultaneously functioning in the same economic system. The market system is widespread among peasants, and in Mesoamerica tends to be free, open, and self-regulating. In Haiti the market is free and open, but special bonds of personal attachment grow up between some buyers and some sellers which cut down the risks involved in small peasant trading. Rotating market centers, with a central market and several subsidiary markets (the solar system analogy), are a fairly common feature in Burma among the Shans, in several parts of Africa north and south of the Sahara, and in many parts of the Middle and Far East. These market systems usually operate without the presence of firms and lack investments in expensive exchange facilities, including the spread of information. The single complex of markets, firms, capital investments, entrepreneurs, deliberate technical investments, and property rules to facilitate accumulation and exchange—in short, capitalism—is apparently a historical precipitate peculiar to the West. In the ethnographic record it does not appear as a necessary bundle or sequence of events.

Reciprocity of exchanges is prototypically linked to gift-giving. Reciprocal exchange rests on fixed sets of trading partners, occurs between equivalent units of the social structure, and is either close-term, delayed reciprocity or an unbalanced form which may, over the long term, eventually be evened out. One interesting form of reciprocal exchange is the undischargeable debt. This is modeled on the kinship bond, and the Japanese notion of *on* (the gift of life from the parents) and as such is an unrepayable exchange. In the nonkinship sphere many southeast Asian societies have undischargeable debt mechanisms, like the "debt of the inside" in the Philippines. This unrepayable debt forms the basis for a "patron-client" structure. The rules of symmetry, equivalence, and balance characterize a reciprocal exchange network. Redistributive trade or exchange needs hierarchy, centrality, and imbalance to work. A political center gathers goods and claims services and then distributes these on the basis of social status, which carries with it a series of economic entitlements. An African paramount chief may collect tribute in the form of goods and redistribute it down the social hierarchy through his clients and kinsfolk. Administered trade at fixed prices with a political center exchanging with its peripheries is another example. There appears to be an increasing trend for redistributive exchange as the wealth of a society increases. The progressive income tax of modern industrial societies, the payments to the disadvantaged, the child-support systems are all redistributive devices. There are also the phenomena of redistribution upward in complex societies, such as government granted monopolies, license systems, or other forms of giving the well-to-do an extra competitive advantage. Redistributive systems rest on a series of notions of legitimacy of product claim, apart from economic performance. A mobilization system delivers goods into the hands of, and demands payment of services to, an elite for the broad political or expressive aims of the society. The irrigation empires of the early civilizations apparently had this sort of exchange system, and some of the new nations of Asia and Africa rely heavily on mobilization economies.

The fourth dimension of variation in economic systems is in *the control of wealth and capital*. Generally, investment takes the form of using resources and services to buttress or expand existing sets of social relations. Only recently in the human career have we witnessed the economic thrust of a society bent on social transformation. Land and labor are the chief capital goods in peasant and primitive societies. Tools, machines, terraces, livestock, and other improvements in the productive resources are controlled in a manner derived from the conventions of control and allocation of land and human beings. Land tenure is an expression of the social structure of a peasant and primitive society, and the allocation of land results from the operation of the system of kinship, inheritance, and marriage—and only marginally from the interplay of purely economic forces. Even in those societies where corporate kin groups such as clans do not exist as landholding bodies, special devices such as the establishment of titles or kindred-based landholding corporations may be invented, as on Truk. Manpower, like land, is also organized to flow in terms of given social forms, not to abstract best uses. Kinship and domestic organization and status groups are summaries and refractions of the rules governing the use, allocation, and replacement of the wealth and capital stock of a peasant and primitive society.

If peasant and primitive societies are to be maintained, capital, property rules, or economic chance may not be permitted to work in ways disruptive of the values and norms of the society. A fairly common device for insuring that accumulated resources are used for social ends is the *leveling mechanism*. The leveling mechanism is a means of forcing the expenditure of accumulated resources or capital in ways that are not necessarily economic or productive but conducive to the perpetuation of social forms and cultural integrity. Leveling mechanisms may take the form of forced loans to relatives or coresidents, a large feast following economic success, the ritual levies consequent on office-holding in civil and religious hierarchies as in Mesoamerica, or the giveaways of horses and goods of the Plains Indians. At any rate, most small-scale economies have a way of scrambling wealth to inhibit reinvestment in technical and economic pursuits, and this mutes the crystallization of class lines on an economic base.

This schematic presentation of the major features of peasant and primitive economies serves to place them in a comparative series of economic organizations to show the range of variety in the ethnographic record and to provide novel contexts for economic analysis. But since the economic system is but a subsystem of the total social system, how it relates to other subsystems and to the whole is a question of major theoretical importance. Economic action is only a part of the social action system, and must be integrated with the whole system. There are three major modes of relating economic action to the whole social system. This may be accomplished in three ways: (1) normative integration, (2) functional interdependence, and (3) causal interaction.

The ends sought in the economic sphere must be consonant or complementary, with goals in other spheres. Economic activity derives its meaning from the general values of the society, and people engage in economic activity for rewards often extrinsic to the economy itself. From this viewpoint, there are no economic motives, only motives appropriate to the economic sphere. The economy and technology, as the adaptive aspects of the social system, seem inherently to stray from the norms of the general society. To keep the economy normatively constrained there are economic activities which are legitimate, responsible, and socially useful. These are often derived from the major integrative aspects of a social system (religion, ethics, and expressive systems), on the one hand, and from the threat system (politics, law, public good), on the other. The economic system makes for organic cohesion and needs to be surrounded and confined by both values and force in order not to corrupt social integration and cultural cohesion.

The functional interdependence of economy and society

stems from the fact that economic actors are also actors in the other subsystems of organized social life, and that there are empirical limits to role incompatibility. The father's role must fit in some way with the believer's role in the ancestor cult, and these must fit in some way with the farmer's role, and these must all fit with the authority position in the lineage, to take an example from the Tallensi. This functional interdependence means that there are limits to the types of economies and societies that can coexist in the same time and space continuum. The marriage and descent system of the Nayar of Malibar (where husbands were warriors who lived away from wives and descent was matrilineal) is an instance of the functional compatibility of an occupational and status system with a marriage and descent system.

The causal interaction of economy and society turns on the pivot of the provision of facilities for the rest of the social system. The means of production and of reproduction are the basic subsystems of a society and enter intimately in determining the limits of the form and content of other subsystems. But the interactions are mutual—for a given social structure a given variety and volume of goods are required, and if there are shifts in available facilities, there will be shifts in the rest of the society. Conversely, shifts in social structure will change the volume and variety of goods and services a society produces. In times of abundance the polar Eskimo are kind and gentle with their aged; in times of near famine the old volunteer to die. The rate of infanticide is a direct function of economic levels of performance.

The empirical way of establishing causal interactions is to study peasant, primitive, and modern societies undergoing change. The facts of change, the actual historical continuum in a real world of time and space, not models or grand evolutionary guesses, are the only sure guides to generalizing on the sequences, forms, and processes of economic and social change.

Much of the observable economic changes in the life of primitives and peasants comes from the expansion and spread of Western forms of economic activities. This expanding economic frontier has some typical consequences, as in Orissa, the hilly tribal region of India. Here economic opportunity in the wake of the spread of the money economy has permitted some castes to move quickly up the status ladder and forced some traditional high castes downward. The economic frontier can most generally be viewed as a more or less dramatic change in the opportunity structures facing the small-scale society. Who can seize the new opportunity, who can benefit from it, and who will suffer from it, is of course a function of the social structure of the impacted small-scale society. But there have been some general across-the-board consequences. The spread of money and new opportunities tends to reduce the role of corporate kin groups and places more emphasis on smaller familial units. It also brings in its wake a growing division into wealthy peasants, poor peasants, and landless laborers, with the wealthy peasantry having a national orientation and the poor and landless becoming either a rural proletariat or the urban mob of new migrants.

Involvement in the world economy, however marginally, tends to make for increased economic instability, wider wealth differentials, pressure on traditional authority, and changes in religious and ethical concepts. The peasants of Kelantan in Malaysia own small rubber-producing holdings. The fluctuations in the world price of rubber determine the lavishness of their feasts, the frequency of visits to Thailand for entertainment, and even the number of sarongs a person owns. A boom in peasant agriculture often involves a change in religious and ethical concepts and an increase in economic activity relative to other forms of social activity. One other consequence of the economic frontier is usually to push the weakest economically to the wall. So peasants and primitives may wind up as the poor backwater of a developing nation, gradually getting depopulated as its young leave for greener economic opportunities. Peasant and primitive economies are not so much transformed as they are depeopled and hence collapse because there are not enough individuals to enact a viable role structure, though some societies have managed to weather this very general effect.

In the modern world the small-scale economies are facing problems of integration into national economies, while the national economies are facing similar challenges to productive integration into the international economic structure. The days of the typical "export" economy, usually within a colonial political system with an ethnic division of labor and an economy distorted for the needs of the metropole, seem over. But the international trade system in part perpetuates international economic stratification and, within nations, the marginality of the poorer peasants and primitives. It is one of the challenges of economic anthropology to do a close, empirical analysis of these situations, to lay bare the contexts of economic opportunity and those in a position to seize them, in order to understand better these contexts of economic change, perhaps even with a view to suggesting ways out of this unapplauded consequence of the spread of the money and industrial economy to the remotest reaches of human habitation.

What the studies of economic change have taught is that modifications in economic activity, usually engendered by exogenous forces, set up a series of pressures and tensions in the society and culture and that there are limited possibilities for their resolution. There is no generally agreed upon sequence of change and hardly more consensus on final forms, but the evidence seems to indicate that economic systems are among the most dynamic subsystems, and that economic activity, in the sense of provision of facilities for the organization of the rest of society, is one of the most pervasive and determinative aspects of social life. It sets the limits within which social structures and cultural patterns may fall.

In the coming decades economic anthropology will move more and more into the problems of economic and social change and the relations of the economy and society in modern, industrial societies. It will move toward a theory of causal interaction of economic variables with other parts of society and culture. Its greatest challenge and potential are the fashioning of a theory encompassing both economic and noneconomic variables in a single explanatory system. If successful, it will transform itself from economic anthropology to a *scientia rex*, a true political economy, as the major anchor of social science which is truly comparative and historical.

BIBLIOGRAPHICAL NOTE

Since the pioneeting studies of Bronislaw Malinowski's *Argonauts of the Western Pacific* (Reprint. New York: E. P. Dutton & Co., Inc., 1961), Raymond Firth's *Primitive Polynesian Economy* (Reprint. New York: W. W. Norton & Co., Inc., 1975), and Melville Herskovits's *Economic Anthropology* (Reprint. New York: W. W. Norton & Co., Inc., 1965), there have been a number of good summaries of the field: Manning Nash, *Primitive and Peasant Economic Systems* (New York: Chandler Publishing, 1966), Cyril S. Belshaw, *Traditional Exchange and Modern Markets* (Englewood Cliffs, N.J.: Prentice-Hall, Inc., 1965), and several collections of readings: E. E. Le Claire and Harold K. Schneider (eds.), *Economic Anthropology: Reading in Theory and Analysis* (New York: Holt, Rinehart & Winston, Inc., 1968), and Marshall D. Sahlins, *Stone Age Economics* (Chicago: Aldine-Atherton Publishing Co., 1972).

17.
SOCIAL ORGANIZATION

James L. Gibbs, Jr.

EPIGRAMMATISTS MAKE MUCH of the fact that man is the only animal who knows that ultimately he must die, and of the impact that this has on man's actions. Man is also the only animal who studies himself and his way of life. Clyde Kluck-hohn has called anthropology a "mirror for man" in which he can see himself in his infinite variety. Since the early workers in our discipline first silvered that mirror, we anthropologists, along with laymen, have been interested in describing the variations in the form of the human family and in human social groups and relationships. Why do some peoples inherit posi-tion and property through the mother while others inherit through the father? Was a matrilineal form of the family its earliest form? Is father-right or patriliny identical in all socie-ties in which it exists?

We anthropologists have always asked ourselves questions like these, but the answers we have given have varied between one of two extremes. On the one hand, we have explained man's family forms and kinship behavior in terms of some factor external to family and kinship—a factor in another segment of culture or even apart from culture itself, yet something which is part of the matrix or setting in which the family and kinship rests. Such an explanation accounts for matrilineal residence—where a man goes to live with his wife and her family after marriage—in terms of economic patterns. For example, where women are the owners of fields, and agriculture is largely in their hands, men will live with their wives' families. Such a theory we can call a "matrix-centered theory" because it explains family forms in terms of an element in the wider matrix in which they are found.

At the other extreme we have explanations that are narrower, which explain the family and kinship in terms of themselves, in terms of some inner dynamic. Such theories are tight and well ordered because they relate significant features of the family to other features of kinship or to very closely related institutions. Such an explanation uses the residence pattern to explain another feature of kinship, unilineal descent, which is the transmission of important social rights more through one parent than the other. For example: where men live in their wives' households, children will come to acquire the most important social rights through their mothers rather than their fathers. Such a theory we may call a "kinship-centered theory" because it explains one aspect of kinship in terms of another.

Which kind of explanation is right? Actually, the two types of theories are not mutually exclusive, but at different periods in the history of social anthropology one or the other type of explanation has been predominant. In recent years kinship-centered theories have been very dominant, but there is a current move in the other direction which is gathering momentum.

The matrix-centered theories which are re-emerging in American social anthropology represent a trend established by our early colleagues, the social evolutionists of the last century. These men, strongly influenced by Darwin's theory of organic evolution, were dominated by two concerns: to explain the variations in forms of marriage and the family in human society and to explain the development or evolution of human culture through time.

A view firmly held by most of the evolutionists was that matriliny, where descent is traced through the mother, is a very primitive form of family organization. It was found, they suggested, in societies in which the biological role of the father was unknown or where mating was so promiscuous that paternity would necessarily be in doubt. Moreover, many of them held, matriliny would lead to matriarchy or the concentration of economic, political and ritual power in the hands of women. That would be a natural reflection of the fact that matriliny was stronger in gardening societies where women performed most of the labor. In their unilineal view of human history, matriliny would, everywhere, ultimately be succeeded by patriliny, supposedly a higher form of family organization in which women hold a less exalted position.

The evolutionists were imaginative in framing matrix-centered theories to explain the presence of matriliny. We have seen that in turning to factors outside of kinship they noted beliefs about conception and the mode of subsistence. They placed a lesser stress on narrow kinship-centered explanations.

However, later advances in our knowledge proved the evolutionists to be wrong in some major ways. It was proven that matriliny is not associated with the simplest forms of subsistence and technology, nor with promiscuity, nor with the concentration of power in the hands of women. Finally the conclusion that matriliny preceded patriliny in the history of human society was also overthrown.

When evolutionism died out in the 1890s social anthropology in America veered off in a new direction. The evolutionists who had used broad, matrix-centered interpretations were wrong. Consequently, many anthropologists seemed to conclude not that those particular theories were faulty, but that *all* wide-scale systematic theories would probably prove to be incorrect unless they were based on more adequate knowledge of nonliterate societies.

Under the strong leadership of Frank Boas, American anthropologists energetically turned to the firsthand study of nonliterate societies, especially those of the vanishing North American Indians. These men did not deny the importance of seeking theoretical explanations of human behavior, as some have claimed; they simply felt that this task was so important that it should be postponed until they had gathered adequate descriptions of nonliterate societies from which *sound* deductions could be made.

While many evolutionists had been especially interested in the family and kinship, Boas and his followers were interested in man in each of his aspects. As field workers they concerned themselves with physical anthropology, archeology and linguistics. With such breadth of interest, the problem of understanding family and kinship was no more important to them than many other problems such as the role of folklore or the historical spread of American Indian cultures in the New World. Thus, studies of family and kinship were usually made only as a part of wider studies.

Both in their empiricism and in their moderate, cautious theorizing, the anthropologists of the Boasian period were reacting against the evolutionists. They avoided matrix-centered theories and turned to less speculative kinship-centered theories. Why, in some societies does a person call his mother's sister by the same kinship term that he uses for his mother? The evolutionists would have explained this first in terms of residence, saying that where my mother and mother's sister live in the same household they both care for me. Thus, I think of them as being alike and call them by the same term. Moreover, the residence pattern would, as we have seen, be explained in terms of economic matrix-centered notions. Kroeber, re-examining this question during the empiricist reaction, took a much more cautious view which some years later he renounced. He said that the use of kinship terms is really a matter of linguistics, of the way in which a language categorizes the world, and has nothing to do with either household composition or economic patterns.

The empiricists left us full descriptions of kinship practices in many societies, but they provided only incomplete answers to such questions as *why* people who speak widely divergent languages categorize their relatives in identical ways, or *why* in some matrilineal societies a man lives with his wife's people while in others, he takes his wife to live at his mother's brother's house.

In the 1930s American anthropology veered in still another direction. At this time in England Radcliffe-Brown and Malinowski were pioneering figures in a new approach in anthropology which can be called the comparative sociology of nonliterate societies. The impact of this school on America was intensified when both men came to teach in this country: Radcliffe-Brown at the University of Chicago, and Malinowski at Yale.

Social anthropology brought a blending of systematic theory building and systematic empiricism which led to a great refinement in the sophistication of explanations of social organization, especially of the family and kinship. This development of a specialized concern with social organization was given unique impetus and flavor by the fact that many American academic departments of anthropology were and are departments where anthropology and sociology are taught together.

The central concern of social anthropology is social organization, which has two aspects. One aspect is social structure, i.e., the network of social relations. This is the total pattern or repertoire of social position or statuses which a society offers its members and to which it fits them. The other aspect of social organization is the behavior or roles associated with the statuses or positions. Social organization, then, is a network of recognized statuses and the behavior patterns followed by people who occupy those statuses.

It was clear even to the evolutionists that most of the statuses that comprise social structure in nonliterate societies are kinship statuses. Thus, in studying social organization in the simpler societies, social anthropology is concerned largely with kinship, and kinship studies came to the fore again as social anthropology rose as a separate subdiscipline within cultural anthropology. The kinship organization of a society, like its general social organization consists of two parts: (1) a *structure* of kinship roles *and* (2) associated behavior. We have discovered that kinship organization has the attributes of a system. That is to say, the statuses and roles are arranged in an orderly pattern such that changes in one aspect of the system will lead to changes in other aspects. In recent years social anthropologists have discovered and stated rules about such changes—about the conditions that precipitate them and about the directions they will take under given circumstances.

Lewis Morgan, the evolutionist, first noted that the key to the system which underlies any kinship organization is its terminology. The kinship terms which members of society use for each other are themselves ordered in such a way that they reflect other features of the kinship organization such as the

types of kinship groups and the kind of descent. It is by
analyzing kinship terms as a kind of cryptogram that we social
anthropologists have gained many insights into kinship *as a
system.*

Such analyses are very detailed and abstract—almost mathematical. Detractors refer to them as "kinship algebra," while
others use the more neutral term, "componential analysis."
Thus, explanations of kinship organization in the 1950's were
in terms of highly refined kinship-centered theories, not
matrix-centered ones.

An influential classic study which demonstrated that kinship
organizations are systems which therefore change in predictable ways was George P. Murdock's research on kinship in a
sample of 250 societies. Professor Murdock demonstrated that
kinship organization as a system is arranged in such a way that
when the residence pattern changes, the form of kinship
groups changes and this in turn leads to a change in descent
which finally leads to a change in the kinship terms which
people use for each other. For example, if in a matrilineal
society most couples begin to reside after marriage with the
husband's family rather than with the wife's, this leads to a
change in the composition of households, later to a change to
bilateral descent and perhaps later still, a change to patrilineal
descent. Finally, there will be a change in the kinship terms
with which people refer to each other.

The systematic quality of other aspects of kinship organization was studied by other writers. For example, the interest in
matrilineal kinship organization which first aroused the evolutionists continued in the fifties. In 1954 the Social Science
Research Council sponsored a summer research institute on
matrilineal kinship systems and the papers which were prepared for that institute have recently been published in a
lengthy monograph. Part one of the monograph is by David
Schneider and it describes the features which characterize
matrilineal kinship systerms in general and explains, in
kinship-centered terms, why these features occur together. For
example, matrilineal societies everywhere are characterized by
a very close tie between brother and sister, and a weak tie
between husband and wife. In a matrilineal society a man's

children do not belong to his kinship group, but to his wife's, because they trace their descent through their mother—his wife. They inherit major property from their mother's family, not from his family. As a result, he has limited authority over them. In some ways he has stronger ties to his sister's children who do belong to his kin group because their mother does. As an adult male of their kin group he has authority over them. Moreover, as their mother's brother he will leave his property to them. These characteristic allegiances and cleavages are also reflected in kinship terminology.

From Schneider's analysis, we note that in matrilineal societies it is men, not women, who make the major decisions with regard to property and other matters, although the men are related through women. When we understand the reasons for the weak link between husbands and wives in matrilineal societies, we can better understand why such societies generally have higher divorce rates than patrilineal societies.

We have here a kinship-oriented explanation for the nature of sibling ties and marital ties. They are explained in terms of other connected kinship features, namely the type and locus of authority over women and children, and descent group membership.

Marital ties, in fact marriage in general, is an element in kinship organization which has always interested anthropologists. It remained a significant focus of analysis in the fifties. Some of the most sophisticated attempts to gain new insight into the role of marriage in kinship organization have started with an examination of kinship terminology which as we have already noted is a key to the way in which kinship organization is a *system*. As the evolutionists, the empiricists, and contemporary social anthropologists have all noted, there are a limited number of patterns of kinship terminology which recur again and again in human societies. We classify the patterns of kinship terminology in terms of the way in which they categorize cousins. Other research has shown that these basic patterns of kinship terminology are partly influenced by marriage customs.

A deduction from this principle led to an important insight into the function of a preferred form of marriage among the

Algonkian-speaking hunters of the northern regions of North America. These North American hunters have a kinship terminology in which cross-cousins, the children of one's father's sister or mother's brother are called by a special term. All the other cousins are called by the same term as a brother or sister. In these societies, one can*not* marry a cousin who is called brother or sister, just as one cannot marry one's real brother or sister. Similarly, one *can* marry a cross-cousin whom one does not call brother or sister. This suggested to some anthropologists that the Algonkian hunters practiced cross-cousin marriage, a type of marriage in which a man marries a woman who is his cross-cousin. An examination of kinship terminology for in-laws gave further evidence for this.

One might ask: what difference does it make what form of marriage is preferred by the Algonkians? Anthropologists had been puzzled as to what held together the small hunting bands of the Algonkians. There was no inherited political office and even no unilineal descent groups to assume important duties, and a constant shifting of families from one band to another. Fred Eggan has suggested that these bands were given unity and strength by the presence of cross-cousin marriage which enables them to remain small and isolated and thus able to successfully exploit their traditional hunting territories. This is because cross-cousin marriage is a way of linking related families over and over again in matrimony. Other studies such as that of Kimball Romney and P. J. Epling of the Kariera in Australia have also indicated the way in which marriage patterns can be strongly integrative in social organization.

Such an interpretation would not have been possible without componential analysis and the slow accumulation of precise principles concerning the interrelationship of terminology and other aspects of kinship.

However, the amount of range in kinship organizations is inherently restricted by the limited variation in the elements which are part of kinship organization. Because of this, we have reached the point of diminishing returns in making involuted studies of kinship organizations as relatively self-contained systems. In graduate seminars, at professional meetings, and in prophetic articles in professional journals critics of the work of the fifties have suggested that kinship processes and behavior have been neglected in favor of a narrow concern with structure. This restlessness is reflected in a current trend to studies which attempt to understand kinship not in terms of itself, but in terms of matrix-centered elements such as other aspects of culture or even environment.

Francis Hsu has recently reminded us that kinship organizations with identical *structures* may, nevertheless, be different in actual operation and feeling. This is because kinship organizations are partially shaped by the values or basic premises which pervade and direct each culture. Thus, individuals who live in societies with identical patrilineal kinship structures may behave quite differently even though they occupy parallel positions in those kinship structures.

To document this view, Professor Hsu uses a more intuitive and literary approach than that characteristic of most kinship studies in the fifties. He compares China and India and notes that while their kinship organizations are almost identical in structure they are very different in content, content which is molded by each society's basic values. The pervading value in Chinese culture is continuity of traditional ways from generation to generation. In the patrilineal kinship organization this results in a stress on the ties which link father and son in a chain of father-son bonds stretching far into the past. It results in a mutual dependence between father and son which inculcates submission to authority within the individual. It also leads to a very subordinate role for women whose primary duty is not to their husbands or even to their brothers, but to their husband's parents and their sons.

In India, on the other hand, with a virtually identical patrilineal kinship structure, the behavior patterns of kinship organization are quite different. There, one major value is diffuse spirituality or supernatural dependence. In the proper Hindu household there is segregation of the sexes which means that the young Indian boy spends his early years primarily with his mother or other women who answer all his needs. In the kinship system, this leads to a stress on the mother-son tie. Moreover, Hsu argues, the implication is that the dependence on the supernatural is first learned as this dependence on one's mother in the household. A related outcome is the lack of strong father-son tie in a society which is apparently heavily male centered. Although there is a male-centered descent group, it is one which is oriented about a pantheon of deities, many of whom are female. Thus, we see a strong contrast to the Chinese descent group centered on the ancestor cult.

I have simplified Dr. Hsu's argument which is very subtle and most provocative. We are left with the intriguing chicken-and-egg aspects of his problem. Is kinship behavior strongly shaped by a society's general values or are the values in the family generalized out to other social institutions? In any case, it is clear that values influence the patterning of kinship behavior.

Robert LeVine in a study of political behavior in East African societies makes a similar point, that values are similar both within the kinship organization and outside of it. He points out that in relatively homogeneous nonliterate societies, this makes it possible for early socialization and training in the family to serve equally well as training for political behavior outside the family. Thus, a stress on deference to elders is a strong value in many patrilineal East African societies. One learns this in the family with regard to one's older brothers, father, uncles, and granduncles. Later the same principle serves one in good stead as one becomes a member of the age-grades or a chief's council. We see again that values influence behavior both within the kinship sphere and outside of it, although we are still left with the question of whether kinship values or other values come first.

Values, then, form one aspect of the matrix in which kinship operates. Other recent studies by Service, de Gonzales, Foster and Barnouw have suggested further elements in this matrix which may also affect kinship—elements such as the total level of technological complexity, and the degree of stress in the form of acculturation. Gough and Aberle in the concluding sections of their monograph on matrilineal kinship mentioned earlier similarly related structures to outside factors such as mode of subsistence and ecology. In turning to these as explanatory factors, anthropology of the sixties returns to broader, matrix-centered theories in favor of the narrower kinship-oriented ones which have carried us to this threshold.

This trend indicates eclecticism, which has always been characteristic of American anthropology. It also indicates a self-conscious concern with theory, just as the choice of societies in which to gather data shows both a continuing concern with the American Indian and a parallel international focus as indicated by the wave of field studies in Africa, Asia, Latin America, the Middle East, and Oceania.

BIBLIOGRAPHICAL NOTE

A stimulating and clear presentation of the concepts and substance of social anthropology which provides insightful comments on the "meaning" of social organizational studies is in Paul J. Bohannan, *Introduction to Social and Cultural Anthropology* (New York: Holt, Rinehart & Winston, Inc., 1963). Sol Tax, "From Lafitau to Radcliffe-Brown," in Fred Eggan (ed.), *Social Anthropology of the North American Tribes* (2nd. ed., Chicago: University of Chicago Press, 1955), includes a concise historical treatment of most aspects of the treatment of social organization. A longer treatment of the work and lives of some of the earlier theorists appears in Robert Lowie's *The History of Ethnological Theory* (New York: Henry Holt & Co., 1937). A useful, concise, and astute overview of kinship appears in an article by John A. Barnes entitled "Kinship," in *Encyclopedia Britannica*, Vol. 10 (1974). Two works which are basic to the work of most contemporary American anthropologists who deal with social organization—especially kinship—are both oriented to the martix-centered approach to kinship; they are George P. Murdock, *Social Structure* (New York: Free Press, 1965), and A. R. Radcliffe-Brown and Darryl Forde (eds.), *African Systems of Kinship and Marriage* (New York: Oxford University Press, 1950).

Noteworthy examples of newer studies in social organization which reflect some of the recent trends noted in the present article include Fred Eggan *et al., Social Anthropology of the North American Tribes* (Rev. ed. Chicago: University of Chicago Press, 1955), and David Schneider and Kathleen Gough (eds.), *Matrilineal Kinship* (Reprint. Berkeley: University of Calif. Press, 1974). Shorter contributions such as journal articles reflect new trends in research more quickly than monographs, and they contain some of the most substantive and provocative contributions to the professional literature. Such social organizational studies are abstracted and commented upon in Harry Basehart, "Social Organization," in Bernard Siegel (ed.), *Biennial Review of Anthropology* (Stanford: Stanford University Press, 1959).

18.

EQUALITY AND INEQUALITY IN
HUMAN SOCIETIES

Lloyd A. Fallers

INEQUALITY APPEARS TO BE AN inescapable feature of the human condition. Thus far, the efforts of utopian reformers to eliminate it have failed, leading most students of the subject to conclude, with Robert Michels, that the life of man in society is bound by a kind of "iron law of oligarchy." And yet, in modern times particularly, the pursuit of equality has persisted, in both the aspirations of individuals and the goals of political movements, especially in the Western world. Most observers, while doubting the possibility of complete equality, would at the same time agree that these modern egalitarian movements and aspirations have met with an important degree of relative success. Today, furthermore, they are spreading to an ever widening circle of the world's people in the new states of Asia and Africa.

In what sense, then, is inequality universal and in what sense is equality possible? How far is the somewhat longer Western experience with the modern urge to equality an accurate guide for contemporary Asian and African peoples with similar aspirations—or for Western observers who wish to understand those aspirations? Anthropologists and other students of human society and culture try to answer these questions through the comparative study of societies of diverse kinds. Their investigations suggest that equality and inequality, like most social and cultural features which engage our attention, are complex phenomena which can best be understood by breaking them down analytically into their constitu-

257

ent elements. In this way we are able to see more clearly the different combinations of elements which produce the differences in actual social life that interest us.

Clearly one universal source of inequality is the tendency of every human community to develop, as part of its body of common culture, a system of values in terms of which persons may judge themselves and each other. These values commonly define for the community's members an image of the "admirable man"—the kind of man everyone would like to be. Such an image holds up both a standard of moral evaluation and a goal for personal ambition—a definition of what is worth doing and being, and why. Judged by such standards, persons are always in some measure unequal, though the qualities admired differ greatly from society to society.

But of course inequality is a more complex matter than this. If one primary root of inequality is moral judgment, another is the division of labor or—to use a broader and more accurate phrase, since what is divided is not always "labor" in the usual sense—the differentiation of social roles. Societies are never completely undifferentiated; they always distinguish behavior appropriate to people who differ with respect to sex, age and kinship, and usually with respect to other criteria as well. Moral evaluation takes account of these differentiations, holding up somewhat different images of virtue for husband and wife, elder and youth, farmer and priest. The result is a kind of two-dimensional moral evaluation among a society's members: Persons judge each other according to how well they perform their particular roles; but, because a people's system of values tends to have a degree of coherence, roles themselves are evaluated with respect to some central conception of excellence and virtue. We know of no people who do not have views concerning the relative merit, for example, of youth and age, of masculinity and femininity, and of various occupations.

Of course societies differ greatly in the number of roles they distinguish and in the number of distinct statuses, or bundles of roles, which are commonly combined in one social person. The societies which have been called "simple" or "primitive" are so called, in part at least, because they distinguish relatively few roles and, even more important, because these roles are typically combined into a very few statuses. Societies of hunting-and-gathering peoples often have quite complex systems of kinship roles, for example, as compared with those of modern Western societies, in the sense that they distinguish, and assign distinct behavior to, many more different kinds of kinsmen. But because the occupational structure is simple— because there may be only one adult male occupation, that of hunter and warrior, for example—there are very few distinct statuses. Since there are no occupational alternatives, each male and each female moves through the same complexes of age and kinship roles as his or her life progresses. In such societies there is essentially only one kind of man. The possibilities for inequality, apart from the age, sex, and kinship roles into which a person is born and grows, are for the most part limited to differences in the excellence with which he performs in the one occupational role which the society provides. Aboriginal Australian and most North American Indian societies were relatively egalitarian in this sense.

We usually think of modern societies also as being relatively egalitarian; certainly they have often aspired to be so. But their egalitarianism, insofar as it exists, must clearly be of a very different order from that found in aboriginal North America or Australia. For one of the characteristic features of modern societies is precisely the intricate differentiation of occupational roles which they exhibit—the wide range of occupational choices which they offer to their people. In such societies there are many different kinds of men: physicians and lawyers, farmers, priests and industrial managers, white collar and manual workers of many kinds. With this proliferation of alternative life careers—of relatively distinct statuses—the problem of equality and inequality becomes more complex in at least two important respects: On the one hand, this vast range of occupational roles invites relative evaluation in terms of society's common values, thus greatly increasing the possibilities for inequality. And, on the other hand, it also raises the problem of how all these alternative positions are to be filled—the problem of equality and inequality of opportunity to occupy the more highly valued roles. Modern egalitarian ideologies have sought both to reduce the inequality of evaluation of occupational roles and to increase equality of access to them.

But of course this comparison of very simple societies with very complex ones, while it teaches us something about the different meanings equality and inequality can have in different kinds of societies, nevertheless has a certain lack of relevance because it is so very unhistorical. Modern, highly differentiated societies have generally not developed out of very simple ones of the aboriginal North American type; they have rather grown out of the quite complex, but not yet modern, societies which occupied much of Europe, Asia, and Africa in ancient and medieval times. These have sometimes been called "peasant societies," sometimes "traditional civilizations." They were—and are, for some of them still exist—the most *un*egalitarian societies known to us—societies in which the different orders of men were sometimes so unequally evaluated as to be regarded almost as different kinds of creatures. Because they have provided the setting out of which, and against which, modern egalitarianism has grown, we may learn something about the modern urge to equality by examining the nature of inequality in these traditional peasant societies.

Characteristically, these societies were much more differentiated than the simple societies of which we spoke earlier, but still a good deal less differentiated than modern societies. More important, the kinds of differentiation which they exhibited served to maximize inequality. If we make use of the common image of the pyramid in thinking about inequality, these societies may be described as sharply "peaked" in form, with very small elites at the top and very large masses of peasants at the base.

Part of the gulf between elite and common folk was cultural. Most of these societies lay within the ambit of one or another of the literary world religions—Christianity, Islam, Hinduism, or Buddhism. Religion lay at the center of these cultures and everyone participated in it, but elite and peasants commonly participated in very different ways and degrees. Literacy, and hence direct access to the literary religious tradition, was limited to the elite and their servants. As a result there commonly developed, as Robert Redfield has reminded us, relatively distinct elite and folk variants of the common tradition—a phenomenon represented in medieval Europe, for example, by the aristocratic Christianity of nobility and knighthood, with its emphasis upon honor, *noblesse oblige* and military prowess, in contrast to the submissive piety of the peasantry, organized about the cycle of the agricultural year. The elite variant—more closely associated, as its bearers were, with the leadership of the church—was regarded as the higher or purer one—the one more nearly representative of the common values—and this judgment was in large measure accepted by peasants as well as aristocrats. Similar kinds of cultural stratification are revealed by studies of India and the Islamic world.

In some cases the traditional culture, with its religious foundation, added to this tendency toward cultural stratification a positive ideological defence of hereditary inequality. This was true of medieval Christianity, despite the egalitarian emphasis of the primitive gospel message. Medieval Christian philosophers could view the ranks of society as immutably fixed by God's will, like the parts of the human body, and could advise their people to avoid worldliness by serving faithfully in the statuses into which they had been born. Traditional Hinduism was even more explicit: Membership in the castes, ranked in relation to the proximity of their ritual practice to that of Brahmins, was in theory fixed for life. Closer approximation to the religious ideal, and hence social advancement, could come only through reincarnation.

On the other hand, Islamic ideology was apparently more egalitarian in both theory and practice: In the Koran and in the traditions, Muslims found a body of law—the *sharia*—which they sought to make a full and sufficient rule of life in this world for all believers without distinction. Islamic education was relatively accessible, and elites appear to have been more open to lowly-born persons who managed to acquire it. Something like the same situation seems to have prevailed in traditional China, where the acquisition of Confucian learning might enable a capable peasant lad to enter the ranks of the imperial bureaucracy.

However, though these differences in cultural attitude toward hereditary inequality were not unimportant, their practical effect was lessened by the kinds of economic and occupational structure which prevailed in the peasant societies. Where elites are very small and the common folk very numerous, the chances of any particular peasant boy's rising into the elite may be quite infinitesimal, whatever the culture may say about the rightness of his doing so.

(We may note, parenthetically, that the practical effect of such differences may be much greater at the elite level. Because of the small size of the elite, the recruitment into it of even relatively small numbers of persons of lowly origin may greatly affect its character—a phenomenon familiar in the history of the Islamic world.)

Elites in the peasant societies, then, were small and they were supported economically by the surplus beyond their own subsistence needs produced by numerous peasants. Intermediate groups—the traders and the craftsmen, whose products often exhibited marvelously high levels of specialized skill and aesthetic expression—were few, like the elite. They were, in fact, few essentially because they produced *for* the elite. There were no mass markets for their products. Peasants produced most of what they consumed and consumed much of what they produced—or as much of it as they could retain in the face of elite demands for taxes, dues, and tribute.

There was yet another feature of the occupational structure of the peasant societies which tended to fix a man in the social station into which he had been born. A man's occupation was very largely learned and carried out within his household. Both peasant lad and prince learned their occupational roles at home. The king's household was the government; the peasant's homestead was his enterprise. Traders and craftsmen taught these occupations to their sons and other young kinsmen through apprenticeship. For the most part there was neither an educational system nor a labor market external to the family to channel the young man into an occupation other than his father's. For the vast majority of people, family, school and work-place were one.

Thus, while the traditional peasant societies were quite

differentiated occupationally—while they contained many different kinds of men—these kinds of men were very unequal, both in the way they were evaluated with reference to the common culture and in their opportunities to occupy the more highly esteemed positions in society. It was out of sharply stratified societies of this kind, as they began to change into societies of the sort we recognize as modern, that the contemporary urge to equality developed.

It happened first in the West, in the lands of medieval Christendom. The reasons for this have been the subject of much debate among historians and others, but for present purposes we need not concern ourselves with this problem except to note that, because modern societies first developed in the West, and because the Western experience with modernity is more extensive, we are apt to fall into the habit of thinking of modernity as a peculiarly Western possession. We can easily come to identify as Western social and cultural features which may in fact be characteristic of modern societies wherever they develop, and vice versa. Let us, then, try to abstract from concrete historical experience those features of generic modernity which seem to be associated particularly with the modern urge to equality.

First of all, there is a cultural dimension of modernity which we may perhaps characterize as a commitment to the idea that human life is subject to unlimited improvement through systematic scientific investigation and its technological application. The roots of this idea clearly lie in classical antiquity, but its pervasive dominance over men's minds is, equally clearly, quite modern. Only in modern societies does innovation become routine and only in modern societies is it regularly applied to society and culture as well as to technological problems. Such an attitude is only with difficulty, if at all, reconcilable with the great religious systems which lay at the heart of traditional cultures. In the West, to the extent that it remains religious, a kind of deistic modus vivendi appears to have been arrived at, in terms of which the universe is viewed as the handiwork of a rational God, so that the attempt to understand its complexities may be regarded not only as permissible, but even as a religious duty. It would, however, be rash indeed to assert that the reconciliation between science and faith is complete. Outside the West, the outcome is perhaps still more problematical. For our purposes, however, the essential point is that the scientific attitude is incompatible with cultural conceptions in terms of which men were regarded as irrevocably unequal, irrespective of their needs and capacities. Instead, it tends to apply both to social roles themselves and to candidates for them the universalistic test of utility. This does not, of course, mean equality, but it does mean a constant questioning of the bases of inequality.

This attitude of innovative utilitarianism is given particular scope in modern societies by a second great differentiating characteristic—the modern type of occupational organization. It seems to have been Karl Marx who first pointed out the manifold consequences for society of the growth of occupational organizations distinct from the family and the resulting separation of work life from domestic life. Marx was preoccupied with one particular manifestation of this phenomenon—the factory worker and the insecurities which he suffered by virtue of having to sell his labor on an impersonal market, unshielded by the personal ties of mutual responsibility which had pervaded the peasant village. In the light of a further hundred years' experience, it is apparent that his insight, while profound, was incomplete. Modern societies have accepted responsibility for securing the worker's place in the labor market, but meanwhile his occupational situation—his position as a paid employee of an extra-familial organization—has spread to an ever increasing proportion of society's members. His employer, who in Marx' time was the owner of a family firm, has become a salaried manager. Civil servants—the employees of government—have become more numerous as the state has assumed wider responsibilities, and an increasing proportion of the practitioners of the learned professions have become employees of either state or industry. Even those islands of family enterprise, the farm and the small business, are increasingly treated—by the tax laws, for example—as organizations in which the owners employ themselves.

In short, there has come into existence a vast complex of organizations, outside the family, devoted to specialized tasks and employing persons in terms of their contributions to those tasks. At the same time, there have developed separate educational organizations charged with selecting and training persons for such tasks. The upshot is a kind of society in which the old connection between family and social status is broken. Not completely, of course, for so long as the family has any part in the training of children more highly placed persons will be in a position to confer differential advantages upon their offspring. But to a very marked degree in modern societies the allocation of occupational roles, and in turn general social status, depends upon performance in relatively impersonal educational and occupational structures. Again, this does not mean equality. The system is highly competitive and offers markedly differential rewards as inducements to achievement. But the logic of the modern industry or bureaucracy does involve continuous reassessment of both roles and persons in the light of technically-defined tasks. They are thus the institutional embodiment of the scientific-technological attitude of which we spoke earlier.

But the kind of equality to which modern societies aspire, and which their institutions enable them to achieve, is not merely a matter of providing scope for occupational achievement. It also has a political side: the demand, expressed in the ideologies of political movements, for some kind of popular participation in the state. This "politics of equality" has expressed itself in two principal directions. On the one hand, the state has been pressed to assume over-all responsibility for the progress of society in the directions defined by the scientific-technological attitude. Differences in view concerning the best means of fulfilling this responsibility—whether through direct state action or through securing the conditions for free competition, for example—tend to obscure what is basically the common attitude of all modern states: All assume the burden of both overseeing the technical efficiency and progress of the occupational structure and supplying their citizens with such services as education and health as means of participating in the occupational system on the basis of a rough equality of opportunity. The other principal expression of the "politics of equality" is the demand that these and other actions of the state reflect the will of the people. The modern state is populistic; whether or not its citizens actually participate in the formation of public policy, it must find means of securing at least the symbols of popular approval. It is precisely in this respect that modern authoritarianisms differ from traditional ones. The rulers of traditional peasant societies required only that their people obey; modern political leaders, whether democratic or authoritarian, must justify their acts as reflecting the popular will, even when this will must be determined by undemocratic means.

Thus the politics of equality in modern societies does not necessarily involve political democracy. Indeed, as Alexis de Tocqueville and others have shown, there is a sense in which equality may work against democracy. When egalitarianism takes the form of an insistence upon the elimination of all loyalties and groupings within society which differentiate individuals and stand between them and the state, the citizens become a mass of political atoms, more readily manipulable by the leaders of the state. Democracy appears to require a compromise with equality: a tolerance of differences among persons, of loyalties based upon occupation, economic interest, ideology, religion, or locality—loyalties which inevitably add to inequality, but which also diffuse the power of the state and provide the individual with the means to express his will within it.

These appear to be the major dimensions of equality and inequality in modern societies. In the past, students of society and culture have inevitably been greatly influenced in their thinking about such matters by the particular historical experience of the West, where modernity is older. But the contemporary spread of this complex outside the limits of the Western cultural tradition holds out the intellectually very exciting prospect of a natural laboratory in which our ideas concerning the nature of modernity, and the place of equality within it, may be tested. We may learn, for example, that different traditional cultures are differentially hospitable to egalitarian ideas, and that they find different kinds and degrees of difficulty in dealing with the scientific-technological attitude. We may discover that kinds of group loyalties unfamiliar to the West are capable of mediating between individual and state in a manner which nourishes democracy. Thus we may come to understand a bit more clearly, and perhaps be able to inhabit with greater comfort, a world in which modern egalitarianism, its privileges and responsibilities, are no longer the monopoly of people of Western culture.

BIBLIOGRAPHICAL NOTE

Robert Michels sets out his "iron law of oligarchy" in *Political Parties* (New York: Free Press, 1949). The most ambitious attempt to systematize the theory of social stratification is that of Talcott Parsons, "Revised Analytical Approach to the Theory of Social Stratification," in R. Bendix and S. M. Lipset (eds.), *Class, Status and Power* (New York: Free Press, 1953). This volume also contains many other important papers on the subject. The "fathers" of the study of social stratification are Karl Marx and Max Weber. The best selections from their writings on the subject are in T. B. Bottomore and M. Rubel (eds.), *Karl Marx: Selected Writings in Sociology and Social Philosophy* (London: C. A. Watts, Ltd., 1956), and Hans Gerth and C. W. Mills (eds.), *From Max Weber: Essays in Sociology* (New York: Oxford University Press, 1946). The best discussion of stratification in simple societies is that of Gunnar Landtman, *The Origin of the Inequality of the Social Classes* (Reprint. Westport, Conn.: Greenwood Press, Inc., 1968), while the best on peasant societies is that of Robert Redfield, *Peasant Society and Culture and the Little Community* (Reprint. Chicago: University of Chicago Press, 1960). Louis Dumont's *Homo Hierarchicus: The Caste System and Its Implications* (Chicago: University of Chicago Press, 1970) provides the best general account of the caste system of India, while Hamilton A. Gibb and Harold Bowen, *Islamic Society and the West: A Study of the Impact of Western Civilization on Moslem Culture in the Near East* (New York: Oxford University Press, 1950) describe the less rigid inequalities of Ottoman society. Alexis de Tocqueville's influential ideas concerning social stratification and modern politics may be found principally in his *Democracy in America*, 2 Vols. (New York: Alfred

A. Knopf, Inc., 1946) and his *Old Regime and the French Revolution* (Garden City, N.Y.: Anchor Books, 1955). My own views on the subject as a whole are presented more fully in *Inequality: Social Stratification Reconsidered* (Chicago: University of Chicago Press, 1974).

19.
THE STUDY OF POLITICS IN ANTHROPOLOGY

Morton H. Fried

FOR THE PURPOSES OF this article, *politics* is defined as the total complex of power relations within and between societies. Politics refers to the differential possession and application of power, and the symbols and surrogates of power, by individuals, groups, aggregates, whole societies, and coalitions of whole societies. At whatever level political phenomena are manifest, they are directed at the behavior of individuals and groups, manipulating it by a wide variety of means to a great diversity of ends. For the most part, those ends have real content, so that one outstanding political scientist defined politics as "Who gets what, when, and how." The remainder of this essay is devoted to an explanation of these remarks of definition, plus an attempt to show where anthropologists enter the study of politics and some of the things they have learned as well as some of the questions they continue to pursue.

Some definitions of politics are so broad that they literally include every facet of behavior—at least the behavior of *Homo sapiens* or, for that matter, what we can reconstruct of the behavior of nonsapiens culture-bearers (for example, *H. erectus, Australopithecus*). *Webster's Eighth New Collegiate Dictionary*, for example, includes: "5. the total complex of relations between men in society." (Let us charitably assume that the use of "men" in that phrase is the generic for people—a tough assumption because of the tremendous downgrading of women specifically in the political realm.) The phrase is so broad that it has to include, off the top of my head, the use of kinship terminologies, dining etiquette, behavior at ball games, seat selection at the airline counter, and interaction with the checkout clerk at the supermarket. The trouble, of course, is that any of these things can be carried out in a thoroughly political way. In the early and middle 1950's references to the Soviet Union in the People's Republic of China frequently were couched in kinship terms, the USSR being conceded a favored age status ("older brother"); with the subsequent dramatic change in Sino-Soviet relations, the kinship terminology was dropped in favor of epithets, "revisionist" and "fascist." As for dining etiquette, few situations are more latently political than those involving commensality. Who eats with whom is a political question as old as politics. Modern states have specialized officers of protocol who make out guest lists and seating arrangements and choose politically informed menus. An Irish politician in New York expands his base of support by eating *knishes*; his Jewish colleague poses with a slice of pizza. A president of the United States solidifies his relations with the electorate by feeding the king and queen of England hot dogs at Hyde Park. Which reminds us of the political use of sports and behavior at ball games. The American president used to open the baseball season, of course, by throwing out the first ball. This has been curtailed by the exile of the Washington team and the flurry of political assassinations. Incidentally, for any political official to leave a game before the outcome is pretty well sealed is to court a serious drop in popularity, although supplying plays to a professional football coach is considered endearing by the populace. In fact, concrete examples can be given of the use of almost any conceivable human activity as a political event.

So protean are political phenomena that the development of a coherent discipline of political science has been inhibited. As noted by David Easton, from ancient times almost to the present century "the study of political life remained not a discipline in the strict sense but a congeries of inherited interests." Even now, for similar reasons, Easton describes his field as still in search of its identity. It is worthwhile to harp on these views of Easton because, as Edwin A. Winckler has noted, "Easton is the political scientist most often referred to in anthropological writings on politics." I think it particularly interesting that Easton worries so about the identity of political science, because he has taken a leading role in the attempt to strip politics of the central element in its definition, namely, *power*. Early in his career, Easton came out heavily against the concept of the state, asking that the word be totally abandoned. Although Easton's reasoning is complex, I think his basic motivation for requesting elimination of the concept of the state is simple. The analysis of the state makes sense only when it is viewed in terms of power and exploitation; the concept of state is inherently one of classes, differential access to strategic resources, varying standards of living and unequal access to force and power. In many forms of the state, however, the ideological underpinning of the system, its legitimation, requires the denial of all of these things. Such states claim to be free of class divisions, unequal access (opportunity) and class conflict and deny the existence of raw power by which the conduct of all is finally directed into approved channels. The house philosophers in such systems (which, incidentally, include those in the socialist camp as well as the bourgeois or capitalist camp) align their theories to support the official myths. I do not wish to characterize particular scholars as "house philosophers," but I cannot refrain from noting the development of Easton's thought on this matter. While Easton recognizes an earlier utility of the power concept in the analysis of political phenomena, he has been consistent in following his previous rejection of the concept of the state by voicing growing dissatisfaction with continued employment of the power concept.

Although possibly sharing final conceptions of political organization, certain other social scientists present a view of power diametrically opposite to that of Easton. This contingent of scholars sees a drive for power as a universal characteristic of human (and some include prehominid) social life. It is declared to be an intrinsic feature of the human "biogram" rooted in physical evolution. To hold this position it is necessary for these scholars to disregard major portions of contemporary evidence drawn from primate ethology. It is by such means, for example, that Lionel Tiger and Robin Fox can sweepingly pronounce that "whatever the details of the system, certain underlying processes are obvious despite the diversity of surface structures." Tiger and Fox then assert that hierarchy and status competition are universal among terrestrial primates, determining access to resources and sex; that dominance is a universal phenomenon in these populations; that females play political roles by furthering the progress of particular males; that the whole social fabric is dependent on male "bonding" and the possibility that "charismatic individuals can upset the hierarchical structure, and by the same token, retain power." It is not surprising that in their next sentence Tiger and Fox find that "these rules apply to human beings as well."

Having come so far into power, I had better say quite directly what I mean by it. Power is the ability to compel the behavior of others. At the root of the concept of power is the notion of force, but the use of force is an ultimate recourse; it may not be brought forth at once and, indeed, may not be concretely manifested in some behavioral sequences at all. Quite often force is represented symbolically or is exercised by intermediate figures, referred to in my original definition as *surrogates* or substitutes. One of the main reasons anthropologists have become deeply enmeshed in the study of political systems is because they are interested in the almost inextricable intertwining of political and general cultural systems. In parallel fashion, social anthropologists seek to tease out what is political in the general fabric of relations within and between societies.

In a simple model of force we confront the image of the physically strong individual whose violence, or the threat of whose violence, can induce or lead to the suppression of specific behavioral manifestations on the part of associates. We move quickly beyond such a model, however, because simple size and strength do not always identify leading animals even where there is a dominance hierarchy. And, it should be stated right now, dominance hierarchies are not universal, certainly not among primates. As a matter of empirical fact, those primates that are regarded as being phylogenetically closest to

hominids, chimpanzees and gorillas, show the fewest indications of dominance in their social patterns. Even among
primates showing strong dominance hierarchies, however,
other factors intrude in addition to size, sex, and strength. Most
interesting is the shifting coalition, the possibility that two or
more animals that can be identified as relatively weaker than
one or more others in physical terms, can use their combination to offset or neutralize the potential force of those others.

Rather than go further with such excursions in comparative
ethology, it might be better to question the basic premise that
selected observations on nonhuman societies can be a useful
guide to the understanding of political events and structures in
human society. Once again it becomes necessary for us to step
back a bit to ask how our patterns of thought are shaped by our
existing sociocultural milieu. It may well be that the tendency
to see dominance hierarchies and power struggles everywhere
is a reflection less of universal truth than of our own social
system and its antecedents of the past few thousand years. Nor,
as indicated earlier, is this merely a matter of academic
interpretation, because the insistence on the universality of
power conflict is a highly active contemporary political doctrine that serves to legitimate the present unequal distribution
of power with regard to individuals, classes, and nations.

To the extent that power is used in interpersonal relations,
we may say that a political event has occurred. In this broad
usage there is a politics of friendship, of family relations, of
sex. It is frequently useful, however, to narrow the concept.
This is often attempted by restricting the field of political
events to those which involve public rather than private
aspects of a society or have public effects. The briefest consideration of this public/private distinction will reveal many
difficulties, even with due consideration for the qualification
that it is the effects that are critical. Thus, there are few things
more political than the secret cabals of power holders and
power seekers; while it is true that such activities have broad
public significance, no one may ever know that they occurred.
The highest political official in a state may forever deny
starting in motion (or covering up) a process of theft, obstruc-
tion of justice, perjury, and so on, while the alleged actions

have the most ramified political consequences. Conversely, the sudden appearance of a number of naked people streaking across the campus, through the bank, or in any other thoroughly public place (just to take one recent popular craze) may reflect important things about the state of public morale, but it is basically devoid of particular political significance. Still, there are those who associate such activity with a general defiance of authority, which seems unlikely, although we know that the Dukhobors, a religious sect, have used nakedness as a political weapon.

In any event, the duality "public/private" is very much a cultural artifact. While every culture provides some social distance-setting mechanisms that loosely fill out the rubric of privacy, the actual mechanisms are so diverse as to make distillation of a valid cross-cultural standard exceptionally difficult. I, for one, cannot readily apply the dictum of some anthropologists, that declares "a political process is public rather than private." (Swartz, Turner, Tuden 1966, p. 4) Let me illuminate my problem with privacy by offering a specific instance which, I think, critically challenges our own conception of privacy and does so in a clearly political context. It was reported from the Soviet Union some years ago, when students from the People's Republic of China were still present in large numbers in Moscow, that one such student desired to keep a photographic record of his stay. So he skipped meals and purchased a camera and film with the money he saved. When his fellow students discovered this, they took him through a number of struggle sessions until he finally sold his camera and turned over the money to the group. He did this because he was brought to agree that, being a student sent by the PRC, it was his obligation to the Chinese people to keep his strength at maximum and therefore not to forego meals, particularly not for a personal acquisition such as a camera. It is an integral part of this cross-cultural note on privacy that the anecdote was apparently told and retold with horror by Russians who with it sought to confirm some of their worst fears about the Chinese.

Having mentioned the Chinese, we can turn to none other than Mao Tse-tung to tip us again into the question of the relations between power and politics. One of Mao's most famous aphorisms is "Political power grows out of the barrel of a gun." Mao, citing Lenin, says that "war is the continuation of politics by other . . . means." However, the remark does not originate with Lenin, but, as Lenin indicated, with the old Prussian militarist, Carl von Clausewitz, who said: "War is not merely a political act, but also a real political instrument, a continuation of political commerce, a carrying out of the same by other means."

Many political anthropologists have joined ranks with colleagues in other disciplines—among them David Easton and Talcott Parsons, and Edward A. Shils, to deplore the placing of force at the center of the concept of politics. As Swartz, Turner and Tuden state:[1]

> Despite its undeniable importance, insuperable difficulties confront the view that force is the sole, or even the major, basis of political behavior. These difficulties arise from the fact that force is a crude and expensive technique for the implementation of decisions. More importantly, force itself has to depend on interpersonal relationships that are based on something other than force.

One of the logical paradigms behind such reasoning is that of the infinite receding network of police believed to be required to maintain a society by force alone, for surely even police, in turn, have to be policed. This is rather like the Eleatic paradox of mobility: How can anyone take even one step, because before taking a full step one must take half a step, before half a step one must take a quarter step, and so into infinity, negating any steps at all? This was long a stumper, though it never interfered with anyone's taking all the steps he or she wanted to. Finally, Bertrand Russell suggested that if one wished to make an infinite number of divisions of a step, so one should simultaneously make equivalent divisions of the time elapsed in taking the step. The two infinities cancelled each other; hence the step could be taken.

If force seems so finite as to be "crude" and too "expensive" for extensive use, terror is infinitely expandable and can be generated on relatively small capital. It is also necessary to call into question the seemingly ahistorical thrust of the previously

1. Marc J. Swartz, Victor M. Turner, and Arthur Tuden, *Political Anthropology* (Chicago: Aldine Publishing Company, 1966).

quoted remarks by Swartz and his colleagues. Unless those remarks intend to say only that force is not continuously exerted in any known society, a statement with which it is impossible to disagree, the spokespeople miss the point, for no one, to my knowledge, has ever asserted that any society is built about the unceasing application of violence. That is a straw man. What is arguable is that in all state societies the power that maintains the state rests ultimately upon force and violence to which such states usually claim monopoly of access. The myth of the monopoly of violence claimed by the state is one aspect of its legitimacy and authority. A closely related aspect is the intertwining of legal norms, whether specified in codes or not, police power, legislation, adjudication, and other paraphernalia of jurisprudence, whether conducted in marble courts or yamens or beneath a tree deemed sacred. Most decisions made in such systems will be followed by individuals who are found against, without any suggestion that failure to comply will ultimately unleash a terrible power that will crush resisters or change their life in ways they would rather not. Yet, ultimately, in all such systems there is the original catch: If you are good, you will admit you are wrong and take your punishment; if you are bad, you will deny it and take your punishment.

Although this is a survey article, we have still come too far, too fast. Further explanations are needed of things already said. Let me begin, however, with a view contrary to that of Tiger and Fox. In my view, the growth of political power was a very slow process. I believe that the vastest portion of the period of existence of hominids and cultural society knew little or no political power. The combined evidence of archeology and ethnology suggests to me that at the earliest it was only in very late Paleolithic times, say twenty thousand years ago, that a regular economic basis began to develop for concentrations of political power in specific individuals and groups in some ecosystems, although not in others. Let me explain.

While details of the organization of specific human societies probably showed some variety even in the earliest cultural times, certain gross patterns, characteristics, and trends can be described for the entire period running from the advent of cultural society to the present. To begin with, there is no doubt that political society has evolved. We can be specific about what has evolved. Social units have increased in demographic mass, in the complexity of their divisions of labor and other divisions of role. They have evolved in the degree of separation and the increasingly hierarchical arrangement of statuses, the association of some statuses with preferential rights of access to strategic resources and the concomitant birth of exploitation, and the growing separation and specialization of political roles in society. These evolvements, which by no means exhaust the list, are among the key sociopolitical changes since the inception of massive cultural processes. It is obvious, but worth mentioning, that not all societies underwent parallel development; some world regions saw rapid advances for a time, then a slackening, with the next general evolutionary steps occurring elsewhere. Other areas saw few advances of a general kind. [2]

One conventional way this evolution has been described with reference to political organization has been from family to band (or horde) to tribe to confederacy to state. A frequently encountered Marxist formula begins with primitive communism, proceeds through classical slave city-states and empires to feudalism, through capitalism (bourgeois state) to socialism, with communism regarded in the offing as the end of the state. [3]

There are a number of such "ideal type" schemes, but I should like to give a synopsis of my own, which takes its departure from a hypothetical model of "egalitarian society," proceeds through "rank society" into "stratified society," and culminates in the emergence of the state. For the purposes of

2. The concept of general evolution here used is that which, in tandem with the concept of specific evolution, was refined by Marshall Sahlins and others. Briefly, specific evolution is Darwinian "descent with modification," a change of ramification of types to fit shifting selection pressures. General evolution is not necessarily viewed phylogenetically but emphasizes any quantum leap in organization, such that a higher degree of energy flow or a conspicuously more efficient one is achieved or a grossly larger biotic mass is supported, and so on.

3. We have no space to go more deeply into the matter, but it has to be noted that Marx himself indicated another view in which the unilinear sequence just rendered is broken by a specific alternative, namely, the "Asiatic Mode of Production" associated with the great agrarian/irrigation/despotisms such as Persia, India, and China.

this chapter, the model will be pared to its political and economic essentials.

The earliest and simplest form of human society I call *egalitarian,* but that is in some sense a misnomer, since no real society composed of our kind of animal can ever be completely egalitarian. Take the matter of our biosocial means of bringing forth and developing young; quite evidently a three-months-old infant is poorly equipped to fill a decision-making status (but some three-months-old infants have occupied such statuses—in which cases an adult substitute, we sometimes call them "regents," actually carried out the political work in the child's name). At times a very old person may encounter equal difficulties. In any event, I do not have to work too hard to convince you that age is a ubiquitous factor leading to at least temporary inequality in all human societies.

Sex seems to have played a similar role in the differentiation of all human societies, but its functioning is much less obvious, much more complex, than age. With the political consciousness of women becoming a major political factor in our own society, the question of the history and evolution of female status has become increasingly controversial and also increasingly important.

Despite some feminist assertions, there is a mythology, but no hard evidence, of any archaic system of matriarchy, political dominance of females, in any human society. Even in known societies with matriliny and matrilocality, such as Iroquois and Nayar, men have tended to dominate political sectors of the culture. Yet the problem is knottier than such simple statements suggest. If sex has operated as an ubiquitous factor leading to at least temporary inequality, I think it is not because of any differences of size, strength, or endurance. Rather, it has to do with the total social patterning of early human society and its subsequent historical development. Given the sharp differentiation of female and male roles in procreation, we have a marked predisposition toward the development of a similarly differentiated sexual division of labor. This is underlined in those societies in which chronic needs for defense require some degree of specialization for carrying out violence. For reasons advanced by Marvin Harris, it is likely that such specialization would devolve upon males, at least until the technological revolution of recent times which has obviated such a concentration of specialization.

Even in the face of such reasoning, however, I find that I cannot quite take seriously the view that ancient society was characterized by the unqualified political dominance of men. I am plagued with doubts that arise from wondering if this is not a view developed out of more recent cultural experience. It seems to me that in truly primitive society the distinction between male and female spheres are too profound and at the same time too fundamentally based in survival pressures for the question of higher and lower status to make much sense. I therefore tend, at least provisionally, to agree with Peggy Sanday, an anthropologist, who says that "there was probably a relative equality between the sexes initially." I have some difficulty following her, however, when she says, "but . . . men were in a strategic position to gain power as resources began to accumulate, since they had easier access to such resources." For one thing, as far as my own understanding of this matter has developed, I believe that the process of individual or group accumulation of strategic resources is a very recent invention, perhaps of the past twenty thousand years. The inferential evidence, based on comparative ethnography, is that cases of inferior female status are much older.

Having perhaps whetted your appetite for deeper discussion of this major and intriguing problem, I may irritate you by suddenly dropping it. It may well be that the sexual division of population is the original class division, that women, as a class, are the original exploited mass, that their exclusion as primary parties from the emergent political process may be the first major watershed in the emergence of the political process itself. I see these as important hypotheses, but I cannot presume to discuss them adequately in a chapter as brief and circumscribed as this, though the reader should keep them in mind while considering what follows.

Though egalitarian society is imperfect in its equality, it is characterized, by and large, by the presence at any particular

time of as many positions of valued status as there are
individuals in the society capable of and willing to assume
such positions. [4]

Thus, in an Eskimo encampment, there is no fixed number of
ermecin ("strong men"), certainly not *one*, the paramount one,
top dog, king of the hill, but as many as there happens to be.
Some encampments have two or three, others one, but the
actual number is a transient figure. What is more, Eskimo
society knows competition and killing, too. But the contests
and murders do not usually act to thin out a population of
contenders for status. Quite to the contrary, it is likely that
threat of desertion, of losing human company, was a major
sanction within Eskimo social groups.

In an egalitarian society there is little or no power, but there
may be some recognition of influence and authority. [5]

The absence of power is readily spotted because there are no
commands in such a society. People may or may not bow to
suggestion, but no one can control the behavior of another. Our
own experiences in this area are so massive as to make it
difficult to imagine such a world, devoid of power and command. Our world, by contrast, is one where coercion is conspicuous among the means of regulating an infant's control over
its bowels and sphincter, of conducting family life, and of
adjusting differences between nation-states classified into violence categories as *powers* and *superpowers*. On the contrary,
in the ethnography of egalitarian societies we see almost
nothing of violence as a means of getting a group to run

4. While the overall organization of specific societies may show an evolution
from the egalitarian form to the ranking form, to the stratified form, to the state
form, enclaves of egalitarian organization or egalitarian ideology may remain.
For a lovely example in our society, showing how conflict over egalitarian
ideology and the actualities of ranking and stratification played a major role in
vitiating the New Left, particularly in its student aspect, see John C. Leggett,
Taking State Power: The Sources and Consequences of Political Challenge
(New York: Harper & Row Publishers, Inc., 1973).

5. The distinction between these things, often indicated in dictionaries as
synonyms, is neatly conveyed in Lord Acton's memorable remark: "Power
tends to corrupt and absolute power corrupts absolutely. Great men are almost
always bad men, even when they exercise influence and not authority." Which
bears comparison with a remark by George Washington made when he was
exasperated at the ineffectiveness of government between the time of the
British surrender at Yorktown and the establishment of the Constitution and
the republic in 1789. Washington wrote: *"Influence* is no *government."*

smoothly. This pertains with particular strength to the conduct of infancy and childhood. In such societies, parents do not coerce their children into doing or not doing things. For the most part they are unconcerned. Kids are not ordered to bed or commanded to rise; they are not hounded to eat; they are not supervised in their games and play; they are not criticized for hanging out with certain associates. To some extent young ones exist under the eyes of older children, but these rarely interfere in any direct way. One grows up in a milieu totally different from that which most kids in our society know. It is not surprising that adult behavior should be different too.

In such societies the process of decision making occurs without seeming to. Consensus is as close as we can get to it. Such a regime has no chief. Indeed, as I argue elsewhere, in such a social setting there are no tribes—certainly not as the "tribe" is conventionally understood, as a population sharing a common heritage and a common political structure. Instead, there are, on the ground, so to speak, communities, shifting encampments, probably with shifting populations as well. Some people move into a group, others leave. The group becomes attached to one or more other groups for a time; then the larger aggregation breaks up again, but probably into smaller groups not quite the same as those that originally joined to form it. In some instances, there could be violent interaction, even killing. Usually, however, it is likely, particularly in the remote, less populous past, that threats and insults would suffice if, indeed, generally peaceful relations did not prevail. It hardly seems necessary to say that the economic arrangements underlying such a society would be devoid of mechanisms of individual accumulation, on one hand, and of exploitation, on the other.

As a consequence of various congeries of factors, including increasing population density, technological development, mounting ecological specialization, and the like, human society probably began to go through a set of economic changes that had major consequences for the organization of social relations and, of course, politics as well. One of the decisive changes seems to have involved the great increase in significance of a second kind of economic integration, by which we mean the systematic organization of the patterns of exchange by which any given society is pulled together. The earliest widespread form of economic integration in cultural society was what we usually call reciprocal—exchanges between individuals, implying a simple to-and-fro movement of goods and services, without the formation of significant nodes (clusters of exchanges). The system is considered reciprocal because each act of giving is theoretically balanced by an act of getting, although this aspect varies in different types of reciprocal system. In such systems restrictive access to strategic resources simply does not exist and all goods tend to circulate, making them relatively available. Accordingly, there are proportionately few bases for conflict in an egalitarian society. The absence of nodes also correlates with the absence of political power; there are no individuals in such societies who can function to command settlements when disputes arise. There may be individuals who have some influence, but this, the least substantial of terms relating to the interpersonal determination of behavior, is completely advisory, mediating and neither compelling nor binding.

The second form of economic integration does not put in a late appearance, for in some form it is probably as old in human society as is reciprocity. I refer to *redistribution*, which is characterized by the flow of goods into a center (usually in simple situations by coming to one particular person) and subsequent flow out of that center (for example, through a feast organized by the redistributor). In a sense many familial economies run on this model. Of great interest is the observation that in simple redistributive setups the individuals serving as the centers often work harder and consume less than anyone else. Such individuals are powerless but may well develop influence and even authority beyond anything known in reciprocal/egalitarian society. Still, in the final analysis, such roles are extremely limited in decision-making and decision-implementing force. Any effort on the part of such primitive redistributors to command the behavior of others would likely send fellow producers off after more lenient colleagues. Precisely lacking power, arrogant redistributors would be unable to retain their clientele.

Out of such germs emerges what I call the rank society, one in which there are fewer positions of valued status than individuals desirous and capable of filling them. The limitation of access to status is often based upon accidents of birth. Thus the first son (such systems usually display marked preference for males in such statuses, even if the society in question has matrilineal descent and uxorilocal residence) of the first son, and so on, is not infrequently the occupant of such a status. As just indicated, the original position of redistributor is devoid of or quite weak in political power, but it seems evident that with various concatenations of events (differential productivity, varied environments, differential sizes and densities of population, and so on) the role of redistributors was enhanced and transformed. From self-exploiters, redistributors ultimately developed into managerial specialists and either began to command real political power themselves (as an extension of their role in the organization of production as well as distribution) or saw the emergence of a separate set of social functionaries carrying out these roles.

Further complexity was added when stratification appeared. Rank societies are not necessarily characterized by differential access to strategic resources among their members. But in some societies, again under differing sets of conditions, there emerged a concept of exclusive access—some form of private property in strategic resources. Sometimes the privacy of property relations was completely obscured by the vesting of title exclusively in the ruler. All others would pay for the privilege of access in some way. The systems vary greatly and the details cannot concern us here; suffice it to say that with such a development there arose concrete systems of exploitation—basically, the return to a producer of only a portion of the product of the producer's labor. Societies characterized by such unequal access I term *stratified.*

Stratified societies require increasingly elaborate mechanisms of power in order to maintain themselves. Some force is derived directly from control of resources, which is to say that some people accept lesser status in return for limited access rights. But social contract is not sufficient to hold such a society together, now or ever. Behind all the understandings which comprise the charter of legitimacy in such a society there lies the force of violence. But stratified, nonstate societies lack sufficient means of violence, or the organizational means of bringing it efficiently into action, to provide a secure and continuous legitimacy to the social order. In the face of real inequality and exploitation, such an order can be sustained in a simple and stratified society only for a relatively brief period of time, a few generations at most. The most devastating contradiction faced by such a society is that between its once and yet continuing kin basis and the new demands for the exclusion, wholesale, of relatives from rights of primary access to strategic resources. The new order, which is to say the state order, is one in which kinship is relegated to a minor role so far as the distribution of wealth and power is concerned, except for a handful, the elite. A stratified society, then, to a greater extent than any other kind of society specified in this series of types, is structurally in crisis and therefore ephemeral. Such a society must quickly—say, in a few generations—develop the specialized institutions of state organization, or it faces a structural compulsion to retreat, succumbing either to internal forces of dissolution (that is, return to the form of a ranking or even an egalitarian society) or to external forces (conquest, annexation, absorption by a fully state-organized society).

The state, then, is a system of organization of the power of a society on a nonkin basis. By extension, state refers to any society so organized. At the crux of the state are two characteristics: first, the division of the population into at least two classes, those with privileged and direct access to strategic resources and those who are dispossessed, hence exploited; second, the claim, realized to varying extents, that the state apparatus itself has a corner on, if not a monopoly on, violence. It uses violence as the ultimate means of upholding the orders of stratification and of ranking that it contains. All other decisions of state functionaries, qualified by the variety of forms of structure and ideology, are supported in the same ultimate sense by state force. It should never be forgotten, however, that the study of politics is confined not to the analysis of the application, maintenance, and manipulation of such force but also to all means of obtaining, transferring, or transforming it. In other words, the political arena is inhabited not merely by power-wielders and those it is wielded against, but also by power-seekers, including revolutionaries as well as candidates, those who want to fit into the system, reform it, or destroy it.

As a matter of fact, there is a portion of political behavior that presents itself almost as the antithesis of power. In the presence of truly great power concentrations in state-organized societies, some political actors, who are themselves devoid of power, nonetheless compete in political interactions. Often in such common, unbalanced power situations, the behavior is marked by pretense, bluff, and fraud. Trickery, manipulation, co-optation, payoffs, and wheeling and dealing—these are the kinds of activities that the society begins to identify with political behavior. This is particularly true of societies that dissimulate about power, pretending that the institution of the state is a benign device for the protection of the populace at large. Ironically, in such societies the political office and career are widely regarded as tainted, something a good person does not pursue, and the politician is a figure of suspicion, distrust, and contempt.

In a complex political system such as a state, there are many problematic areas that have drawn the scrutiny of social scientists. Anthropologists, in particular, have contributed with regard to particular questions and by contributing certain methods of study and analysis. With reference to the former, anthropologists, more than political scientists and political sociologists, have kept alive an interest in the evolution of culture and have always paid special attention to the evolution of the political sector. In line with this, anthropologists pioneered the study of political behavior in simpler societies, although in recent years more political scientists have turned their attention to such investigations. Yet, even now, such political science studies tend to be oriented toward problems of *development* (in the technical modern sense) and the emergence of new nations.

Rather distinct from the evolutionary approach to political phenomena is the structural/functional one. Part of this approach is essentially descriptive and comprises a major portion of the traditional field of political science. Where anthropologists have made interesting input, however, is in the realm of comparison, again with regard less to modern states, especially those of Europe and America, than to a much wider range of forms drawn from all over the world and different periods of time. Thus, the previously mentioned concept of "Asiatic mode of productions," or "hydraulic state," while not originated by anthropologists, has seen perhaps greatest excitement among anthropologists and archeologists, pro and con.

Anthropologists are also interested in a variety of more or less straightforward questions about political organization such as have to do with the form of the polity, the structure of office, and the chains of command, as well as with the symbology of all of these. There is also very great interest in the problem of factions and parties, partially from an abstract scientific interest in the structure of society, partially as a means of interpreting the political significance of such phenomena as class and ethnicity. Thus, anthropologists are involved in field studies of the translation of older societal loyalties into party formation and participation in, say, a new African state. On the other hand, an intrepid anthropologist friend of mine is currently studying political factionalism in Northern Ireland.

Finally, more closely related to the structural/functional approach than to evolutionary or historical studies, there is the so-called behavioral approach to politics. Here emphasis tends to be placed upon the nature of participation in particular political systems. Questions asked include the following: How are political decisions actually made? How are they carried out? How are political personnel recruited? How are they trained? How are political ideas instilled into the population at large? Such investigations quickly move into the intellectual domain normally associated with sociology and psychology, but anthropologists have shown great interest as well. This relates to aspects of anthropological method; anthropologists come to such studies with techniques for making deeply penetrating studies of small communities. Rather than obtain information through the ready distribution of questionnaires, the field anthropologist settles into the community and begins an extended process of penetration. At times the quality and intensity of anthropological work is such that extraordinarily difficult ethical problems emerge, particularly in the political sector, since the revelations of the anthropologist can be used by existing government to tighten control over a population or it can show weaknesses in a system and advise its opponents.

The field of political anthropology is one of the most fascinating of the subareas of the discipline as a whole. Work in this field, however esoteric it may seem, is usually not far from the main pulse of society. Its complexities are such that no brief article such as this can do the field justice. Fortunately, those whose interest has been whetted will find a large, if disputatious, literature awaiting them.

BIBLIOGRAPHICAL NOTE

The *International Encyclopedia of the Social Sciences*, edited by D. E. Sills, 17 Vols. (New York: Macmillan Publishing Co., Inc., 1968), has several articles of general interest to our subject; see especially "Political Anthropology: The Field," by Elizabeth Colson, and "Political Organization," by M. G. Smith, both in Volume 12. There are now a number of general volumes providing overviews of the whole field, although they tend to stint the analysis of contemporary states and associated phenomena, such as colonialism and imperialism. Among these general works are Lucy Mair, *Primitive Government* (London: Penquin Press, 1962), Isaac Schapera, *Government and Politics in Tribal Societies* (New York: Schocken Books, Inc., 1967), Max Gluckman, *Politics, Law and Ritual in Tribal Society* (Oxford: Blackwell, 1965), and Georges Belandier, *Political Anthropology* (New York: Random House, Inc., 1970).

A number of volumes of collected papers take up different theoretical problems of political anthropology and sociology at various levels of complexity. Among them are S. N. Eisenstadt, *Political Sociology* (New York: Basic Books, Inc., 1971), Reinhard Bendix (ed.), *State and Society* (Boston: Little, Brown & Co., 1968), Irving L. Horowitz, *Foundations of Political Sociology* (New York: Harper & Row Publishers, Inc., 1972). Those with more ethnographic interests will find other collections rich in problems relating to particular cultures. Meyer Fortes and Edward E. Evans-Pritchard (eds.), *African Political Systems* (London: Oxford University Press, 1961), is one of the best known, while among the more recent collections are J. Marc Swartz, Victor W. Turner, and Arthur Tuden, *Political Anthropology* (Chicago: Aldine Publishing Co., 1966), J. Marc Swartz, *Local Level Politics* (Chicago: Aldine Publishing Co., 1968), and Ronald M. Berndt and Paula Lawrence (eds.), *Politics in New Guinea: Traditional and in the Context of Change, Some Anthropological Perspectives* (Seattle: University of Washington Press, 1973).

The classic works of the nineteenth century concerning political evolution are not merely extant but in many instances in current editions—for example, Lewis Henry Morgan, *Ancient Society* (Reprint. New York: World Publishing Co., 1968), and the famous work of Frederick Engels, *The Origin of the Family Private Property, and the State* (Reprint. New York: New World Press, 1972), inspired by Morgan's work. In both these reprint editions there are introductions by Eleanor Burke Leacock which are very much worth reading. There is also a very interesting edition of Herbert Spencer, *The Evolution of Society: Selections from Herbert Spencer's "Principles of Sociology"* (Chicago: University of Chicago Press, 1967), edited by Robert Carneiro, whose article, "A Theory of the Origin of the State," *Science*, 169:733–38 (1970) gives a more recent view. A survey of state origin theories is given in Lawrence Krader's *Formation of the State* (Englewood Cliffs, N.J.: Prentice-Hall, Inc., 1965).

A view of political process and development that differs from mine yet shares some common ground may be found in Elizabeth Colson, *Tradition and Contract: The Problem of Order* (Chicago: Aldine Publishing Co., 1974). While the Colson book speaks to problems in American political culture as well as to more conventional anthropological topics, there are others that either are more concentrated on the contemporary United States or take a more radical political stance: John C. Leggett, *Taking State Power: The Sources and Consequences of Political Challenge* (New York: Harper & Row Publishers, Inc., 1973) and Marvin Harris, *Cows, Pigs, Wars and Witches: The Riddles of Culture* (New York: Random House, Inc., 1974).

For a more detailed presentation of my own views, see *The Evolution of Political Society* (New York: Random House, Inc., 1968) and *The Notion of Tribe: Social Science or Slander* (Menlo Park, Calif.: Cummings Publishing Co., 1975).

20.

ANTHROPOLOGY AND THE LAW

Paul J. Bohannan

THE GOLA PEOPLE, OF the hinterland of Liberia, have a
proverb that "the law is like a chameleon—it changes form in
each place and can be controlled only by those who know its
ways." That proverb can be matched with an aphorism by one
of the foremost twentieth-century Western jurists, who tells us
that the law has no subject matter of its own, but is as broad as
life itself.

If the law is as changing as a chameleon, and as broad as life
itself, its entirety is obviously beyond the competence of any
one man, or even of any one profession. There must be many
specialists to study it, understand it, and apply it. These
specialists fall into two broad groups; there are those who are
concerned with the law in its relation to behavior, and there are
those who are concerned with the law in its intellectual and
philosophical aspects. The first are the lawyers, judges, police-
men, and legislators. The second sort of people are the students
of jurisprudence, of the history and art of government, and
those anthropologists who have concentrated on the ways in
which different peoples throughout the world settle their
disputes, and maintain at least a modicum of political order.

Lawyers are the specialists who are brought into situations
in which people dispute about their rights or even about the
correct path of conduct. Lawyers and judges settle cases of
trouble in accordance with the written or customary law, and
with the deeper basic values to which the society subscribes.
These are men who, with many others, provide a means for

290

minimizing the upset which trouble and disputes cause. They are also the people who are the guardians of the most basic and valued moral and ethical precepts of the culture. And like all specialists who deal in morally charged matters, they are sometimes considered suspect.

Jurisprudence, in its way, and legal anthropology, in its way—and the two ways are quite different—deal with the same subject matter as do lawyers and judges. But they do not aim at practical ends, with programs of behavior for maintaining the society or ordering its change and growth. They want rather to understand the ways in which a society's law works to uphold its basic values, and also to change them. They might be called the moral preceptors of the judges and legislators, just as the judges are the preceptors of the people. Jurists also want to compare the basic values from one society with those of the next, and to understand and analyze the institutions by means of which different societies provide for their citizens a set of norms within which it is possible both to find rewards and to predict the behavior of others seeking their rewards.

· Therefore, the student of legal anthropology has to take into consideration two initial matters. He must discover first of all what a people say that they should do. He has at the same time to discover what it is that they actually do. In the process, he will find that some people in the world are very strict about making individuals live up to the social ideals. Others are lax. Some people have high standards and high demands; others with the same standards do not make nearly the same demands.

Jurists and anthropologists, thus, are interested not so much in whether in a specific case a person broke the law. That is to be determined by the lawyers and the judges. The jurist and the legal anthropologist rather are concerned with the ways that the law maintains the institutions of society, in the way in which breaches of law are defined in relation to the rest of the ideals of the culture—ideals so deep that they often, in fact usually, cannot be stated in words by the people who hold them.

Thus we can see that it is the lawyer's law to which the Gola proverb refers. Lawyer's law does indeed change color and quality from one culture to the next. It is a real chameleon. It is on the other hand to the jurist's and the anthropologist's law, that the statement about the breadth of the law refers, for although any single system of law may have only a fraction of the ethical, moral and other required behavior encapsulated within it, it can draw from the entire range of the culture.

Thus, the jurist and the anthropologist approach the chameleon of law not in terms of its color, or of its capacity for blending into the background and ultimately to camouflage itself into the totality of its surroundings. Rather, jurists must study the structure of the chameleon: its skeleton, its circulatory system, and the very device which allows it to change color, and to seek camouflage among its surrounding moralities.

However, jurists have not always been successful in studying the legal systems of peoples other than those in the direct line of legal tradition of the West. Jurists of the Western world are experts in the common law and in the Roman law, and in the present-day manifestations of those legal systems. They know and deal in the *Code Civile* of France, the Roman-Dutch tradition in South Africa, and in the Common Law of Britain and the American and Australian versions of it.

Yet, too often these very jurists have taken the categories and ideas found in Roman law and in the Common Law to be universals. They have tended to overlook the fact that the subject matter and even the legal processes involved in these laws were tightly associated with the cultures of which they were a part. There has been, therefore, some tendency to create false analyses of African, Oceanian and American Indian law by the mere device of raising the legal peculiarities of the West to the place of a universal analytical device.

In order to avoid this kind of trap, which anthropologists call ethnocentrism, it is well to look at the legal situation stripped of any particular cultural context. Instead merely of defining law, which is a sticky business at best, as a glance into any good English dictionary will show, it becomes advisable to examine the kind of social acts by means of which individuals or groups within a society make the members live up to agreed expectations.

For a legal situation to exist, there must be a social act which people regard as a wrong way to behave, so wrong that unless something is done the most valued institutions of the society may be undermined. Laws obviously are not social acts. They are precepts in terms of which people are supposed to act. Now there are many kinds of precepts which govern behavior. The social scientist can afford to beg the question of whether a precept is a "law" or some other sort of demand. Indeed, he cannot afford not to beg it. He begins rather by examining the acts which follow upon a breach of the standard of behavior which the society has set for itself, whatever that may be. Following the commission of an act which is in violation of the recognized standards of conduct, there may or may not be a reaction on the part of society, or some institution of it. As we have seen, every culture allows its people a certain range of deviation from its own standards—that is, the law does not expect that all of us always live up to all of the ideal norms. However, once we overstep the accepted permissible range of deviation, if the standard is indeed a law, some sort of social mechanism will swing into action so that the breach of standards can be corrected. In modern nation-states, this counteraction takes the form of specialist lawyers, of complex police systems, and of courts. Either the police of their own volition or on the recognized demand of a citizen, or a private citizen himself, bring wrongdoers before the courts.

Counteractions against crimes are much easier to illustrate than are counteractions against breach of contract or agreement. Contract law not only came late in our own society, it is still more precarious than is the criminal law. We shall, here, for the sake of clarity, deal primarily but not entirely with what we would call the criminal law.

There are, besides courts, many kinds of counteracting institutions. One of the most common—it is found in all societies—is "self-help." Within certain defined limits, a wronged person every place has permission from general society to bring about the correction of the situation by which he was wronged. Modern peoples in all legal systems are expected to help themselves against burglars, for example. There are, however, certain lengths beyond which they must not go in applying self-help. These boundaries can be writ very much more precise in the presence of a police system than they can in the absence of such a system. Many societies of the world, for example, not merely allow but demand that a man who has suffered robbery must go out, if there is to be any retribution, and steal back, so to speak, his own property. If a dispute or fight ensues, he will have moral right on his side, and therefore the backing of his community. Such institutions of self-help are commonly found throughout the world.

Another widespread type of social counteraction to breach of law is the "game" solution, found in very widespread areas. Indeed, modern courts have been compared to games in which we take the whole of life, and reduce the range of rules to a controllable span. Disputes which cannot be settled in the wide arena of life can be examined in the narrower arena of the courts, and settlements made which can then be sent back to the wider stage. More to the point, however, are the gladiatorial contests and ordeals which were and are commonly used to solve disputes.

Still another form of counteraction is the town meeting. In many parts of the world a whole community meets to discuss the problems of some of its members and ultimately to provide the solution for them. The town meeting sort of arrangement is a very different from a court. The court is a specialist body appointed in a stable political system—a specialist body which has the task of settling disputes. The town meeting is not a specialist body; it is a gathering of all the citizens of the community.

When a counteraction of one of these sorts occurs, we can be sure that a law of the society has been broken. The counteraction, as we have called it, and under which we have classified courts and police systems, gladiatorial contests and ordeals, town meetings, and self-help, is the way that we can begin to define a situation as legal. Like the original breach of norm, the counteraction is a series of social acts. The social acts can be observed, and they can be discussed at length with the people who participate in them.

If the counteraction is successful, it is followed by another series of acts that we can call the correction. This English word "correction" has a neat ambiguity in it, which it is wise for us to utilize. There are really two ways in which a deviant act can be corrected. First of all, the person who committed the original wrong may be required subsequently to carry out the action in terms of the norm which he violated. Thereupon, the community can pretend that no breach of the standard ever occurred at all. The other way in which correction can come about implies some sort of penalty. It is this use of the word correction which we underline when we speak of a prison as a house of correction. Thus the word "correction" within itself means both that restitution is made or, if that is impossible, that some sort of retribution must be made.

It is these three social acts, one following upon another, that creates the legal behavior in any society: first, the breach of standard, next, the counteraction, and finally, the correction. Lawyers, jurists and anthropologists all study this same series of acts, but they do so for different purposes, and in somewhat different ways.

Legal anthropologists take the standards as well as the acts which are violations of them, as their data. They then investigate the ethical axioms that lie behind the standards, at the same time that they focus on the institutions of counteraction rather than upon the law, or standard, itself.

Here we will take a series of disputes from several societies to show different ways in which the institutions of counteraction work to apply the law and maintain the moralities that underlie the law. One of the most famous cases in anthropological jurisprudence is the case of Qijuk, an Eskimo who, after his wife died, stole the wife of a neighbor in another community. Being without a wife in Eskimo society is an extremely serious situation because getting a living is so demanding that there *must* be two persons, a man and a woman, to divide the labor in order to do it at all. Qijuk, accompanied by two of his brothers, stole the woman while her husband was out hunting. Qijuk had obviously broken the law, and it is obvious not just because the Eskimo say that a husband has certain rights in his wife, but more specifically because of the fact that certain recognized customs of counteraction came immediately into play. This one was simple. The wronged husband, with the help of friends from his own community, in this case, killed Qijuk; they also killed one of Qijuk's brothers, although the other brother escaped.

Now in this particular case, the matter ended there. Qijuk

had broken the law, and he got his comeuppance. The counter-action was self-help, carried out with the consent of the community. For had Qijuk not been in the wrong when he was killed, the Eskimo society would ultimately have formed a resolve, probably taken informally and over a period of time, to execute his killer. The ritual head of the community would have gone to the killer's closest kinsmen and charged them on behalf of the community with carrying out the execution. Ultimately, it would have been up to the brothers of the killer to perform the execution in the name of the community. They may, or may not have done it, but there are several instances in the records of Eskimo cases in which kinsmen have carried out such a charge—in one case, it was even carried out by the mother. Obviously, the reason that it is the next-of-kin who must carry out the execution is that only so can it be assured that feuds will be avoided.

There is another kind of concerted counteraction that an Eskimo community can take. Either the principals to a dispute or the community itself can decide that the dispute must be settled in terms of a song or "buffeting" contest. Sometimes, they even combine the two, and the two disputants sing insults at one another, at the same time that they bump foreheads till one cries a halt.

At the other end of the world, in central Nigeria, I have myself seen singing contests used as a legal device. In this instance, which happened among the Tiv people of central Nigeria, a dispute arose between Torgindi and Mtswen. Mtswen's ward had been married to a son of Torgindi. When the marriage proved to be unsuccessful, there was some difficulty about the return of the bride-wealth that had been paid. The two men were neighbors, and rather than disgrace himself by calling a close neighbor before the courts, Torgindi hired a song-maker and brewed a great supply of beer. When the beer was ready, and the song-maker had had time to perform his task, Torgindi threw a big party. The song-maker taught his songs to all of the guests. They were scurrilous attacks on the behavior of Mtswen. They were sung loud, long, and lustily into the night. Everyone in the countryside for as much as a mile or so about could hear, and Mtswen was among the listeners. Mtswen did the only thing that an honorable man could do under the circumstances. He too hired a song-writer and began to brew beer and to give parties in direct competition with Torgindi. This situation continued for about three weeks. Thereupon, the most influential elder of the community invited, indeed demanded, that Torgindi and Mtswen come, each with his song-writer and his guests and partisans, and submit both the songs and the original dispute about the bride-wealth to decision by the elders. It is interesting that the elders of the community decided the dispute about bride-wealth in favor of Torgindi, but agreed that Mtswen had the most entertaining and best songs.

Africa is, however, one of the homes of advanced legal institutions. Perhaps the most famous of these institutions is the court found among the Bantu in the southern third of the African continent. Here the head of the community, be he chief or king, was one of a number of judges on a large and inclusive bench. The bench included men who represented all of the important pressure groups and segments of the community. There was a pronounced and well-known hierarchy. The headman sat in the middle, and at his immediate right was the second most senior person. To his left, the third most senior, and so on, right and left, until the whole court was deployed more or less in an arc. Then, after the principal disputants had each told his side of the dispute, and after witnesses had been heard, the most junior member of the bench, down at the far end, pronounced a decision. His decision probably included a moral lecture, statements about the proper kind of behavior that should have been carried out in the situation, and he may have cited precedent. His judgment was then followed by that of the man at the other end of the line, the next junior, who might disagree, and who added new views and new opinions. The third most junior man followed, and so on until they arrived at the middle where the headman pronounced the final decision and sentence. He had heard everything that the representatives of the community had to say. He had a chance to weigh the evidence, the judgments, and the opinions of his junior judges. His word on the decision became law.

The law is indeed a chameleon. It changes to fit in with its surroundings, but like the chameleon there is underneath it all a recognizable animal. Its very changeability is one of its most important and strengthening capacities. The law, whatever it may be in any particular society, is, for the student of anthropological jurisprudence, always to be studied by first discovering the way people handle disputes and cases of trouble; that is, the ways in which they organize the institutions of the society to cope with deviations which, if they were allowed to go unchecked, would destroy the very fabric of the society. At the same time, the law must look out in the other direction to avoid any opportunity for tyranny. In this sense, every community we have ever discovered has a pronounced system of legal institutions. There are always institutionalized counteractions to repeated breaches of standards of behavior. Ultimately they swing behavior back into recognized and accepted channels so that social life can preserve. Law is society's way of healing and maintaining itself.

BIBLIOGRAPHICAL NOTE

The literature in legal anthropology is small and almost all good—neither claim can be made for very many other branches of the subject. Background classics are Henry Maine's *Ancient Law* (Reprint. New York: E. P. Dutton & Co., Inc., 1954); Paul Vinogradoff's *Common Sense in Law* (Reprint. New York: Arno Press, 1975); and Roscoe Pound's *An Introduction to the Philosophy of Law* (Rev. ed. New Haven, Conn.: Yale University Press, 1954). For comparative purposes, I find the following particularly helpful: Joseph Schacht, *The Origins of Muhammadan Jurisprudence* (New York: Oxford University Press, Inc., 1950); Anthony Allott, *Essays in African Law* (Reprint. Westport, Conn.: Greenwood Press, Inc., 1975); Hubert S. Box, *The Principles of Canon Law* (London: Oxford University Press, 1949).

Of anthropological writings, the best general book is E. Adamson Hoebel, *The Law of Primitive Man: A Study in Comparative Legal Dynamics* (New York: Atheneum Publishers, Inc., 1968). Bronislaw Malinowski's *Crime and Custom in Savage Society* (Reprint. Atlantic Highlands, N.J.: Humanities

Press, Inc., 1970), a short book about the Trobriand Islands, has been influential among both anthropologists and lawyers, not always for the better. Some noteworthy ethnographic reports are Northern Rhodesia—Max Gluckman, *The Judicial Process Among the Barotse of Northern Rhodesia* (2nd. ed. Atlantic Highlands, N.J.: Humanities Press, Inc., 1967); Nigeria—Paul Bohannan, *Justice and Judgement Among the Tiv* (London: Oxford University Press, 1957); Philippines—R. F. Barton, *Ifugao Law* (Reprint. Berkeley: University of California Press, 1969); New Guinea—Leonard Posposil, *Kapauka Papuans and Their Law* (Reprint. New Haven, Conn.: Human Relations Area File Press, 1964); and North America—Karl Llewellyn and E. A. Hoebel, *The Cheyenne Way: Conflict and Case in Primitive Jurisprudence* (Norman, Okla.: University of Oklahoma Press, 1967).

21.

THE ANTHROPOLOGY OF LAW AND ORDER

Klaus-Friedrich Koch

IN THIS COUNTRY "law and order" has come to mean quite different things for different people. To some it is a battle cry—a call for better police control and surveillance of political and cultural "deviants," for longer prison terms and the death penalty for criminal offenders. To others the slogan implies a dreadful antithesis. They have realized that the "law and order" advocates break laws and violate constitutional rights or condone such violations to consolidate an order to be made in their own image—an order that works to the advantage of a privileged and powerful "establishment" and thus creates the very conditions that the established seek to maintain by repression and punishment.

These problems are, of course, not new in American society; nor are they unique to this country. But "Watergate" has brought to the consciousness of all citizens, except the apparently irredeemably naive, one simple fact: although the lady with the scales is supposed to be blindfolded, in reality she is cock-eyed and squints at economic interests and political power.

The anthropology of law, unlike jurisprudence, is not concerned with what Lady Justice should be; it investigates what she is and what she does. This orientation directs research to the operation of a legal system. Anthropologists study the total cultural matrix in which legal transactions take place, the conditions that engender disputes, and the social and political contexts in which disputes are settled or which prevent people from obtaining redress for grievances.

Every society—in fact, every social group that has some permanence—must cope with three interrelated problems: (1) the definition of rights and duties that regulate the relationships between its members; (2) the management of disputes that arise from conflicting interests; and (3) the allocation of responsibility for actions or events that have injured people or abrogated their rights.

This article outlines an anthropological perspective on these problems and provides some illustrative ethnographic data.

To say that *every group must define the rights and duties of its members* means that the group must order the myriad of social relations inherent in its organization according to rules. The group may be a family, a country club, a village, or a nation. A group, in more general terms, is an aggregate of people who share an identity that derives from their residential association and/or their joint participation in regular activities.

All social relations are governed by rules. The rules of a football game regulate the behavior of the players on the field and the rules of etiquette and propriety distinguish polite and proper manners from rude and uncouth conduct. These two kinds of rules differ. The rules of a game are circumscribed by the place of the event and its duration. Rules of propriety apply in a much wider context, but their content differs from one situation to another depending on the occasion and on the status relationships between the persons involved in an interaction. Thus, rules regulating bodily contact at a church service are quite different from those observed at a dance. And the rules covering appropriate behavior among strangers are not those for college students living together in a dormitory.

Since all individuals play several distinct roles in the various contexts in which they interact each other, these contexts or occasions also prescribe modes of conduct. A judge and a lawyer meeting at a cocktail party or a class reunion follow rules of interaction quite different from the rules that prescribe their behavior toward each other in the courtroom. While a breach of either rules may be sanctioned, the nature of the sanctions differs. A lawyer's misconduct at a social gathering may lead to his or her exclusion from subsequent gatherings of the people who were offended. But if a lawyer violates the rules of courtroom behavior, he or she may be fined, suspended from practice, or jailed.

The line between improper social conduct and illegal behavior is neither straight nor clear. For example, whether a derogatory remark about another person remains an objectionable indiscretion or constitutes slander cannot easily be known from the linguistic form of the remark. In any case, a third kind of rule defines a person's *jural* rights and duties. These are contractual in nature in that they imply a party's claim to have its rights respected by others and a party's liability to perform its duties. Many societies have formalized these rules by legislation in much the same way as the rules of a football game have been codified. In other societies many rules are also expressed in the opinions of judges whose decisions constitute a large part of the people's common law. Still other societies, especially those without courts and writing, have not formulated any abstract norms defining specific rights and duties of their members. In the past, anthropologists and historians have mistaken the absence of such substantive legal rules and formal legal institutions for an absence of law.

Today few anthropologists find it interesting to debate whether or not all societies have law or to speculate how law developed in the course of cultural evolution. The answer to these questions depends on one's definition of what is law. Since a definition is a conceptual invention, an objectively true definition is impossible. Thus, one's definition of law depends entirely on the nature of the phenomena that one chooses to observe, compare, and explain. A scholar who identifies law by the presence in a society of an authority whose office entitles the incumbent to enforce norms will find no law in a society where official authorities do not exist, unless one extends the meaning of "official" to any individual who enforces norms with general public approval. The general public, however, is an elusive constituency and very difficult to discern, especially in societies where any dispute between two people often divides their "public" into two partisan camps.

On the other hand, authorities in totalitarian states can enforce laws without much public support.

The prolonged debate about the nature of law has hardly been more than a dispute in semantics. Each new ethnographic study on law increases our suspicion that semantic arguments are an inept way to advance our research. Whether an author's definition of law is universalistic or restricted, it sidetracks the main problem in the anthropology of law: How do members of a particular group regulate their conduct and how do they deal with breaches of rules and with incompatible interests? This question deflects the ethnographic search for familiar legal institutions in other societies to the investigation of ideas and activities dealing with preventing and settling disputes.

An analogy may serve to clarify this point. Imagine a scientist is interested in the study of human habitation. Narrowed down a bit, this study would investigate the kinds of buildings people have in different societies. If this research is broadly conceived as a worldwide survey, our imaginary scholar would gather information from Alaska to Patagonia and from the Sahara to Tahiti. Yet nobody would go about this task in an ethnocentric fashion, describing only buildings that are made of bricks, cement, or wood and that have doors and windows. No doubt the sample would include the igloo of the Eskimo, the yurt of the Lapp, the hut of the bushman, and the wagon of the gypsy. Why would the sample lump together such different structures? The answer is quite simple. What would attract scientific attention is not a building similar in design and shape to mansions in Cambridge, Massachusetts, but something that these structures have in common—a technological solution for protecting people and property against rain and wind, heat and cold, and for regulating residential distance and privacy. A scientific study of buildings would thus explore how people live. To understand the observed differences our scholar would then consider the ecological and economic conditions that determine the kind of homes found around the world and the relationship of their design to the people's social organization.

This focus on the cultural context of man's activity and reasoning has always been the distinctive feature of anthropological research. In the study of law this focus has found its full recognition in the *case method.* When ethnographers record cases of actual conflicts, they do more than write up little stories. A complete case study contains information about the relationships between the parties, the circumstances in which their dispute arose, their own activities, and the actions of other people aimed at doing something about the matter, the resolution of the dispute, and the consequences of this resolution. As the case develops, is talked about, and perhaps, is finally settled at a hearing before a third party, the pertinent ideas that are jurally relevant to the case emerge. Thus, by observing antagonistic behavior and by listening to arguments and, perhaps, to the decision of a third party, ethnographers get to know the ideas that define right-duty relationships among group members. Especially in societies where no judicial authorities exist and where the peculiarities of a case rather than its general nature determine the outcome of a dispute that is acceptable to both parties in that particular situation, these right-duty relationships are often not specified by abstract rules. More important than strictly defined behavior norms are the principles that define the procedures to achieve a settlement. Certain procedures may actually prevent a dispute from becoming a "case" in the sense of an open confrontation. As one recent field study of conflict management on a small Fijian island by A. Arno has shown, *strategic gossiping* can be an effective method to solve disputes.

Historically, the emphasis on cases in the anthropological study of law has been a reaction against the earlier rule-oriented research that sought to describe a society's legal system in a record of *substantive laws.* The case method guides the study of the process of dispute settlement. But it elucidates a society's substantive law only within the range of the issues that emerge in the cases which ethnographers can record. Consequently, the comprehensive study of law requires, in addition, the exploration of the rules which are rarely broken and the norms which most people most of the time follow. This is a more difficult task. Because all social relationships entail notions of right or wrong conduct, a complete description of legal rules is theoretically synonymous with a description of social organization. Especially in societies whose organization is largely structured by kin relationships, *structural self-regulation* operates as an effective system of social control.

Consider, for example, a society, patrilineally organized, where marriage is prohibited between agnatic kin, is contracted by the payment of brideprice, and entails specific duties toward the offspring on the part of both father's and mother's kin. If any man married in disregard of the first rule, the others would fail to work also. The brideprice would have to be paid within the same descent group, while in the people's conception it is a payment suitable only between such groups. . . . The offspring of such an irregular union would forfeit the double assistance from two kin groups since the father's and mother's kin now coincide, and would be less advantageously placed than the offspring of customary marriages. And there would be various other, minor but no less confusing, complications; for example, rules of avoidance (obligatory toward in-laws) and intimacy (toward blood relations) would now apply to the same people. In short, one breach of routine disrupts routine all round, and the individual is faced with a wide loss of social bearings. [1]

Without empirical evidence of how the infraction of a rule is treated, the distinction between rules of "customary" behavior and "lawful" behavior must remain, to some extent, a matter of definition. In societies that have a bureaucratic court system, statutes, and records, this problem of identifying lawful and illegal actions is, of course, less severe; but an exclusive emphasis on litigation even in this country would produce a biased view of the nature of its legal system. It would exclude the study of a large area of legitimate grievances of ordinary people who are often ignorant of their rights as consumers and citizens, as well as outright criminal activities of a political and corporate elite who manage to succeed in avoiding prosecution. Nevertheless, in my view, the empirical study of disputes remains the only productive way to explore law in societies that do not have written records and statutes and lawyers to interpret and administer the law, though it remains also an indispensable technique for exploring how the legal system actually operates in countries such as the United States.

1. S. F. Nadel, "Social Control and Self-Regulation," in *Social Forces*, 31(3):265–273(1953).

This focus on actual disputes has one great advantage. It removes the possibility that an anthropologist studies the legal system of another culture from the perspective of a lawyer, who is likely to equate law with the existence of formal legal institutions. But this view is wrong even for the study of our own legal system. In this country, a very large number of cases are either settled *out of court* or are handled more according to customary procedures in the lower courts than by diligent reference to written statutory provisions. The prevalence of reaching a verdict by negotiation between the defense attorney and the prosecutor with the collusion of the judge has become known as *bargain justice*. The very expression contradicts, of course, our idealized notion of what law is all about. On the other hand, many societies consider a negotiated or mediated bargain the ideal outcome in litigation.

While ethnocentric concepts are unsuitable to the comparative study of legal institutions, they are distorting in the domain of jural ideas. A case heard in a court of the Kaguru people in Tanzania, as described by T.O. Beidelman, illustrates how difficult, if not erroneous, it can be to use Anglo-American legal concepts in describing the jural ideology of other cultures. A young man had been observed copulating with a sheep belonging to another man. When the accused denied the offense, the court elders ordered the disputants to return the next day and bring the sheep in question before the court. After several people present at the hearing had testified that the animal was the sheep in question, the defendant admitted his guilt. The court then ordered the offender to pay one goat and one kid to the sheep's owner. Both disputants accepted the verdict.

The interesting point of this case concerns the nature of the offense. The issue did not involve any punishment for bestiality, which the Kaguru regard as unnatural and ridiculous. Rather, the offender was guilty of infringing the proprietary rights of another person. He had used the sheep for his enjoyment without its owner's permission. He thus became liable to compensate the owner in the same way as a man found guilty of adultery with a married woman must compensate her husband who has exclusive rights to sexual relations with the woman. The court elders were aware that the young man could have been convicted of bestiality and sent to prison if this case had reached a higher court, which administered imposed English law. But they refused to judge the offense according to a foreign morality, which makes a foolish act a crime and, at the same time, fails to respect the owner's claim to compensation from the person who violated his property rights.

The task of describing jural concepts indigenous to another culture is a formidable ethnographic problem. Even if we succeeded in rendering native ideas into English without impairing their meaning, we still have to find a way in which to compare "folk concepts" in a "scientific" frame of reference needed to develop our theories. Anthropologists have at least recognized this problem, and one of the most intriguing, if so far inconclusive, debates in the ethnology of law has dealt with its methodological implications.

The second problem that all groups must solve if they are to maintain their order and promote or accommodate change without violent upheavals has already emerged in the preceding discussion. All groups must institutionalize procedures by which disputes are settled and conflicts are resolved. A dispute or a conflict—I make no semantic distinction between these terms—is any antagonistic state between parties that arises from at least partially incompatible interests. Potential consequences of incompatible interests include strife for the control of resources or positions of power and dissension over values and norms.

By and large, anthropologists have succeeded in their efforts to study law by describing the process of conflict resolution. However, very few comparative studies exist that could provide a basis for formulating general theories of conflict management. I suspect that this lack of comparative research has been due to inadequate descriptive models. No cross-cultural and intrasocietal comparison is, in fact, possible without a typology that prescribes how to classify observed phenomena. One model that I have developed in my own work distinguishes six basic types of procedure, each identified by a distinct combination of two factors: (1) the presence or absence of a

third party in the dispute process and the mode of its intervention, and (2) the nature of the outcome. Outcome means some
resolution of the conflict, but it need not be an actual settlement by which the original problem is solved. If no settlement
in this sense occurs, the resolution merely marks an intermediate phase in the history of a conflict.

Let us assume that a conflict refers to a relationship between
two parties, the principals. Certainly not all conflicts involve
only two sides, but the kind of conflicts anthropologists
usually describe are bilateral.

1.   One way in which the principals may attempt to settle
their dispute is by discussing it with each other or through
partisan representatives or supporters. This procedure we call
negotiation, a method by which both sides seek a mutually
acceptable settlement without the intervention of a third party.
A recurrent element in this procedure is a settlement by
compromise.

2.   When a third party intervenes in a dispute, he or she can
do so in three distinct ways: by mediation, adjudication, or
arbitration. As a mediator, this party can have any influence on
the outcome only if both principals want to help in achieving
an agreement. Both parties, ultimately, must consent or, at
least, acquiesce to the intervention, whether it was requested
by only one of the principals or whether the third party
initiated it because of a personal interest in a resolution of the
conflict. Depending on how strong these interests are, the
mediator may even threaten or impose sanctions on both sides
to force them toward an agreement. A classic ethnographic
example of mediation is the method of conflict resolution used
by the *monkalun* among the Ifugao of Luzon in the Philippines.

> To the end of peaceful settlement he exhausts every art of Ifugao
> diplomacy. He wheedles, coaxes, flatters, threatens, drives, scolds,
> insinuates. He beats down the demands of the plaintiffs or prosecu-
> tion, and bolsters up the proposals of the defendants until a point be
> reached at which the two parties may compromise. If the culprit or
> accused be not disposed to listen to reason and runs away or "shows
> fight" when approached, the *monkalun* waits till the former ascends

into his house, follows him, and war-knife in hand, sits in front of him and compels him to listen.[2]

As in negotiation, in *mediation*—which one may view as negotiation by brokerage—the outcome is often a compromise, an agreement that requires a mutually satisfactory adjustment of each principal's initial demands. The mediating third party need not be a single person. Many societies practice a form of mediation where the principals and their supporters argue their case before a neighborhood council or a similar body whose members as a group attempt to solve the dispute.

3. If a third party's intervention in a dispute derives from an office that gives the incumbent the power to decide the case, we may properly speak of *adjudication*. Historical and cross-cultural evidence reveals that the institutionalization of this method tends to formalize the norms of conduct, establish rules of judicial procedure, and develop means to enforce compliance with a verdict. On the whole, through its emphasis on the violation of a rule in a particular past instance, adjudication is a much less flexible procedure than mediation and less likely to secure a settlement that reestablishes amicable relationships between the disputants.

4. Another way in which a third party intervenes in a dispute combines elements of mediation and adjudication. This procedure, *arbitration*, is similar to mediation in that both principals must consent to the arbitrator's intervention. It is similar to adjudication in that the outcome is a verdict, though it is one which both principals have agreed to accept along with the intervention of the third party. This procedure includes situations where a prior contract between the parties provides for the appointment of the arbiter by only one of the principals or by an administrative office. In this country labor disputes between unions and management are often settled by arbitration. Many societies use a special form of arbitration to determine guilt or innocence, when they defer the decision to a nonhuman agent in the performance of an ordeal or in divination.

2. Roy F. Barton, *Ifugao Law* (Reprint. Berkeley: University of California Press, 1969).

5. When no third party intervenes and negotiation fails or is not even attempted, the principals may resort to *coercion*. Either side then seeks to impose the outcome and alone determine its concession, if any, to the opponent. In this situation the threat or use of force often aggravates the conflict and impedes a settlement altogether. In many societies as well as in international relations warfare is the most extreme form in which coercion is employed. Ostracism represents another widespread coercive technique of dealing with conflicts. In this case the offender does not suffer any physical assault; rather, the coercion consists in abrogating some of his or her rights. In rural Japan, for example, this practice constitutes a formally institutionalized method to enforce adherence to norms of communal cooperation and neighborly obligations. Patterns of violent class conflict (euphemistically called "urban riots" or "racial strife") and other forms of militant protest in recent U.S. history manifest attempts to promote the solution of social, economic, and political inequities through coercive tactics to which people have resorted when the established legal order failed to do justice to their grievances.

6. An aggrieved party can also resort to a method that is the obverse of coercion. In using *avoidance* as a procedure the party takes no direct action to obtain redress by any of the methods outlined above. In societies where avoidance is a recognized tactic of conflict management, it demonstrates an existing grievance and may result in a settlement offered by the opponent.

These six distinct procedures are, of course, ideal types. Most processes of conflict management include, to a greater or lesser degree, several procedural phases. An industrial dispute, for example, may go through an initial period of negotiation between labor and management, enter a phase of coercive action by strikes or lockouts, and end with an arbitrated settlement after a court order has terminated the work stoppage. Different procedures need not be limited to consecutive phases of a dispute. The principals may employ several methods concurrently. As negotiations in industrial conflicts during strikes repeatedly demonstrate, and as the Paris peace talks during the Vietnam war showed, the relative failure or success of the parties in their coercive strategies influences their attitudes and efforts in negotiation and vice versa.

The methodological advantage of studying conflict management through an analysis of procedures derives from their conceptual status. The six basic types do not confuse the criteria of an office, such as that of an appointed judge, or the form of an agency, such as that of a court, with the performance of a role, that is, with the activities of the people engaged in the management of the conflict. Observing what people actually do permits the anthropologist to study when and how judges work as mediators and elders without an office act as arbiters. Furthermore, the study of procedures is singularly useful to comparative research, so little of which has been done until now. We can ask the kinds of questions that have traditionally preceded the development of anthropological theories. In simple terms these questions ask: "What cultural institutions hang together?" and, "What is the logic of their empirical association?" We need to know, for example, what are the political and economic structures that promote, hinder, or eliminate the settlement of disputes through mediation, which facilitate or require adjudication, and how do conditions of socioeconomic change alter traditional patterns of conflict resolution.

It appears, for example, that a universal function of mediated conflict resolution is the beneficial effect of this method on the preservation and support of amicable cooperation among members of a local community. This effect follows from a concern with the future relationship of the disputants and their status within the community. In contrast, adjudication is predominantly retrospective and strict rules of evidence and protocol often prevent a complete evaluation of the circumstances that led to a dispute. In different parts of the world, ethnographers have discovered similar changes in patterns of conflict resolution when peasant villages emerge from their traditional relative isolation by becoming politically and economically more integrated in the national society. In the countries of the Middle East and in Taiwan—areas in which mediation has been the preferred method for settling disputes—the effectiveness of private mediation has declined and the people's reliance on adjudication in government courts has increased along with the erosion of reciprocal collaboration and the weakening of communal solidarity. A similar change has occured in the patterns of dispute settlement in the Chinatowns of this country. After the Chinese immigrants had successfully adapted their customary mediation techniques, largely based on Confucian ethics, to metropolitan life in America, the gradual emancipation of the younger generation from the constraints of the traditional family associations has channeled many disputes into government courts for litigation under an adversary system.

All societies use each of the six basic procedures, but the kind of social relationship between the parties, the type of their dispute, and the structural level on which the dispute occurs very much determine which particular procedure people commonly use. In our society disputes between family members are usually resolved by negotiation or coercion; when someone on this level seeks an outcome by adjudication, he or she often merely wants a *de facto* severance of familial relations confirmed by official verdict. And it is not by chance that arbitration is particularly adaptable to labor disputes. The dependence of the workers on their jobs and the dependence of their employer on their work call for an equal participation of both sides in the settlement process. In criminal cases the power to prosecute and to punish is the government's, and adjudication is the only legitimate way of dealing with such offenses. As the case of the Kaguru youth who copulated with a sheep indicated, there are few, if any, actions that all societies consider "criminal." In fact, a distinction between civil and criminal wrongs is of dubious analytical validity in comparative legal research. In many societies homicide is not an offense against society but an injury inflicted upon the dead person's relatives, who—according to the norms of their culture—not only have a right to exact vengeance or demand compensation but have a personal duty to obtain redress.

One question that has puzzled me a great deal concerns the political prerequisites that facilitate the transformation of a dyadic dispute between two parties into a triadic relationship between the opponents and a third party who is capable of doing something about the conflict. Many societies have not developed procedures of third-party intervention, and very much like conflicts in international relations disputes among their members have a pronounced tendency to escalate into warfare.

In a recent monograph, I have tried to explain the inability of the Jalé people in the mountains of western New Guinea to settle many of their disputes by peaceful means. In their society even minor grievances between neighbors may lead to violent confrontations between the principal parties and ultimately engulf several villages in a prolonged war. This pattern of escalation occurs because economic, social, and ritual activities do not require any cooperation of people beyond small coresident groups of kinsmen, who acknowledge no leadership or judicial authority even on the village level. The extreme political fragmentation of Jalé society and an ideological emphasis on revenge and retribution have impeded the development of triadic procedures of conflict management.

Similar impediments to effective third-party intervention appear also in nations that have an established bureaucratic court system. In southern Italy, as described by J. Brögger, peasant villages often lack a workable local government and disputes between families that remain unresolved by the neighborhood council tend to lead to retaliation and further escalation in vendetta. Here, as in New Guinea, "revenge in some form or another is the sanction on which public order rests."

No society can maintain public order by any procedure of dispute settlement unless its members agree on the grounds that establish rights to demand compensation for an injury and punishment for a wrong. Every society, in other words, has rules for allocating responsibility. A logical distinction exists between *responsibility*, as subjective moral fault or mental disposition, and *liability*, as a jural obligation to suffer the consequences of an injurious action or a breach of duty. Consequently, some rules must define a party's guilt for damaging another party's reputation, health, or property, and other rules must translate a party's responsibility into its own or others' liability to compensate the injured party and/or to suffer punishment. However, in its broadest scope the question of liability involves not only a great variety of damages caused to the welfare of others but also the consequences of a person's self-inflicted harm (by committing suicide, for example) or of a curtailment of his or her interests and privileges (by failing to exercise one's rights in a given situation). Intent, volition, mistake, ignorance, accident, provocation, inadvertence, and negligence are some key concepts to distinguish circumstances that imply personal guilt or innocence.

In the history of Western jurisprudence, the logic of aligning responsibility with liability has been a central problem in the writings of philosophers and legal scholars since Aristotle's *Nicomachean Ethics*. The importance of this problem goes far beyond its place in jurisprudential analysis. It is the core issue in any debate about the purpose and reason of law enforcement. Whether the treatment of a wrongdoer should serve as a deterrent to others, as a retribution for an offense, or as a method of reform depends on a society's beliefs about the relationship between personal responsibility and objective liability.

Whether a person's liability coincides with his or her responsibility varies from society to society and according to the type of injury and the social context in which the injury occurred. For example, in English common law, with certain provisions, an innkeeper is liable for the theft of a guest's property, even if the article has been stolen by someone in the innkeeper's employ. Many societies hold witches liable for the harm they cause, even though their evil doings stem from an affliction beyond their control. In contrast, our modern jural ideology accepts insanity and other forms of "diminished responsibility" as conditions that either exculpate an accused killer or reduce the charge from murder to manslaughter and thus mitigate the punishment. Juries often deliberate for many days whether a defendant acted with intent or negligence, or whether the injury in question followed from some inadvertence, provocation, or impaired mental capacity. A verdict that must recognize these factors cannot be reached by formal legal reasoning alone. Consequently, the deliberations rely to a large extent on nonjudicial opinions—scientific beliefs as they appear in expert testimony—and on a rather dubious creature, the mystical "reasonable man of ordinary prudence," whose cross-cultural manifestations several anthropologists have recently debated.

Realizing the enormous costs of trials involving traffic accidents, the legislatures of some states have instituted insurance regulations that incorporate the notion of liability without fault. This idea does not presume that somebody could not be blamed for any given accident; it simply ignores this question in the interest of legal and bureaucratic expediency.

Although we cannot really understand how different societies settle disputes without knowing how they determine liability, anthropologists have only lately explored the whole idea in any systematic or comparative fashion. We know so little about this fundamental legal concept because it can only be fully elucidated through the study of a people's morality, psychological and nosological beliefs, and natural science, in addition to their jural ideology. So far, only the classical study of this belief complex among the Azande of the Sudan by Edward E. Evans-Pritchard has explored the logic of its jural implications in some detail, but his work has inspired several recent studies on the idiom of responsibility in other societies.

Killing is perhaps the most conspicuous injury that demands a determination of liability. All societies distinguish between different types of homicide. These distinctions may derive from an evaluation of the killer's responsibility or depend on the context in which the killing took place. To destroy an enemy in battle may be a heroic act of patriotism; to slay an attacker in self-defense, a justifiable homicide; and to execute a convicted felon, an occupational duty. To abandon the sick and feeble may be a virtue among the Eskimo, while to terminate benevolently the suffering of an incurable patient is still a crime in Western societies. Other distinctions may derive from the relationship between the killer and the victim and decide both the range of people liable for the killing and the extent of their liability as measured by the amount of indemnity to be rendered to the victim's relatives.

The Jalé people of western New Guinea have a doctrine of liability typical of societies that rely on retaliation as a dominant mode of conflict management. Jalé jural ideology deduces liability from what I call the "doctrine of effective action." The Jalé do not distinguish between intent, negligence, and accident as aggravating or extenuating circumstances in establishing a person's formal liability, that is, the obligation to provide compensation to the kinsmen of the victim. Their doctrine resembles the famous dictum of Chief Justice Brian of the Common Pleas who, in 1477, asserted that "the thought of man is not triable; the devil alone knoweth the thought of man."

The recognition of responsibility, a person's guilt or innocence, however, influences the procedure by which the injured party seeks to obtain redress. Particularly, kin and residential relationships between the parties determine if and how a person's responsibility devolves upon one's liability to indemnify the victim's relatives or to suffer revenge. For example, a man who invited a neighbor to come along on a trading trip during which the neighbor fell from a cliff and a husband whose wife died in childbirth are as liable to pay the customary indemnification in the form of "guilt pigs" as a man who killed somebody in a fight. The Jalé reason that the fatal fall would not have occurred if the deceased had not been induced to make the trip and that the unhappy husband caused the woman's death "by his penis" (had he not copulated with his wife, she would not have become pregnant and thus would not have died). However, while all three men are liable to provide the same compensation, the way the Jalé handle this problem varies according to the social context. The kinsmen of the woman will be most lenient with her husband and give him time to furnish the required pig, especially if they want to continue their affinal gift exchanges. The kin people of the dead trader will insist on immediate compensation from their neighbor, with whom they share less tangible interests. If their claim remains unsatisfied, they will attempt to seize a pig from the neighbor by stealth. And the kinsmen of the man killed in a fight may not even accept a "wergild pig" from the slayer—if, indeed, such an offer is made—and instead contemplate blood revenge.

In Jalé law liability is absolute, but it also is corporate when the parties belong to different kin groups. Liability is then shared by the agnates of the person whose action caused the death. I suspect that the correlation between absolute and corporate liability, also found in many other societies, follows from a necessity of settling disputes by coercive self-help. If, in the absence of some form of judicial review, an offender's abscondence and alleged or actual accidents were to confer immunity, the maintenance of social order would become a precarious enterprise. However, to allocate responsibility also poses great procedural problems in the courts of complex industrial societies. There the recent extension of absolute or strict liability in tort legislation probably relates to the difficulties of securing evidence to determine whom to blame for injuries caused by defective or unsafe products that reach the consumer through a long chain of intermediate commercial transactions.

Because of the crucial importance of liability to an understanding of how people evaluate claims to redress, the future comparative exploration of this concept in its psychological, metaphysical, and legal dimensions will significantly advance our knowledge of the relationship between jural ideology, legal procedure, and social organization.

BIBLIOGRAPHICAL NOTE

The following articles provide cursory reviews of the field discussed in this chapter: S. F. Moore, "Law and Anthropology," in B. J. Siegel (ed.), *Biennial Review of Anthropology* (Stanford: Stanford University Press, 1969), and Laura Nader, "The Anthropological Study of Law," *American Anthropologist*, 67: No. 6, Part 2 (1965). Four other publications present both general introductions and ethnographic case studies: E. Adamson Hoebel, *The Law of Primitive Man: A Study in Comparative Legal Dynamics* (New York: Atheneum Publications, 1968), Laura Nader (ed.), *Law in Culture and Society* (Chicago: Aldine Publishing Co., 1969), Leopold Pospisal, *Anthropology of Law: A Comparative Theory* (Reprint. New Haven, Conn.: Human Relations Area File Press, 1974), and *Law and Society Review* 7:No. 4(1973).

Monographs published after 1960 that describe legal systems in different societies include Jane F. Collier, *Law and Social Change in Zinacantan* (Stanford: Stanford University Press, 1973), Lloyd A. Fallers, *Law Without Precedent: Legal Ideas in Action in the Courts of Colonial Busoga* (Chicago: University of Chicago Press, 1969), Max Gluckman, *The Judicial Process Among the Barotse of Northern Rhodesia* (2nd. ed. Atlantic Highlands, N.J.: Humanities Press, Inc., 1967), P. H. Gulliver, *Social Control in an African Society: A Study of the Arusha, Agricultural Masai of Northern Tanganyika* (Boston: Boston University Press, 1963)., and Klaus-Friedrich Koch, *War and Peace in Jalémó: The Management of Conflict in Highland New Guinea* (Cambridge, Mass.: Harvard University Press, 1974).

22.

THE STUDY OF RELIGION

Edward Norbeck

MAN'S EXAMINATION OF HIS own behavior in a systematic and objective way is one of the newer developments of science, which first examined the inanimate world and only later included among its subjects man as a member of the animal kingdom. The social sciences studying man's learned or cultural behavior developed still later, and the last of these to appear was the science of culture. As one of the categories of culture—the manmade part of the universe—religion was thus a late addition to the roster of scientific subjects, and until recent times the progress of its study was slow. Primary obstacles standing in the way of the scientific study of religion were the interpretations of the world provided by Western religions themselves, and these were not seriously challenged until the second half of the nineteenth century. Western religious philosophies share a common ancestry and have common themes, interpretations of existence that became articles of faith and were vigorously defended. The teachings of Islam, Judaism, and Christianity were held to be divinely revealed, and they declared human beings to be a special creation. These views allowed no place for the scientific investigation of the genesis and development of either the human species or religion.

Modern science began and has had its greatest development in the Western world among Christian nations. As the scope of science enlarged during the nineteenth century, skepticism was concomitantly directed toward Christian theological interpretations. The reaction is well-known history, a fiercely emotional defense of traditional dogma that seemed to be threatened by science. In view of the strength and emotional depth of Christian opposition to science in general, it is not surprising that the scientific study of religion was slow to develop. Nevertheless, during the period of greatest opposition many of the basic data required for the objective, comparative study of the religions of the world were made available, placed on record by early travelers, missionaries, historians, and, later, scholars in the social sciences. The beginnings of a comparative study of religion were in fact made in the nineteenth century, but the greatest interest in the subject has developed in the past few decades. The first scholarly journal devoted solely to the scientific study of religion was established in 1961, in the United States. All of the social sciences are presently interested in religion, but the comparative or cross-cultural study of religion remains principally an anthropological endeavor. The recent growth of anthropological studies of religion is in part a reflection of the quantitative growth of anthropology as well as of the progressive weakening of the opposition toward scientific views. A large majority of the professional anthropologists of the United States, and thus also of the entire world, were awarded professional degrees after 1965. The manifold increase of anthropologists, departments of anthropology, and degree programs in anthropology during the past decade has been accompanied by a corresponding increase in studies of religion. Old problems for investigations have been reexamined, and sometimes recast, and new problems continue to be formulated.

A perennial problem in scholarly research on religion that needs discussion at the outset is the definition of the subject of study. The traditional scholarly conception of religion centered on supernaturalism as its primary distinguishing trait, often drawing a distinction between the sacred and profane or between supernaturalism and naturalism. *Religion* was viewed as ideas about mysterious forces and entities which control the universe and the affairs of man that are unexplainable in conventional, naturalistic terms and the behavior or customs associated with these beliefs. During the twentieth century, as

human life became increasingly secular, some tendency has
developed among scholars to define religion as *ultimate
values*—ideas and ideals that are the most highly cherished
and are surrounded by the most intense emotional feelings.
This view of religion, which has some currency today among
social scientists and educated citizens, imputes religion to all
mankind, allows, but does not require, supernaturalism, and
uses as its central focus the trait of intensity of emotional
feelings. An examination of actual studies of religion, however,
shows little use of this definition, which may be seen as an
ethnocentric projection of Western ideas of the intimate and
inherent association between cherished moral values and religion, an association which does not exist in many societies of
the world. As in the past, anthropological studies of religion
generally continue to rest upon a definition of religion as ideas
and acts of supernaturalism.

Another problem with a long history in the study of religion
has been the distinction between magic and religion. Many
scholars have sharply distinguished magic and religion, defining magic as signifying supernaturalistic control by man
through mechanical formulas or recipes and religion as meaning a concept of control over man by supernatural entities with
manlike qualities which must be treated as sentient beings
rather than as impersonal objects, substances, or forces. A
problem encountered in using this definition is that ideas and
acts of both magic and religion are often included in a single
rite. The Christian rite of communion, for example, includes
theophagy, god-eating, a practice followed elsewhere in the
world that is ordinarily classified as magic. Anthropologists
have generally regarded both magic and religion as forms of
supernaturalism, *magic* referring to concepts of impersonal
supernatural power and *religion* signifying behavior based on
a personified conception. Procedures of interpretation of magic
and religion have been the same.

Like anthropology in general, from its beginnings the anthropological study of religion has examined and attempted to
explain similarities and differences. Early examination of
non-Western religions seemed at first to reveal much diversity
and many inexplicable customs of supernaturalism. Closer

examination showed fundamental similarity in the seeming diversity and removed some of the mystery. Anthropological study of the physical traits of human beings as a biological species which was conducted at the same time led to the early conclusion that all living forms of *Homo sapiens* are essentially alike in biologically inherited traits. The study of differences in religion among world societies accordingly deals only with differences in culture or learned ways of life. Similarities in religion are, of course, seen as reflecting in part the essential uniformity of human nature and, in other part, similarities in culture. Although anthropological conceptions of problems of religion meriting investigation and certain specific interpretations of religion have changed since the beginning of anthropology, these early ideas about the human species, religion, and culture continue to prevail.

The history of trends and emphases in the anthropological study of religion follows the general pattern of the historic development of the field of cultural anthropology since its beginnings about a century ago. This pattern consists of an early emphasis on cultural and social evolution, a period of reaction toward evolutionary interpretation, beginning at the turn of the century, during which studies were primarily descriptive, and a return to interpretation, beginning in the nineteen thirties, which has seen the development of various lines of interpretive study.

Early theories of the origin and evolution of religion were generally discarded by the beginning of the twentieth century. Certain interpretations which saw an evolution from magic to religion or from polytheism to monotheism were set aside as ethnocentric projections of the cultures of their anthropological formulators, who placed the traits of the religions of their own societies at the peak of the evolutionary chain. All theories of religious genesis were looked upon as being at best speculative and unverifiable. These early ideas were not valueless, however, and they have led to modern studies. Characteristically, the early theories saw religion as a form of human interpretation of and adjustment to the universe, a view which anthropologists continue to hold. Certain interpretations stressed the social value of religion, seeing it as a means of promoting social solidarity and continuity through joint beliefs and acts and through the support it often if not always gives to moral codes and other social values. The role of religion in providing psychological support for individuals, and thereby indirectly promoting social harmony, was also noted. These lines of thought have had their greatest elaboration in modern times.

Modern anthropologists look upon supernaturalistic beliefs and associated acts as human creations, expressions of human desires, hopes, doubts, hates, and fears and as interpretations of the otherwise unknown. Cast into comprehensible form as supernatural forces and beings, hopes, problems, anxieties, and questions become intelligible and ways of dealing with them are suggested. Supernatural forces and whole theologies are then conceptualizations of the traits of human beings, their social life, and their experiences with the world about them, all cast into a special framework of supernaturalism. The *origin* of religion thus lies in the process of human interpretation of the universe by which people create the realm of the mysterious supernatural on the model of everyday or mundane life.

Following this view, anthropology sees theologies and accompanying practices of supernaturalism as being molded into their particular forms by peoples' habitats, their ways of gaining a lifelihood, the manners in which their societies are ordered, and the whole of their cultures. It is not simple coincidence that the warlike ancient Aztecs gave primary importance in their pantheon of supernatural beings to a god of war, that peoples who raise rice and corn as principal crops worship important deities called the "Rice Mother" and the "Corn Mother," and that Christians traditionally have worshipped God the Father. The activities and social roles which the names of their deities imply were all matters of great importance to the societies concerned. Similarly, critical events in the life cycles of individuals, such as birth, physical maturity, marriage, parenthood, serious illness, and death, have tended strongly to become the subjects of religious observances.

In their attempts to observe and account for similarities and differences in religious creeds and acts such as those described above, anthropologists have not been concerned with the question of the validity in a scientific sense of people's religious beliefs. Instead, their goals of study have been gaining an understanding of the role of religion in human life, the relationship of religion to other parts of culture, and the ways in which religion undergoes change. To reach these goals they have gone beyond the study of theology to give attention to the observable acts of religion—the identity and social relations of participants, what they do, and when the acts are performed. In particular, studies have tried to deduce unintended effects of religious acts, effects not ordinarily perceived by the participants. From the view of the participants, for example, the goal of ritual may be to worship a god for the reason that he is thought to have power over man and to require propitiation. Unintended and generally unperceived effects include the binding of society through common acts and beliefs; the encouragement of smooth social life through adherence to moral precepts when these are interpreted as commands of the gods; and the psychological assurance given to the individual by the belief that divine aid is available.

Much of the foregoing may be restated in somewhat more technical terms. Contemporary anthropologists customarily take a view of culture as constituting a system made up of interrelated parts. As is customary in physics, chemistry, astronomy, and other sciences that use the concept of systems, anthropologists implicitly or explicitly use the idea of equilibrium. Like any other system, the parts of culture—technology, economy, social structure, social institutions, and ideology—are conceptually seen as enmeshing and working together. Change in any important element of the system then results in change in other aspects, leading to a new enmeshing or state of equilibrium, or otherwise to disequilibrium. The term *equilibrium* does not, however, necessarily imply perfect harmony of the parts. Many societies may be seen to limp along in poor states of cultural articulation, like defective but still-operating mechanical motors. A fair measure of congruence or functional consistency of parts is seen as essential for continued maintenance in any given form of a society or culture.

Equilibrium implies functional relationships between parts

of the whole, and it is this subject which has long been a principal interest of anthropological studies of religion. Many such studies have presented interpretations of function as the part played by any element of culture in maintaining the social order and the psychological well-being or integration of the individual. For the most part, these interpretations call attention to positive or supportive effects, a procedure that accords with the view that systems are composed of functionally compatible elements. Much less attention has been given to negative or dysfunctional aspects. Functional relationships or covariations are also sought between and among religion, social and political organization, technology, and other distinguishable categories of human culture which scholars have chosen for attention.

Following these lines of functionalist thought, the successful pursuit of studies of religion has depended strongly upon progress in similar studies of subjects other than religion—in particular, upon the increase of anthropological observation and understanding of human social organization. As examples of these assumptions about religion and culture and the associated procedures of study we may use interpretations that have been offered of rites of passage, witchcraft and rites of reversal, and human work and play in their relationship to religion.

Rites of passage, such as rites at birth, coming of age, marriage, and death, that mark the movement of individuals from one social status to another, vary considerably among world societies. In general, the degree of elaboration of ceremonial may be seen to accord with the social importance of the transitions they concern. The death of a king is obviously more important to the entire society than the death of a commoner. But the social importance of events celebrated by rites of passage in foreign societies is often not obvious, at least not until the social relationships which the rites involve are examined. Where lasting unions of marriage are not vital to the upbringing of children and the welfare of mothers, and thereby the continuance of society, for example, rites of marriage tend to be simple and the incidence of divorce is high. In about one-fourth of the historically known societies of the world, kinship has been reckoned through female lines only, and social units—lineages and clans—that are important throughout life are composed only of matrilineal relatives of both sexes. Spouses come from outside lineages or clans. Divorce does not change the most important social identity of mothers and children; that is, they are lifelong members of their matrilineal kin groups. In many of these societies, the father does not economically provide for or rear his children. These roles are filled by the mother's brother, who is a member of the mother's kin group (and thus the father has these roles with respect to his sister and her children). In patrilineal societies, however, where the vitally important lineages and clans are composed of relatives united through male lines of descent, lasting marriages are very important to the birth and rearing of children. Only females give birth to children and, ordinarily, the roles of mother and father's sister with respect to children are not easily interchangeable. Strong sanctions for lasting marriages are common in these societies, including elaborate ceremonies of marriage which may involve much supernaturalism.

Rites of passage are also seen to have many other functional aspects. For example, rites at coming of age ease the individuals through the social transition to adulthood and publicly announce and approve the new status. Such rites are incongruous with societies such as our own, in which there is no established age of social maturity and where the growth of culture has progressively lengthened the period of the life span until one becomes economically productive and thus, in a social sense, a fully mature member of society.

Witchcraft is an example of beliefs and practices that seemingly are only disruptive, but many studies have seen in them socially supportive effects. Customs of witchcraft are seen to promote social conformity by sanctioning norms of behavior, including the rules of morality and etiquette, that govern interpersonal relations. Accusations of witchcraft are not made randomly but indicate social relationships of hostility or tension, often fostered by the nature of a society's social structure, which puts some categories of people into stressful relationships with others. Among the Navaho Indians, for example, the most common accusation of witchcraft has been by women who so accuse their fathers-in-law. In many societies the deviant from moral or other norms of behavior is prone to either the accusation of witchcraft, and attendant punishment, or the misfortune of becoming the target of witchcraft. These circumstances may instill fear, but they also serve to foster conformity.

Rites of reversal, a class of ceremonial acts that is widespread throughout the world but uncommon in the United States and Europe except in such lingering echoes of the past as Mardi Gras, are also examples of seemingly disruptive customs. Like witchcraft, these rites have been seen to have positive effects. Rites of reversal are acts performed on ritual occasions which in some way reverse everyday practices. Reversals may be the central theme of grand rites of upside-downing or they may be simple elements of ritual complexes otherwise involving no reverse behavior. One may be expected or required to wear clothing backward, to say yes when no is meant, or to don the clothing and the demeanor of the opposite sex. In grand ceremonies of reversal, rules of proper moral conduct may be turned upside down. Obscenity, lewdness, theft, sexual license, and the mocking, insulting, and reviling of social superiors may all be permitted or expected. Interpretations of these rites has seen them as safety valves, controlled releases of tension that promote social harmony. These rites are also seen to be special forms of symbolism, a subject that will later be discussed.

The relationship of forms of play to religion is a recent subject of study, although the relationship of religion to work was long ago made a noted topic of study by Max Weber's interpretation of the "Protestant ethic." Weber used this name for the set of values said to characterize Protestants, which may be described as ascetic devotion to work as a religious and moral duty, and he held that the great economic achievements of capitalist Protestant nations were fostered by these values. Motivation toward achievement continues to be a subject of modern study in anthropology and other social sciences, and the link between work and play in this connection has also come to scholarly attention. Traditional Protestantism frowned upon play and honored work. Anthropological examination of attitudes toward work and play in non-Western societies has shown them to differ from the Protestant conception, and the subject of play has tardily become regarded as a proper subject for investigation by the social sciences.

As a universal trait of human beings and of the entire class of mammals, play is genetically based behavior which, among human societies, is culturally molded so that it varies from society to society. As with many of the rites of reversal, the role of religion with regard to play has been both permissive and controlling. During most of human history, the great times for play have been religious occasions, and religious customs have given instruction in when and how to play and when to stop playing. The religious control of play may prohibit certain kinds of play and permit others, sometimes under the guise of acts of piety. Protestantism has been notable in this respect, manifestly discouraging or prohibiting play in favor of work but nevertheless allowing such forms of play as certain kinds of music and art and, by interpreting this behavior as a religious phenomenon, psychic states of ecstasy that involve seizures and trance.

Like other customs, the religious control of play may have functionally negative effects, and Protestantism is also notable in this respect. We are all familiar with the current social and psychological problems of the United States connected with our inability to play and with illegal forms of play. The use of drugs that induce psychic transcendence has probably been the most troublesome of these problems. In many societies of the world this form of play has been institutionalized and controlled since ancient times as an act of religion or in a religious context. Under this permissive-controlling mantle, psychic transcendence has not been a social problem.

Other subjects of study that directly or indirectly concern religion have long included mythology, religious therapy, especially its faithhealing or psychiatric aspects, and the thousands of religious movements, periods of heightened and otherwise changed religious activities, that have occurred during the past few centuries among societies at all levels of cultural development throughout the world. Religious movements are seen as responses to stress, and, during the past two centuries, the source of stress has been principally changes in culture, often brought about by contact with powerful foreign cultures.

A strong current trend of anthropological interest is the symbolic significance of human behavior as expressed in myth, dogma, and acts of supernaturalism. These studies often assume the existence of pan-human "structures of thought," the idea that, as a single species, all human beings think in characteristic ways which have structure or pattern. As a class of behavior particularly strong in symbolic significance, religious ideas and acts have been included in this scrutiny. One very commonly recurrent and possibly universal "pattern of thought" appearing again and again in religious symbolism is what is called *dualism* or binary opposition, a conception of pairs of things in a complementary relationship. Examples are good-evil, virtue-sin, love-hate, god-devil, heaven-earth, sacred-profane, and the dualisms in the entire complex of uncounted thousands of institutionalized rites of reversal.

If we review these and other anthropological studies of religion of the past five or six decades, the major trends of study and the principal hypotheses about the nature of religion may be summarized briefly. The principal guiding concept in study has been the systemic nature of society and culture. Religion is examined in its relationship to the whole of culture, not as a separate element that can be removed from its cultural matrix. Religion is seen to offer both interpretations of the universe and congruent courses of action. It also often provides motives and validations for human existence as well as human action. It is seen to be socially and individually supportive in many ways, through the bonds of joint action and belief, as a sanction for social values, and by providing assurance, comfort, and solace. Religion has been an important vehicle for expressing and controlling human emotions, predispositions, and "drives." During most of the human past it has been the principal channel for forms of art, dancing, singing, and all other branches of aesthetics and an important channel for sports, games, and all other forms of play including transcendental psychic states. In this capacity it has also been a major source of human entertainment. As exemplified by witchcraft and many of the rites of reversal, religion has permitted and controlled potentially disruptive human emotions of anger, hate, envy, hostility, aggression, and resentment. Similarly, through supernatural sanctions, it has aided in the control of human impulses toward sexual activities. Perhaps its most outstanding negative effect has been to inhibit the development and acceptance of nonreligious interpretations of the universe which might have greater human value. As exemplified by Christian history, this negative influence has sometimes been deliberate or conscious; but it is also an unintended effect since the mere existence of one kind of interpretation inhibits the formulation of any other. Anthropological consensus sees religion as having had survival value in human life. Consensus also notes a general trend of religious change toward secularization of life, a trend that reflects changes in other parts of culture and may be regarded as evolutionary. Many of the former functions of religion in human life are today performed by functional counterparts that are secular displacements of supernaturalistic ideas and acts which have become incongruous in the modern cultural context. Accordingly, consensus does not see religion in the form of supernaturalism as an indispensable feature of human life in the future.

BIBLIOGRAPHICAL NOTE

For the earliest detailed anthropological study of religion, see E. B. Tylor, *Primitive Culture*, Vol. 2 (3rd. ed. New York: Henry Holt & Co., Inc., 1889), which presents an evolutionary interpretation. The appendix to William J. Goode's *Religion Among the Primitives* (New York: Free Press, 1951) provides a review of nineteenth century theories of the origins of religion and of ideas concerning the distinction between magic and religion. Important works in the formulation of modern functionalist interpretations of religion are Emile Durkheim, *The Elementary Forms of the Religious Life* (New York: Free Press, 1954), A. R. Radcliffe-Brown, *The Andaman Islanders* (Reprint. New York: Free Press, 1964), and Bronislaw Malinowski, *Magic, Science and Religion and Other Essays* (New

York: Free Press, 1948). Later functionalist interpretations of single societies include A. I. Richards, *Chisangu* (New York: Grove Press, Inc., 1956), and M. G. Marwick, *Sorcery in its Social Setting: A Study of the Northern Rhodesian Cewa* (Atlantic Highlands, N.J.: Humanities Press, Inc., 1970). Noteworthy American studies of witchcraft are Clyde Kluckhohn, *Navaho Witchcraft* (Boston: Beacon Press, Inc., 1962), and Keith H. Basso, *Western Apache Witchcraft* (Tucson: University of Arizona Press, 1969).

The classic study of rites of passage is Arnold Van Gennep's *The Rites of Passage* (Chicago: University of Chicago Press, 1960). For a later functionalist interpretation of rites at coming of age that incorporates psychological concepts, see Frank W. Young, *Initiation Ceremonies: A Cross-Cultural Study of Status Dramatization* (Indianapolis: Bobbs-Merrill Co., Inc.). A classic and essentially descriptive account of supernaturalistic ideas and acts is provided by the numerous editions of Sir James G. Frazier's *The Golden Bough* (Abridged ed. New York: Macmillan Publishing Co., 1922). Modern general works on the anthropological study of religion include Edward Norbeck, *Religion in Primitive Society* (New York: Harper & Row Publishers, Inc., 1961) and *Religion in Human Life: Anthropological Views* (New York: Holt, Rinehart & Winston, Inc., 1974). Max Weber's well-known work, *The Protestant Ethic and the Spirit of Capitalism* (London: George Allen & Unwin, Ltd., 1930), has been the foundation of many later sutdies of smaller scope that concern the relationship between religion and motivation toward achievement. *The Forest of Symbols: Aspects of Ndember Ritual* (Ithaca, N.Y.: Cornell University Press, 1967) and other writings by Victor W. Turner exemplify the modern attention given to symbolism in its relationship to religion. For references to other modern trends of the anthropological study of religion, see Edward Norbeck, *Religion in Human Life: Anthropological Views* (New York: Holt, Rinehart & Winston, Inc., 1974), and Agehananda Bharati, in Bernard Siegel (ed.), *Biennial Review of Anthropology* (Stanford University Press, 1971).

23.

ANTHROPOLOGY AND THE ARTS

Alan P. Merriam

THE RELATIONSHIP BETWEEN anthropology and the arts—
what that relationship should be, how it is best expressed, and
what kinds of study would most sharply delineate it—has
seldom received the kind of fruitful discussion and debate
accorded other aspects of anthropological investigation. Yet
anthropologists have long shown interest in the arts, particularly among nonliterate peoples, and they have contributed
enormous amounts of raw materials; indeed, various kinds of
investigators have accumulated knowledge of the arts in a
more or less systematic fashion for several centuries. Herta
Haselberger tells us that "specimens of ethnological art had
been included in European collections as early as the fifteenth
century," and references to African music extend well back
into the seventeenth century. The study of European dance
forms received impetus from the research of Cecil Sharp in
England early in the twentieth century, but a survey of studies
made in the Soviet Union shows materials dating back to 1848.
Concentrated investigation of oral literature was begun in
Germany by the Grimm brothers early in the nineteenth
century, and the word "folklore" was coined by William John
Thoms in 1846. The earliest publication in ethnomusicology as
such is Theodore Baker's 1882 doctoral dissertation at the
University of Leipzig, and the study of the visual arts among
peoples other than ourselves began to receive significant
impetus in the decades surrounding the advent of the twentieth century.

332

We can thus look back on the study of the arts in societies other than our own at least four hundred years, though it is not until the turn of this century that extensive and serious studies begin to appear. And it is not until very recent times that a major attempt has been made to deal with anthropology and the arts in more than descriptive terms.

Interest in specific arts as aspects of anthropology has also varied enormously. The study of drama, for example, had hardly been touched upon in anthropology since Melville J. Herskovits's pioneering study until recent specific works such as those of Raymond Firth and James L. Peacock cast new light upon a fascinating series of problems. Similarly, architectural studies have played an extremely small part in anthropology; although a description of house types is found in almost every ethnography, summarizing and theoretical works are virtually absent. Even dance has received nowhere near the attention it deserves, although it, too, shows recent signs of increased attention on the part of anthropologists. On the other hand, the anthropological literature is full of references to the graphic and plastic, or visual, arts, to music, and to oral literature.

So it is that the study of the arts remains unbalanced, with much emphasis on some forms and very little upon others. It is reasonable and accurate to say that with the possible exception of oral literature, the study of the arts in anthropology has been seriously neglected and undervalued. The average text in anthropology, for example, devotes a single chapter or a portion of a single chapter to all of the arts taken together, and the contrast between this allotment and the space given to problems of social structure or political organization is indeed striking.

This relative neglect of the humanistic aspects of culture derives primarily from two major misunderstandings about the arts and how they should be handled in anthropological investigation. The first of these stems from the failure to comprehend, or at least to act upon, the essential nature of the content of the social sciences, on the one hand, and the humanities, on the other, and the basic relationship between them. I have argued this point at some length elsewhere, but, in sum, the content of the social sciences—that is, the subject

matter which is of concern to them—derives from the institu-
tionalizing behavior of man through which he solves the
problems which arise from his own biosocial existence. That
is, man must regulate his economic, social, political, and
enculturative behavior with his fellow men, and these problems arise, on the one hand, from the needs of the biological
organism and, on the other, from the group life to which man is
so irrevocably committed. The essential nature of the content
of the humanities, however, seems to arise from man's need to
supply himself with what A. I. Hallowell has referred to as
". . . mediative factors in man's cultural mode of adaptation
. . . whereby a world of common meanings has been created in
human societies." In other words:

> Through the humanistic elements of his culture, man seems to be
> making pointed commentary on how he lives; he seems in the
> humanities to sum up what he thinks of life. In short, man lives as a
> social animal, but he does not live as a social animal alone. For his
> social life in itself seems to bring about conditions under which he
> is unable to restrain himself from commenting upon himself and
> enunciating and interpreting his actions, his aspirations, and his
> values. [1]

The social sciences, then, deal with man as a social animal
and the ways in which he solves his social and biological
problems in daily living, while the humanities take man
beyond his biosocial living into his own distillations of his life
experiences, which he uses, in turn, as an expression of his
basic values.

It may conceivably be argued that the social sciences are
necessarily prior to the humanities because they deal with
absolute fundamentals of existence. I think this is a proper
conclusion only in the sense that man as a social animal *is*
basic; that is, men do live together. But at the same time, both
the social and the humanistic aspects of man's life are universals in his culture and experience, and thus the question is not
at all one of priority but rather one of unity. If man cannot live,
as apparently he cannot, without either his social institutions
or his humanistic responses, then the two become merely two

1. Alan P. Merriam, *A Prologue to the Study of African Arts* (Yellow Springs,
Ohio: Antioch Press, 1962).

sides of the same coin and neither can be examined without involving the other.

The problem here is that the assumptions anthropologists made in the past about the arts led them with considerable consistency to analyses which were much more humanistic than anthropological. In so doing, they followed the strong tendencies in Western culture which set art aside as something unique and special to be discussed in its own terms, and they failed to realize that art can be viewed as human behavior and that, indeed, this is the special skill which the anthropologist has to contribute. Thus the humanistic and social scientific approaches have relatively seldom been merged in anthropological studies of the arts; since we do not think of looking at a kinship system aesthetically (but why should we not?), neither do we think of looking at a music system politically (but of course we should). In effect, anthropologists most often abandoned the very approaches which were unique and important to their discipline; instead of being social scientists, they became substitute humanists.

Contributing further to this confusion is the second major misunderstanding about the arts and their anthropological context, and this concerns the nature of the arts themselves. The arts differ from man's other cultural creations in that the behavior involved in their creation produces a product which, as an object of study, can be treated quite apart from cultural context. The same, of course, is true of tools and house types, but argument exists as to whether these may not also most logically be treated as arts. What the anthropologist treats as *crafts* seem to me to be of such a nature as to be classed with the *arts*, and it is but a convention of our own culture that prevents us from doing so, leading us, instead, to set them apart as something different. In any case, what is important here is that in the Western view, the art product is conceptually, and in certain ways practically, separable from its cultural context. Thus musicians, no matter in what society they are found, produce a product—musical sound—which can be recorded, transcribed to paper, and analyzed as a structural entity. Dance movement is visual pattern which can be objectified by a system of graphic shorthand; oral literature is reduced to writing; the visual arts cannot exist without a tangible product; architecture results in buildings; and drama, reduced to writing after observation, shows structural characteristics of sequence in time, plot, climax, and the like.

This characteristic of the arts seems to set them apart from those organizations of society which we call its institutions, for in the case of institutions what is important is how the organization itself shapes the behavior of the individuals concerned. With the arts, on the other hand, the importance lies in the product, and artistic behavior is directed toward it; without musical sound, music does not exist, but society is behaving. But neither does musical sound exist without behavior, and thus the two facets are but different aspects of the same thing. While artists produce products, and while this is their ultimate and direct aim, in doing so they behave in certain specific ways.

The unity of the product, on the one hand, and the behavior which produces it, on the other, are connections which have been made infrequently in studies of the arts, and most anthropological investigations have tended to concentrate exclusively, or almost exclusively, upon the product, which is visualized as a structure or system, the parts of which interact with each other to form a cohesive whole. Studies of the visual arts are primarily concerned with the painting or sculpture itself, not with the artist; studies of oral literature concentrate upon the tale or proverb or myth, not on the teller; investigations into music deal almost exclusively with the musical sound, not with the musician.

Behavior, then, is separable from the product analytically, but in reality it is inseparable, because no product can exist except as the result of the behavior of some individual or individuals. Similarly, behavior is always underlain by a series of conceptualizations which concern the product, the behavior that goes into making the product, the role played by the product in the society, and so forth. While these conceptualizations are analytically separable from behavior and product, in fact they form part of the single complex that is artistic activity and result. Finally, the product as such has a feedback effect upon the artist's conceptualization. If the art object produced is pleasing to the performers and their audiences, then that particular concept is reinforced; if it is not pleasing, artists are forced to change their concept, which in turn means changes in behavior, resulting finally in a changed product— that, or they lose social acceptance as artists.

A fourfold organizational pattern is thus involved in the arts: concept, leading to behavior, resulting in product, which in turn feeds back upon the concept. Of these four aspects of the art process, only the product has been studied in any detail; concept, behavior, and feedback upon concept have been almost totally neglected. In these terms, it is perhaps not surprising that the study of the arts has not been of central concern to anthropology, for studies of product are essentially descriptive in nature. And any descriptive study must develop a technical terminology which quickly surpasses the competence of individuals who are not primarily concerned with the object of the study at hand. Thus in dealing with the music product, ethnomusicologists speak of "melodic level," "modal analyses," or "triadic split fifths," and they use a large number of further special terms incomprehensible to those not directly involved in this kind of analysis. Artists have their own technical vocabulary to describe visual products; students of dance deal in special ways with dance forms; and so forth. The study of artistic product is a highly technical field of inquiry, and it is also a restricted one.

But if we look at art as behavior in the kinds of terms I have suggested, then it becomes apparent that the product is only one part of art, and our frame of reference immediately stresses precisely the kinds of inquiry which are of primary interest to anthropology. Anthropology seeks descriptive facts, it is true, but of much more importance are the reasons that lie behind these facts. The description of a kinship system is not our ultimate aim; what we want to know is how this system works and, particularly, why it works in the ways it does. But in the study of the arts, the major emphasis has been placed upon the product, with the result that systemic, structural, or synchronic descriptions dominate the literature, leaving little room for studies which help us toward an understanding of the how and why of human behavior. In turning their attention toward the

description of product and away from the understanding of
product as the end result of process, anthropologists have
entered the critical world of humanists and left the analytical
world of social scientists. Product for the anthropologist is
primarily of interest either as the result of process or as it
creates new process in the form of human behavior and
concept. If we look past the product as a product and consider
some of the deeper manifestations which it and the behavior
which underlies it represent, we arrive at an understanding of
the kinds of questions which are beginning to preoccupy more
and more students of the arts and human behavior.

These questions are both numerous and complex, but, taken
broadly, they concern three spheres of interest: the cross-
cultural applicability of the concepts of *art* and *aesthetics*; the
descriptive-analytic study of the arts in given societies and the
application of the results to broader theory formulation; and
the techniques by which the arts can be successfully studied.

The problems concerning the cross-cultural applicability of
the various concepts of the arts may be essentially philosophic
and semantic, but they are nonetheless real for those who must
grapple with them. Those who argue for the view that these
concepts are not cross-culturally valid reason more or less as
follows. "Art" and "aesthetics" seem to be especially difficult
terms to define, much more difficult, apparently, than other
kinds of terms used in anthropology, such as "lineage" or
"chief." Further, the definitions suggested are inevitably
couched in Western conceptual terms, and since we have not
yet tested them on a world scale, as has been done with many
other anthropologically used terms, certain consequences en-
sue. While all societies have some of the activities and products which Westerners define as *art*—including music, dance,
and (oral) literature—the universality of other arts, including
visual art, drama, and architecture, is definitionally doubtful.
Further, where these arts are present, the processes involved
are by no means necessarily regarded either as "creative" or as
"arting," and the products are not necessarily regarded as art.
Indeed, we have reasonably good evidence to indicate that in
some societies, and perhaps in many, these activities are
regarded simply as normal human activities, ranked alongside
hunting, farming, repairing a bicycle, and so on.

Similarly, the argument continues, some cultures include a category of conceptualization which Westerners call "aesthetics," that is, a particular constellation of attitudes, beliefs, and responses toward activities and objects that we call art—and some clearly do not. Thus, from the Western point of view, all societies have at least some of what we call the arts, but not all the arts; and not all societies have aesthetics, though some do. The evidence for the presence or absence of art and the aesthetic, however, is relatively meager on the cross-cultural level, and much basic data gathering remains to be done.

This being so, at least three major groups of questions and further speculations arise.

1. Why should this be so? Do some underlying organizational factors exist in social organization, or ideation, or another structure of human society and culture which can account for this?
2. Can we isolate a universal constellation of attitudes and behaviors which we can call aesthetic in the widest sense, and of which the Western aesthetic concept is simply one manifestation? If so, how can we best probe for, and understand, the broader human concept?
3. Is what we call art in fact a special aspect of culture, separable from the rest of the sociocultural system in a special way, operating in special terms under special conditions for special ends? It is thus that Westerners regard the arts, but it is apparently not necessarily so in other societies.

Approaches to the solution of the philosophic-semantic questions posed by the concepts of "art" and "aesthetics" have not been particularly promising. Anthropologists and others have taken a number of courses, among them simply refusing to deal with the problem; using simple and essentially Western definitions which allow the writer to proceed to analysis but which do not solve the problem; substituting new sets of terms for the old; suggesting new meanings for old terms, such as the idea of the "unvoiced aesthetic" or "functional aesthetic"; or, potentially most fruitful, establishing broader cross-cultural meanings for the terms by seeking internal criteria through indigenous responses to what are taken to be art objects.

The ultimate solution of the definitional problems surrounding the terms "art" and "aesthetics" is not yet in sight, but it seems evident that it will result from careful analytical cross-cultural study involving artists, their activities, and their own concepts and evaluations of what they are doing, such as has been carried out in a few societies to date.

The second broad problem area in the study of the arts and anthropology concerns the specific arts in specific societies, and the application of the results to broader theory formulation. While it is not my purpose here to present a roster of successful and unsuccessful studies, it is worthwhile pointing out that studies undertaken from an anthropological perspective are notably lacking. While the literature is choked with descriptions of art products, studies of art processes are few and far between, and even basic anthropological descriptions of the arts as sociocultural phenomena in given societies are rare. The result is a wide gap in fundamental arts ethnography. We have little information on a world scale, for example, about musicians and the social groups in which they work and interact, about basic postulations concerning color relationships, about internal evaluations of dance movements. While we can divide the traditional North American Indian continent into a given number of music style areas, for most Indian societies we lack even the most fundamental knowledge of what music means to the people who play and hear it, or how the composer works, or the relationship between music and power. Notable exceptions occur, of course, but anthropologists simply do not have the basic kinds of information needed either to carry out comparative studies or to formulate additional theory.

Furthermore, when studies such as these are achieved, it is evident that a strong tendency exists to banish all concern for the initial set of problems noted above, that is, what are "art" and "aesthetics". Instead, investigators act as though these questions had already been answered; the unspoken assumption is that since "dance" and "music", and "drama" are considered to be arts in Western society, they must also be arts in other societies. Thus the two sets of problems are often compartmentalized with consequent loss of potential solutions to both.

In any case, what we know best about the arts in other societies lies on the technical or formal level. In contrast, we know very little about the behavioral and conceptual levels, and thus the information we have at hand tends to be essentially nonanthropological in its usefulness.

The third general sphere of interest in the study of the arts in anthropology concerns the various approaches which can be used, and here the potential is exceptionally wide. Indeed, those interested in the field find themselves currently in the midst of a revolution of techniques and methodologies.

Structural studies, for example, have been applied in a number of ways to various art products, and the work of Lévi-Strauss and others, particularly in respect to myth, legend, and tale, has stimulated many new and complex approaches. The application of Birdwhistell's system of kinesics to the analysis of dance is a further extension of structural analysis. Among functional approaches, new applications of statistical and computer techniques have led to the development of correlational statements about the arts and other aspects of culture and society. A few studies have looked at the arts as human behavior and attempted to understand music, for example, or the arts in general as aspects of culture and society. The special methodology of ethnoscience has hardly been applied to the study of the arts, but beginnings have been made in research into color; and investigations of music by Charles Adams among the southern Paiute and Basotho, for example, are as yet unpublished. Some attention has also been turned toward perception on a cross-cultural basis, but such studies are rare.

The field of semiotics, in general, and linguistics, in particular, has provided new stimuli in several directions. Unpublished studies have been made of various kinds of sign systems in the arts, such as dance, and Peacock's analysis of drama both as communication and as symbol has had considerable influence. New theories of art using communication theory are being developed, and transformational and generative analyses of the various arts are reasonably well established.

The future of the study of the arts from an anthropological perspective depends upon the extent to which they are viewed not as isolated bits of culture which are simply reflections of other sociocultural behavior or systems but as ongoing social and cultural subsystems in themselves. The arts are not passive in their sociocultural dimensions; rather, they are action systems which inform behavior, order behavior, and cause behavior. They are also highly effective symbolic systems, expressions of ideas, and highly redundant repositories of knowledge, values, and expressions of man in his multifaceted human dimensions. The approach argued here is anthropological in nature, as contrasted to the more common approaches which emphasize the formal art product. In the slowly growing awareness of what is anthropological about anthropological investigations of the arts lies the future of this field of study.

BIBLIOGRAPHICAL NOTE

No general work on the arts in anthropology exists, and the literature for the specific arts varies considerably both in quality and quantity. Anthropological approaches to music are to be found in Alan P. Merriam, *The Anthropology of Music* (Evanston, Ill.: Northwestern University Press, 1964), Alan Lomax, *Folk Song Style and Culture*, Publication Number 88 (Washington, D.C.: American Association for the Advancement of Science, 1968), and John Blacking, *How Musical Is Man?* (Seattle: University of Washington Press, 1973). Broad references in the field of dance are few and far between, although Gertrude P. Kurath, "Panorama of Dance Ethnology," *Current Anthropology* 1:233–54 (1960) and Alan P. Merriam, "Anthropology and the Dance," in Tamara Comstock (ed.), *New Dimensions in Dance Research: Anthropology and Dance—The American Indian* (New York: Committee on Research in Dance, 1974), have attempted overviews. Herta Haselberger's discussion surveys visual art study in "Methods of Studying Ethnological Art," *Current Anthropology* 2:351–84 (1961), and Robert P. Armstrong's *The Affecting Presence: An Essay in Humanistic Anthropology* (Urbana, Ill.: University of Illinois Press, 1971), while purporting to be general, is, in fact, a novel anthropological approach to visual art and its impacts. Franz Boas, *Primitive Art* (Reprint. Gloucester, Mass.: Peter Smith Publishers, Inc., 1962), has long been a classic in the field. Folklore, taken broadly, is represented by Alan Dundes, *The Study of Folklore* (Englewood Cliffs, N.J.: Prentice-Hall, Inc., 1965), and the new approach by Americo Paredes and Richard Bauman (eds.), *Toward New Perspectives in Folklore* (Austin: University of Texas Press for the American Folklore Society, 1971). Maria Leach (ed.), *Standard Dictionary of Folklore, Mythology and Legend* (New York: Funk & Wagnalls Co., Inc., 1972), includes discussion and summary of a great variety of folklore topics. Although specific studies of drama are to be found, they are not abundant, and Melville J. Herskovits, "Dramatic Expression Among Primitive Peoples," *Yale Review* 33:683–98 (1944), remains virtually the only attempt at a general statement.

24.
THE PSYCHOLOGICAL APPROACH IN ANTHROPOLOGY

Edward M. Bruner

THE FIELD OF CULTURE and personality has been one of the most controversial in contemporary anthropology. After taking off in the late nineteen twenties with a flourish, inspired by such pioneers as Edward Sapir, A. Irving Hallowell, and Margaret Mead, the field came under increasingly severe criticism in the nineteen fifties and went into a partial eclipse in the nineteen sixties. Possible reasons for the decline include a lack of scientific rigor, a preoccupation with intuitively derived depictions of national character, and departures into such methodological blind alleys as projective testing. But the central problems of psychological anthropology have remained with us, and there is evidence that the continuing sound investigations of John Whiting, Mel Spiro, and Anthony Wallace, among others, as well as increasing interest in universally human processes of thought and affect may well generate a resurgence of interest in the field.

Some social and cultural anthropologists, particularly followers of A. R. Radcliffe-Brown and Leslie White, still take the position that we should study only social and cultural systems. They say that anthropologists should not be concerned with either psychology, personality, or individuals, even in a cross-cultural framework. They fear that the psychological anthropologist will offer naive explanations of social institutions and events in terms of individual motivation—for example, that war is caused by man's aggressive instinct—without reference

344

to the complex historical, political, and economic factors which precipitate warfare in any given instance.

Modern students of culture and personality, on the other hand, well aware of the excesses of their predecessors and the cautions of their critics, contend that the psychological dimension is an essential component of human existence and, further, that adequate understanding of relationships among men and their cultural institutions must include statements about what goes on within an individual's mind—about what he or she thinks and feels—with due attention to irrational unconscious processes as well as to the rational conscious ones. There is recognition that individuals interpret experience based upon culturally defined symbolic systems and indeed, it is the acknowledgement of the importance of unconscious and symbolic processes which characterizes culture and personality research.

Psychiatrists also study unconscious processes, and it was, in fact, "the encounter of anthropology . . . with psychoanalysis that gave rise to culture and personality studies." Many contemporary workers in the field today do rely upon one or another variant of the Freudian psychoanalytic model. But there are basic differences in objective and approach between psychiatry, and culture and personality. Our discipline is not a mere extension of psychology applied cross-culturally, and we are not clinically oriented, in that no attempt is made to help or cure the mentally ill. Nor are we primarily interested in particular individuals in all their uniquenesses; individuals are studied for the light they shed on regularities in the social process. Indeed, *psychological anthropology* takes as its field of investigation the study of culture as such, only it does so from a special point of view and with reference to a limited number of problems.

In this chapter we shall examine some of the premises of the psychological approach starting with universal aspects of the human condition and ending with the analysis of specific cultures. Let us begin by viewing the origins of man and culture in evolutionary perspective. As Clifford Geertz (Chapter 2) and Clark Howell (Chapter 5) have pointed out, the emergence of modern man from the lower animals did not occur all at once, as if by divine or legislative act, but was a slow, gradual, possibly painful process that took place over many hundreds of centuries during and even before the ice ages. In some respects, the hominization of our species is relived, or recapitulated, by every one of us and our children, as each newborn infant is slowly, gradually, and painfully transformed from an animal-like being into a more or less fully socialized adult member of some particular human society. For at birth, children have much in common with our primate ancestors in that neither can talk, love, laugh, believe in ghosts or gods, nor reflect upon themselves in relation to the larger environment that surrounds them. The frustrations and joys of childhood are, in a very real sense, the residue and inheritance of man's imperfect and incomplete biological and cultural development in the past.

I do not wish to push too far the analogy between the hominization of our species and the socialization of children, as the mechanisms involved, the time depth, and other aspects of the two processes are certainly different. A basic difference is that the genetic potential for humanization, acquired over the last few hundreds of thousands of years, is immediately present in every human infant, and the infant is ready and eager to actualize this potential in the family context. The essential similarity, however, is that culture made us human phylogenetically and culture makes us human ontogenetically. But culture was not a gift from the gods, nor did it just grow by itself. It was achieved at great psychic cost. All of us, all humanity, past, present, and future, pay the price of civilization.

Let us be more specific about those universal aspects of a cultural mode of adaptation which exact this psychic cost. Infants are helpless at birth and immature for a relatively long period; and they are born with or soon develop aggressive, sexual, and acquisitive desires which must be controlled in the socialization process. There is no known human society in which men can kill, rape, or rob at will, and there is no known human society in which children and adults, at one time or another, and in one way or another, have not experienced such desires. Every culture must control the expression of aggression; otherwise society would be disrupted. And every culture must regulate the allocation of women and property, simply because there are never enough of these resources to satisfy everyone. Individuals who cannot adequately control their aggressive, sexual, and acquisitive needs can never adjust to any human society. Persons who approach this extreme are either killed, ostracized, or placed in mental or penal institutions.

On the other hand, it is difficult to imagine a society in which all personal desires of all individuals were gratified. Such a hypothetical society would probably be without suicide, or neurosis, or crime as we know it, but it would also lack passion, creativity, and change. Our imaginary culture would, I think, be a rather dull place, inhabited by fully satisfied vegetable-like beings instead of by human beings. But to return to this, the real, world: if all the aggressive, sexual, and acquisitive needs of an individual were immediately and completely gratified, then that individual would never become fully human. We develop ego strength, self-awareness, and a sense of reality as a consequence of external controls and inhibitions. Some degree of frustration is necessary for survival and maturity.

The psychic cost to which we have referred, the inherent frustration associated with the socialization process, is even more specific. There is a necessary delay between wish and gratification, the wishes and desires themselves may be ambivalent, and cultural goals are often contradictory. Children are universally reared in a nuclear family unit or in some culturally stipulated substitute, and the transition from complete dependence upon the parents or parental surrogates to independence in the larger community is often difficult and awkward. This is so because prolonged intimate association in the family context leads to extremely complicated interpersonal bonds. From the point of view of the child, Lawrence Z. Freedman and Anne Roe have pointed out, "the beloved person is the frustrating agent, and the pleasure-giving object inflicts pain." Children develop strong sexual and aggressive feelings toward one or both parents, feelings which are frequently reciprocated and which are only partially controlled by the incest taboo. Further, family units are never exact duplicates of one another. Thus what children learn at an early age from their parents may be in conflict with what they learn at a later age from their peers.

The inherent conflict between personal desires and cultural demands is resolved in slightly different ways by each individual and by each society, although there are some universally human regularities in the process and in the techniques of resolution. One means is by a variety of unconscious defensive mechanisms. We repress culturally unacceptable desires by banning them from consciousness; we project and displace some by attributing our own desires to outsiders or to scapegoats in our own society; we deny the existence of other desires or sublimate them, thereby placing the released energy to work for the benefit of society. We may reverse incompatible wishes, for example, by expressing approval when we really feel hate, or we may direct an aggressive impulse against ourselves with a consequent loss of self-esteem.

Society provides disguised means of gratification in fantasy, literature, drama, folk tales, play, or religious ritual. Such forms of fantasy have a variety of social and individual functions, but by directing potentially harmful impulses into approved or at least acceptable channels, some measure of vicarious satisfaction is provided for the participants. Satire, cartoons, and jokes almost universally perform similar functions. For the individual, the content of dreams both reflects and expresses culturally patterned stress.

Society must, of course, directly fulfill some personal needs, but in every instance it rigidly defines the appropriate objects, goals, and techniques of gratification. Most societies carefully define those persons whom it is proper to hate, precisely specify approved sexual objects, and develop a complex series of rules regulating the acquisition of wealth and property. It is indeed remarkable how elaborate are the cultural norms governing aggressive, sexual, and acquisitive aspects of human behavior.

We have some comments to make about the means of resolving the basic human conflict between personal and cultural needs. The first is that these varied mechanisms, taken together, must be investigated on the individual and on the societal level simultaneously. The nature of the problem is such that it cannot be adequately studied entirely from the perspective of individual psychology, without regard for the sociocultural context in which individuals develop and in which their needs are expressed, nor can it be studied entirely from the perspective of the cultural system, without regard for individuals and the mechanisms they employ to adjust to their society. Neither the psychiatrist nor the cultural anthropologist alone can satisfactorily handle all dimensions of the problem within the framework of one single discipline. It is such problems that give rise to psychological anthropology, to anthropologically-oriented psychology, and to cooperative interdisciplinary research.

Our second comment merely gives emphasis to what has already been implied. We have seen that a major function of the emergence of culture was to direct, channel, and prescribe how our aggressive, sexual, acquisitive, and other needs were to be gratified. From the viewpoint of our species, man is more flexible than any other animal in that his behavior is more dependent upon learning than upon biology or inherited predisposition. But this potential variability is never allowed free spontaneous expression within the boundaries of any given society. Human behavior is universally patterned by cultural norms and prohibitions. Man may be infinitely plastic but particular cultures are not. Each culture has its own special variant of what it means to be fully human and civilized, its unique ways of handling children and of socializing them, and its own model of the good life. This variety of present-day cultures and social structure proves that the human experiment is a continuing process.

The members of a society do not, of course, reconstruct or recreate their culture every generation. They are born into an existing system and they inherit a cultural tradition from their parents and elders. Psychological anthropologists are very much interested in the process by which culture is transmitted from one generation to the next. One means by which this is accomplished is through the application of social and supernatural sanctions. Children who conform to their culture are rewarded and those who do not are punished. The agents of punishment in addition to the parents may include other relatives, neighbors, peers, teachers, or political authorities. They may utilize a variety of techniques including beatings and other forms of physical punishment, threats of bodily harm by supernatural beings, the withdrawal of food or love, and the inculcation of guilt or anxiety. As a consequence of these and other techniques children internalize some, but not all, cultural norms; they develop a conscience which serves as a constant reminder of parental and cultural prohibitions. In the later years it is the internalized anticipation of punishment which serves as a substitute for sanctions applied by the real parents or other authority figures.

This process is not completely negative, however, in that it is not dependent entirely upon frustration, sanction, and punishment. In the course of growing up children come to identify with their parents or with others who serve as models of the cultural ideal. They emulate the behavior of these models, and they evaluate themselves with reference to the standards established by them. To paraphrase Erich Fromm (1944), eventually the members of a society want to act as they have to act; they come to desire what is socially necessary. Most people in most societies most of the time strive to achieve their particular culture's definition of the good life, because they find it personally and socially rewarding.

But not all people do so. Thus far in this paper we have dealt with particular cultures as if they were constant monolithic entities, and we have talked as if the personality structures of all members of a given society were relatively uniform. These are obvious oversimplifications, and it is now time to correct them. Many of us, in popular speech, commit a similar error when we say, for example, that Americans are materialistic, Englishmen are formal, or Italians volatile. Irrespective of whatever element of truth there may be to these stereotypes, it is perfectly clear that not all Americans are equally materialistic, and there are informal Englishmen and passive Italians. The problem we have raised is this: how can we make statements about those aspects of personality shared by an entire group or nation in view of the personality differences that exist between individuals and subgroups within the society? The more fundamental question here concerns the nature of the correspondence between culture on the one hand and personality on the other.

In 1970, in a short but incisive book, Anthony F. C. Wallace has contributed to our understanding of this problem. He does so by contrasting two different points of view which he calls the replication of uniformity and the organization of diversity. In the first view, the aim is to describe how the character structure of one group differs from that of another, and the emphasis is on the uniqueness of each. The members of a society are considered to have learned the "same things" because of similar early experiences and because of common participation in the same cultural system. The culture is considered relatively homogeneous, individuals are thought to share a uniform personality organization, and one expects to find a nearly perfect correspondence between culture type and personality type. Industrialization, urbanization, revolution, and other forms of rapid culture change are seen as leading to personal breakdown and social disorganization. It is assumed that each new generation becomes a replica of the preceding one in both cultural tradition and character structure. The research problem is to investigate the mechanisms of socialization by which this is accomplished.

In the second view, which is Wallace's own, culture is, in fact, characterized by diversity of individuals and groups, each acting to further their own interests, and socialization is not considered to be a perfect mechanism for ensuring the replication of either culture or character from one generation to the next. Individuals differ because of variations in genetic constitution and because of unique experiences in the life career. Society is stratified, regimented, and diversified due to age-sex differences, occupational specialization, the necessary inequality in social life, and differential participation in the total culture. Rapid culture change does not necessarily lead to disintegration; as Wallace says, it is the natural condition of man. In view of the above, the research problem is to investigate the basis of orderly social life. How do diverse individuals organize themselves so as to maintain a cultural system which is itself constantly changing, shifting, and oscillating?

The crucial distinction is between *behavior* and *motivation.*

To take an example from my own profession, the students who attend my lectures behave in strikingly similar ways. All are dressed more or less alike, all arrive and leave at approximately the same time, most prepare their reading assignments, and unfortunately, even their answers to the examination questions are quite similar. But it is a commonplace of university life in America and probably elsewhere that the underlying motivations of the students are highly variable. One student comes to the university because of an inner compulsion to learn; another because of parental pressure; a third out of expediency—he or she hopes to make contacts which eventually will be beneficial in his or her later business or political life; and a fourth, because of social expectation, comes to college because his or her friends do. Of course, the motivation in any given case would be much more complex than I have indicated, but the general point should be clear; common participation in a social institution does not imply psychological uniformity among the participants. Individuals may conform to their culture because of a wide variety of different motives. In other words, the same behavior may satisfy different personal needs, and the same needs may be satisfied by different behavior.

In Wallace's view, the basis of societal functioning is complementarity, not uniformity. In any social interaction it is not necessary that motivation be shared or even that one party understands the motives of the other; it is only necessary that the behavior of each be more or less predictable. To paraphrase Wallace, the relationship between professor and student does not depend on mutual conformity to one role, but on a complementarity of different roles. Complex human social systems are able to function precisely because each person is relieved of the burden of understanding the motivations of others and of acquiring the appropriate skills and knowledge necessary for the performance of others' roles. Nor is it necessary for individuals to reveal many aspects of their own personality to those with whom they interact. To some extent, each of us lives in our own private world.

As we have seen, it cannot be assumed that the members of a society share a common social character. But does this imply that each individual is unique? Certainly not. In the words of

Clyde Kluckhohn and Henry A. Murray, every man is in certain respects like all other men, like some other men, like no other man. There may not be a perfect one-to-one correspondence between the culture of a society and the personality of its members, but some correspondences do exist. In order to study them, as well as the areas in which no correspondences occur, we must make detailed analyses of subgroups within a society and of the primary social units which have significance in personality formation and cultural transmission. We cannot infer personality from social institutions or overt behavior alone, but must investigate the shared aspects of emotional and cognitive patterning based upon detailed study of individuals and of their significant social relationships. We must continue to study the varied means by which culture structures and channels the expression of universal human needs, and we must turn our attention to the bases of conformity and change in social life. These are complex problems, but they are among those that will continue to be of crucial importance for psychological anthropology.

BIBLIOGRAPHICAL NOTE

Culture and personality are generally associated with such early studies as the trilogy by Margaret Mead, *Coming of Age in Samoa* (Reprint. New York: New American Library, 1928), *Growing Up in New Guinea* (Reprint. New York: New American Library, 1930), and *Sex and Temperament in Three Primitive Societies* (Reprint. New York: New American Library, 1935). These books may be obtained in paperback editions at almost every campus bookstore. Another early and highly original thinker is A. Irving Hallowell; see his *Culture and Experience* (Philadelphia: University of Pennsylvania Press, 1974).

Although almost all modern anthropologists would disagree with one or another aspect of Freud's culture and personality writings, two of his books in particular, *Totem and Taboo* (New York: W. W. Norton & Co., Inc., 1952) and *Civilization and Its Discontents* (New York: W. W. Norton & Co., Inc., 1962), are most suggestive treatments of problems that have retained their significance.

Historical developments are described in the following surveys: Milton Singer, "A Survey of Culture and Personality Theory and Research," in Bert Kappan (ed.), *Studying Personality Cross-Culturally* (Evanston, Ill.: Row Peterson & Co., 1961), Melville E. Spiro, "An Overview and a Suggested Reorientation," in Francis L. K. Hsu (ed.), *Psychological Anthropology* (Homewood, Ill.: General Learning Press, 1971), and Anthony F. Wallace, "The New Culture-and-Personality," in Thomas Gladwin and William Sturtevant (eds.), *Anthropology and Human Behavior* (Washington, D.C.: Anthropological Society of Washington, 1962). Each of these papers appears in volumes that contain other important articles and extensive bibliographies.

The best introductions to psychological anthropology are Anthony F. Wallace, *Culture and Personality* (2nd. ed. New York: Random House, Inc., 1970) and Robert A. LeVine, *Culture, Behavior, and Personality* (Chicago: Aldine Publishing Co., 1973).

25.

POPULATION AND ENVIRONMENT

Steven Polgar

THESE DAYS, WHEN there are so many people commenting on population and environmental problems, one may well ask what distinguishes anthropologists who would add their voices to the fray. The main contributions we can make are based on our knowledge of human evolution and our habit of looking at human communities from an ecological or "systems" perspective.

Evolution and the Regulation of Human Numbers

More than two million years ago, groups of primates first started to make tools, to run on their hind legs, to establish home bases, and to obtain a considerable part of their protein intake from the flesh of animals. These changes were accompanied by changes in physiology. The human reproductive system permits pregnancy to occur more frequently than was the case for earlier primates. The change from a single breeding period each year to twelve or thirteen cycles during which fertilization could occur was one important factor in this; the other was the possibility for a female to become pregnant before she stopped breastfeeding her young. After these physiological changes took place, and even with 50 percent of the young dying before they reached the reproductive period and more dying before they completed the childbearing phase, the number of offspring born to each mother would probably have resulted in a substantial population increase. But there was a more immediate problem for early humans: among nomadic hunters and gatherers a woman could not carry more than one child who was unable to walk or feed itself. Therefore, we surmise that voluntary measures for spacing and limiting births, which have been found in all cultures surviving to recent times, may have arisen very early in human evolution.

To say that such measures were voluntary is not the same as saying they were deliberately aimed at regulating population growth. They probably included infanticide, abortion, the killing of adults by members of their own species, prohibitions on the resumption of sexual intercourse for long periods after delivery, delaying beyond menarche the age at which full sexual intercourse could begin, periods of abstention from intercourse, termination of intercourse before the physiological capacity to reproduce had itself ended, and restrictions on who could mate with whom. All of these practices had other and more immediate consequences, but in the long run they all helped to keep the population well below the fluctuating supportive capacity of the environment. Cultures that did not moderate reproduction sooner or later became extinct, leaving the field to those that did regulate their population.

The equilibrium between humans and the environments in which they lived remained relatively stable throughout almost all the two million years of human evolution. While rapid periods of growth and dispersal probably took place as new types of humans and new techniques of getting food evolved, simple arithmetic demonstrates that before the invention of agriculture the population could not have increased at more than an annual growth rate of about 0.002 percent per year. Hunters and gatherers created few changes in the environment, except for the possible extinction of some large animals and burning down some forests.

With the change from food gathering to food production some ten thousand years ago a new relationship was established between humans and their environment, and a great spurt—amounting to perhaps as much as a hundred-fold increase—took place in their numbers. So long as agriculture and animal husbandry remained in the village economy stage, the average increase may have been on the order of one additional person every thousand years (an annual growth rate of 0.1 percent). Producing food required that humans make substantial changes in the vegetation, soil, watercourses, and animal life in their surroundings.

The feudal period of history, marked by supravillage political organization and—later—by preindustrial cities, is notable for great fluctuations in numbers of people. Population increased rapidly under the stimulus of centralized authorities, such as chiefs, priests, and kings, who collected and redistributed large amounts of food and labor as they carried on their prestigious activities. But great epidemics often decimated the concentrated populations, which seem often to have exceeded the safety point in their relationship to the environment. Still, improvements in the technology of agriculture permitted a long-term increase of between 0.2 percent and 0.5 percent per year during feudal times in Europe, China, and Japan.

The current period of history is characterized by colonialism and the emergence of industry, culminating in the economic domination of third world nations by those that can export large quantities of manufactured goods. With regard to population, colonial expansion can be divided into two phases. In the first, the population size of subject peoples decreased abruptly under the impact of slavery, the importation of new diseases, and intensified warfare. In the second, population moved up toward previous levels of density, and went even higher in some cases, not only because people suspended or decreased the voluntary practices that had limited reproduction, but also due to discouragement of tribal warfare by colonialist authorities, the pronatalist influence of missionaries, the establishment of transportation networks over which food supplies could be carried in greater bulk and over longer distances, and the demands of colonial administrators for labor and taxes.

Many people mistakenly share the belief that the recent rapid growth of population in Asia, Africa, and Latin America is primarily due to the use of various health measures since 1945, which suddenly reduced the mortality rates of nonindustrial people below the high levels where they had presumably stood since time immemorial. However, under the colonial rule of the Dutch in Java, for example, population increased during the nineteenth century by 2 percent per year without the benefit of any modern medical services or drugs. The recent diffusion of these innovations merely reinforced a long-term trend that resulted from internal forces compensating for depopulation and from the external forces of colonial exploitation.

Just as the presence of large numbers of poor people in early industrial Europe had been of great benefit to the industrial entrepreneurs who were seeking a supply of cheap labor, the creation of a substantial demand for manufactured goods and the large pool of manpower available for mining and plantation agriculture were of great utility to those who wanted to invest in overseas trade. For peasants in the third world today it also makes good sense to have several heirs, some of whom may try their fortune in urban areas while others remain on the farm to help their parents produce a larger crop. Such a "spreading of one's bets" makes sense when there is little certainty that either route will ensure prosperity for the family.

Recently, many countries have moved toward greater democracy, and in industrial states laws have been passed to protect the health and welfare of workers as higher productivity increased the value of each trained worker. Also, the maintenance of armies in faraway places and the institution of foreign aid by industrial states have diminished the net inflow of goods and money from international ventures. As such changes occur, members of the elite tend to rediscover Malthus and express increasing concern about the population problem among the poor, whether at home or abroad. In translating such concerns into policies, elitists tend to favor negative and repressive measures, rather than programs that would directly benefit health and welfare while they also slow population growth.

Democratization in industrial countries has also led to the creation of a large middle class, for whom continued upward mobility can be better achieved if each family has a relatively small number of offspring so each child can be given a good start in life with high educational attainment and perhaps some capital. Living conditions have also been much improved. Thus, in a number of countries that have undergone industrialization we have witnessed rapid decreases in both birth rates and death rates for substantial segments of the population.

When the advantages of reducing the size of one's family are substantial (as in late-nineteenth-century England), people are willing to undergo the considerable danger or inconvenience of such methods of reproductive control as clandestine abortion, infanticide, withdrawal, and abstinence. When the advantages and disadvantages of having a third (or fourth) child are more nearly equal, the relative safety, effectiveness, availability, and cultural acceptability of birth control methods can make a large amount of difference in the use of family planning.

In industrialized countries such as Japan and Hungary, where legal abortion under medical supervision is easily available, the population growth rate now fluctuates around zero. In the United States, although knowledge about contraceptives is now widespread and almost every couple uses contraception for at least some period of time, one-fifth of all births were unwanted in the period 1960–1965 and two-fifths of wanted births were the result of timing failures. The gross inadequacies of the way in which health care is organized in this country can be blamed for many of these unwanted births. Most unintended pregnancies—meaning both unwanted births and timing failures—could be prevented if abortion upon request and good contraceptive methods and services were made easily accessible and acceptable to everyone. And preventing all unintended births would reduce the level of natural increase of the U.S. population just about to zero. The main problem, then, is not to cajole or coerce people to have fewer children but to help them plan their families effectively and in accord with their own wishes.

In the long run there is no absolute certainty, of course, that greatly improved family planning services (including abortion everywhere available on request) will keep the U.S. population from growing, that there will not be conditions which once again may make it advantageous for families to have more children than is compatible with a stabilized population. It would be good, therefore, if more supportive facilities were provided to women who wish to obtain employment in full equality with men. Equality between women and men is an important goal on its own, and women in the labor force usually have fewer children than housewives. And builders, city planners, and psychologists should not continue to assume that the best way of life centers upon a suburban, child-centered, nuclear household.

Resources

If population growth in the United States were to stop immediately, most of our problems of resource use and environmental pollution would still remain. But if our manner of using resources and discarding wastes is not changed, it is also true that further growth in population will worsen our difficulties. It is necessary to evaluate the impact of these two factors—the *per* and the *capita*—separately.

The rate at which Americans use various resources has grown much faster than has the population. With regard to metals, for example, per capita consumption of iron and steel has risen from thirty pounds at the beginning of the nineteenth century to half a ton in 1960. In recent years, in fact, the U.S. has accounted for one-third to one-half the consumption of all the principal metals in the entire world outside the socialist countries. While the population of the United States has increased one and one-half times in the first half of the twentieth century, total energy consumption grew four and one-half times. On a per capita basis, taking 1900 as the base, the consumption of energy went from 100 to 225.

Some scientists are optimistic about the availability of resources sufficient for continued expansion of both the population and per capita demand. The general philosophy, however, which assumes that private enterprise may withdraw as much of the available resources from the environment as it pleases, switching to new technologies to tap resources more difficult to get when those more easily available are exhausted, pays little attention to the indirect costs that will be borne by future generations. Our descendants will have to pay a great deal, not only to clean up the mess we are leaving, but also to obtain something near the level of comfort in which most of the U.S. population now lives.

Business economists usually assume that the American economy will remain healthy only as long as total production and total consumption continue to increase. Some are even doubtful that if population growth were to halt, continued increases in per capita consumption alone could keep the present system going. Indeed, many of our current practices, such as allowing tax exemptions for depreciation but not for restoration of productive resources and selling bonds on which our descendants will pay interest charges, are based on the assumption of a never-ending expansion in the gross national product. There is no reason, however, to accept this assumption as eternally valid. If we decide that it is in the best long-term interest of humankind to level off average material consumption in industrialized countries and at the same time help the poor in these countries and in the third world improve their level of well-being, economists and lawmakers will have to devise new policies to these ends. Such redistribution and conservation policies are well within the realm of the possible.

The concept of the stationary state has a respectable history in economics. The earlier economists, however, thought that this stationary state would be made necessary by increasing scarcity, both in absolute terms and in terms of increasing costs per additional unit produced. It now turns out, as we shall see, that the pinch is first becoming felt at the other end, in terms of pollution.

Scarcity on the input side remains a possibility for the future. Ecologists have made many studies of the way in which a community of plants and animals becomes established in a new environment; they call this process *succession*. During the early state of ecological succession, both the production of organic matter and the amount of energy used grow very fast. The *biomass*, which is the accumulation of organic matter that has been produced in the past and which remains in organic form, grows steadily. Later, when the ecosystem *matures*, the rate of production and the rate of energy use level off; the biomass continues to grow, but more slowly. E. P. Odum has compared the relationship between humans and their environment to the early state in the ecological succession process. Since the origin of agriculture, humankind has prevented the ecosystem of which it is a part from maturing. And in more recent times we have started to deplete the considerable reserves of the biomass and its derivatives that had accumulated during past times in organic evolution.

By keeping the ecosystem producing at a level as high as it can be made to go, humanity has succeeded in converting a great deal of available energy from current and past organic production into a large "standing crop" of human beings. Were this crop to multiply ten times, in order to survive people would have to displace all other terrestrial animals from the face of the earth and convert vegetable matter to their own needs as efficiently as herbivorous animals do now. It would be the better part of wisdom, it seems, to change our relationship with the environment into one resembling the mature phase of ecological succession long before we reach this point.

Anthropologists have described one type of agriculture, often regarded with scorn by Western technicians, the kind that used to be called "slash and burn" but is more appropriately termed *swidden agriculture.* This involves a craftful imitation of ecological complexity, by the planting and encouraging of a wide variety of different species. This kind of food production is, in the short run, less *efficient* than monocrop agriculture but much less risky in the long run, particularly in tropical climates.

Whether we want to describe the eventual situation we seek in terms of the stationary state of economists or the ecological stability of biologists and anthropologists, a realistic look into the future requires us to abandon the notion that increasing the production of material goods is a goal next to which other desirable goals have to be considered secondary. Activities that do not involve the consumption of larger and larger amounts of energy and matter, such as the "human care of human beings," artistic creation, active sports, and certain types of scientific pursuits, will surely keep busy all those who abhor idleness. And in the realm of material consumption, we will have to move much faster toward a more equal distribution of wealth and certainly reinstitute the old value of thrift.

Pollution

Pollution of the environment is not restricted to Western capitalist societies; it is also a problem in the USSR. When the number of humans was small relative to the total land surface, there was less need to worry about the waste that human activities entail. Disease resulting from the excretions of people and domestic animals has, of course, been a problem ever since settled village life began. But the greatest pollution problems of our time are largely a consequence of dumping the unused byproducts of industrial processes and mechanized agriculture into the air, the water, and the soil.

Air pollution is not merely an annoyance; it is a definite health hazard. While scientists have not yet identified all the harmful substances involved, it appears that brief periods of high concentration of several chemicals are likely to create acute disturbances of the human respiratory system. Chronic conditions of ill health, such as bronchitis and asthma, have been shown to be related to long-term air pollution in such diverse places as London, Jersey City, and Yokohama. Human welfare is affected in other ways, too; organic peroxides, present in smog in Los Angeles among other places, are likely to damage such sensitive plants as spinach, sugar beet, alfalfa, endive, oats, and pinto bean. Other types of atmosphere problems include radioactive fallout, depletion of ozone, and noise.

Water is useful to humanity not only because we drink it, wash in it, irrigate our crops with it, and use it for many industrial processes but also because it is a cheap way to carry away our wastes. Some disease organisms can persist in water for a long time, and some parasites are carried by intermediate hosts such as snails or fish from one infected person to the next. But the hazard to health is usually small when only a few people live near a river or a lake, particularly if there is enough time and distance between the deposition of urine or feces in the water and the time and place where people use the water again. In the United States, moreover, we have learned to deal with most waterborne disease organisms by methods such as chlorination and immunization. Our water sanitation technology, however, geared to deal with disease organisms, has shown itself totally incapable of taking care of industrial waste, hard detergents, and the byproducts of mechanized agriculture.

The organic life of streams can be destroyed either by outright killing, when the added substances are toxic to aquatic species or remove the oxygen they need for respiration, or by *overfeeding* the stream with such chemicals as nitrates and phosphates. The addition of these chemicals brings about a tremendous growth of aquatic plants, and when these die off suddenly, which often happens, the organic life of the stream will be choked by the resulting waste.

Pollution of the soil and of the entire terrestrial ecosystem is almost entirely the result of large-scale agriculture. The mindless spreading of lethal pesticides was dramatically brought before the public in Rachel Carson's *Silent Spring*. Insects, fungi, and other pests easily reach epidemic proportions when they adapt themselves to feeding on crops planted uniformly over large fields. Chemical control agents are just one more condition to which such pests can rapidly adapt by genetic mutation. In line with the tendency of humans since the invention of agriculture to maximize productivity and to prevent ecological succession from proceeding to maturity, and in line with the general "big stick" approach of Americans to any annoying problem, we have moved in on these pests with chemical overkill.

Research on alternatives to chemical pesticides is just getting under way. Some of the most promising approaches are the further development of genetically resistant plants and the breeding and repeated dispersal of male insects that are incapable of generating offspring. In the long run it seems not unlikely that a more permanent solution will have to include the reintroduction of practices similar to swidden agriculture. We will also have to develop an attitude which allows some insects and other organisms to get a small share of our crops. To aim for total eradication is in most instances too expensive and ecologically too dangerous.

To sum up: the effect of human activity on the environment during the later stages of human evolution has generally been in the direction of reducing ecological diversity. At the intake end of the production system, technological innovations have brought us closer and closer to the ultimate sources of energy and minerals. To accomplish this, many other organisms relying on these resources had to be eliminated. At the other end of the production process, industry and agribusiness have treated the environment as an apparently limitless dumping ground.

In the agricultural system of the preindustrial village, a great deal of organic matter is cycled back to the production end; animal and human feces as well as kitchen refuse and the unusable parts of plants are returned to the soil as fertilizer. But in the economic system of industrial societies it is more profitable to plunder accumulated resources wherever they can be found, transport them to locations where production processes are highly concentrated, and dump the refuse into the air, water, and soil without regard to consequences.

One motto for the future will have to be "recycling." Activities which recycle what are now considered useless byproducts into the production process will have to be rewarded. And we will have to stop such foolishness as granting depletion allowances to the pollution-prone oil industry and subsidizing the development of supersonic monster planes.

From what has been presented so far, it should be obvious that the continuing growth of the U.S. population is not what we need to worry about most for the present. First, better health services for everyone and better facilities to enable women to work in full equality with men will help to stabilize population. Second, population growth has been far less important in creating our environmental problems than has the unintelligent use of technology and the institution of economic policies that reward wastefulness rather than thrift.

Is there then a current population problem in the United States? The answer is yes, but the problem is not population growth but the distribution of people.

Urban Congestion and Segregation

The transition from societies at the level of village agriculture to feudal societies does not involve a major change in the sources of human subsistence. Rather, the significant element is a great increase in the degree of political centralization. In the sense that *feudal* is used here, there have been many feudal societies. But in only a few did urbanization occur before the impact of Western expansion.

We may consider an urban society one that has at least one settlement of great density, where one thousand or more adults live whose occupations are not in agriculture. Other than in a few commercial city-states such as Athens and Venice, the inhabitants of preindustrial cities represented a minor fraction of the total population of their state. The proportion of the U.S. population classified as urban—as opposed to rural—rose from 5.1 percent in 1790 to 59.0 percent in 1950. In 1950 the definition of *urban residence* was changed to include all those who lived in places with at least two thousand five hundred inhabitants, leading to a revision of the latter figure to 64 percent; in 1960 by the new definition the proportion was 69.9 percent.

The U.S. Bureau of the Census makes a further distinction, classifying as *metropolitan* residents the people who live in a central city and the contiguous counties which are socially and economically integrated with the central city. We have a great deal of demographic information on two types of metropolitan inhabitants: those who live in the core area and those who live in the suburbs. The population in the suburban rings of metropolitan areas has increased considerably in the last few decades and is expected to continue to grow; the population of the central city, by contrast, has just about reached a stable level and is not expected to increase in the future.

There is an immense body of writings on the problems of cities and suburbs, encompassing such a variety of concerns as transportation, health, recreation, and the location of businesses. In this chapter, one topic will be singled out: the distribution of blacks and whites in metropolitan areas. This topic is timely and sheds considerable light on many of the other problems of cities.[1]

1. My thanks are due to Carl Flemister, Executive Director, Planned Parenthood of New York City, who helped me realize that urban congestion and segregation are the most important population problems in the U.S. today.

Between 1900 and 1960, the proportion of all metropolitan inhabitants who lived in central cities decreased from 62.1 percent to 51.4 percent. Karl E. Taeuber and Alma F. Taeuber point out, however, that the percentage of central city dwellers who were white diminished from 93.3 to 82.4 percent in this period while the percentage of blacks grew from 6.5 to 16.8 percent. In the expanding suburban rings, by contrast, the proportion of whites increased from 90.7 to 95.0 percent, while the proportion of blacks decreased from 8.9 to 4.6 percent.

When describing the changing composition of metropolitan areas it is important to dispel some common misperceptions about birthrates among black people. There is no doubt that for the last few decades the natality rate of nonwhites has been higher than that of whites. The postwar baby boom was marked among both groups, but the increase was even more dramatic among nonwhites than among whites. We have very few clues to what caused the baby boom, but the sharper increase in births among nonwhites was due in large degree to improvements in maternity care over the dismal conditions that prevailed before World War II and the increased stability of marriages during the relatively prosperous nineteen-fifties. Since 1957, and even more since 1961, birth rates for both groups have sharply decreased. The differential between the two groups is still sizable, but the decline since 1957 has been steeper for nonwhites.

Statistics on birth rates often do not differentiate among whites and nonwhites according to socieconomic status or urban-vs.-rural background. It is generally known, however, that poor people and farm dwellers have higher natality rates than middle-class and urban populations. Proportionately fewer whites are poor than nonwhites. Survey results in 1960 already clearly showed that, among married couples, for nonwhites who were not raised on a farm in the south and had a high school education (and these accounted for nearly two-thirds of the sample population) the number of births was no different from that of whites. It is obvious that opportunities for upward social mobility, although severely restricted for blacks even with a high school education and a city upbringing, are minimal for those pushed out from school and those who live in the rural south.

While considerable improvements had been made in maternity services for southern blacks in the last few decades, family planning had until recently been provided on a token basis, if at all. A comparison of birth control methods used before 1960 by whites and nonwhites showed that, among users, more nonwhites than whites used nonprescription methods and fewer used methods requiring a prescription from a doctor. Several surveys on the number of children wanted have demonstrated that blacks are not likely to desire more children than whites, even though on the average they have more, which is not surprising given the lesser effectiveness of the nonprescription methods of birth control. These data reinforce the point made early in this chapter, that many unwanted pregnancies can be attributed to the inadequacies of the medical care system in the United States.

Let us now return to the question of residential segregation. The stark fact is that, despite a number of legal victories in the last fifteen years, the residential segregation of black people has increased rather than decreased. Although restrictive covenants—which prohibited a person buying real estate from selling it later to someone who was nonwhite—were struck down by the courts, more subtle ways of preventing blacks from breaking out of the ghetto have been effectively substituted. Even the recently passed federal fair housing law gives little promise of substantially changing the situation. The burden of proof remains on the person who feels that he or she has been discriminated against, and it takes a tremendous amount of planning, time, and money to press a claim to a successful conclusion. Furthermore, these laws and their enforcement have not been complemented by an effective program of metropolitan housing for low and moderate-income families, both black and white.

Institutional racism in the United States helps to account for both the continued pattern of housing segregation and the lack of governmental commitment to its elimination. It also explains the recent trend toward increasing allocations for the police (not to mention the National Guard and the Army), who are often seen as an occupation force ruling over desperate people tightly encircled by hostile suburbia.

One consequence of the demographic situation in central cities is the prospect that in more and more places, as blacks become the voting majority, blacks will become the mayors and city council members. It would be hazardous to assume that this turn of events will make a great difference in the welfare of central city residents. Demographic and political circumstances severely limit the potential gains for black people and for poor city dwellers regardless of color. For the foreseeable future, federal and state legislatures will remain under the control of affluent whites. Municipal governments are heavily dependent on state and federal allocations since their taxing power is severely limited. Many manufacturing plants and even more service industries have moved, with the white exodus, to the suburbs and other locations far away from the large industrial centers of the northeast. There is unfortunately every reason to believe that this trend will accelerate when black people win the powers of government in many more central cities. Real estate and sales taxes are already inadequate to meet the needs of the central cities, needs which have been neglected for decades.

Economic policies have frequently abetted the exploitation of labor without regard to the complex questions of human welfare, in a situation not unlike that described for resource use and pollution. The rapid urbanization of black people since 1940 is to be understood both as a consequence of mechanized agriculture and as a byproduct of the rapid rise and fall of requirements for cheap labor in manufacturing. Blacks are the successors in this respect to immigrants from Ireland, southern Europe, Poland, and other places. Their political rise in central cities also follows in many ways what happened to European immigrants. But the same racist forces that are preventing their movement into the suburbs are keeping them from effectively using the positions of power that were the springboard for advancement of the European immigrants.

Policies to redress the wrongs created by colonialism in the third world are applicable also in the central cities, which have sometimes been referred to as the "internal colonies" of the United States. New measures to improve health and to halt the wasteful use of resources by business enterprises and by the rich, and which would attempt to distribute more equitably the fruits of technological progress while attempting to keep the total through-put of materials from expanding, might elicit a more positive response from the black community and from the poor.

Conclusion

Population history and current population problems are quite different for the prosperous segments of industrialized nations and for the poor of the third world. The very large increase in the numbers of people during the early stages of industrialization leveled off in the fifty years 1880–1930. But per capita consumption accelerated. After the conquest of the third world, with the great decrease in non-European populations this brought about, raw materials were imported, and the conquered people were used as a huge labor pool and—later— as a market for industrial goods. The rapid growth in the number of third world people after 1800 was advantageous until very recently for the well-to-do in the United States and other nations engaged in economic colonialism.

Internal problems in the United States today are not so much related to population growth, which currently is very close to the replacement rate anyway, as to waste, maldistribution, and depersonalization. Institutional forms and values have developed during the period of industrial expansion which led to the degradation of resources, the serious pollution of air, water, and land, and the dehumanization of personal relationships. Huge discrepancies developed in the distribution of wealth and population. Minority groups—like the people of Asia, Africa, and Latin America—were very useful to form a cheap labor pool. Slavery, immigration, and discrimination helped to keep wages down. But the growth of the black population, the largest visible minority at this time, has come to be strongly disfavored by the elite and the white majority, as mechanization reduced the need for cheap labor and the demands for equality became stronger. In the last few decades the black population has shifted from mostly rural to mostly urban, but blacks have been restricted to the central core of metropolitan areas. Thus, the compaction of black people into city slums has become one of our most serious problems. Like resource degradation and pollution, the problems of our cities have been aggravated by past population growth; but instituting forceful measures now to limit births would be totally irrelevant to solving these problems.

BIBLIOGRAPHICAL NOTE

Recent books on population dynamics in human evolution include Brian Spooner (ed.), *Population Growth: Anthropological Implications* (Cambridge, Mass.: M.I.T. Press, 1972), and Steven Polgar (ed.), *Population Ecology and Social Evolution* (The Hague: Mouton Press, 1975). Of the many publications on resource use and pollution, further exploration of the points raised in this article may be found in Preston Cloud (ed.), *Resources and Man: A Report by the U.S. National Academy of Science* (Oklahoma City: Gloria Foreman Publishing Co., 1969) Fred S. Singer (ed.), *Global Effects of Environmental Pollution* (New York: Springer Publishing Co., Inc., 1970), Barry Weisberg, *Beyond Repair: The Ecology of Capitalism* (Boston: Beacon Press, Inc., 1971).

On the problems of population distribution by color in the United States, see Charles Abrams' "The Housing Problem and the Negro," in Talcott Parsons and Kenneth B. Clark (eds.), *The Negro American* (Boston: Houghton Mifflin Co., 1966), and P. M. Hauser and P. L. Hodge, *The Challenge of America's Metropolitan Population Outlook 1960-1985*, Research Report No. 3, U.S. National Commission on Urban Problems (Washington, D.C.: U.S. Government Printing Office, 1968).

26.

ANTHROPOLOGY AND THE BODY POLITIC

Cyril S. Belshaw

ANTHROPOLOGISTS BELIEVE, RIGHTLY, that a great deal of their knowledge and many of their perspectives have considerable value for the interpretation and guidance of affairs of state.

The interaction of applied and fundamental interest has always been present in the discipline, although at all times some scholars have maintained the purist stance that their work is detached and value-free. According to this view, the more objective their work is, the more it is removed from policy concerns. For example, the structuralists and functionalists in Britain in the twenties and thirties often resisted involvement in applied studies, or even studies of social change, on the grounds that it was impossible to be scientific under such circumstances. That objective studies of social organization and ritual were not in fact as value-free as the argument maintained was nevertheless demonstrated by contemporary counter-arguments and related developments.

Thus indigenous nationalist leaders were inclined to accuse *pure anthropology* of placing a harmful value upon the functioning of traditional systems, in contrast to the value of revolution. Yet, as the later events of the Mau Mau revolution in Kenya possibly demonstrated, anthropological knowledge about traditional ritual, social organization, and sources of power could be used and manipulated by leaders of a variety of political persuasions. Further, very few anthropologists maintained a completely puristic and nonapplied stance throughout their careers. A concern with well-being, adjustment, and the

372

ability of a people to control its own destiny, was a major motivation for nascent studies of social change, as distinct from evolutionary studies. A humanistic concern for the fate of peoples, and a search for clues about the nature and future of mankind, was important to most anthropologists and was reflected in their work. As someone brought up in the British tradition of social anthropology, I am well aware of the disdain with which applied studies were often treated. Yet it is probably true that a greater proportion of anthropological work had an influence on policy and political movement, usually in a liberal direction, than is the case today.

Sometimes the influence has been indirect, a part of the general movement of humanism. Thus anthropologists can claim to have played a major part in the world acceptance of racial and ethnic tolerance, even though this continues to be attacked and threatened in many countries. Sometimes the contribution is more technical, as when anthropologists interpret customary land tenure for administrative purposes or involve themselves in poverty programs. *Fundamental* academic studies, not designed for any applied use, nevertheless figure as sources of data in government departments concerned with any of the myriad issues affecting the lives of cultural groups within the nation-state or with the understanding of foreign countries. When such studies are linked to observations and generalizations about the human condition, and the processes which affect it, anthropologists discover that their work is used in a wide range of contexts, such as the analysis of socialization or creativity in a public school system or the factors bearing upon space use in a program of urban renewal.

One might think that the growing utility of anthropology as knowledge and data would lead to such satisfaction and sense of purpose in the profession; that, in addition to the intellectual profits which come from the handling of difficult questions with discipline and imagination, anthropologists would have the satisfaction of knowing that their work was relevant and that it had some important bearing upon the future of mankind. Alas, this is not so. The profession, nationally and internationally, has been engaged in a traumatic, and often naive, process of soul-searching. Anthropology is information, and information is power—however objective, impartial, biased, or incomplete it may be. Anthropologists as individuals see power used by government, the military-industrial complex, cultural attaches, school teachers, and even clandestine military-political units such as the CIA. Very frequently anthropologists have their own views about the objectives of the power games and disagree strongly about the uses to which their knowledge may be put, whether that knowledge was developed through a consultation role or quite independently in the public domain of the literature. At the very least, they are worried about the false position that can arise through no fault of their own, when elements of the public, cultural minority groups, the politically active, and even their own colleagues stereotype the discipline as a whole, or a major part of it, as the handmaiden of imperialism, of repressive capitalism, or of a government which, at a given time in history, is out of favor. It is indeed disturbing that much of this criticism *is* stereotyping. Anthropology itself is becoming subject to the same process of role-assignment and emotionally loaded labeling that its practitioners have observed and protested against when it has been applied to other professions or social groups.

What has been happening appears to be more hurtful and disturbing in anthropology than in most other professions. This is no accident. It could be argued, for example, that our colleagues in economics and political science have tended to work with two assumptions which orient their work and ease their consciences. The first is that they are concerned with functionally operating systems, of which they themselves are a part and which they can identify. The normative orientation is to make the system work better. The second is that, despite concerns for such matters as world trade or international organizations, the reference point for the system is the nation-state.

For anthropologists, matters are different. First, it is true that a major intellectual tool for anthropologists is, and has been, the idea of functionalism. We have searched for ways in which to interpret phenomena in the context of equilibrium systems, and we have tended to see change as a dynamic equilibrium model. But there are major exceptions to this, and in any event anthropologists are usually *strangers* to the system they are interpreting, with the strengths and weaknesses such a position brings to their observation. Furthermore, it is usually this drive to understand something of which they are *not* a part that motivates anthropologists as scholars. Something has occurred to move anthropologists to detach themselves from their own society, to seek to observe it through their knowledge of other societies, to think of other societies as representing *alternative* modes of living. While most anthropologists experience this detachment in mild ways, and some perhaps not at all, in extreme cases we are talking of a form of alienation.

Second, the way in which anthropologists define a system at work, or see a unit of study even if they are not attuned to the idea of system, very rarely coincides with the boundary of the nation-state. Most usually they deal with a small part of it—a linguistic or cultural entity, a tribe or minority group. While it is true that etymologically the word "nation" was once most commonly used to refer precisely to a culturally distinct tribe, the modern nation-state has almost always been founded on some kind of political control of diverse or variable linguistic and cultural entities. It has had to overcome such diversity through the creation of a myth of unity. The intellectual foundations of anthropology build an apparatus of analysis which does not start with the nation-state, but with units which have interacting, even opposing, elements.

For these reasons, anthropologists do not necessarily accept the ideology, the policies, or even the functional primacy of given nation-states. Even where they may raise such important questions as "How can minority interests be linked to a sense of national identity?" they will not necessarily presume that the nation-state has either a functional or a moral need to dominate the minority from a position of power, however much that power may be exercised paternally. The tension inherent in this situation is most important for those who believe in the defense of the cultural and other rights of minorities. In unwary hands, it can also lead to romanticizing about cultural values, can tempt anthropologists to become self-appointed speakers for others, and can produce irritating and counter-productive political action and policy mistakes.

It is clear that the combination of self-selection of anthropologists and their later field experiences produces a wide variety
of political positions and moral stances. A few major themes do
influence the profession internationally—a concern for cultural preservation and viability, a similar concern, not always
compatible with others, for the well-being of the people with
whom one works, a commitment to the value of variety and
diversity in the human experience—but none of these is
necessarily regarded as a "ticket of entry" and there is no law
(despite attempts at codification of professional ethics) which
states that one must share such assumptions to be an anthropologist.

Indeed there is little, if anything, in the *technical apparatus*
of anthropology which leads to a corporate posture on important matters relating to public policy, unless it be that the field
experience reinforces a certain range of moral attitudes. This is
in contrast, let us say, to the state of affairs in economics. While
political views among economists are as varied as in any other
discipline, there is a predominant acceptance of the use of
macrostatistics attached to formal modeling for the calculation
of alternatives, which influences the economist to accept the
environment of the bureaucracy which is necessary to produce
much of the data. The anthropologist's bias is almost diametrically opposed to this.

The consequence is that the anthropologist's view of issues
of public policy is a highly personal matter, which may or may
not be well informed. It is likely to be best informed if it is
based on research oriented specifically to the issue in question.
Most often, the anthropologist's basis of specialized information falls short. It is, nevertheless, different from, and, in its
own way, deeper than, that of other specialists and exercises a
powerful influence on the position of the fieldworker. Thus,
those anthropologists who are engaged in highly technical
studies of kinship, which will result in esoteric theoretical
papers, are nevertheless drawn into situations in which they
learn a great deal about land tenure and agriculture, about
exchange relations and household wealth, about taxation and
marketing as it affects daily life, about strife, justice, and social
schism, and about the impact of the wider world on the daily

lives, the hopes and aspirations, and the pains and troubles of ordinary men and women. This *is* special knowledge, which may not be shared by other outsiders. It is not *total* knowledge, for it may not be systematic or related to relevant information about such humdrum matters as capital supply, agricultural or forestry management, or the cost benefit implications of a wider national policy.

Anthropologists tend thus to differ from others in their perspectives of the world and to differ among themselves as individuals. Many are, of course, able to operate with minimal conscious political involvement. It has been pointed out that even this is a kind of political stance; to see pain and allow it to have the status of social fact to be recorded and analyzed rather than removed through a change of policy is indeed a choice. But it is not by any means a simple one. For better or worse, anthropologists are *not* trained for political action. They are not normally even very good at it when they decide to engage themselves. Where they do have action skills, they can be extraordinarily effective because of their different knowledge and insight. But mostly they are ordinary men and women appalled perhaps by what they see. When this is the case, moral indignation can be heavy-handed and ineffective, creating as many difficulties as it solves. The world is littered with well-meaning reforms, particularly in areas of poverty and depression, based on false technical and human knowledge, which have failed because advisers—anthropologists and others—have been trapped into believing they had more certain answers than was the case in fact.

But the differences in personal perspective have a special functional significance. The problem is sharpened by asking the question: Should anthropologists work for governments? If they do, should there be a code which defines the circumstances? The point of relevance here is that if one recognizes that anthropologists are individual citizens, and that there are very few, if any, absolute policy truths which emerge from the discipline as such, for all policy statements embody variable value elements, then any professional restraining code is going to hamper somebody's political freedom. Under these circumstances, a professional code is a political instrument, too.

I do not think that anyone in his or her senses would argue that anthropologists have any professional business to engage in military activity resulting in civilian death, on behalf of any government or political group. Having said that, I must record that I know of anthropologists who have been so caught up in their concern for the human condition that they *have* engaged themselves in political-military action and in so doing have placed their special analytic skills at the service of authority, whether governmental or revolutionary. This was very widely done during World War II, when anthropologists worked with others in defense of a concept of democracy. It has been done in southeast Asia by others who also believed they were helping innocent rural people to defend themselves against totalitarian aggression. It has been and still is being done in Africa, Asia, and Latin America by those who believe that revolutionary movements are the necessary means to an equitable freedom, and that foreigners who share this view have a duty to lend a hand and, in some instances, to expiate the guilt of their own governments.

These are extreme instances, but they point up sharply the fact, which may be obscured in the commoner involvements, that the judgment as to what is right and wrong, and as to which side to be on, is not professionally determined. It is an individual political issue. It may also be argued that much of such activity is extraprofessional. But it is often difficult to draw the line, and if one engages in extraprofessional involvements one is influenced by one's special knowledge.

It is one thing to adopt a political stance and follow through with the consequences. It is quite another to drift into a situation in which your skills are used and manipulated for objectives with which you would thoroughly disagree. Very serious accusations have been made on this score against agencies of the U.S. government involving other social science disciplines in addition to anthropology. The U.S. Defense Department, the Agency for International Development, and others have had elaborate organization for major research involvement in other countries, coupled with specialist consultation, on issues ranging from rural welfare to police organization and security and thence to actions affecting the degree to which the social climate was hospitable to revolution or to government policy. In part, the scandals which ensued were affected by the supposition that many social scientists who participated were unaware of the consequences and implications of their involvement, and that the actions represented an interference by the United States in the internal affairs of other countries.

These scandals came to a head at a time when the academic community and, increasingly, the general public were alarmed at U.S. government action in Vietnam and were losing confidence in the legitimacy of government in conditions of moral corruption. It is understandable that, 'for many, the moral indignation translated itself into a suspicion of *any* service for *any* government. It also helped to reinforce suspicions held abroad about the legitimacy of anthropologists working in other countries. But the translation of these moral principles into absolute rules of conduct can have as reprehensible a set of consequences as the evils the rules are meant to deal with. The interpretation of the validity of government conduct, even of the question of secrecy or openness in its dealings, is dependent not only upon one's personal political preferences and values but upon the circumstances of time and place.

Thus, for a large number of American anthropologists, acts of secrecy and clandestine activity, both international and domestic, are ideologically, morally, and practically abhorrent. Yet for other social scientists, including anthropologists, in some other countries, the issues may appear very different indeed. If you are, for example, defending a democratic government being attacked in war, if you believe in liberal values which are attacked by stealth by right or left revolution, if, in short, you wish to defend some political system because you believe in it, you will not hold back *merely* because knowledge is analyzed or produced behind closed doors. And indeed there are numerous instances in which minority groups, to defend themselves *against* governments, or other more powerful interests, need knowledge, and need to keep it to themselves until it is tactically right to use it. Anthropologists who committed themselves to help, and then refused to maintain appropriate confidences, would be rather untrustworthy creatures.

The patterns become even more complex when we consider

the implications of anthropological research and consultation activity across international boundaries. To set the scene for the understanding of this it is necessary to make some points about the rapidly evolving nature of world society. We are all aware of the important functional mystique which attaches to the idea of nationalism, particularly as it is interpreted by national governments who are defending their own powers or trying to create viable societies and economies. The mystique is based upon what I call an *ethnosocial science* theory, that is, a set of principles interpreting the world based not on scientific analysis but upon common sense interpretations, often misinterpretations. One ethnosocial science position is that nation-states represent "peoples." It is, however, in the interests of governments to try to make this a reality by forging unifying links between "disparate" cultures, stratified groups, and other interests, and there is no doubt that this drive to what is often called national independence is a very strong force in the contemporary world. It can also be valued because it assists in the maintenance of world diversity and as a counterbalance to other tendencies which might lead to "great power" hegemony. Here, of course, we enter the realm of political judgment. But nationalism in this form is a political artifact.

Working at cross-purposes to this principle is another reality, which is the existence of a great variety and influence of cross-national interest and power groups. These have existed for centuries in one form or another. Attention has recently been extended to the multinational corporation, which is one manifestation of the phenomenon, but, of course, influential cross-national enterprises predate the conception of the nation-state. Migrant groups, sometimes, as with overseas Chinese, maintain highly significant cross-national communication, frequently linked to familial structure. Continental national borders, more frequently than not, cut through cultural, linguistic, and kinship networks. Labor unions, professional associations, and scientific meetings have their own international momentum. Channels of communication spread ideas, music, television programs, which often have the effect of establishing and reinforcing subcultures which are internationally connected. Political movements, whether revolutionary or not, often have more in common with their connections in other countries than with their rivals in their own. The study of nearly all these phenomena, and the values, organization, social structure and communications channels, is in its infancy. But it is just as important to the contemporary world as is the study of national social organization, for it is in tension with it.

Let us place, to some extent, professional anthropologists in this context. They are not yet very aware of the fact that, whether they like it or not, they are part of the scene of world social organization. They are more aware of the relations they have with the various national bodies politic and with the smaller political system with which they have direct contact. Their actions contribute to the smoothing or exacerbating of international tensions. They contribute to the success or failure of nation-states seeking to establish a functioning unity. They are part of a world network of professionals, not, it is true, highly organized, but yet existing *de facto*.

I shall use as illustration an imaginary situation which refers to an increasingly common and distressing reality. Anthropologists formulate an important empirical research project dealing with the social organization and conceptual world of a relatively isolated people. In doing so, they establish close intellectual and cooperative contact with other anthropologists and institutions concerned with the region. The project is not set up to have direct applied relevance. Yet in the field they note evidence of extreme pressure by government on the way of life of the people. The government itself is operating in response to pressures and drives: to increase control in order to convince world authorities that it is able to prevent opium poppy cultivation and traffic; to relocate peoples in order to permit massive hydroelectric or irrigation schemes to improve a poor nation's income; to open up forests and mineral deposits to exploitation by building roads and railways. Anthropologists see things from the viewpoint of the people being affected, often without any power to represent or articulate their concerns. Whether or not they are engaged as consultants, anthropologists, if they are at all sensitive, make representations, write applied papers, and in extreme cases use political influence or public opinion.

If they are foreigners, they may find that their views are

considered wild or heretical by their local colleagues, who have a different set of balances linked to the issues of national development. They may find their ability to speak out resented. They may find that they create a reaction in the seat of bureaucratic power which regards self-appointed speakers for depressed groups as troublemakers or romantics, and that this affects the policy governing the granting of permission for foreign scholars to work on academic projects within the country. Out of respect for their local colleagues, or for the future of academic work, they may compromise in what they say.

And if they are indigenous anthropologists, they may be in even greater difficulty. Anthropology as such may be very much out of favor in government circles, not understood, or resented. To embark upon such a career may involve following a most sensitive and difficult path, without the funds, the backup, or the political support to enable them to say effectively what needs to be said.

Of course, these situations are by no means universal, and there are many countries where enlightened cooperation is possible and effective. But there are others—and unfortunately they are common—where, despite the existence of well-established government-supported universities and research institutions, no support whatsoever is given to social and cultural anthropology or to those branches of sociology which are close in applied interest. In such countries, those anthropologists who have managed to get themselves trained must follow alternative careers or live abroad or must skirt the issues circumspectly and quietly.

Now with respect to many of the questions of politics, morality, ethics, and ultimate effects of public policy upon minority peoples, subcultures, or depressed groups, there is, of course, a great deal of room for argument. Truth is seldom absolute. And one of the most intriguing and difficult chapters in the judgment of human history is that which might analyze the legitimacy or impropriety of *forcing* changes in the ways of living of less powerful people. From one point of view, the whole of human history is a saga of dramatic interactions in which peoples and cultures find themselves threatened or engaged in reactions to external forces over which they have no control. In most situations, the ability of the human group to react and reestablish itself has been extraordinary; but we also know of the total disappearance of peoples through deliberate acts of genocide and of the effective destruction of ways of life through what is now known as ethnocide. World opinion is now no longer ready to shut its eyes to ethnocide, and there are forces which are willing to intervene on behalf of cultures which are threatened. But, except in extreme cases, it is still not clear when public policy designed to change behavior and institutions is legitimate and when it constitutes a threat to the "right to culture." After all, public policy which does not influence behavior and institutions, through law, taxation, public works, redistribution of property, and the like, is hardly policy at all.

Let us return to field anthropologists. They can find themselves, often quite accidentally, in the most bizarre and tragic situations. They obtain indications that well-educated professionals (lawyers, engineers) working for the welfare of indigenous groups have a conflict of interest and use their position to advise governments on paths of action which bring benefits to them at the expense of their clients. They find themselves witnesses to situations in which indigenous hunters or shifting agriculturalists are forcibly removed from terrain with heavy and brutal loss of life, to make room for new settlers, without compensation. They see that development projects are being rushed through with only the most cursory consideration for the medical, educational, and proprietary interests of the local people. What should they do?

In the very nature of things, it would be most difficult for them to establish any kind of rapport or influence with a government already committed to such extremes. It is likely that to work with their local colleagues in any formal way would hurt them rather than help the cause. Such courses of action are not impossible, and they do in fact occasionally bear fruit where conditions are ripe. But the anthropologists may be forced into the international arena, to mobilize or influence some form of world public opinion, which in turn can influence government action. Their instruments for doing so are extremely weak, and the experience of anthropologists in making use of such procedures as exist leaves a great deal to be evolved. The U.N. Charter of Human Rights, UNESCO conventions dealing with the preservation of and right to culture, the activities of the International Committee of the Red Cross, and the existence of numerous organizations formed to marshall evidence, publicize reports, and build an influence are precarious life rafts to which anthropologists cling.

Such situations present conundrums of a dramatic nature. Fortunately, perhaps, most of life is more prosaic. There are huge areas of government concern in which social science knowledge is desirable and where anthropological analysis can be useful to the solution of problems, as governments and the public they serve think of them. Yet the lack of drama does not remove the existence of serious problems in constructive cooperation. It is very common indeed to hear, even in the most enlightened of governmental circles, complaints about the inefficiency or unreality of anthropological advice and the near-impossibility of using anthropologists as consultants. And it is equally common to hear complaints among anthropologists that the implications of their work, whether as consultants or as detached academics, are ignored or misapplied. There is nowadays too much of this misunderstanding to shrug off.

The curious thing is that this situation is not based on a great deal of experience. Whereas governments have become used to using economists and, in limited fields, psychologists, anthropologists in government service are relatively rare birds. This means that not very much is known, particularly within government, about what they can or cannot do, and there is little skillful innovative thought applied to developing new techniques of using them. Most anthropological advice, deliberately sought for defined purposes (as distinct from that which is provided as a result of academic research), either uses standard field inquiry or amends it to establish short-term quick answers. Possibly the most useful part of this consists in the presentation of data, with some interpretation. But governments tend to find the data discursive and uneconomically presented, are disappointed when the conclusions are not clear and concise, disillusioned when anthropologists tell them things they do not really want to know, and angered when they appear to be overly critical without taking other factors into account. Their political masters are impatient at the length of time that patient field inquiry takes in anthropological hands, and their other consultants (engineers, economists, for example) find the humanism and detail of anthropologists' reports "subjective" and "lacking in clarity," and hence "unscientific."

Unfortunately, there is enough truth in these criticisms to be worrying, and there is not very much evidence that anthropologists know how to meet it. The application of index-construction to complex anthropological issues is in its infancy, and the ability to translate the richness of field data into the aridity of abstract models suitable for mathematical systems analysis appeals as yet to only a minority of our colleagues. We do indeed often replace careful conclusions with intuition and opinion, particularly when pressed for immediate answers. We are perhaps on strongest ground when we use the consultative position to enable the people who are most directly concerned to voice their own opinions, and help them place those opinions in a field of data and in the text of a persuasive argument. Anthropology then becomes less of a disciplined science and more of a political art, for which, as academics, we seldom have the skills, the diplomatic aptitudes, or the training.

But to make such points is to accept the current structure of research and consultancy and to fail to identify the most serious institutional lacks. Three facts are paramount as assumptions for the successful creation of an applied anthropology of real utility for governments, public policy, and the body politic in its widest sense. These are:

1. *No* problem of policy significance lies solely within the domain of one discipline—*all* are interdisciplinary;

2. Most important problems require *long-term* cumulative research, a mix of the *fundamental* and the *applied*, perhaps lasting decades, before we can have confidence in the answers; and

3. Society and culture are in constant movement, so that both data *and theories* capable of application require constant revision and updating, a condition which is much less significant in fields of analysis outside the social sciences.

These facts are not novel, but the structure of applied research in anthropology does not reflect an acknowledgment of them. There is a considerable need to supplement the important and essential self-directed university research with permanent mission-oriented research institutes specializing in the coordinated interdisciplinary examination and monitoring of selected issues of policy concern. In the absence of such organizations, a great deal of social science advice will continue to be picayune and on occasion misleading. Nor will we have in the profession a sufficient body of experience to guide the education of anthropologists able to work confidently in applied fields, as distinct from academic research.

Many informed readers will immediately object that such a structure could only come about through fairly massive governmental support, and that, therefore, there would be dangers that the work would be biased in favor of governmental definitions of policy issues, with insufficient attention given to alternative priorities. Further, the very existence of powerful research institutes in the gift of government places other elements of society at a grave disadvantage, for, as we have said, information is power. It is, however, not beyond man's skill to devise modifications which, if not completely an answer to the criticism, at least go some way to meeting it. The Centre National de Recherche Scientifique of France operates a large network of research institutes. Its power structure and system of professional promotion are largely in the hands of the research staff, and its distribution of resources reflects a dialectic between governmental definitions of priorities and the proposals of individuals in the research establishment. Indeed, in some respects it may be too much like a university system, despite its apparent centralization of funding, to meet the criteria I have in mind.

Again, if the major private foundations were to align themselves with this objective, they could have a powerful independent influence. In Canada it has proved possible to create, with federal funds, an independent Institute of Public Policy, which could, theoretically, develop into an umbrella organization for continuing research institutes. Yet another possibility would be to build on the example of the International Development Research Centre of Canada, funded by federal legislation but with the status of an independent crown corporation, and with a board the members of which are, by constitution, largely drawn from *outside the country.*

No such devices fully meet the issue, for it is the poor, the dispossessed, the groups far from the seats of power and influence who have need for access to research and the skills of applying the research to their own needs. Many anthropologists are able to help from their own university bases. The more this happens, the more the discipline becomes influenced by political commitments of a variety of kinds. When these intersect, as they do, with a disparate range of intellectual interests and methods, with a spectrum of national and individual personal styles, and with an almost infinite variety of human conditions and concerns, the kaleidoscope reflects blindingly confused patterns. What is anthropology? What do anthropologists stand for? There can be no agreement, and to force an agreement would be to threaten seriously the ability of the subject to attract diverse skills, to fuse and synthesize superficially disparate themes—in short, to search for creative innovation.

Yet, when they are faced with confusion, and with important and emotionally charged issues, it can be no wonder that anthropologists seek to find some order. Of recent years, particularly in North America, there has been a trend to find an ordered identity in the notion of annual meetings of professional anthropologists to establish criteria of ethical behavior. Codes of conduct have been proposed, largely as a result of dissatisfaction and argument about interactions between anthropologists and government agencies.

The ideal of ethical behavior is one that is difficult to qualify, but it also is difficult to define in universalistic terms, which is what codes usually do. All professions which have effectively adopted codes have, as a result, blinded themselves to alternatives and, on occasion, found that the code has established a

posture which many would regard as *un*ethical. The effect of
the Hippocratic Oath upon the position of medical professions
with regard to euthanasia and abortion is an obvious, if
extreme, example.

For anthropology, the debate about ethics is of major importance. Many would argue that the debate and discussion,
revealing issues as they do, are more positive and influential
than any code; for it is doubtful if anthropology is or ought to
be a profession, in the sense that the practice of medicine is a
profession. Anthropologists serve a great variety of clients, in
quite different ways, and with quite different implications.
Most of us are university teachers, and in that context we are
part of the general profession of university teachers; our
anthropology is not and ought not to be something special and
apart. It is when anthropologists are research workers that our
special difficulties and problems become defined. It is true that
for the majority, the academic enterprise of inquiry has a
certain unity. But we relate to such different groups in such
different contexts that even the most innocuous or
undebatable-sounding principle turns out on many occasions
to backfire when it is applied literally.

For example, the current important and widespread American concern for openness in academic and public dealings has
influenced the American Anthropological Association to include a clause requiring general availability of all anthropological research reports and censuring "secret" research or communications made secretly to some and not to others. As
general principles governing normal academic conduct and
expressing ideal conditions of academic scientific communication, these are clearly cornerstones. All academic anthropologists, in my view, should hold to them as ideals and should not
depart from them without very good reason.

Unfortunately, the conditions under which anthropologists
might wish to depart from them are seldom normal, and they
are conditions which the code does not adequately forsee. The
problem is less with the principles than with their absolutism.
Anthropologists would never agree that they had the right to
publish the private details of tax information, particularly if
such publication were to harm their informants. Indeed, other

parts of the code make it clear that anthropologists should not harm their informants, and this principle *requires* secrecy and confidentiality, on occasion. There are many occasions on which anthropologists may make it clear to their clients that any information they receive must be published freely, and that they, the anthropologists, must determine the nature of the publication. But if they are to consult for minority groups, if they are to enter the world of policy formation, they must be prepared to assess the constraints of confidentiality that an action role may imply. They cannot lean on an automatic code to help them. They must decide themselves whether the constraints are functionally necessary, reasonable, and legitimate, and only through the responsible exercise of that decision can they be said to be ethical. If they are not prepared to exercise such judgment, they should not enter the world of advice and action, and they should not complain if their advice is not sought or if they fail to have influence in the shaping of policy. They should be prepared to be forced back onto a nonrelevant anthropology.

Indeed, so particular is applied anthropology to the specific groups and conditions defined by the anthropologist's client relationships that I can fully understand the view of many anthropologists that applied anthropology is, somehow, impure, because of the intrusion of questions of interest as distinct from those of scientific impartiality. But surely the critics of *pure* anthropology have by now shown that the "impartial" discipline is not value-free. A self-controlled applied anthropology is capable of making the value judgments clearer and more explicit.

I also suspect that there is a certain amount of anxiety and fear among those who look with alarm at recent developments. Some of this is justified. Amateurish or naively motivated policy comment from anthropologists, or anyone else, can do the reputation of the discipline considerable harm. The likelihood of this happening seems very high, given present levels of inexperience and inadequate training in policy analysis. The profession is being forced to relearn the principles of tolerance of diverse, even contradictory, value stances. If it does not, it will fly apart. There are critical dangers.

Yet there are other aspects to the question which are more positive. We are social and cultural scientists whose work forces us to consider the human condition from its specific detail in almost microscopic intensity to the broad movement of peoples. We are humanists concerned with man's values, goals, and purposes. A few, very few, of us have the power of olympian detachment exercised in the confines of the study. Most of us need the checks and balances of the real world to bring reality and order to our observations. It is as the real world evolves and changes that we can see whether our propositions hold true. Public policy is an applied social science, whether or not social scientists are involved in its formation and application. It is in the world of public policy that new questions are being formulated, as much as in the academic world. The union of policy concerns and academic discipline leads to a stormy marriage, but at least one productive of new generations. Celibacy, on the other hand, could lead to the establishment of a comfortable priesthood of insignificant theologians. Each anthropologist is now, in his or her own way, engaged in making the choice.

BIBLIOGRAPHICAL NOTE

A good discussion of the kinds of topics of applied concern which anthropologists deal with is contained in George M. Foster, *Traditional Societies and Technological Change* (2nd. ed. New York: Harper & Row Publishers, Inc., 1973). Articles in *Human Organization*, the journal of the Society for Applied Anthropology, also give a useful perspective.

Two of the most interesting accounts of ethical issues are Irving L. Horowitz, *The Rise and Fall of Project Camelot: Studies in the Relationship between Social Science and Politics* (Cambridge, Mass.: M.I.T. Press, 1974), and Ralph L. Beals, *Politics of Social Research: An Inquiry into the Ethics and Responsibilities of Social Scientists* (Chicago: Aldine Publishing Co., 1969). A sensitive book which shows that it is not easy to be Simon-pure in politics is Maurice Cranston, *The Mask of Politics* (LaSalle, Ill.: Open Court Publishing Co., 1973). The International Work Group of Indigenous Affairs, Frederiksholms Kanal 4A, DK-1220 Copenhagen K, Denmark, publishes a series of brief reports on ethnocide and similar questions. Although they are uneven, they contain much useful data and analysis.

Those who believe that the social sciences have all the answers should read Pitirim Sorokin's classic *Fads and Foibles in Modern Sociology and Related Sciences* (Chicago: Aldine Publishing Co., 1956) and the later, and perhaps less temperate, book of Stanislav Andreski, *Social Science as Sorcery* (London: Andre Deutsch, 1972).

I have completed an overview of some of the analytic issues, including the ethical and professional, in *The Sorcerer's Apprentice: An Anthropology of Public Policy* (Elmsford, N.Y.: Pergamon Press, Inc., 1976).